First World War
and Army of Occupation
War Diary
France, Belgium and Germany

51 DIVISION
Divisional Troops
401 Field Company Royal Engineers
1 December 1915 - 31 March 1919

WO95/2855/2

The Naval & Military Press Ltd
www.nmarchive.com
Published in association with The National Archives

Published by

The Naval & Military Press Ltd

Unit 10 Ridgewood Industrial Park,

Uckfield, East Sussex,

TN22 5QE England

Tel: +44 (0) 1825 749494

www.naval-military-press.com

www.nmarchive.com

This diary has been reprinted in facsimile from the original. Any imperfections are inevitably reproduced and the quality may fall short of modern type and cartographic standards.

© **Crown Copyright**
Images reproduced by permission of The National Archives, London, England, 2015.

Contents

Document type	Place/Title	Date From	Date To
Heading	WO95/2855 Dec 1915-Mar 1919 401 Field Co Royal Engineers		
Heading	51st Division 401st (H'Land) Fld Coy RE. Dec 1915-Mar 1919 From 7 Div Troops		
Heading	7 Div Transferred To 51st Divl-Dec 6th 1/2nd Highland F.C.R.E Dec 1915 Vol XI		
War Diary		01/12/1915	27/12/1915
Heading	1/2nd Highd Fd. Co. R.E Jan 1916 Vol XII		
Heading	1/2 High Fd Coy R.E Vol XIV		
War Diary		01/01/1916	18/03/1916
War Diary	Mirvaux	01/03/1916	30/03/1916
Heading	War Diary For May 1916 Vol No.16		
War Diary		01/05/1916	28/05/1916
Miscellaneous	Officer i/c A.G Office G.H.Q	28/05/1916	28/05/1916
Diagram etc	Diagram		
Miscellaneous	1/2nd Highland Field Coy R.E		
Diagram etc	Machine Gun Emplacement		
Miscellaneous	1/2nd Highland Field Coy R.E		
Diagram etc	Machine Gun Emplacement & Radial Mounting		
Miscellaneous	1/2nd Highland Field Coy R.E.		
Diagram etc	Diagram		
Heading	War Diary Of 1st/2nd Highland Field Coy R.E. for June 1916 Vol No. 17		
War Diary		01/06/1916	30/06/1916
Map	Map		
Miscellaneous	The Officer i/c Adjutant-Generals Office G.H.Q. Base	31/07/1916	31/07/1916
Heading	War Diary Of 1st/2nd Highland Field Coy R.E. (T.F.) For July 1916 Vol 18		
War Diary	Anzin St Aubyn	01/07/1916	31/07/1916
Map	Map		
Heading	51st Divisional Engineers 1/2nd Highland Field Company R.E August 1916		
War Diary	Ravine Between Fricourt And Becourt	01/08/1916	31/08/1916
Miscellaneous	A Form Messages And Signals.		
Miscellaneous	Report on Work Carried Out By 1st/2nd Highland Field Company R.E during Period From 2nd July-6th August inclusive		
Map	Map		
Diagram etc	Diagram		
Heading	War Diary Of 1st/2nd Highland Field Co. R.E. (T) For September 1916 Vol. No. XXI		
War Diary	Armentieres	01/09/1916	30/09/1916
Heading	War Diary Of 1st/2nd Highland Field Company R.E. (T.F.) For October 1916 Vol.21		
War Diary	Candas	01/10/1916	31/10/1916
Heading	War Diary (With Plan) of 1st/2nd Highland Field Company R.E.T For November 1916 Vol: No. XXIII		
War Diary	Forceville	01/11/1916	30/11/1916
Map	Map		
Miscellaneous	Appendix 2		

Miscellaneous	Stores in R.E. Dumps reserved for "Z" day. Appendix "3"		
Miscellaneous	Instructions In Alignment Posts		
Miscellaneous	O.C. No. 1 Section 1st/2nd Highland Field Co. R.E		
Miscellaneous	O.C. No. 2 Section 1st/2nd Highland Field Co. R.E		
Miscellaneous	O.C. No. 3 Section 1st/2nd Highland Field Co. R.E		
Miscellaneous	O.C. No. 4 Section 1st/2nd Highland Field Co. R.E		
Miscellaneous	Office In Charge R.E Store Mailly		
Miscellaneous	Notes On Attack		
Heading	War Diary Of 1st/2nd Highland Field Company R.E (T) For December 1916 Vol No. 23		
War Diary	Wolfe Huts Ovillers-La Boisselle X14.b.2.9	01/12/1916	31/12/1916
Diagram etc	Diagram		
Map	Map		
Heading	War Diary Of 401st (Highland) Field Company R.E For January 1917 Vol 24		
War Diary	Ovillers Post	01/01/1917	31/01/1917
Heading	War Diary Of 401st (Highland) Field Company R.E For February 1917 Vol. No. 1917		
War Diary	Anzin St. Aubin	01/02/1917	28/02/1917
Map	Map		
Heading	War Diary Of 401st (Highland) Field Company R.E. For March 1917 Vol. No XXVII		
War Diary	Anzin St. Aubin	01/03/1917	31/03/1917
Map	Map		
Heading	War Diary Of 401st (Highland) Field Company R.E For April 1917 Vol: No. XXVIII		
War Diary	Anzin St Aubin	01/04/1917	30/04/1917
Miscellaneous	Officer i/c No.I Section 401st (Highland) Field Co R.E	06/04/1917	06/04/1917
Map	Map		
Heading	War Diary Of 401st (Highland) Field Company R.E For May 1917 Vol. No XXIX		
War Diary	Anzin St Aubin	01/05/1917	31/05/1917
Diagram etc	Diagram		
Map	Map		
Diagram etc	Diagram		
Heading	War Diary Of 401st (Highland) Field Company R.E For June 1917 Vol. No XXX		
War Diary	Bailleul Aux Cornailles	01/06/1917	04/06/1917
War Diary	Antin	05/06/1917	05/06/1917
War Diary	Hezecques	06/06/1917	07/06/1917
War Diary	Clercques	08/06/1917	15/06/1917
War Diary	Camp At A.29 B 6.0	16/06/1917	17/06/1917
War Diary	Canal Bank	18/06/1917	30/06/1917
Heading	War Diary Of 401st (Highland) Field Coy R.E. For July 1917 Vol. XXXI		
War Diary		01/07/1917	31/07/1917
Miscellaneous	DAG 3rd Echelon Base	15/10/1917	15/10/1917
Heading	Report On The Operations Of The 51st (Highland) Division N.E Of Ypres July 31st To August 1st 1917		
Miscellaneous	Index		
Miscellaneous	Preliminary Summary		
Miscellaneous	The Battle		
Heading	War Diary Of 401st Highland Field Co R.E For August 1917 Vol XXXII		
War Diary	Canal Bank 1000 Yds N Of Ypres	01/08/1917	07/08/1917

War Diary	A.27.b.35 Ref Map Belgium Sheet 28 N.W. 1/20,000	07/08/1917	17/08/1917
War Diary	B.24 D.3.7 Ref Map Belgium Sheet 28 N.W. 1/20,000	18/08/1917	28/08/1917
War Diary	Canal Bank 1000 Yds N. Of Ypres	29/08/1917	31/08/1917
Heading	War Diary Of 401st Highland Field Coy. R.E. For September 1917 Vol XXXIII		
War Diary	Yser Canal C.25.a.3.8	01/09/1917	24/09/1917
War Diary	Peselhoek	25/09/1917	30/09/1917
Heading	Report On The Advance Towards Poelcappelle By The 51st (Highland) Division 20th Sept 1917		
Miscellaneous	Section I Preparations And Dispositions		
Miscellaneous	Reference Map: Poelcappelle, 1/10,000		
Map	Map		
Map	Map No.2		
Heading	War Diary Of 401st (Highland) Field Company R.E. For October 1917 Vol. XXXIV		
War Diary	Courcelles Le Comte	01/10/1917	05/10/1917
War Diary	Boiry Becquerelle	06/10/1917	29/10/1917
War Diary	Beaulencourt	30/10/1917	31/10/1917
Heading	War Diary Of 401st (Highland) Field Coy. R.E. For November 1917 Vol. XXXV		
War Diary	Ytres	01/11/1917	10/11/1917
War Diary	Havrincourt Wood	11/11/1917	21/11/1917
War Diary	Flesquieres	22/11/1917	30/11/1917
Heading	War Diary Of 401st (Highland) Field Coy R.E For December 1917 Vol: XXXVI		
War Diary	Bertincourt	01/12/1917	02/12/1917
War Diary	Boursies	03/12/1917	05/12/1917
War Diary	Doignies	06/12/1917	31/12/1917
Heading	War Diary Of 401st (Highland) Field Company R.E For January 1918 Vol XXXVII		
War Diary	Doignies	01/01/1918	18/01/1918
War Diary	Beugny	19/01/1918	19/01/1918
War Diary	Courcelles	20/01/1918	20/01/1918
War Diary	Bailleulmont	21/01/1918	26/01/1918
War Diary	Ablainzevelle	27/01/1918	31/01/1918
Heading	War Diary Of 401st (Highland) Field Coy R.E. For February 1918 Vol XXXVIII		
War Diary	Ablainzeville	01/02/1918	13/02/1918
War Diary	Lebucquiere	14/02/1918	28/02/1918
Heading	51st Divisional Engineers 401st Field Company R.E March 1918		
Heading	War Diary 401st (Highland) Field Coy R.E March-1918		
War Diary	Lebucquiere	01/03/1918	19/03/1918
War Diary	Trench J.19.C.3.7. 57.C.N.W.	21/03/1918	23/03/1918
War Diary	M.V.S. Camp At N.4.b.4.3. Sheet 57.c.	23/03/1918	24/03/1918
War Diary	Loupart Wood 3 Miles W Of Bapaume Lens II & 57.c.S.W.	24/03/1918	24/03/1918
War Diary	Loupart Wood 3 Miles W Of Bapaume	24/03/1918	25/03/1918
War Diary	Fonque Villers 10 Miles N.W. Of Bapaume Lens II	25/03/1918	25/03/1918
War Diary	Pas 7 Miles E. Of Doullens Lens 11	26/03/1918	26/03/1918
War Diary	Ransart 3 Miles N.W. Of Doullens	27/03/1918	28/03/1918
War Diary	Ransart	28/03/1918	31/03/1918
Map	Map		
Heading	51st Divisional Engineers War Diary 401st (Highland) Field Company R.E. April 1918		
Heading	War Diary 401st (Highland) Field Coy R.E. April-1918		

War Diary	Gonnehem	01/04/1918	04/04/1918
War Diary	Auchel	05/04/1918	07/04/1918
War Diary	Cense La Vallee L'Ecleme	08/04/1918	13/04/1918
War Diary	Robecq	13/04/1918	24/04/1918
War Diary	Bourecq	24/04/1918	30/04/1918
Map	Map		
Heading	War Diary For May, 1918 Of The 401st (Highland) Field Company, R.E.		
War Diary	Bourecq	01/05/1918	03/05/1918
War Diary	Maroeuil	04/05/1918	11/05/1918
War Diary	Ecurie	12/05/1918	28/06/1918
Map	Map		
Heading	Divisional Engineers 51st (Highland) Division 401st Field Co., R.E. July 1918		
Heading	War Diary 401st (Highland) Field Coy. R.E For July 1918		
War Diary	Ecurie	01/07/1918	17/07/1918
War Diary	Chouilly	19/07/1918	19/07/1918
War Diary	Bellevue	20/07/1918	20/07/1918
War Diary	Nanteuil.	21/07/1918	31/07/1918
Heading	War Diary 401st Highland Fld Co. R.E. August-1918		
War Diary	Nanteuil.	01/08/1918	05/08/1918
War Diary	Aubigny	06/08/1918	15/08/1918
War Diary	Ecurie	16/08/1918	16/08/1918
War Diary	Ecurie & Bailleul	16/08/1918	27/08/1918
War Diary	Point Du Jour & Scarpe Valley To North	28/08/1918	31/08/1918
Map	Map		
Map	Fampoux		
Heading	War Diary Of 401st (Highland) Field Coy. R.E. For September 1918		
War Diary	Ecurie & Fampoux Area	01/09/1918	13/09/1918
War Diary	Petit Servins	14/09/1918	14/09/1918
War Diary	St. Nicholas Fampoux Area	23/09/1918	30/09/1918
Map	Map		
Heading	War Diary 401st (Highland) Field Coy. R.E October-1918		
War Diary	St. Nicholas Fampoux Area	01/10/1918	01/10/1918
War Diary	Le Pendu Camp	02/10/1918	11/10/1918
War Diary	Thun St Martin (N. Of Cambrai)	12/10/1918	18/10/1918
War Diary	Auesnes Le-Sec	20/10/1918	21/10/1918
War Diary	Noyelles Sur Selle	24/10/1918	30/10/1918
Heading	War Diary 401st (Highland) Field Coy R.E November 1918		
War Diary	Noyelles Sur Selle	01/11/1918	01/11/1918
War Diary	Paillencourt	02/11/1918	30/11/1918
Heading	War Diary 401st (Highland) Field Coy R.E. December-1918		
War Diary	Paillencourt	01/12/1918	31/12/1918
Heading	War Diary Of 401st (Highland) Field Company R.E For January 1918		
War Diary	Paillencourt	01/01/1919	01/01/1919
War Diary	Houdeng Goegnies	02/01/1919	31/01/1919
Heading	War Diary Of 401st (Highland) Field Company R.E. For February 1919		
War Diary	Houdeng Goegnies Belgium	01/02/1919	28/02/1919

Heading	War Diary 401st (Highland) Field Coy. R.E. March-1919		
War Diary	Houdeng Goegnies Belgium	01/03/1919	21/03/1919
War Diary	Manage	22/03/1919	31/03/1919

WO95/2855

Dec 1915 – Nov 1919

401 Field Co Royal Engineers

51ST DIVISION

401ST(H'LAND) FLD COY RE.
DEC 1915-MAR 1919

FROM 7 DIV TROOPS

51ST DIVISION

7 D.
(Transferred to 51st Div - Dec 6th?)

1/2nd Highland F. C. RE

Dec 1915
Vol XI

Dec '15
Mar '19

Army Form C. 2118.

WAR DIARY
or
INTELLIGENCE SUMMARY

(Erase heading not required.)

Instructions regarding War Diaries and Intelligence Summaries are contained in F. S. Regs., Part II. and the Staff Manual respectively. Title pages will be prepared in manuscript.

2nd HIGHLAND FIELD COY. R.E.

Hour, Date, Place	Summary of Events and Information	Remarks and references to Appendices
1st December	Company left LE TOURET, after handing over work and billets to 222 Coy. R.E. and marched via BETHUNE and LILLERS to billets at GUARBECQUES. All details rejoined Company. 2 NCOs and 9 men transferred to Company from 2/2 HIGHLAND FIELD Co. R.E.	
6th December	Left GUARBECQUES at 1 p.m. and entrained at BERGUETTE Stn. Time taken to entrain 42 minutes. Arrived PORT REMY near ABBEVILLE at midnight 6th/7th and detrained. Marched to billets at SAISSEMONT via ARRAINES, CAMPS EN AMIENOIS and MOLLIENS-VIDAMES arriving 1 p.m. Company engaged in construction of latrines; ablution benches; cooking shelters; stables and cadievs and improvement of billets at MOLLIENS-VIDAMES, CAMP EN AMIENS, SAISSEVAL, BOXICOURT, FOURACHES and OISSY; also in the construction of a bath house at MOLLIENS-VIDAMES, including drainage room, drying room, fitting up pumps and necessary fitting and drains.	
14th December	2nd Lieut W. COWAN CLEGG attached to Divisional Training Headquarters at MONTAGNE, as Instructor in Military Engineering and 1/2 Company left SAISSEMONT at 10 a.m. and marched via AILLY and LONGPRE to TAIRPS on AMIENS - DOULLENS road arriving 5 p.m.	
21st December	Class at MONTAGNE. Commenced work on 3rd Army Putting Scheme. Overhauled and retained lauriomi engine and boiler; fitting new packing to pistons; checking glands; fitting new tubes and bolts; fitted 3 workshops and bunches also Net Built foundation	

Army Form C. 2118.

WAR DIARY
or
INTELLIGENCE SUMMARY

(Erase heading not required.)

Instructions regarding War Diaries and Intelligence Summaries are contained in F. S. Regs., Part II. and the Staff Manual respectively. Title pages will be prepared in manuscript.

O.C. 2nd HIGHLAND FIELD COY., R.E. (D)
MAJOR, R.E. (D)

Hour, Date, Place	Summary of Events and Information	Remarks and references to Appendices
	and installed heavy circular cast iron and fitted force plant for same.	
	Constructed latrine frame, ablution trestles. Commenced installation of a deep well pump in well near Church. 186 feet deep.	
19th December	Repaired walls, floors and roofs of billets and drew up a billeting scheme for the village of TRENAS.	
20th December	Watchful action of HM.C.O. and 8 men reported for duty. C.Q.M.S. McINTYRE, military foreman of works reported for duty. 1 dism. FYFE and RITCHIE went on leave.	
24th December	Remaining 1/2 Company reported Unit. No. of NCOs and men in Base detachments = 60.	

1/2nd High'd. F.C. Rig.
Jan 1916
Vol XII

6/1/16

51

1/2 High 2ª Coy
R.E.

Vol XIV

Army Form C. 2118.

WAR DIARY
INTELLIGENCE SUMMARY
(Erase heading not required.)

Instructions regarding War Diaries and Intelligence Summaries are contained in F. S. Regs., Part II. and the Staff Manual respectively. Title pages will be prepared in manuscript.

Hour, Date, Place	Summary of Events and Information	Remarks and references to Appendices
1st January 1916.	Fitting up high well pumps at	

I. TALMAS.

Wells Nºˢ 1 & 2. Both twenty-two feet. Fixed pumps and laying bearers, pistons and cams on steel posts to carry it from window platforms built at ten ace at elevation from the well. 6 H.P. Petrol Engine supplied to pump water. Owing to the fact of there being a history of breaking with water through nuts not actually tight. This was avoided by bolting on through rod bared to be too in a successive direction in stages.

At Wells Nºˢ 8 and 10. Fitted identical frames and constructed hoisting gear, etc. Assembled plant and constructed hoisting gear.

II. VAL DE MAISON.

Well. 118 feet deep to water level. Erected pump, piping, head-gear and power plant.

III. LA VICOGNE.

Erected flying "ISLER" pump, headgear and power plant.

Erected workshops at TALMAS. Repaired and overhauled hand saw engine and boiler. Fitted new boiler tubes, repacked all bearings and steam pumps. Reassembled valves by means of spring and new levers. Tuned up turbine and completely overhauled engine. Fitted up circular saw bench and 30 H.P. motor for same. Fixed blacksmiths shops with forge and vertical drills and put same into working order.

O.C. 2nd HIGHLAND FIELD COY.
MAJOR, R.E. (T.)
2ND HIGHLAND FIELD COY.
Nº 15 Date 1-2-16
R. E.

Army Form C. 2118.

WAR DIARY
or
INTELLIGENCE SUMMARY
(Erase heading not required.)

2/2nd HIGHLAND FIELD COY.
No. 13
Date. 1-2-16
R.E.

Hour, Date, Place	Summary of Events and Information	Remarks and references to Appendices

Established fitters and joiners and painters workshops. Constructed a loading bank at store.
Work done during month:-
Refined reconnaissance in THOMAS by planning known and existing banks for H.500 men, including flooring of barns at
 VAL DE MAISON for 1,400 men
 at LA VICOGNE for 1,000 men
 at FERME DE ROSEL for 1,000 men
Repaired all wells in THOMAS and fitted up a horse haulage arrangement on Well No 11.
Reported on all wells and tanks in our area.
Billet 35 large huts, could come to cover huts and cut into required sizes.
Repaired roads in THOMAS, straining flints by quarrying near LA VICOGNE. Repaired lanes and siding schedule for all villages in our area and inspected and marked up to lists on buildings towards accommodation.

No 3. Company 9th Devon Regiment attached to/for duty.
C. Company 2/10th Manchesters (4th Division) attached for duty 29/1/16
L3 Infantry. enlisted (4th Division) deleted for duty 29/1/16
4 Chilled R.G. from 149th Heavy Trench Coy. R.E yellow/red for duty 29/1/16
1 Motor Lorry attached from 15/1/16 to 31/1/16
4 G.S. Waggons attached from 15/1/16 to 31/1/16
2 Lts. Eyre and Ritchie attached from lease on 10/1/16
2 Lt. Oxell on leave from 11/1/16 to 21/1/16
Lt. Gordon on leave from 22/1/16 to 1/2/16
Sapper Mitchell on leave from 26/1/16 to 5/2/16
Distributor M.L. Hutchings on leave from 1/1/16 to 25/1/16
H.E.W. Comp. Gregg with details of joined Coy on leaving Blair 30/1/16.

Additional training Blair.

O.C. 2nd Highland Field Coy. R.E. (D.)
MAJOR, R.E. (D.)

Army Form C. 2118.

WAR DIARY
or
INTELLIGENCE SUMMARY

(Erase heading not required.)

Instructions regarding War Diaries and Intelligence Summaries are contained in F. S. Regs., Part II. and the Staff Manual respectively. Title pages will be prepared in manuscript.

2nd HIGHLAND FIELD COY.
No. 13
Date 1-2-16
R. E.

Hour, Date, Place	Summary of Events and Information	Remarks and references to Appendices
31st January	Company left THOMAS at 2.30 pm and marched to CO15V1. arriving 51st (Highland) Division's new place of 1st & 3rd DURHAM FIELD CO. (R.E.) No. of N.C.O. and Men on leave during month - 42. 2 N.C.O & 1 Sapper time expired sent to Base for disposal. Draft of 14 others from Base joined Company on 12-1-16 " " 1 " " " " " " 30-1-16 " " 1. 16. "	[signature] O.C. 2nd HIGHLAND FIELD COY. R.E.(T) MAJOR, R.E. (T).

Army. Form C. 2118.

1/2nd HIGHLAND FIELD Coy, R.E.
No. 14
Date 1/3/16

WAR DIARY
or
INTELLIGENCE SUMMARY
(Erase heading not required.)

FEBRUARY 1916

Instructions regarding War Diaries and Intelligence Summaries are contained in F. S. Regs., Part II. and the Staff Manual respectively. Title pages will be prepared in manuscript.

Hour, Date, Place	Summary of Events and Information	Remarks and references to Appendices
1st February	Company billeted in COISY and engaged in company training and drill; rifle exercises, physical exercises, & C.O's communication drawing and visiting card, lecturing and erecting wire trestles and clearing up and refitting.	
7th February	Company moved to LA NEUVILLE with 154th Infantry Brigade, arriving there arriving 2 p.m. Fitted up circular arc and axle, engine to drive saw. Constructed wagons in field, others carting to animal and cart lines to animal lines. Built shelter in the village and erected trestle latrines. Field shelters and latrines, repaired wiring & saw and made lines, boxes of same. Constructed a lath house in CORBIE, with 8 bunks; and new gear recovery; ironing room, dining room, and clothes store; but contents have in all been, and erected resting hut complete, also lath huts clothes store cupboards, beds and night canopies for Repaired portions of roads between CORBIE and PONT NOYELLES and draining CORBIE-DOURS road. Carried on construction of return system for pontoon and bridges for instructional purposes.
21st February 22nd February	11 Lieut. T.P. MAITLAND reported for duty and moved with 154th Infantry Brigade to TOUVAUX arriving at 2 p.m. and billeted there. Lieut. J. GORDON returned from leave 2nd February. Major R. MITCHELL " " " 8th " Capt. W.P. BERRON on leave from 14th to 28th February 24 N.C.Os. 11 Lieut. W.C. GREGG " " 21st to 29th February No. of N.C.Os men on leave during month, 19. No. of N.C.Os men discharged on expiry of term of service.
23	Company training continued; also pontooning and trestle practice in pond near CORBIE.	

O.C. 2nd HIGHLAND FIELD COY RE (T)

Army Form C. 2118.

WAR DIARY
or
INTELLIGENCE SUMMARY
(Erase heading not required.)

1/2nd HIGHLAND FIELD Coy., R.E.
No. XV Vol.
Date. MARCH.

Instructions regarding War Diaries and Intelligence Summaries are contained in F. S. Regs., Part II. and the Staff Manual respectively. Title Pages will be prepared in manuscript.

Place	Date	Hour	Summary of Events and Information	Remarks and references to Appendices
at MARŒUIL	16		Company horse shies and mounted orderly killed, orderlies & horses killed and 6 wounded.	
	18		Lieut. T.J. GORDON admitted to hospital, rejoined unit 25/3/16	
			1 Sapper on leave during month	
			3 NCOs and 3 men sent to Base tins officer.	

W.P. Barron
O.C. 2nd HIGHLAND FIELD COY, R.E.(T.)
Capt R.E. (T)

Army Form C. 2118.

WAR DIARY
or
INTELLIGENCE SUMMARY

(Erase heading not required.)

1/2nd HIGHLAND FIELD Coy., R.E.
No. .... Vol. XV
Date .... MARCH

Instructions regarding War Diaries and Intelligence Summaries are contained in F.S. Regs., Part II. and the Staff Manual respectively. Title Pages will be prepared in manuscript.

Place	Date	Hour	Summary of Events and Information	Remarks and references to Appendices
			Relaid 40 cm. Tramway Track from ANZIN to ROUTE DE LILLE.	
			Repaired bridges in ROUTE DE LILLE and in ROUTE DE BETHUNE.	
			Cleared out and built generally and Trench on Trenches from ROUTE DE LILLE to TR. BONNAR and built further steps and Trenches in GRAND COLLECTEUR Trench.	
			Repaired and overhauled dug-in dug-outs at ETRUN.	
			Destroyed unexploded shells and aerial torpedoes.	
			Took over and re-arranged Electric lighting plant and wiring system in ANZIN ST. AUBYN and in gun positions. Repaired large water wheel and adjusted dynamos and switch boards.	
			Cleaned out and fixed in workshop portable workshop with electric boring machine, lathes, emery buff, planing machine and forge with rotary blower.	
			Repaired steel boxes and built trestle cradles for horse haulage.	
			Altered bogies trucks to 40 cm. gauge, turned new faces on wheels, and fixed up flanges, made spindles and bearings for new bogies.	
			Commenced erection of Electric Lighting Plant at ETRUN.	
			Built grenade and ammunition stores at SABLIERE.	
			Removed dangerous TM at ETRUN.	
			Repaired ammunition director	

2449 Wt. W14957/M90 750,000 1/16 J.B.C. & A. Forms/C.2118/12.

WAR DIARY
or
INTELLIGENCE SUMMARY

(Erase heading not required.)

Army Form C. 2118.

1/2nd HIGHLAND FIELD Coy., R.E.

No. ....XV...vol.........
Date ....MARCH................

Place	Date March	Hour	Summary of Events and Information	Remarks and references to Appendices
MIRVAUX	1		Company engaged in drill, shooting and lecturing etc.	
	3		Inspected by General HARPER, G.O.C., 51st (Highland) Division.	
	6		Left MIRVAUX and marched to BRETEL near DOULLENS.	
	8		Left BRETEL and marched to WAMIN. Two officers met French Engineers of 23rd French Division at ANZIN-ST-AUBIN and reconnoitred sector of front with view to taking over.	
	9		Left WAMIN and marched to ETRUN.	
	10		Left ETRUN and marched to ANZIN-ST-AUBIN. Major R. MITCHELL, D.S.O., Officer Commanding this Company, took over duties of acting C.R.E. from 10th to 23rd March. Headqrs. billeted in MARCEUIL. Company billeted in dug-outs vacated by French Engineers.	
			Took over R.E. charge of sector from 23rd French Division. Company engaged in construction of sector works in conjunction with 154th Infantry Brigade and in sector held etc. Work done by Company during the month:-	

O.C. 2nd HIGHLAND FIELD COY. R.E.(I)
CAPT. R.E. (I)

Army Form C. 2118.

WAR DIARY
or
INTELLIGENCE SUMMARY
(Erase heading not required.)

1/2nd HIGHLAND FIELD Coy., R.E.

XV Vol
Date March 1916

Place	Date	Hour	Summary of Events and Information	Remarks and references to Appendices

Constructed in joiner's shop:- trench boards, trench/steel-hemmed apertures, nose-boards, Machine-gun loopholes. Dug-out frames for moved dug-outs and temporary shelters for front trenches.

Constructed and placed in position, latrine shelters - 50 seats.

Constructed bath-house at ETRUN, complete with dressing and undressing rooms, drying room, boiler and baths, all with concrete floors.

At ECURIE, work done on deep dug-outs and Grenade and extractor.

Commenced mining forward with a view to constructing machine-gun emplacements at end of galleries.

Reconstructing fire-steps and traverses on parts of the defences breezy.

Water in ECURIE was handed over to 130th Field Company R.E. on 24th March 1916.

Repaired and improved all machine-gun emplacements in GRAND COLLECTEUR trench.

New platforms with hinged posts for rapid mounting up and piece of platform in position.

Constructed ventilation shafts in dug-outs under ROUTE DE LILLE.

O.C. 2nd HIGHLAND FIELD COY., R.E.

Army Form C. 2118.

WAR DIARY
or
INTELLIGENCE SUMMARY

(Erase heading not required.)

1/2nd HIGHLAND FIELD Coy., R.E.

Vol: XVI.
No. ....
Date APRIL 1916

O.C. 1/2nd Highland Field Coy: R.E.
[signature] Major, R.E. (T)

Place	Date	Hour	Summary of Events and Information	Remarks and references to Appendices
	1/30		Conclusion killed (dug-outs) at ANZIN-ST-AUBYN near ARRAS.	1
			The Company engaged in the following work:— Deepening BONNAL trench between L.20 and L.24; Dug-out for TRENCH MORTAR OFFICERS in trench PLACE D'ARMES ANCIENNE — with two entrances; Dug-out under ARRAS—BETHUNE ROAD for MIDLOTHIAN BATTERY R.F.A.; Camouflage Artillery Observation Post, near MADAGASCAR—ECURIE road; Framework erected ready for superstructure of steel; Boathstore in LA SABLIERE — enlarging and framing with wood and making new door; Setting up and to a certain consider tearing Radial Mountings for Machine Guns in B9 10 & B11 D. traverse CHARLES; Deepening trench ASR.CENTRAL for extra cover and constructing and framing manholes; Weeing of damaged trenches in old frontline and instructing infantry. Repairing framing and building Spit-traverse for protection of well at ROCLINCOURT. Making concrete well to prevent one from going down well and cleaning drains of well at BARRICADE on ROCLINCOURT road.	

Army Form C. 2118.

1/2nd HIGHLAND
FIELD Coy., R.E.

No. .... Vol: XVI
Date ..... APRIL 26.

WAR DIARY
or
INTELLIGENCE SUMMARY

(Erase heading not required.)

Place	Date	Hour	Summary of Events and Information	Remarks and references to Appendices
	1/30		Making a deep well sump for well at ROCLINCOURT and placing it in position. Sump carried on wooden framework, lined transversely and strutted to sides and delivery to trunk with taps.	
			Constructing Concrete machine gun Emplacement in NEW COLLECTEUR Trench, Roof front and sides made of concrete and roof reinforced with 8. 5"x3" R.S.B.	
			Two other concrete machine gun Emplacements to commence in COLLECTEUR Trench at Boyau CHARLES and Boyau BIDOT.	
			Re-siting NEW COLLECTEUR Trench, and revetting same with 3ex 73 and turfing	
			Constructing two visual signalling stations — one in SABLIERE and one on LILLE ROAD. Both consist of dug-outs with kinescope carried to surface of ground and funnels on top for signalling lamps.	
			Making Cooking Shelter in Boyau FANTOME. Reconnaissance of Trench 8'x 8'.	

Major, R.E. (T.)
O.C. 1/2nd Highland Field Coy: R.E.

Army Form C. 2118.

1/2nd HIGHLAND
FIELD Coy., R.E.

No. VOL. XVI
Date APR 12 1916

WAR DIARY
or
INTELLIGENCE SUMMARY

(Erase heading not required.)

O.C. 1/2nd Highland Field Coy: R.E.
Major, R.E. (T)

Place	Date	Hour	Summary of Events and Information	Remarks and references to Appendices
	1/30		Forward R.E. Store at FERME MODELE, making entrance from communication trench leading into old cellar and constructing a flight of steps in opposite side of trench to new LILLE ROAD	
			Strengthening Gun Emplacements of 2nd CITY OF EDINBURGH and 1/1 MIDLOTHIAN Batteries	
			R.F.R. (LOTHIANS BDE) laying new corrugated iron roof, water proofing and making shelter in Ammunition Shelter, framing and fitting new roof in Telephone Dugout.	
			Building concrete Sentry Posts in GRAND COLLECTEUR - 20 yards syd	
			Boyau BIDOT intersection, in NEW COLLECTEUR at point L.29, in TRENCH BOYAU 4 and in BOYAU FANTOME	
			Constructing reinforced concrete Machine Gun Emplacement in GRAND COLLECTEUR on right arm of LILLE ROAD. Reinforced with channels and steel joists with layer of expanded metal near outside surface. Angle for Bullets wide in front and sides.	
			Framed and erected three temporary shelters in left sub-sector between L.27. L.29. the dimensions being 9'6" x 9'0"	

WAR DIARY or INTELLIGENCE SUMMARY

Army Form C. 2118.

1/2nd HIGHLAND FIELD Coy., R.E.
No. XVI
Date APRIL 1916

O.C. 1/2nd Highland Field Coy: R.E.
Major, R.E. (T)

Place	Date	Hour	Summary of Events and Information	Remarks and references to Appendices
	1/30		Began Cautier shelter erected at ETRUN.	
			The following dug-outs completed:-	
			1 for Machine Gun Section in COLLECTEUR TRENCH at PT 219 (two entrances)	
			3 (with two entrances each) in Main Fire Trench at L.29 and L.27.	
			3 (with two entrances) in COLLECTEUR TRENCH at PT 56. (two entrances)	
			1 for Company Headquarters in COLLECTEUR TRENCH at PT 403.	
			2 in Main Fire Trench at L.29 and L.26. (two entrances).	
			Erecting New Stokes Gun (double) emplacement near CRATER PT 403.	
			Laying 600 yards Pipe Line to 1º SOBLIÈRES up CHEMIN CREUX; semi-rotary pump	
			placed at well in ROCLINCOURT to pump water; 3 - 200 gallon tanks placed in 1º	
			SOBLIÈRE. Pipe line placed in separate trench with 12" of cover.	
			Laying trench pipe line (length 150 yards) from CHEMIN CREUX to PBK CENTRAL.	
			Trench from trench line with alternate valves and two tanks placed at PBK CENTRAL.	

Army Form C. 2118.

WAR DIARY
or
INTELLIGENCE SUMMARY

(Erase heading not required.)

1/2nd HIGHLAND FIELD Coy., R.E.
No. VOL: XVI
Date. April 1918

Instructions regarding War Diaries and Intelligence Summaries are contained in F.S. Regs., Part II. and the Staff Manual respectively. Title Pages will be prepared in manuscript.

Place	Date	Hour	Summary of Events and Information	Remarks and references to Appendices
	1/30		Building Concrete Machine Gun emplacement W; making frames for roof and putting in shuttering and placing concrete walls. Erecting new spray heater and partitioning off enclosing place at Bath house at ETRUN. Making frames and hurdles at ETRUN; Revising and instructing infantry in making of same. Work done in R.E. Workshops during month:- Supplying Trench doors and making dug-out frames, trench board, portable closets at frees, notice boards (including printing frames); Trench shelters, rifle racks, Trench ladders; machine gun rocket recentacle forms; swivelling machine gun turrets, fixed rifle mountings. Preparing all necessary material and fittings for work on water supplies, railways and deep-mined dug-outs.	

O.C. 1/2nd Highland Field Coy: R.E.
Major, R.E. (T)

Army Form C. 2118.

1/2nd HIGHLAND FIELD Coy., R.E.
No. Vol. XVI
Date April 1916

WAR DIARY
or
INTELLIGENCE SUMMARY
(Erase heading not required.)

Instructions regarding War Diaries and Intelligence Summaries are contained in F.S. Regs, Part II. and the Staff Manual respectively. Title Pages will be prepared in manuscript.

Place	Date	Hour	Summary of Events and Information	Remarks and references to Appendices
	1/30		Making steel storage tanks.	
			Constructing bogies for 40 cm track	
			Laying 40 cm railway line to FERME MODELE.	
			Relieving bogie wheels. Erecting a new circular revetment and coveraging sieve for same.	
			Major Westhill on leave from (1) 12-4-16 to 20-4-16 and (2) 24-4-16 to 1-5-16	
			3 Other ranks on leave during month.	
			Transport lines and billets at MOREUIL shelled on 28th. 2 Drivers being connected and 1 severely injured. 1 horse killed and 6 wounded.	
			Transport engaged in carting stone during April	
			2 Officers and 2 N.C.Os said attended an ANTI-GAS course.	
			Reinforcements from base, reported for duty on the following dates: 6/4/16 .... 1.O.RONK
			16/4/16 ..... 14. O.RANKS.
			1 Sapper sent to Base, time expired.	

2449 Wt. W14957/M90 750,000 1/16 J.B.C. & A. Forms/C.2118/12.

O.C. 1/2nd Highland Field Coy: R.E.
Major, R.E. (T)

51

Vol 16

1/2nd HIGHLAND
FIELD Coy., R.E.

WAR DIARY

for

MAY - 1916

Vol. No ~~XVII~~

Army Form C. 2118.

WAR DIARY
or
INTELLIGENCE SUMMARY

(Erase heading not required.)

1/2nd HIGHLAND FIELD Coy., R.E.

Vol. XVII
Date MAY 1916

Place	Date	Hour	Summary of Events and Information	Remarks and references to Appendices
	1st / 31st		Company in billets in ANZIN-ST-AUBIN.	
			Company engaged on the following work throughout the month:-	
			ECURIE defences:- Wiring at different points round the defended locality. Constructing and improving fire and communication trenches, ammunition shelters and dug-outs constructed.	
			Progress made with reinforced concrete machine-gun emplacements and arranging steel vertical mountings for machine guns fitted in same.	
			Water supply improved by laying pipes, fitting up pumps and storage tanks etc.	
			Work done in front trench system:- Construction and repair of deep dug-outs continued, with 2 new dug-outs and	
			seven shaft entrances to same and fitting all dug-outs with gas curtains and small proof screens.	

[signature]
Major, R.E. (T)
O.C. 1/2nd Highland Field Coy: R.E.

Army Form C. 2118.

WAR DIARY
or
INTELLIGENCE SUMMARY
(Erase heading not required.)

1/2nd HIGHLAND FIELD Coy., R.E.
No. VOL: XVII
Date 12th May 1917

Place	Date	Hour	Summary of Events and Information	Remarks and references to Appendices
			Mac Roberts Gun emplacement and shelter etc.	
			Constructed deep store for grenades and trench mortar shells at FERME DES CAVES	
			Also other dug-outs and deep mined Tunnel entrances.	
			Constructed 8 reinforced concrete sentry posts in front trenches and dug-in.	
			Constructed 4 reinforced concrete machine gun emplacements with one mountings, loopholes etc.	
			Completed light line from ROCLINCOURT to ABRI CENTRAL and other tanks in position.	
			Keeping deep well trench in order and resetting displaced pump, for semi-rotary pump.	
			Completing machine gun emplacement in W.	
			Making machine gun emplacement L.S.B. with dome mountings	
			Making second entrance to dug-out in CHEMIN CREUX	

[signature] Major, R.E. (T)
O.C. 1/2nd Highland Field Coy: R.E.

WAR DIARY or INTELLIGENCE SUMMARY

Army Form C. 2118.

1/2nd HIGHLAND FIELD Coy., R.E.

No. VOL: XVII
Date MAY 1916

Summary of Events and Information

Making second entrance to and enlarging dugout in W.

Driving shaft and making dugout chamber at WELL at FERME DES CAVES.

Making gas proof doors to AID POST at LILLE ROAD.

Making Machine gun emplacement No. 12 at ECURIE

Laying Pipe line to Headquarters ECURIE and putting in tanks and pump

Wiring and blocking disused trenches

Constructed 3 Trench Mortar Emplacements and dug-outs

R.E. Workshops:- Constructed medical mountings and ironwork and fittings for same including graduated cane-well in erection.

Cutting oak and Rolled Steel Joists, making bolts, corg. iron rods and iron buckets

Fitting up gheeting tube system in 2 Battery positions 256th BDE. R.F.A. including boring holes through ground, cutting trenches, cutting, bending and

(signed) Major, R.E. (T)
O.G. 1/2nd Highland Field Coy. R.E.

Army Form C. 2118.

WAR DIARY
or
INTELLIGENCE SUMMARY
(Erase heading not required.)

1/2nd HIGHLAND FIELD Coy., R.E.
No. .... VOL: XVII
Dated July 1916

Instructions regarding War Diaries and Intelligence Summaries are contained in F. S. Regs., Part II. and the Staff Manual respectively. Title Pages will be prepared in manuscript.

Place	Date	Hour	Summary of Events and Information	Remarks and references to Appendices

and securing W.I. tubes and fitting mouthpieces etc.

Repaired wagons and constructed trolleys for light tramway track, including turning frees on wheels, making spindles and superstructure.

Pury's. Forging fittings, making plungerods and spent cartridges.

Fitting cocks on water tanks of 300 gallons capacity.

Made fused inflicents and ignitors for firing rifle grenades.

Constructed large numbers of trench floorboards, dug-out frames, foleys, chevaux de frise.

Repaired and manufactured 40 cm. track to BARRICADE and 60 cm track to ARIANE. Repaired power station Dynamo by cutting out broken cooling tape, white metal powered, finishing up same complete with oil grove and rebaring.

Fitted up CAMOUFLAGE O.P. near MADAGASCAR, act'd on string wire-frame.

Began and commenced construction of a deep dug-out at avenue ....

[signature]
Major, R.E. (T)
O.C. 1/2nd Highland Field Coy: R.E.

Army Form C. 2118.

WAR DIARY
or
INTELLIGENCE SUMMARY

(Erase heading not required.)

1/2nd HIGHLAND FIELD Coy., R.E.

No. .... VOL: XVII
Date .... MAY 1916

Place	Date	Hour	Summary of Events and Information	Remarks and references to Appendices
			Cutting timber in sawmill, 5,000 lineal feet cut per day.	
			Constructed dug-outs below BÉTHUNE ROAD for R.F.A. and constructed concrete O.P. in ECURIE.	
			Completed Visual Signal Station at ECURIE.	
			Constructed dug out for dressing station in ANZIN.	
			On May 31st the Company took over the M. SECTOR, as far as ANNIVERSAIRE TRENCH in addition to L. SECTOR and commenced work of repair and improvement there, including machine gun emplacements, dugouts, water supply etc.	
			Instructed infantry parties in revetting — 2 parties of 25 men each day throughout the month.	
			Constructed 100 yards of trench tramrail for G.O.C.'s inspection.	

[signature]

Major, R.E. (T)
O.C. 1/2nd Highland Field Coy: R.E.

Army Form C. 2118.

WAR DIARY
or
INTELLIGENCE SUMMARY
(Erase heading not required.)

1/2nd HIGHLAND FIELD Coy., R.E.
No. Vol. XVII
DATE MAY 1916

Place	Date	Hour	Summary of Events and Information	Remarks and references to Appendices
	21		Monte too action engaged in eretingations both by rove and in light railways.	
	15	May	3 Officers and 3 NCOs attended Anti Gas Courses at FREVIN CAPELLE during month	
			M.O. & Logost. E. Hutchings, Interpreter transferred to 153rd Infantry Brigade on 2.19th May.	
	9		Sergeant George FORTROT arrived and took up duty on 15th May.	
			Lieut. (temporary Major) R.W. JOHNSTONE, 2/2nd Highland Field Coy R.E. attached on 6th May.	
	6		Coy. Company for instruction for 3 days from 9th May.	
			Coy. Acetylene Generic of 2 N.C.Os. and 10 Sappers sent to base to be trained as ordinary reinforcements in accordance with instructions regarding withdrawal of daylight sections from Field Companies R.E.	
	2		Lieut. Major Mitchell, D.S.O, Returned from leave on 2nd May.	
	6		11th Lt. A.B. Fyfe went on leave from 7th to 15th Returned from leave on 15th May.	
	6		Interpreter Hutchings went on leave. Returned 15th May.	

[signature]
Major, R.E. (T)
O.C. 1/2nd Highland Field Coy: R.E.

Army Form C. 2118.

WAR DIARY
or
INTELLIGENCE SUMMARY
(Erase heading not required.)

1/2nd HIGHLAND FIELD Coy, R.E.

No. VOL: XVII
Date 1st MAY 1916

Place	Date	Hour	Summary of Events and Information	Remarks and references to Appendices
	13		11/= F.B.RITCHIE. Went on leave 14th to 22nd. Returned on 23rd May.	
	20		11/= C.OKELL. Went on leave 21st to 29th. Returned on 31st May.	
	24		Lt T.J.GORDON Went on leave 28th to 5th June.	
	28		1 Sapper sent to Base time expired on 12th June.	
			Lt T.J.GORDON. Promoted Temporary Lieut dated 19/9/15) Announced in London Gazette	
			Lt W.C.GLEGG. Promoted Temporary Lieut. dated 24/8/15) of 16/5/16.	
			4 N.C.Os Men on leave during the month.	

J M Mitchell Major, R.E. (T)
O.C. 1/2nd Highland Field Coy: R.E.

— SECRET —

OFFICER i/c
A.G.'s Office
G.H.Q.

Herewith WAR DIARY for
month of April last.

1/2nd HIGHLAND
FIELD Coy., R.E.
№ 30
Date 28/5/16

[signature]
Major, R.E. (T)
O.C. 1/2nd Highland Field Coy: R.E.

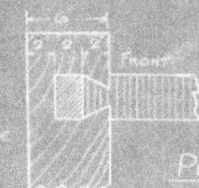

Sentry Post

Scale 1/4" = 3"

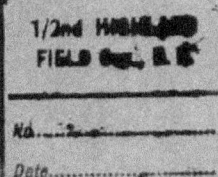

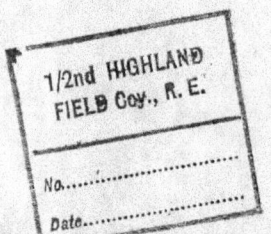

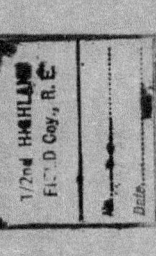

PLAN.

MACHINE GUN EMPLACEMENT
&
RADIAL MOUNTING

Scale ½ in = 1 Foot

1/2nd HIGHLAND
FIELD Coy, R.E.

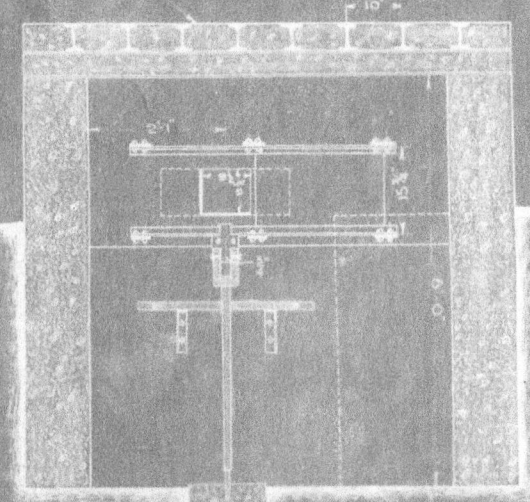

BACK ELEVATION

SECTION THRO' A-A

1/2nd HIGHLAND
FIELD Coy., R. E.

No..............
Date............

Fire Trench Shelter

Scale $\frac{1}{2}" = 1'$

Quantities

4	Uprights 5'·0" × 6" × 6"
2	R.S.J. 10'·0" × 5" × 3"
11	R.S.J. 7'·0" × 3" × 1½"
12	Flat Iron 10'·0" × 1" × ¼"
5	7'·0" Sheets G.C.I.
400	Sandbags (approx)

30 Men to carry one up

Approx Weight 220 Kgs.

Section thro' A·B

Parapet — Parados

Filled in with Sandbags &c.

Corrugated Iron — Flat Iron 10'·0"×1"×¼"
R.S.J. 7'·0" × 3" × 1½"
R.S.J. 10'·0" × 5" × 3"

Seating for 13 men

1/2nd HIGHLAND FIELD Coy., R.E.

(Army Form C. 2118.)

WAR DIARY
or
INTELLIGENCE SUMMARY

(Erase heading not required.)

War Diary
of
1st/2nd Highland Field Coy RE
for
June 1916

Vol. No. XXX

WITH RELATIVE MAP
and
SKETCH

Army Form C. 2118.

WAR DIARY
or
INTELLIGENCE SUMMARY

(Erase heading not required.)

1/2nd HIGHLAND FIELD Coy., R.E.

No. ....

Date June 1916

Place	Date	Hour	Summary of Events and Information	Remarks and references to Appendices
	1/6/16		Company in billets as follows:— 4 Sections R.E. in ANZIN ST AUBYN. Mounted Section in MAREUIL. The Company was engaged in the following work throughout the month:— In L. SECTOR – RIGHT SUB-SECTOR. Machine gun emplacement L.S.A.–concrete in walls and on roof, recurring shuttering. Machine gun emplacement L.S.C. lowering trophole and putting concrete table. Machine gun emplacement L.S.D. completing mounting and giving up loophole. Machine gun emplacement L.S. putting new doors in place of ore blown away. Commencing to lay pipe line from ABRI CENTRAL – service ABRI CENTRAL to ABRI DU MOUTON.	

O.C. 1/2nd Highland Field Coy: R.E.

Major, R.E. (T)

Army Form C. 2118.

WAR DIARY
or
INTELLIGENCE SUMMARY

(Erase heading not required.)

1/2nd HIGHLAND FIELD Coy., R.E.

No. ......Vol. XVIII......
Date .... 1st April 1916

Instructions regarding War Diaries and Intelligence Summaries are contained in F. S. Regs., Part II. and the Staff Manual respectively. Title Pages will be prepared in manuscript.

Place	Date	Hour	Summary of Events and Information	Remarks and references to Appendices
	1-30 June		Repairing dump at wcc in ROCLINCOURT.	
			Completing fire trench shelter in TRENCH BONNAL where it cuts LILLE ROAD.	
			I. L. SECTOR: RIGHT 2 SUB-SECTOR:- Deep dug-outs.	
			Completing deep dug-out at L.28. Making rear entrance to dugout at L.29	
			Completing telephone dugout in AVENUE FANTOME.	
			Completing dug-out in intermediate line on left of point 54.	
			Commenced construction of dug-out at junction of ORR AVENUE and intermediate line.	
			Water tanks:- making emplacement for three - 200 gallon water tanks at junction of SPOONER AVENUE and ORR AVENUE.	

Major, R.E. (T)
O.C. 1/2nd Highland Field Coy: R.E.

2449 Wt. W14957/M90 750,000 1/16 J.R.C. & A. Forms/C.2118/12.

Army Form C. 2118.

WAR DIARY
or
INTELLIGENCE SUMMARY
(Erase heading not required.)

1/2nd HIGHLAND FIELD Coy, R.E.

No. ...... Vol. XVIII
Date .... April 1918

O.C. 1/2nd Highland Field Coy: R.E. (T)

Place	Date	Hour	Summary of Events and Information	Remarks and references to Appendices
			Main Fire trench.	
			Clearing, revetting and fire stepping and repairing damage by shell.	
			Fire.	
			Support line.	
			Trench boarding, making traverses and fire stepping and deepening	
			Trench.	
			Machine Gun Emplacements.	
			Completed emplacement M.S.A. in support line at F.12, raised mountings	
			Completed emplacement M.S.B. in support line at E.9.12 for ORR AVENUE	
			Completed emplacement M.S.D. in support line at point 210.	
			Lewis Gun concrete emplacement.	
			Constructing Lewis Gun concrete emplacement at M.31.	
			Company Headquarters Dug-out.	
			Constructed Company Headquarters dug-out at WICK AVENUE.	
			Making emplacement for 100 gallon water tank at MINOTAUR AVENUE.	

2449 Wt. W14957/M90 750,000 1/16 J.B.C. & A. Forms/C.2118/12.

Army Form C. 2118.

WAR DIARY
INTELLIGENCE SUMMARY
(Erase heading not required.)

1/2nd HIGHLAND FIELD Coy., R.E.

No. R.E. XVIII
Date. March 1916

Place	Date	Hour	Summary of Events and Information	Remarks and references to Appendices
In M. SECTOR			Reinforced concrete sentry posts:- Construction of the following sentry posts:- 2 in front line at M.30: 1 in shaft at M.30a: 1 in front line at M.32: 1 in front line at M.33: and 1 in TRENCH BONNAL at L.24.	
			ECURIE DEFENCES. Wire Trenches: deepening, revetting fire steps, parapets and parados, building traverses, laying floor boards and widening sumps.	
			Communication Trenches:- deepening, laying floor boards, etc.	
			Strong post barricades and bombing and loophole blocks, lighting up parapets to conceal C⁰ 11 Machine Gun Emplacement.	
			Constructing (Moncrieffe) Post with Cylinder Drop cover at rear. D.3.	
			Deep dug-outs (two entrances):- 5 dug-outs, chambers excavated, framed and shoring driven.	

O.C. 1/2nd Highland Field Coy: R.E.
Major, R.E. (T)

Army Form C. 2118.

WAR DIARY
or
INTELLIGENCE SUMMARY
(Erase heading not required.)

1/2nd HIGHLAND FIELD Coy., R.E.

No. .... Date ....

O.O. 1/2nd Highland Field Coy. R.E.

Place	Date	Hour	Summary of Events and Information	Remarks and references to Appendices
ECURIE DEFENCES (continued).			CONCRETE MACHINE GUN EMPLACEMENTS.	
			No. 15 M.G.E. Concrete work completed, loophole cleared and recess mounting and table fitted. New ladder fitted in entrance shaft.	
			No. 14 M.G.E. Concrete work of walls and roof of group completed. Entrance tunnel and shaft excavated, frames and lintels.	
			No. 13 M.G.E. Loophole cleared, bottom bearing of radial mounting fitted and sliding shutter and table for mounting fitted.	
			No. 12 M.G.E. Concrete work completed, loophole cleared and recess mounting fitted and sliding shutter guides fitted.	
			No. 11 M.G.E. Concrete work completed. Timber centering removed and loophole cleared.	
			No. 18 M.G.E. Wall in front of site of emplacement under shelter filled with concrete and cemented.	
			No. 9 M.G.E. Pit of emplacement excavated and sandbag outer walls partly built.	
			No. 6 M.G.E. Radial mounting table and sliding shutter fitted, outside of loophole cleared.	
			No. 5 M.G.E. Loophole cleared and concrete work partly built.	
			No. 8 M.G.E. Wooden cradle added to radial mounting to raise muzzle of gun.	

Army Form C. 2118.

WAR DIARY
or
INTELLIGENCE SUMMARY

(Erase heading not required.)

1/2nd HIGHLAND FIELD Coy., R.E.

No. Vol. XVII
Date April 1916

O.C. 1/2nd Highland Field Coy: R.E.
Copy – Major, R.E. (T)

Place	Date	Hour	Summary of Events and Information	Remarks and references to Appendices

In P. SECTOR. One section R.E. under Lieutenants OKELL and FYFE attached for work on QUARRIES LINE from 5th to 18th June.

Wiring in front of about 2500 yards and clearing communication fire trenches —

In R.E. Workshops.

Concrete sentry Pots: Construction of timber framing and being carried on continued also the casting of reinforced concrete wall pieces averaging 3 ft × 30 of these have been made.

Machine gun work: (a) Timber bracket mountings nearly mounted work for fittings made. Loophole plates cut in two and fitted with hinges.
(b) Ordnance mountings copied and received in absence of accurate gradients supply.
(c) A few mountings have been supplied to facilitate the use of machine guns against aeroplanes. They allow a travel of 135° in a vertical plane and a complete horizontal travel.

2449 Wt. W14957/M90 750,000 1/16 J.B.C. & A. Forms/C.2118/12.

Army Form C. 2118.

WAR DIARY
or
INTELLIGENCE SUMMARY
(Erase heading not required.)

1/2nd HIGHLAND FIELD Coy, R.E.
Vol. XVIII
Date: March 1916

Place	Date	Hour	Summary of Events and Information	Remarks and references to Appendices
	1/30		<u>Trench Mortar Work</u>. This has consisted principally in erecting emplacements and repairs for the Trench Mortar Battery and also the supplying for very considerable number of rolled steel joists sent to reconnoitre the <u>approaches to Ruined and Wells</u>. I informed the dug-out emplacements, the nature of the materials required in the different trenches, no particulars were obtained in the Brigade Area are not equal to the emergencies of them. From the mapping nature of the repairs required in different trenches, no particulars were obtained. The lifting gear at such will alter care has been replaced repeatedly. Upon one occasion a complete new steel rope has to be supplied. There is every evidence of the walls being very roughly handled by the enemy. <u>Dug-outs</u>. Supplies of dug-out frames, Emergency Enclosures are being continued. Dug-outs constructed near ARTILLERY O.P. and for Ennd Rangers Position 1) A.27.a.2.4. 2) A.27.a.3.1. 3) G.3.a.3.5.	

O.O. 1/2nd Highland Field Coy. R.E.
Major R.E. (T)

WAR DIARY
INTELLIGENCE SUMMARY

(Erase heading not required.)

Army Form C. 2118.

1/2nd HIGHLAND FIELD Coy., R.E.

No. ....
Date ....

Place	Date	Hour	Summary of Events and Information	Remarks and references to Appendices
	1/30		Cutting of Sal Beams & Ruler:— About 300 - 5"x 3" Rolled R.S.J. beams have been cut to order during the month and also several heavy mahogany rulers. Cutting of Timber:— Most of the timber sawed from our own supply of large section went on the revival. It consists of boarding and light battens. Bridge Work:— As one of the bridges on the RUE ROAD was of faulty construction and required frequent repairs — a complete new bridge constructed to carry if necessary, tractors and heavy artillery, was erected. Constructed were recesses for dug-out entrances collapsible elements — free, boxes for ammunition recesses and to hold dirty linen, making and painting notice boards. Maintained 40 cm. and 60 cm light railway to BARRICADE and ZIANE respectively. GENERAL./	

O.C. 1/2nd Highland Field Coy: R.E.
Major, R.E. (T)

Army Form C. 2118.

WAR DIARY or INTELLIGENCE SUMMARY

(Erase heading not required.)

1/2nd HIGHLAND FIELD Coy., R.E.

Date: March 1916

Place	Date	Hour	Summary of Events and Information	Remarks and references to Appendices
	1/30		GENERAL:- New O.3. ECURIE Artillery O.P. constructed.	
			Constructed dug-out at L.29 in AVENUE NEW FANTOME for 2" TRENCH MORTAR Battery.	
			Constructed Dressing Station in ANZIN.	
			Made work on dummy figures mounted on frames. Telephone erected in trenches ready for use.	
			25 figures in communication trenches off SAP 23.	
			25 " in SAPHEAD L.22.	
			30 " in French SENTIER.	
			Completed dug-out at Camouflage O.P. near MADAGASCAR.	
			Completed 2 dug-outs for Army Corps Ranging Station.	
			Erected speaking tubes in battery position in AVENUE DU GENIE.	
			Mounted section engaged in carrying stores from MARŒUIL to ANZIN,	
			running trains of bogies from MARŒUIL to ARIANE and from ANZIN to ECURIE	

O.O. 1/2nd Highland Field Coy. R.E.
Major, R.E. (T.)

WAR DIARY
INTELLIGENCE SUMMARY
(Erase heading not required.)

Army Form C. 2118.

1/2nd HIGHLAND FIELD Coy., R.E.

No. .... Date ....

Place	Date	Hour	Summary of Events and Information	Remarks and references to Appendices
	1/30		Major R. MITCHELL, Officer Commanding, took over duties of acting C.R.E. from 14th to 23rd June. Horse Lines frequently shelled during the month and also bombed by aeroplane. ANZIN shelled daily. Casualties during the month :- 1 Sapper Wounded. Lieut. Gordon returned from leave on 4th June. Interpreter G. FORTRAT returned from leave on 3rd June. Number of N.C.Os. & Men on leave during the month = 6. 2 Sappers and 4 Drivers reinforcement joined from Base. Two Officers and 2 N.C.Os. attended Anti-Gas Course for 5 days.	

O.C. 1/2nd Highland Field Coy: R.E.

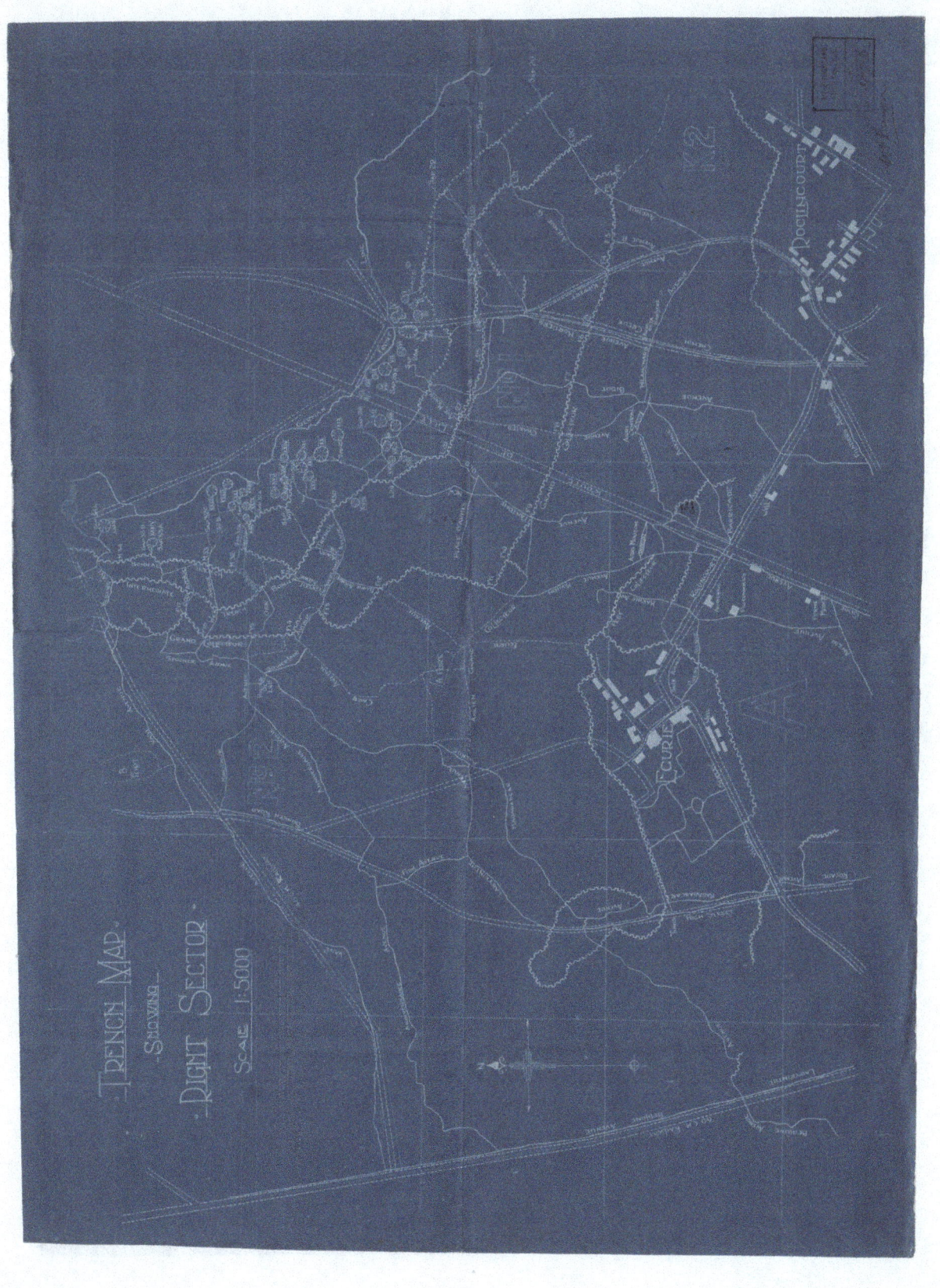

SECRET

The Officer i/c
ADJUTANT-GENERAL'S OFFICE
G.H.Q.,
BASE

Herewith War Diary for month of June 1916.

1/2nd HIGHLAND
FIELD Coy., R.E.
No. 3
Date 31-7-16

W R Barron
Capt., R.E. (T)
O.C. 1/2nd Highland Field Coy: R.E.

CONFIDENTIAL.
No. 3092.A.

Army Form C. 2118.

WAR DIARY
or
HIGHLAND DIVISION INTELLIGENCE SUMMARY

(Erase heading not required.)

Instructions regarding War Diaries and Intelligence Summaries are contained in F. S. Regs., Part II. and the Staff Manual respectively. Title pages will be prepared in manuscript.

Hour, Date, Place	Summary of Events and Information	Remarks and references to Appendices

July 16

WAR DIARY
OF
1ST/2ND HIGHLAND FIELD COY R.E. (T.F.)
for
JULY 1916

VOL. No. ***

WITH MAP

WAR DIARY
INTELLIGENCE SUMMARY
(Erase heading not required.)

Army Form C. 2118.

1/2nd HIGHLAND FIELD Coy., R.E.
No. Vol. XIX
Date July 1916

Hour, Date, Place	Summary of Events and Information	Remarks and references to Appendices
ANZIN ST AUBYN	Instructing 3rd/2nd London Field Co. R.E. 60th Division in	
1st JULY to 11th July	trench work in b SECTOR and M. SECTOR.	
	Company engaged in construction of dug-outs. Repairing	
	Communication trenches for flanking fire. Deepening, revetting and	
	improving trenches. Section of concrete Sentry Posts and concrete	
	MACHINE GUN EMPLACEMENTS. Work on water supply: roads	
	repaired and bridgement erected. Checking tube out. Kent	
	and erected in battery positions.	
	Running workshops and power station as reported in	
	previous diaries.	
	Continued instructing infantry parties numbering 50 Officers	
	and men daily.	
	Handed	

12th July

Army Form C. 2118.

1/2nd HIGHLAND FIELD Coy., R.E.
No. VOL: XIX
Date July 1916

WAR DIARY
or
INTELLIGENCE SUMMARY
(Erase heading not required.)

Instructions regarding War Diaries and Intelligence Summaries are contained in F. S. Regs, Part II. and the Staff Manual respectively. Title pages will be prepared in manuscript.

Hour, Date, Place	Summary of Events and Information	Remarks and references to Appendices
12th July.	Handed over all work and material to 3rd/3rd London Field Coy. R.E. who took over R.E. charge of 154th Infantry Brigade sector prior to relief of division.	M.W.
13th July.	Company moved at 10 a.m. to CHELERS near SAVY, arriving at 4 p.m. — moving by PREAS – 52 POL ROAD. Billeted here.	M.W.
14th July.	1 Section (Lieut. FYFE) detailed to work on work apron of trenches for infantry training. Commenced erection of bath house at ROCOURT. Major R. MITCHELL removed to 42nd Casualty Clearing Station, under M.O's orders.	
15th July.	Orders received at 11.45 p.m. to move to LUCHEUX and to be at CROSS ROADS TINCQUES at 12 midnight 14/15th. Packed up and cleared ground, arriving at rendezvous at 1.15 a.m.	M.W. Barker Major R.E. R.E.(T) O.C. 1/2nd Highland Field Coy.

Army Form C. 2118.

WAR DIARY
or
INTELLIGENCE SUMMARY
(Erase heading not required.)

1/2nd HIGHLAND FIELD Coy, R.E.
No. 1041/X/X 3
Date. 7 July 1916

Instructions regarding War Diaries and Intelligence Summaries are contained in F. S. Regs., Part II. and the Staff Manual respectively. Title pages will be prepared in manuscript.

Hour, Date, Place	Summary of Events and Information	Remarks and references to Appendices
15th July	Surplus stores and kit dumped at CHELERS and left in care of 1 NCO and 2 men. Dismounted men conveyed to LOCHIEUX in motor lorries arriving 4 am.	
16th July	Mounted Section arrived 8.30 am. Company billeted in LUCHEUX.	WB 1
17th July	Company moved at 9 am. to GRIMONT, 18 miles march, arriving 2 pm. Billeted in GRIMONT.	WB
18th July	Company engaged in cleaning and getting foot inspection and general overhaul.	WB
19th July	Engaged in drill and company training. Company engaged in drill, bayonet exercise and a short scheme". Received orders to move at 2.30 pm. to MONTONVILLERS near FLESSELLES.	WB

[Signature]
Major, R.E. (T)
O.C. 1/2nd Highland Field Coy.

Army Form C. 2118.

WAR DIARY
or
INTELLIGENCE SUMMARY
(Erase heading not required.)

1/2nd HIGHLAND FIELD Coy., R.E.

No. 4

Date ... July 1915

Hour, Date, Place	Summary of Events and Information	Remarks and references to Appendices
20th July	Arrived at MINTONVILLERS at 3.30 am and received orders to move at once to MERICOURT 18 miles away. Left at 5 am and marched to MERICOURT. Received orders here to proceed on to MEAULTE and arrived at 5pm, having covered a distance of 41 miles. Officer Commanding the Company was in command of a Column, consisting of our Field Coy R.E., one Field Ambulance, all Transport of 154th Infantry Brigade and 1/4th Machine Gun Company. Men very tired and footsore. 1 horse died on the way. Company trenched near MEAULTE.	
21st July	Moved at 4pm to FRICOURT and trenched beside road.	

O.C. 1/2nd Highland Field Coy. R.E.
M.R. Ross Capt. R.E. (T)
Major, Coy. R.E. R.E.

Army Form C. 2118.

WAR DIARY
— OR —
INTELLIGENCE SUMMARY
(Erase heading not required.)

1/2nd HIGHLAND FIELD Coy., R.E.

No. ....
Date ....July 1916..............

Instructions regarding War Diaries and Intelligence Summaries are contained in F. S. Regs., Part II. and the Staff Manual respectively. Title pages will be prepared in manuscript.

Hour, Date, Place	Summary of Events and Information	Remarks and references to Appendices
21st July.	Old British Support Line.	W.N./
22nd July.	Moved to dugouts in ravine between POICOURT & BECOURT.	
	4 Sections marched to BAZENTIN LE GRAND under heavy shell barrage and worked on defence of village and consolidation of position — returning to billets at 12 midnight. Casualties:— 2 asphyxiated wounded.	W.N./
23rd July	Relieved new trenches at BAZENTIN LE GRAND, taped out and took charge of working parties as follows:— 300 men at ADVANCED REDOUBT - D.5 at 9 p.m.	

SECTION	No. OF INFANTRY	WORK DONE
No 1 (Lt FRAYER)	70.	Commenced digging C.T. marked M.27 on Company's map
No 2 (Lieut. RITCHIE)	30.	Improving trench and relaying GERMAN SUPPORT LINE A5-B5.
No 3 (Lieut. CREAR)	100	Sapping new pit French L.O.
No 4 (Lt G. EGG)	100	Digging new pit French L.O.

Four engineers made.

O.C. 1/2nd Highland Field Coy., R.E. (T)
Major, R.E.

Army Form C. 2118.

WAR DIARY
or
INTELLIGENCE SUMMARY
(Erase heading not required.)

1/2nd HIGHLAND FIELD Coy, R.E.

No. ....
Date ....

Hour, Date, Place	Summary of Events and Information	Remarks and references to Appendices
24th July.	Work on scheme to be continued. 400 infantry arranged for at 9pm. at D.5. but very heavy shell barrage across our front of hostile machine guns and then rifle fire and work were difficult to carry that work had to be abandoned.	W.B.
25th July.	Working parties arranged as follows: 50 men at 4pm. 5pm. 6pm. and 9pm. Heavy shell fire prevented all party and except my party which got through savage and worked on trench L.M. Detailed 2 sections (Nos 1 and 3) to have bivouacs at 3 am.	W.B.
26th July.	and proceed to old German dug-outs at BAZENTIN LE GRAND. Working party of 200 men each, at 9pm., 12 midnight and 12.15am. 26th/27th. Work carried out on L.M. M.T. P.B. Beach wiring of trenches M.N. also improvement of communication trenches.	W.B.

O.C. 1/2nd Highland Field Coy, R.E. (T)

Major, R.E. (T)
O.C. 1/2nd Highland Field Coy, R.E. (T)

Army Form C. 2118.

WAR DIARY
or
INTELLIGENCE SUMMARY
(Erase heading not required.)

Instructions regarding War Diaries and Intelligence Summaries are contained in F. S. Regs., Part II. and the Staff Manual respectively. Title pages will be prepared in manuscript.

1/2nd HIGHLAND FIELD Coy., R.E.

No. ....
Date. ......7 May 1916.......

Hour, Date, Place	Summary of Events and Information	Remarks and references to Appendices
27th July	Work on defences then turned over to lengthening of KEEP and improving village defences. Working parties as follows, totalling 1900 men, working at D.S. every 15 minutes from 8.30 p.m. to 10.45 p.m. carrying R.E. Stores and forming 'Advanced R.E. dumps at HIGHWOOD. Heavy shell fire caused confusion and casualties among carrying parties. Two-thirds of loads were got into dumps. (Units continued in carrying stores (500 infantry) heavy shell fire but all stores were ultimately got through.	
28th July	1 Section R.E. engaged in fitting gascurtain in Divisional Headquarters at FRICOURT and also in deepening dug-outs. Commenced erection of screens of wire netting and twigs along road in front of BAZENTIN LE GRAND to hide road from	M.R.

O.C. 1/2nd Highland Field Coy.
Major, R.E.(T), R.E.B.E.

1247 W 3299 200,000 (E) 8/14 J.B.C. & A.   Forms/C. 2118/11.

Army Form C. 2118.

WAR DIARY
or
INTELLIGENCE SUMMARY

(Erase heading not required.)

Instructions regarding War Diaries and Intelligence Summaries are contained in F.S. Regs., Part II. and the Staff Manual respectively. Title pages will be prepared in manuscript.

1/2nd HIGHLAND
FIELD Coy., R.E.
No. Vol XIX 8
Date 31 VII 16

Hour, Date, Place	Summary of Events and Information	Remarks and references to Appendices
28th July. 29th July.	from enemy of guns etc from DELVILLE WOOD. Relieved Section No 1 & 3 by sections Nos 2 & 4 at 4 a.m. Nos 2 & 4 Sections engaged in carrying stores to dumps, cutting notice and direction boards and completed.	W.P.B.
30th July	Sections on road. Two sections of company placed under orders of G.O.C. 15.3rd Infantry Brigade in connection with operations at HIGH WOOD. One section R.E. engaged in construction of shelter & off dressing station near MAMETZ WOOD	W.P.B.
31st July	1 section R.E. engaged on dressing station and 1 section engaged on road repair near dressing station. Headquarters section engaged in carrying stations, water and stores to site of work, also repairing and overhauling all transport and pontoon equipment, etc.	W.P.B.

Major, R.E.
O.C. 1/2nd Highland Field Coy.,
Major, R.E. (T)

WAR DIARY
or
INTELLIGENCE SUMMARY
(Erase heading not required.)

Army Form C. 2118.

1/2nd HIGHLAND FIELD Coy., R.E.

No. ....
Date ....July 1916......

Hour, Date, Place	Summary of Events and Information	Remarks and references to Appendices
31st July	2 Sections (Lieuts. GORDON and MAITLAND) at work forming 4 kinds of cases in front of "BLACKWATCH" Trench. 2 Sections engaged in repair of wire of approaches under heavy shell fire. No. of Casualties during month :- 1 NCO + 2 Coplrs wounded. 1 NCO + 1 Sapper relieved from forward employment on return to work. The following reinforcements joined the Unit. 6th July .... 1 NCO 12th July .... 4 DRIVERS 23rd July .... 1 FARRIER SERGEANT. 1 SAPPER 5 Drivers attached from 1/2nd Wessex Counties Field Co R.E. returned to Base Depôt. No. of Officers and men on leave during month :- NIL. Roll of OFFICERS with Company at 31.7.16 :- CAPT: W.P. BARRON, LIEUTS: T.T. GORDON & W.E. GLEGG, 2nd LIEUTS C. OKELL, R.FYFE, F.B. RITCHIE & A.M. MAITLAND.	

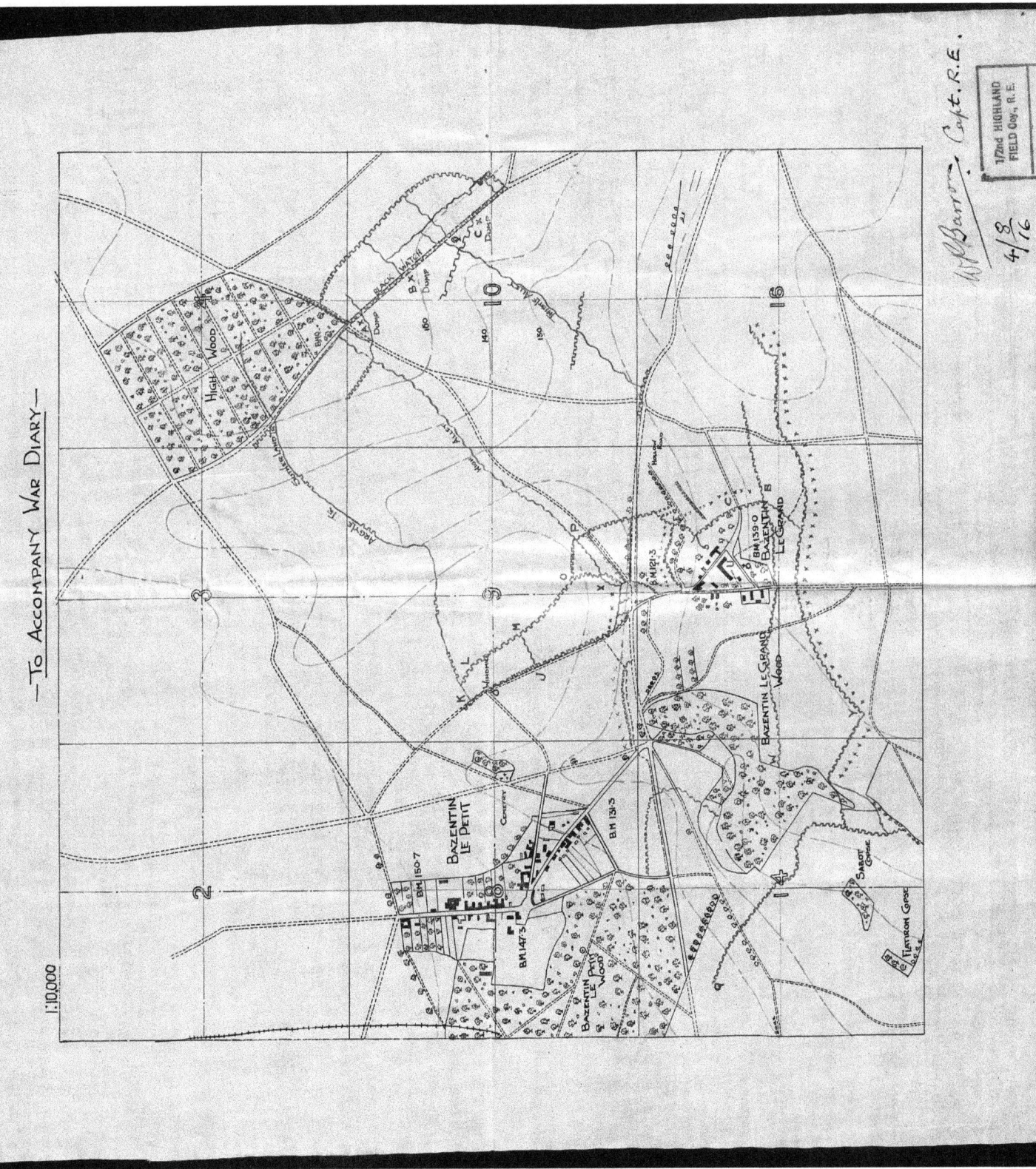

51st Divisional Engineers

1/2nd HIGHLAND FIELD COMPANY R. E.

AUGUST 1 9 1 6 :::::

Appendices attached:-

Report on Work 22nd July to 6th August 1916

WAR DIARY
INTELLIGENCE SUMMARY
(Erase heading not required.)

Army Form C. 2118.

1/2nd HIGHLAND FIELD Coy., R.E.

No. VOL XX
Date August 1.2.16

Place	Date	Hour	Summary of Events and Information	Remarks and references to Appendices
Ravine between FRICOURT and BECOURT.	August 1st		Nos 1 & 3 Sections repairing road between Brigade Headquarters and X dump.	
			Nos 2 & 4 Sections lining in old German dug-outs at BAZENTIN-LE-GRAND.	
			Engaged in siting and digging fire trench 160 yards in advance of BLACKWATCH TRENCH running south from HIGH WOOD. 190 x of fire trench dug to an average of 3' deep.	
			2nd Lieut. A. Mark. Maitland. Killed at night while superintending work with No 4 section on above named trench.	W.C.G.
	2nd		Nos 1 & 3 Sections repairing roadway between Brigade Headquarters and X dump.	
			Nos 2 & 4 Sections working on new fire trench 130 yards in front of BLACKWATCH Trench. 350 yds of trench dug to average depth of 3 ft. Portions of trench commenced on previous night, deepened.	
			Sections Nos 2 & 4 relieved by 2 sections of 1st/1st Highland Field Coy R.E. at 4 A.M.	

W.P.Barron
Capt.
R.E. (T.F.)
Major.
O.C. 1/2nd Highland Field Coy. R.E.

W.C.G.

Army Form C. 2118.

WAR DIARY
or
INTELLIGENCE SUMMARY
(Erase heading not required.)

1/2nd HIGHLAND FIELD Coy., R.E.
No. Vol. XX. 2
Date. August 1916

Place	Date	Hour	Summary of Events and Information	Remarks and references to Appendices
	3rd August		No 1 section repairing roadway between Brigade Headquarters and thence twice and clearing debris from entrance to new dug-out there. Also extending dug-out at support Brigade Headquarters and making a second front shelter. No 2 section making roadway in front of advanced dressing station. No 3 section repairing roadway between Brigade Headquarters and x dump. Making and fitting frame in dug-out and erecting elephant troughing at Rear Brigade Headquarters. Also altering ⟨?⟩ for dug-outs and building sandbag towers at advanced Dressing Station. No 4 section Testing hydraulic pipe forcing jack near billets and loading same into wagon.	
	4th August		No 1 section with carrying party of 200 infantry transported pipe forcing jack stores from D.5. to HIGHWOOD. Company wagon alone reached	

O.O. 1/2nd Highland Field Coy. R.E.
W.P. Warren (Capt)
Major, R.E. (T.)

Army Form C. 2118.

WAR DIARY
or
INTELLIGENCE SUMMARY

(Erase heading not required.)

1/2nd HIGHLAND
FIELD Coy., R.E.
No. VOL XX
Date August 1916

Place	Date	Hour	Summary of Events and Information	Remarks and references to Appendices
			reached D.5. with stores. Two disersal tram wagons with stores failed to cross barrage of shell fire near X dump. Only 100 men of carrying party went to transport pyle forcing pack stores from D5 to HIGHWOOD. Owing to the non-arrival of the horse wagons with stores, second 100 men of carrying party dismissed after waiting for one hour at D5. Sapper Gurdler experienced difficulty in locating site of work of pyle forcing pack at HIGHWOOD, owing to intense artillery bombardment and gas alarm.	
BAZENTIN.			No. 1 & 3 Sections engaged on repair of road from X dump towards No. 2 Section engaged on work on mined dugouts at QUARRY Dressing Station & at allotment Brigade Headquarters. Also construction of heavy sandbag traverse at dressing station.	

O.C. 1/2nd Highland Field Coy: R.E.
Major, R.E. (T)
Wiseman CAPT
W.C.G.

Army Form C. 2118.

WAR DIARY
OR
INTELLIGENCE SUMMARY

(Erase heading not required.)

1/2nd HIGHLAND FIELD Coy., R.E.
No. Vol. XX
Date August 1916.

Place	Date	Hour	Summary of Events and Information	Remarks and references to Appendices
	August 5th		No. 1 Section met working party of 300 infantry at D.5 at 11.30 P.M. 4th Aug. Commenced digging northern half of C.T. from GEORGE STREET to LEITH WALK. C.T. 2'6" wide cut to depth of 3', 150 yards length at forward end. Heavy shell fire. 1 Sapper wounded. ½ No. 4 Section engaged on carrying job. Others to BLACKWATCH TRENCH. 100 Infantry carrying party. No. 3 Section resting in billets. Rifle inspection at 10 A.M. No. 2 Section engaged in road repair & dugouts. Working parties of 100 Infantry at 6 A.M. 10 A.M. & 2 P.M.	
	6th		No. 1 section engaged in enlarging & deepening C.T. Length of 550 yards widened to 3'6" at top & deepened to 3'6". 150 yards cut 3'6" wide by 2'6" deep. Heavy shell fire. No. 2 Section engaged on road repair & dugouts. 100 Infantry working party at 6 A.M. Section engaged loading pontoons, cleaning billets, etc. Company moved up at 4.45 P.M. Arrived at 7 P.M.	

CAPT.
Major, R.E. (T.)
O.C. 1/2nd Highland Field Coy., R.E.

Army Form C. 2118.

WAR DIARY
or
INTELLIGENCE SUMMARY
(Erase heading not required.)

1/2nd HIGHLAND FIELD Coy. R.E.
No. VOL. XX
Date: August 1916
5

Place	Date	Hour	Summary of Events and Information	Remarks and references to Appendices
	August			
	7th		Bivouacked 1 mile N. of DERNANCOURT.	W.C.S.
	8th	10 A.M.	Company parade. Inspection of Rifles Equipment. Trench Helmets — Drill.	W.C.S.
			Cyclists moved off at 10 A.M. en route for PONT REMY.	
			Issue of clothing + small kit. Sappers engaged changing socks and cleaning grounds.	
			2nd Lieut. F.B. Ritchie thrown from his horse when leaving sports bivouac.	
	9th		Left Company for Hospital at PICQUIGNY.	W.C.S.
		3.30 P.M.	Sappers engaged clearing grounds + carrying water. Fall in at 3.30 P.M. + marched to EDGEHILL. Halted midway between + resumed there until 9 P.M.	
		9.15 P.M.	Fallin at 9.15 P.M. + entrained for PONT REMY. Left EDGEHILL about midnight arriving at 8 A.M. on the 10th.	
	10th		Company marched to GRANDSART about 8 kls. from LONGPRE arriving at 11.30 A.M. Company bivouacked.	
			+ Reinforcements join Company at LONGPRE.	
	11th		Sappers resting. Company paid out 5 francs per man.	

C.O. 1/2nd Highland Field Coy: R.E.
Major. R.E. (T)
CAPT.
W.C.S.

Wilson

Army Form C. 2118.

WAR DIARY
or
INTELLIGENCE SUMMARY

(Erase heading not required.)

Instructions regarding War Diaries and Intelligence Summaries are contained in F.S. Regs., Part II. and the Staff Manual respectively. Title Pages will be prepared in manuscript.

1/2nd HIGHLAND FIELD Coy., R.E.
No. VOL XX
Date Aug-Oct 1916.
6

Place	Date	Hour	Summary of Events and Information	Remarks and references to Appendices
	August			
		6.P.M.	Orders to proceed to PONT REMY. En route for STEENBECQUE. Fell in at 9.15 P.M. Whole Company moved off at 9.45 P.M. Wagons halted about 2 Klm. this side of PONT REMY. Cycles & transport continue en route for PONT REMY. Wagons arrived at 12.15 A.M. morning of the 12th. Cyclists and spare wagon load transport. Time taken to entrain, one hour.	W.C.G.
	13th		Left PONT REMY at 1.50 A.M. & arrived at STEENBECQUE at 10.20 A.M. Time taken to detrain at 10.45 P.M. Commenced Offloading transport at 11 A.M. Time taken to offload 30 minutes. Company fell in & moved off at 11.40 A.M. En route for WALLON-CAPPELL. Arrived at 1.30 P.M. Very warm marching. Company bivouacked.	
	14th		Company parade 10 A.M. Inspection of Rifles. Equipment & Musketry Helmets. Company resting. One officer, sergeant and cyclist proceed to ARMENTIERES to arrange for taking over of billets and work. Mounted Section & Cyclist parade at 3 A.M. Fork in at 4.15 A.M. and moved off at 4.45 A.M. En route for ARMENTIERES. Wagons fell in at 2 P.M. and marched to EBBLINGHEM. Entrained for STEENWERK at 4.15 P.M.	W.C.G.

CAPT.
W.C.G. Gordon(?)
Major, R.E. (T)
O.C. 1/2nd Highland Field Coy. R.E.

Army Form C. 2118.

WAR DIARY
or
INTELLIGENCE SUMMARY
(Erase heading not required.)

Instructions regarding War Diaries and Intelligence Summaries are contained in F.S. Regs., Part II. and the Staff Manual respectively. Title Pages will be prepared in manuscript.

1/2nd HIGHLAND FIELD Coy. R.E.
No. Vol. XX
Date August 1916.

Place	Date	Hour	Summary of Events and Information	Remarks and references to Appendices
	August		Arriving here at 6 P.M. Company marched to ARMENTIERES arriving at 8-10 P.M. Transport arrived at 6-30 P.M. 1 horse left at MOLLEN CAPPEL.	W.C.G.
	15th & 16th		Taking over billets, workshops, stores etc. Overhauling pontoon equipment. Washing and greasing wagons. Visiting the line & taking over.	W.C.G.
	17th & 21st		Nos 1, 2, 3, & 4 Sections engaged in construction of reinforced concrete M.E. shelter with double roof in front trenches. (see attached plan). Concrete emplacement and magazine for large trench mortar. Cementing floor of completed shelter to stop leakage. Trolley tracks from TISSAGE and FOCHABERS advanced dumps to front trenches advanced. Top of well at S.P.x covered and access to it improved. India at well at BUTERNE FARM altered. Excavating site for 2 M.G. emplacements in front and support trenches. Constructing log shuttering for cementing same. Transporting concrete materials, trolley track sections and steel rails for roofing shelter to TISSAGE and FOCHABERS dumps. Steel rails carted from railway to Divisional dump. Company wagons employed. Company found for duty.	W.C.G.

2nd Lieut. W.B. Robertson joined Company for duty.

[signature] Capt.
W. [signature]
Major, R.E. (T.)
O.C. 1/2nd Highland Field Coy, R.E.

Army Form C. 2118.

WAR DIARY
or
INTELLIGENCE SUMMARY

(Erase heading not required.)

Instructions regarding War Diaries and Intelligence Summaries are contained in F. S. Regs., Part II. and the Staff Manual respectively. Title Pages will be prepared in manuscript.

1/2nd HIGHLAND FIELD Coy, R. E.
No. Vol. XX
Date August 1916.

Place	Date	Hour	Summary of Events and Information	Remarks and references to Appendices
	August 21st		100 Infantry and 3 Officers from 154th Brigade attached to Company. Work on M.G. emplacements and with object to give preference to construction of concrete H.E. shells, and T.M. emplacement.	M.E.G.
			2nd Lieut. A.G. Mackail rejoined Company for duty.	
	22nd to 24th		Work on H.E. shells continued. Parties working in each in 8 hour shifts. One attached infantryman working with each sapper as his mate. Arrangement of work on H.E. shells:- 3 Sappers and 3 attached infantry on 8 hour shifts. 1 R.E. guide and 25 to 30 infantry carrying party nightly for each shelter to carry stores from advanced dumps to shelter by trolley trucks, carted forward parties and manhandling. Carrying party reporting at advanced dumps at 9 P.M. and working for 8 hours. One attached infantry officer superintending carrying parties at each dump. Average weight of stone carried by empty transport and 2 horse trench waggons from divisional dump to advanced dumps, 25 tons per night.	

CAPT.
O.C. 1/2nd Highland Field Coy, R.E.
Major, R.E. (T.)

Army Form C. 2118.

WAR DIARY
or
INTELLIGENCE SUMMARY

(Erase heading not required.)

1/2nd HIGHLAND FIELD Coy. R.E.
No. Vol. XX
Date August 1916

Place	Date	Hour	Summary of Events and Information	Remarks and references to Appendices
	August			
			Workshops dismantling and moving one portable steam engine to Company workshops, and Plant erecting engine. Overhauling lathe and vertical drilling machine. Pr. Irving shifting for H.E. Drilling cutting steel rails, and cutting strips of steel metal for shuttering blown out rails. Building curved sections of trolley track for relaying Trolley line at FOCHABERS dump.	
	24th		Intelligible Report Transferred to 1/8th A.&S. Highlanders and Intelligible Hutching regimed unit for duty. 1 N.C.O & 2 sappers transferred from 2/1st Highland Field Co. R.E. to this company. Attached infantry from 154th Brigade report augments and as replaced by 2 officers and 100 others from 152nd brigade.	W.E.G.
	24 to 31st		Company engaged on work on H.E. Shelter and T.M. Emplacement as above; 1 Lieut. D.W., 16th seaforth Highlanders superintending carrying parties, and loading of stores at TSSAGE dump and 1 Lieut Plowman, 1/7th Gordon Highlanders closing same at FOCHABERS dump.	W.E.G.

Army Form C. 2118.

WAR DIARY
or
INTELLIGENCE SUMMARY
(Erase heading not required.)

1/2nd HIGHLAND FIELD Coy. R.E.
No. Vol XX 10.
Date August 1916

Place	Date	Hour	Summary of Events and Information	Remarks and references to Appendices
			1 N.C.O. and 2 Sappers sent for duty from Base on 24th Aug.	
			No. of Casualties during month :- 1 Officer killed, 1 Sapper wounded.	
			1 N.C.O. & 3 Sappers released for civil employment in munition workers.	
			No. of Officers & men on leave during month :- 2 N.C.O's	
			Roll of Officers with company at :- 31/8/16 :-	
			Capt. W.P.BARRON. LIEUTS. T.J.GORDON & W.C.GLEGG; 2nd LIEUTS. R.G. MACNEILL, C.O'KELL,	
			A.R. FYFE, P.B. RITCHIE, & W.B. ROBERTSON.	W.C.G.

CAPT.
O.C. 1/2nd Highland Field Coy. R.E.

"A" Form. Army Form C. 2121.
MESSAGES AND SIGNALS. No. of Message............

Prefix...... Code......m.	Words	Charge	This message is on a/c of :	Recd. at............m.
Office of Origin and Service Instructions.	Sent			Date............
	At	m.	............Service.	From............
	To		(Signature of "Franking Officer.")	By............
	By			

TO { C.R.E. 51st (Highland) Division.

| Sender's Number | Day of Month | In reply to Number | AAA |
| W.P. 40. | 6 | | |

Herewith War Diary of this Unit for August 1916. aaa.

Ha 2 d Coy 5▪ 8/16

From O.C. 1/2 Highland Field Co. R.E.
Place
Time

Signature ...... Capt OET

Report on work carried out by 1st/2nd Highland Field Company R.E. during period from 2nd July – 6th August inclusive

22nd July:-

Orders received from General Staff to commence consolidation of positions in front of BAZENTIN LE GRAND, the length of front allotted to this company being from road south of village, to junction with 5th Division on our right.

4 Sections R.E. proceeded to site of work, & commenced work on firestepping & improving fire trench A.B. This trench was a reversed German support trench.

Also on the conversion of trench BC into a fire trench giving flanking fire along A.B.

23rd July

Sited & taped new fire & communication trenches. Working party 300 men at O.S. at 9 p.m. allotted as follows:-

No.1 Section. 70 men. Digging C.T. marked M.S. on plan.

No 2. Section 30 men. Continuing work on trenches A.B & B.C

No 3. Section 100 men. Digging new fire trench L.O.

No 4 Section 100 men Digging new fire trench L.O.

Fair progress made.

24th July

Work on scheme to be continued, but working party of 400 men were prevented by heavy barrage from reaching work. 2 section R.E. proceeded to works, but had to give up work on account of heavy shelling.

25th July.
Working parties of 150 men at 4.pm. 5.pm. 6.pm. & 9.pm.
Heavy shelling prevented all infantry & sappers from reaching works, except 1 party which got through barrage & worked on trench. L.M.

26th July
2 Sections. R.E. proceeded to old German dugouts at BAZENTIN LE GRAND.
Working parties of 200 men at 3.Pm. 12 midnight & 12.15. am. 27th. Work carried out on trenches L.M, M.S, AB., B.C. also wiring to trench M.N. One party engaged in improvement of communications in village.

27th July
Work on consolidation discontinued except on strengthening of Keep & improving defence of Village. Carrying parties, total number 1700 men. reported at D.5. in parties every 15. minutes. from 8-30.pm. to 10-45.pm.
Work done. Carrying R.E. stores from D.5. & forming 3 R.E. advanced Dumps A.B.C. behind BLACKWATCH trench.
Heavy shelling caused casualties & consequent confusion delayed work. Two thirds of stores were placed in position.

28th July. Working party of 500 men. Continued carrying stores. Stores Carried:—

	A. DUMP	B. DUMP	C. DUMP
Screw pickets	500	—	250
Barbed Wire (large coils)	100	—	50
French Wire (small coils)	115	50	—
Plain wire	1	1	1
Wirecutters	10	20	10
Sandbags	3000	11,200	3000
Shovels	900	400	300
Picks	550	—	100
Tracing tapes	10	—	10

1 section. R.E. engaged in fitting gas screens in Divisional Headquarters at FRICOURT & in strengthening dugouts.

1 section R.E commenced erection of screens of wire netting & twigs along low road east of BAZENTIN LE GRAND to hide road from observation from LONGUEVAL.

29th July.

Relieved 2 sections. R.E. by remaining 2 sections at 4.a.m.

Nos 2 & 4 sections engaged in carrying R.E. stores to dump, erecting notice & direction boards & completed screens on road.

30th July.

1 Section. R.E. engaged in construction of splinter proof dressing station near D5. This party worked from 4.a.m. to 5.p.m & completed work.

2 Sections placed under order of G.O.C. 153rd Infantry Brigade in connection with operations at HIGH WOOD.

The work allotted was the construction of two strong points complete with wire, one at E corner of HIGH WOOD & 1 in German trench.

For this work, only 16 infantry per section were detailed, a number totally inadequate for the work proposed.

From previous experience on many similar occasions, the number detailed should be 40 - 50 men with one section R.E. for each strong point.

Instructions were given to commence these works immediately the attack succeeded without regard to the question of light & the

the impossibility of carrying out work of this type in the open in daylight.

The sections, however, were not called upon to carry out the work.

31st July.

1 Section engaged in addition to & improvement of dressing station near D.5.

1 Section engaged on road repair opposite Advanced Brigade Headquarters.

1st August.

2 Sections taped & commenced construction of fire trench 100 yards in advance of BLACK WATCH trench, running south from HIGHWOOD.

Working party of 100 men.

Work done. 190 yards dug to an average depth of 3'.

The working party were not fresh & the amount of work done was therefore lessened.

2 Sections at work on repair of road between Brigade Headquarters & X Dump.

Working party of 100 infantry at 6 a.m., 10 a.m. & 2 p.m.

2nd August.

2 Sections on road repair with parties of 100 men. reporting at 6 a.m. 10 a.m. & 2 p.m.

2 Sections continued work on advanced trench. Work taped out, & a length of 350 yards dug to a depth of 3'.

Work continued on previous nights work. trenches deepened.

Working party of 400 infantry.

2nd Lieut. A. McA. Maitland. Killed.

2 Sections relieved by 2 sections 1st/1st Highland Field Coy. R.E. at 4. a.m. 2nd Aug.

3rd August.
 2 Sections repairing roads.
 Working parties at 6.am. 10.am. & 2.pm. 100 men.
 1 Section commenced construction of dugout at QUARRY dressing station & at Brigade Headquarters, also building sandbag splinter proof walls at dressing station.
 1 Section testing & overhauling hydraulic pipe forcing jack. Making hard wood base plate.

4th August
 Along with infantry party of 200 men, pipe forcing jack & part of the required stores, carried to BLACKWATCH trench.
 2 Sections engaged on road repair from X Dump forwards.
 Parties of 100 men at 6.am. 10.am & 2.pm.
 1 Section at work on dugouts & sandbagging at QUARRY & at Advanced Brigade Headquarters.

5th August
 1 Section with working party of 300 at D.S. at 11-30.pm. 4th Aug. commenced digging northern half of C.T. from GEORGE STREET to LEITH WALK. 550 yards cut 2'6" wide & 3' deep.
 1 Section on road repair & dugouts. Parties of 100 men at 6am. 10.am. & 2.pm.
 1 Section along with party of 100, completed carrying of pipe forcing material & explosives to BLACK WATCH trench.

6th August
 1 Section engaged on 2nd relief on C.T. from GEORGE STREET to LEITH WALK. Working party of 300.
 Length of 550 Yards widened to 3'6" & deepened to 3'6"

150 Yards cut 3' 6" wide by 2' 6" deep.
 1 Section on road repair & dugouts.
1 party of 100 infantry at 6 am.
 Mounted section engaged in carting stores & driving sappers to & from work.
 Practically all above work was carried out under shell fire. Arrangement & handling of working parties was made very difficult by this & infantry officers took the responsibility on several occasions of stopping work on account of the very heavy shell fire.

W.P. Barron Capt.
Major, R.E. (T)
O.C. 1/2nd Highland Field Coy: R.E.

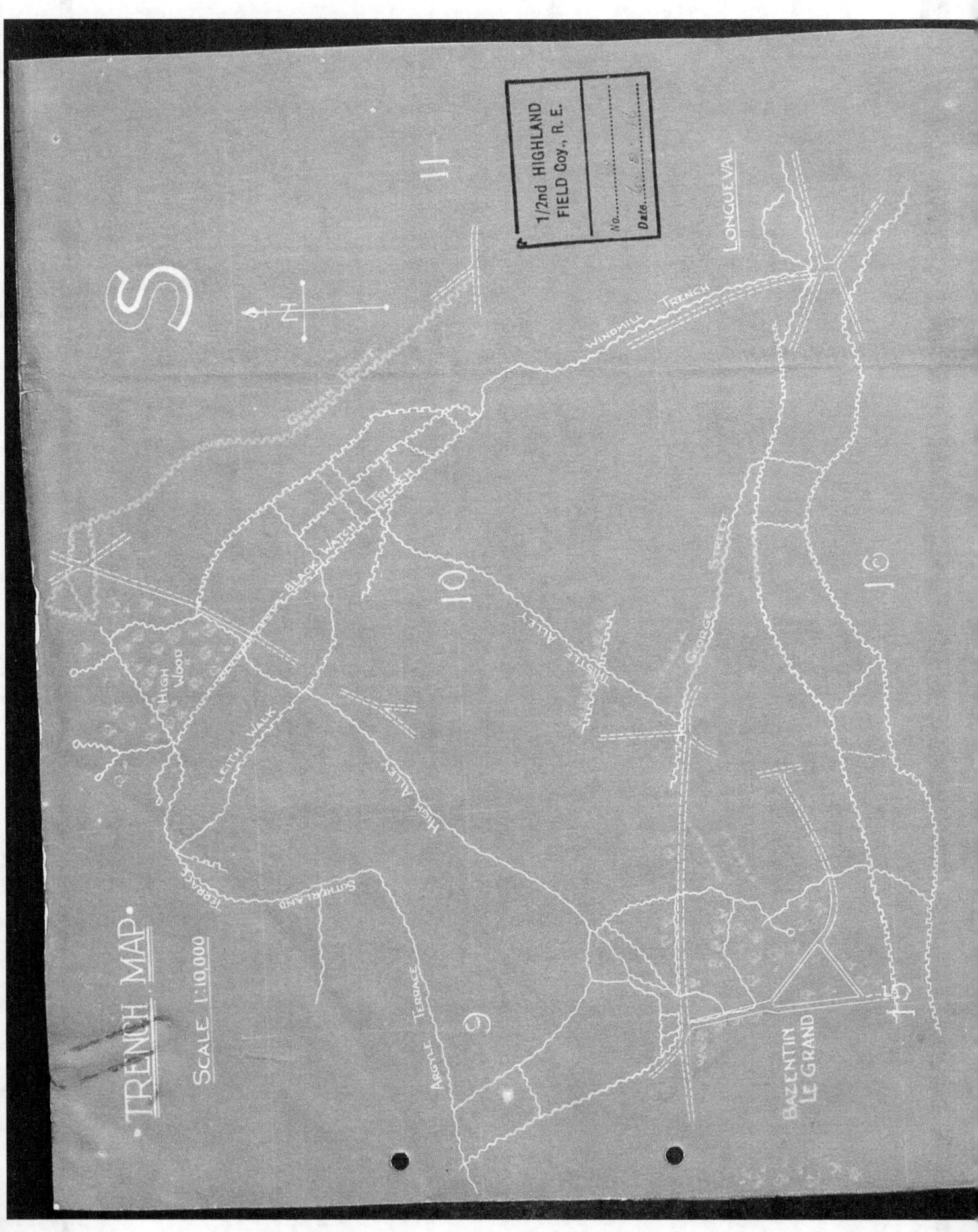

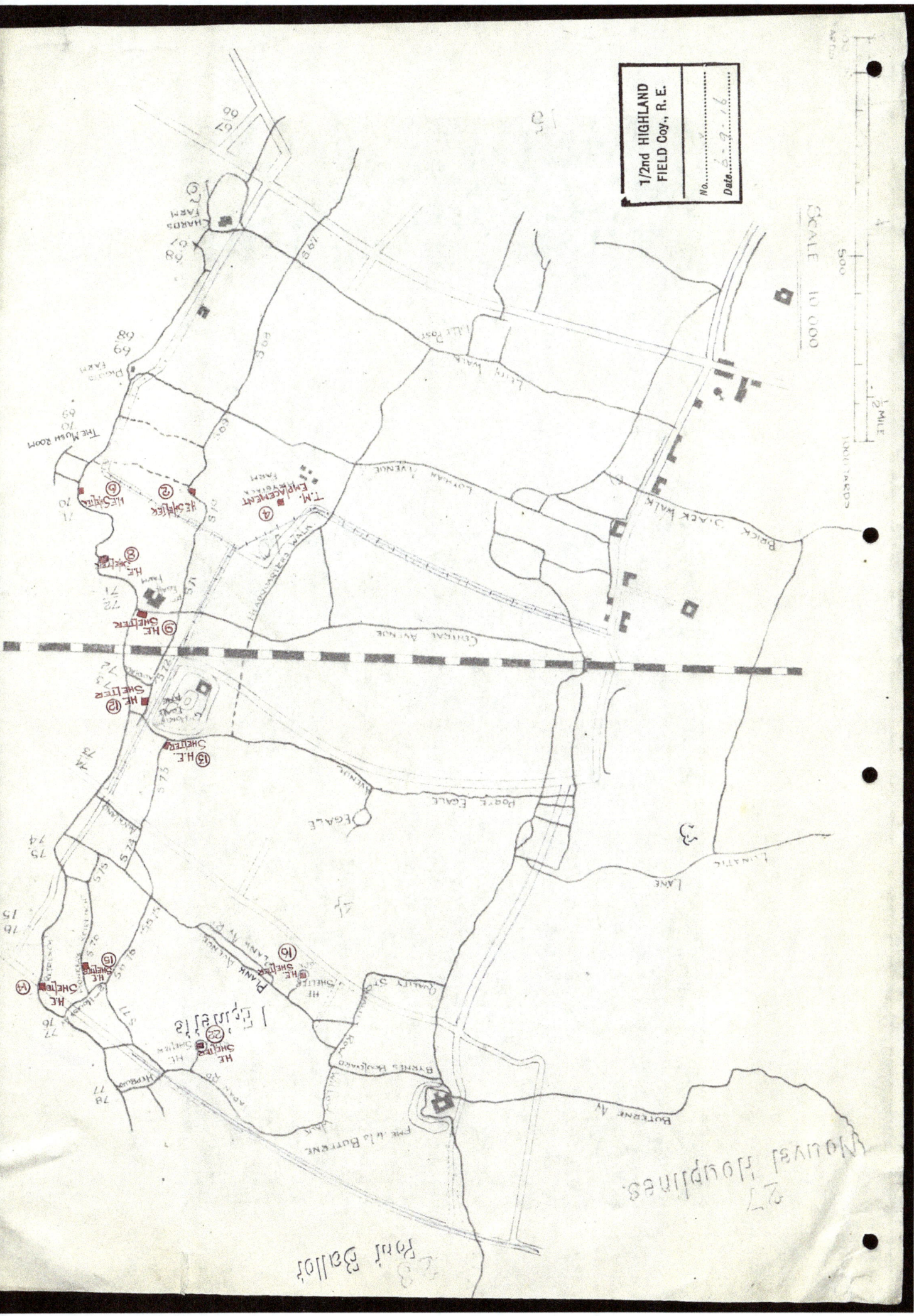

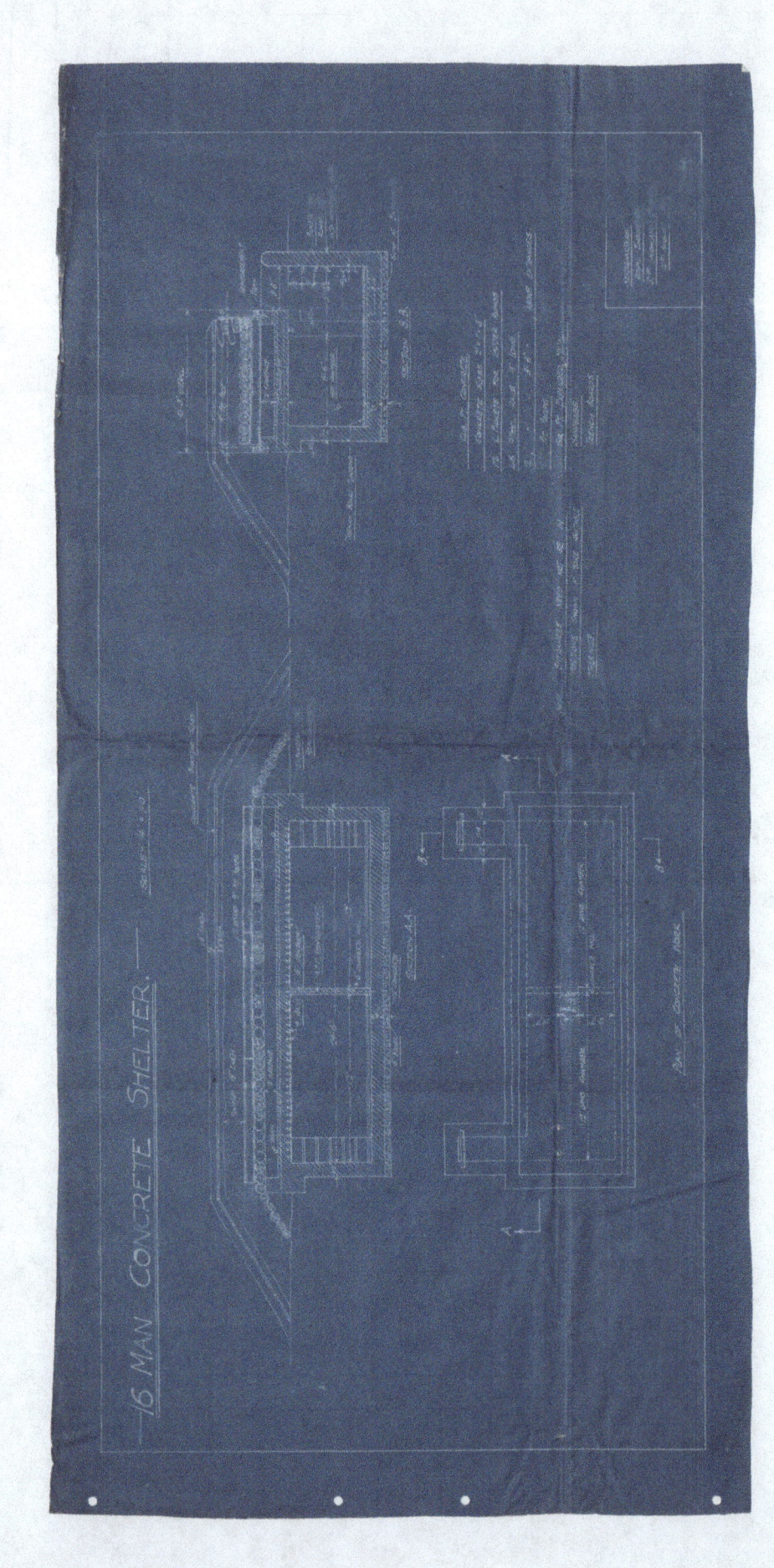

CONFIDENTIAL.
No 21/A.
HIGHLAND DIVISION.

War Diary
of
1st/2nd Highland Field Co. R.E.(T)
for
September 1916.

Vol: No XXI.

Army Form C. 2118.

WAR DIARY
or
INTELLIGENCE SUMMARY
(Erase heading not required.)

1/2nd HIGHLAND FIELD Coy., R.E.

No. Vol. XXI
Date SEPTEMBER 1916

O.O. 1/2nd Highland Field Coy: R.E.
Major, R.E. (T)
Whittaker

Place	Date	Hour	Summary of Events and Information	Remarks and references to Appendices
ARMENTIERES	SEPTEMBER 1st		Company continued construction of reinforced concrete shell proof shelters in front & support trenches & in strong points.	NtB
			Making asphalt & plugging & making watertight the floors & sumps of shelters.	NtB
			Continued work on concrete emplacement & magazine for heavy T.M.	NtB
			Putting kerbs on wells & placing tanks in positions, repairing pumps	NtB
			Carrying gas cylinders & placing in position in front trenches.	NtB
			Repairing trench tramways & laying new steel track	NtB

WAR DIARY
or
INTELLIGENCE SUMMARY

(Erase heading not required.)

Army Form C. 2118.

1/2nd HIGHLAND FIELD Coy., R.E.

No. VOL. XXI.
Date SEPTEMBER 1916.

O.C. 1/2nd Highland Field Coy: R.E.
Major, R.E. (T)

Place	Date	Hour	Summary of Events and Information	Remarks and references to Appendices
	7th		Building horse standings & stables.	
			Running workshops – engaged in making framing notice boards, rifle rests etc.	WB
	12th		Company bills shelled.	WB
			16 Drivers, 30 mules & 5 wagons attached for duty from 51st Divisional Ammunition Column.	WB
	19th		2 Officers & 100 Infantry (Sappers mates) of 153rd Infantry Brigade rejoined their regiments, and were replaced by 2 Officers and 100 Infantry from 152nd Infantry Brigade.	WB
	21st		16 Drivers, 30 mules & 5 wagons rejoined Column.	WB
	24th		Handed over all work and material to Field Co. R.E.	

Army Form C. 2118.

WAR DIARY
INTELLIGENCE SUMMARY
(Erase heading not required.)

1/2nd HIGHLAND FIELD Coy., R.E.

No. Vol. XXI
Date SEPTEMBER 1916.

O.C. 1/2nd Highland Field Coy: R.E.
Major, R.E. (T)

Place	Date	Hour	Summary of Events and Information	Remarks and references to Appendices
	25th		Field Co. R.E. 34th Division, who took over R.E. charge of 152nd Infantry Brigade sector prior to relief of Division. Surplus stores & kit dumped at ARMENTIERES. 2 Officers & 100 Infantry of 152nd Infantry Brigade returned their regiments.	A.P.B. A.P.B.
	26th	2.A.M.	Company moved at 9.30 a.m. to ESTAIRES arriving at 2.A.M. Billeted there.	A.P.B.
	27th		Company engaged in cleaning & refitting & general overhaul.	A.P.B.
	28th		Engaged in drill & company training. Inspection of Gas Helmets, Kits, & 40% of Company inoculated.	A.P.B. A.P.B.

Army Form C. 2118.

WAR DIARY
INTELLIGENCE SUMMARY
(Erase heading not required.)

1/2nd HIGHLAND FIELD Coy, R.E.

No. ....
Date. SEPTEMBER 1916

O.C. 1/2nd Highland Field Coy: R.E.
Major, R.E. (T)

Place	Date	Hour	Summary of Events and Information	Remarks and references to Appendices
	29th		Overhauling wagons and packing up.	A/B
	30th		Company moved at 12-45 A.M. 1st to MERVILLE & entrained there with orders to proceed to CANDAS.	
			No. of casualties during month:— 1 N.C.O. killed	
			1 Sapper killed	
			1 Sapper wounded.	
			2 Horses killed and 6 wounded.	
			1 N.C.O. & 1 Sapper released for civil employment as Munition worker & ships carpenter.	
			The following reinforcements joined the Company:— 2nd September 1 Officer (from hospital) 24th 1 N.C.O. & 1 Sapper.	

WAR DIARY
or
INTELLIGENCE SUMMARY
(Erase heading not required.)

Army Form C. 2118.

1/2nd HIGHLAND FIELD Coy., R. E.

No. V.Q4. XXI
Date SEPTEMBER 1916

Place	Date	Hour	Summary of Events and Information	Remarks and references to Appendices
			No. of Officers & Men on leave during month :- 5.	
			Roll of Officers with company at 30.9.16 :-	
			O.C., CAPTAIN. W.P. BARRON. LIEUTS. T.J. GORDON, & W.C. GLEGG. 2nd LIEUTS. A.G. McNIELL, C. O'KELL.	
			P.R. FYFE, F.B. RITCHIE, W.B. ROBERTSON.	

Major, R.E. (T.)
O.C. 1/2nd Highland Field Coy: R.E.

Secret
Set 2/1

WAR DIARY
- OF -
1ST/2ND HIGHLAND FIELD COMPANY, R.E. (T.F.)
- FOR -
OCTOBER
- 1916 -

VOL: No XXII

Army Form C. 2118.

WAR DIARY
or
INTELLIGENCE SUMMARY

(Erase heading not required.)

1/2nd HIGHLAND FIELD Coy., R.E.
No. V94. XXII
Date. OCTOBER 1916

Place	Date	Hour	Summary of Events and Information	Remarks and references to Appendices
CANDAS	Oct. 1		Company arrived at CANDAS at 10-20 a.m. detrained and marched to AUTHEUX, arriving at 1-30 p.m. Billeted there.	2 P.G
	2		Company inspection & Company training	
	3		2 Lieut S.J. HUNTER joined Company for duty.	1/2 P.G
	4		Company moved at 9 a.m. to THIEVRES, arriving at 3-30 p.m. Billeted there.	1/2 P.G
	5		Company moved at 12 noon to COURCELLES, arriving at 3 p.m. Billeted there. Company takes charge of Divisional R.E. Park, COURCELLES. Officers reconnoitre trenches. Work in line commenced, carrying up trench boards for new trench.	1/2 P.G
	6		Major. R. Mitchell. D.S.O. rejoined company for duty. 2 Officers and 75 men from 154th Infantry Brigade attached to company	1/2 P.G

M.P.Bonar
Major, R.E. (T)
O.C. 1/2nd Highland Field Coy: R.E.

Army Form C. 2118.

WAR DIARY
or
INTELLIGENCE SUMMARY

(Erase heading not required.)

1/2nd HIGHLAND FIELD Coy., R.E.

No. Vol. XXII
Date. OCTOBER 1916

Instructions regarding War Diaries and Intelligence Summaries are contained in F. S. Regs., Part II. and the Staff Manual respectively. Title Pages will be prepared in manuscript.

Place	Date	Hour	Summary of Events and Information	Remarks and references to Appendices
	7-10		for work in R.E. Park. Work in store & workshops continued.	V.C.J.
			Interpreter Hutchings returned from leave.	
			Work in R.E. yard and workshops continued; Constructing eleboards and hooking Bangalore Torpedo tubes, repairing damaged Bangalore Torpedoes, making foot bridges, ripping timber, making camouflage netting screens, making & painting notice boards for trenches & reinforcing and loading stores.	
			Constructing dressing stations.	
			1. At HOME AVENUE. Excavation complete. Timber roofing finished, one kind of steel rails laid on roof and covered with two layers of sandbags, finished on top with 2ft of earth.	
			2. At HOME AVENUE. Excavation complete and 75% of timber on roof	

W. Brown
Major, R.E. (T.)
O.C. 1/2nd Highland Field Coy: R.E.

Army Form C. 2118.

WAR DIARY
or
INTELLIGENCE SUMMARY

(Erase heading not required.)

1/2nd HIGHLAND FIELD Coy., R.E.

No. V.2.4.X.X.11. 3.
Date Oct.1915.F.R.1914

Instructions regarding War Diaries and Intelligence Summaries are contained in F. S. Regs., Part II and the Staff Manual respectively. Title Pages will be prepared in manuscript.

Place	Date	Hour	Summary of Events and Information	Remarks and references to Appendices
	11.		3 & 4. At HOME AVENUE. Excavation almost completed.	
			Lieut. W.C. Gligg returned from leave.	
			Above work in stores and trenches continued. Digging 3 new communication	W.C.G.
			trenches west of PAPIN trench. Burying cable and clearing out NAIRN trench.	
	12.		Notice boards erected in NAIRN trench.	
			Work in R.E. yard and workshops continued, also constructing trench	
			boards & artillery bridges.	
			Construction of dressing stations.	
			1. 470 steel rails laid in position on roof and covered with two	
			layers of sandbags and 2'6" of earth.	
			2. Timber placed in position on roof.	
			3. Excavation completed and sandbags filled ready to be built in position.	
			4. Communication trenches at shelter deepened to 6" below floor level of shelter.	W.C.G.

A.J.Bonner
Capt
Major, R.E. (T)
O.C. 1/2nd Highland Field Coy: R.E.

Army Form C. 2118.

WAR DIARY
or
INTELLIGENCE SUMMARY

(Erase heading not required.)

1/2nd HIGHLAND FIELD Coy., R.E.

No. VOL. XXII.   4.
Date OCTOBER 1916

Place	Date	Hour	Summary of Events and Information	Remarks and references to Appendices
	13.		Notice boards erected in NAIRN and JEANBART communication trenches. Foot-bridges across NAIRN trenches heightened. Above work in R.E. store, workshops, dressing stations and trenches continued. 2 ammonal tubes exploded in cleared trenches by house O/E Chalmers R.E. 10 tubes exploded by X, Y, + Z. T.M. batteries.	
	14.		Work in R.E. store and workshops continued, also construction of trolleys for trench tramways. Completing marking of tracks leading to front, repainting all posts. Bridging trenches, filling in shallow trenches and cutting ramp at side of road. Marking edge of trench on roadsides with posts and painting same.	

A J Bowser
Major R.E. (T)
O.C. 1/2nd Highland Field Coy: R.E.

Army Form C. 2118.

WAR DIARY
or
INTELLIGENCE SUMMARY
(Erase heading not required.)

1/2nd HIGHLAND FIELD Coy., R.E.

No. Vol. XXII
Date. OCTOBER 1916

Place	Date	Hour	Summary of Events and Information	Remarks and references to Appendices
	15.		Construction of dressing stations continued. Benches for 16 stretchers made and fitted at dressing station COLINCAMPS.	W.S.Y
			25 yards Bangalore Torpedo carried to front trench and fitted together ready for use in "No man's land".	
			Work in R.E. store & workshops continued. Also construction of tin caps for Bangalore Torpedo tubes.	W.S.Y
			Work stopped on dressing station in HOME AVENUE.	
			Erecting beds, making wooden floors and walls, and coating with whitewash, in dressing stations at COLINCAMPS.	
	16		Company under orders to move.	
			Work in trenches and workshops stopped.	
			Nathen engaged in loading & greasing wagons and in general overhaul.	

W.S.Bonner
Major, R.E. (T)
O.C. 1/2nd Highland Field Coy: R.E.

Army Form C. 2118.

WAR DIARY
or
INTELLIGENCE SUMMARY

(Erase heading not required.)

1/2nd HIGHLAND FIELD Coy., R.E.

No. Vol. XXII
Date. OCTOBER 1916.

Place	Date	Hour	Summary of Events and Information	Remarks and references to Appendices
	17		Work in R.E. Store continued. Works in trenches handed over to 31st Division.	W.E.G.
	18.		Company under orders to move. General overhaul of equipment continued. Work in R.E. store continued.	W.E.G.
			Company moved at 11 A.M. to hoot west of MAILLY-MAILLET. Arrived 1 p.m. Company bivouacked. Attached infantry returned to their regiments. Material for construction of bivouacs carried into company.	W.E.G.
			2 Officers reconnoitre new sector of line.	
	19.		Company engaged in making bivouacs and canvas huts. Party of joiners sent to workshops at MAILLY. to work under 2/3 Highland Fit Coy RE. Main communication trenches reconnoitred, and front and support trenches reconnoitred and their suitability for use as "forming up" trenches	

W.F. Bower
Major, R.E. (T)
O.C. 1/2nd Highland Field Coy: R.E.

Army Form C. 2118.

WAR DIARY
or
INTELLIGENCE SUMMARY

(Erase heading not required.)

1/2nd HIGHLAND FIELD Coy., R.E.

No. Vol. XXII 7.
Date. OCTOBER 1916

Place	Date	Hour	Summary of Events and Information	Remarks and references to Appendices
	20		reported on. State of trench tramways and artillery bridges over trenches reported on.	W.F.G.
			Carting stores from R.E. store to AUCHONVILLERS.	
			Company took charge of R.E. Hut and workshops at MAILLY-MAILLET.	
			Making trench boards, trench ladders and making and painting mortar boards, unloading & loading stores.	
			Digging out and draining damaged trenches with infantry working parties. Company working on trenches, 2nd AVENUE, BROADWAY AVENUE, WELLINGTON trench, SEAFORTH trench, CRIPPS CUT, CARDIFF STR. and ESSEX STR. Cutting sortie steps in 2nd AVENUE and BROADWAY AVENUE. Fire trenches very wet.	
			Carting stores from R.E. Store to AUCHONVILLERS.	W.F.G.

W.F. Gomer
Major, R.E. (T)
O.C. 1/2nd Highland Field Coy, R.E.

Army Form C. 2118.

WAR DIARY
or
INTELLIGENCE SUMMARY

(Erase heading not required.)

1/2nd HIGHLAND FIELD Coy., R.E.

No. Vol. XXII
Date. OCTOBER 1916

Place	Date	Hour	Summary of Events and Information	Remarks and references to Appendices
	21.		No.3. Section moved to R.E. store. MAILLY-MAILLET. billeted there with 2 Officers.	
			No.1 + 4 Sections moved at 8 p.m. to FORCEVILLE with 2 Officers and took over part of 1/1st Highland Field Co. R.E.'s billets.	
			Work continued in R.E. store and workshops at MAILLY-MAILLET. Work continued on above trenches.	
			Carting stores from R.E. store to AUCHONVILLERS.	
	22.		Transport and Headquarters with 4 Officers moved to FORCEVILLE at 11 A.M. arrived 1 P.M. Bivouacked in canvas huts. No. 2 Section and 2 Officers remained bivouacked at wood west of MAILLY-MAILLET.	
			Work in R.E. store and workshops continued.	
			Constructing 40 Bangalore torpedoes for 152nd + 153rd Infantry Brigades for use in destroying wire engagements.	
			Carting stores from R.E. store to AUCHONVILLERS.	

W.P.Bonner
Major, R.E. (T)
O.C. 1/2nd Highland Field Coy: R.E.

WAR DIARY
or
INTELLIGENCE SUMMARY

(Erase heading not required.)

Army Form C. 2118.

1/2nd HIGHLAND FIELD Coy., R.E.

No. VOL XXII
Date OCTOBER 1916

Place	Date	Hour	Summary of Events and Information	Remarks and references to Appendices
	23		Commenced strengthening dressing stations at AUCHONVILLERS and MAILLY-MAILLET, and construction of new dugout inside dressing station at AUCHONVILLERS.	
			Sites for alignment posts for defining flanks of objective in proposed attack, reconnoitred and fixed.	
			Work continued at R.E. store and workshops, making alignments & sign posts for alignment posts.	
			Construction of new roof in dressing station at AUCHONVILLERS completed.	
			Construction of dugout beside same, continued.	
			Strengthening cellar and entrance, and fitting up toilet-house for drying purposes, at dressing station at MAILLY-MAILLET.	
			Construction of Mortuary at ENGLEBELMER.	
			Position of alignment posts for boundaries of attack, shewn and 3 complete standards and boards carried to each line of posts, and laid ready for	W.B.G

A.J.Bonar
Major, R.E. (T)
O.C. 1/2nd Highland Field Coy: R.E.

Army Form C. 2118.

WAR DIARY
or
INTELLIGENCE SUMMARY

(Erase heading not required.)

1/2nd HIGHLAND FIELD Coy, R.E.

No. Vol XXII
Date OCT 03 ERIGIE 10.

Place	Date	Hour	Summary of Events and Information	Remarks and references to Appendices
	24		for erection. 2 posts to be used and one spare at each site. Alignment set out by prismatic compass. Nos 3 & 4 sections dug 2 shallow trenches 1'-0" deep, 140 yards long from front trenches, and buried continuous lines of tubes of ammonal, ready to make gap by blowing up. Forming dumps of R.E. Stores in trenches and at AUCHONVILLERS. Carting stores from R.E. Store to AUCHONVILLERS. Work in R.E. Store & workshops continued. 50 Bangalore Torpedoes with detonators and Nobel lighters attached. Constructed out of 2" piping. Repairs made to attached mens billets at MAILLY-MAILLET. Work continued on dressing station at MAILLY-MAILLET and on dugout at AUCHONVILLERS. Construction of Mortuary at ENGLEBELMER completed. Site of mortuary at MAILLY-MAILLET selected and materials for same collected at site.	W.E.J.

W.J.Bonner
Capt
Major, R.E. (T)
O.C. 1/2nd Highland Field Coy: R.E.

WAR DIARY
INTELLIGENCE SUMMARY

(Erase heading not required.)

Army Form C. 2118.

1/2nd HIGHLAND FIELD Coy., R.E.

No. Vol. XXII
Date. OCTOBER 1916.

Place	Date	Hour	Summary of Events and Information	Remarks and references to Appendices
	25		Work of forming dumps of R.E. Stores in trenches and at AUCHONVILLERS continued.	
			Major R. Mitchell evacuated sick.	W.C.J.
			Carting stores from R.E. Store to AUCHONVILLERS.	
			Work in R.E. Store + workshops continued.	
			Making standards + sign boards for alignment posts.	
			Forming dumps of R.E. Stores in trenches and at AUCHONVILLERS continued.	
			8 dumps being formed.	
			Work on dressing station, MAILLY-MAILLET and dugout AUCHONVILLERS continued.	
			Site for third line of attack boundary alignment posts reconnoitred & fixed.	
			Construction of mortuary, MAILLY-MAILLET continued.	
			Carting stores from R.E. Store to AUCHONVILLERS.	W.C.J.

A.J.Bonner Capt.
Major, R.E. (T)
O.C. 1/2nd Highland Field Coy: R.E.

War Diary of Intelligence Summary

Army Form C. 2118.

1/2nd HIGHLAND FIELD Coy., R.E.
Vol XXII No. 12.
Date OCTOBER 1916

O.C. 1/2nd Highland Field Coy: R.E.
Major, R.E. (T)

Place	Date	Hour	Summary of Events and Information	Remarks and references to Appendices
	26		Work in R.E. Store and workshops continued. Filling Bangalore torpedoes and lengths of 2" water piping with ammonal, and fitting detonators, fuses and Nobel lighters to same. Forming dumps of R.E. stores in the trenches continued. Position of south boundary alignment posts fixed by prismatic compass, and laid off standards and signboards carried to positions. Strengthening of dressing station MAILLY-MAILLET completed. Work on dugout at AUCHONVILLERS continued. 2 mine to be used as communications to German front line reconnoitred. Construction of mortuary, MAILLY-MAILLET continued. Construction of bivouacs for future use of Company at cross roads west of MAILLY-MAILLET. Carting stores from R.E. Store to AUCHONVILLERS.	

Army Form C. 2118.

WAR DIARY
INTELLIGENCE SUMMARY
(Erase heading not required.)

1/2nd HIGHLAND FIELD Coy., R.E.

No. Vol. XXII
Date October 1916

O.C. 1/2nd Highland Field Coy., R.E.
W. Bowser
Major, R.E. (T)

Place	Date	Hour	Summary of Events and Information	Remarks and references to Appendices
	27		Work in R.E. Store and workshops continued. Carting timber from VARENNES to R.E. Store MAILLY-MAILLET. Forming dumps of R.E. Stores in trenches and at AUCHONVILLERS continued. Dugout beside dressing station, AUCHONVILLERS completed. Construction of Mortuary, MAILLY-MAILLET completed. 3rd Mine proposed for use as communication to German front line, reconnoitred and sufficient approval to blow safe from end of all mines to German front line, carried up and stored in mine shafts. Part of standards and sign boards required for county boundary alignment carried to sites of posts. 2nd Lieut Robertson. W.B. wounded and sent to No 4. Casualty Clearing Station. Construction of bivouacs for future use of Company at wood east of MAILLY-MAILLET continued. Carting stores from R.E. Stn to AUCHONVILLERS.	

WAR DIARY
or
INTELLIGENCE SUMMARY

(Erase heading not required.)

Army Form C. 2118.

1/2nd HIGHLAND FIELD Coy., R.E.

No. Vol. XXII
Date. OCTOBER 1916

Place	Date	Hour	Summary of Events and Information	Remarks and references to Appendices
	28.		Work in R.E. Store and workshops continued; making Bangalore Torpedoes, trench boards, sign boards, bridges and trench ladders.	
			Carting timber from VARENNES to R.E. Store at MAILLY-MAILLET.	
			Experiments made in blowing saps by means of 3", 3ft. tin canisters of ammonal buried in ground.	
			Extra canisters of ammonal carried up and stored in own shafts.	
			Investigations made of water piping required for bake house, MAILLY-MAILLET.	
			Forming dumps of R.E. Stores in trenches and at AUCHONVILLERS continued.	
			Construction of bivouacs for future use of Company at Wood west of MAILLY-MAILLET continued.	
	29.		Carting stores from R.E. Store to AUCHONVILLERS.	
			Work in R.E. Store and workshops continued as above.	
			Position suitable for storing reserve ammonal sufficient for blowing 2 saps already prepared on 23rd October, reconnoitred.	

A.J. Bonner
Major, R.E. (T)
O.C. 1/2nd Highland Field Coy: R.E.

Army Form C. 2118.

WAR DIARY
or
INTELLIGENCE SUMMARY
(Erase heading not required.)

1/2nd HIGHLAND FIELD Coy., R.E.
No. Vol. XXII
Date. OCTOBER 1916

Place	Date	Hour	Summary of Events and Information	Remarks and references to Appendices
	30.		Remainder of standards and sign boards required for south boundary alignment posts carried to site.	
			Formation of 7 dumps of R.E. stores in trenches completed.	R.E.4
			Forming dumps of R.E. Stores at AUCHONVILLERS.	
			Construction of bivouacs for future use of Company at woods west of MAILLY-MAILLET completed.	
			Works in R.E. Sltn Workshops continued. Timber carted from VARENNES to R.E. Store MAILLY-MAILLET.	
	31.		Stores carted from R.E. store to AUCHONVILLERS.	R.E.4
			Reserve supply of ammonal in canisters sufficient to blow two gaps as above, carried to allotted site and stored.	
			Forming dumps of R.E. stores at AUCHONVILLERS continued.	
			Fitting up water piping in bath-house, MAILLY-MAILLET.	
			Carting timber from VARENNES to MAILLY-MAILLET R.E. Store & carting R.E. Stores from MAILLY-MAILLET to AUCHONVILLERS.	

W.P. Bonner Capt
Major, R.E. (T)
O.C. 1/2nd Highland Field Coy: R.E.

Army Form C. 2118.

WAR DIARY
or
INTELLIGENCE SUMMARY

(Erase heading not required.)

1/2nd HIGHLAND FIELD Coy., R.E.

No. Vol. XXI.
Date OCTOBER 1916

Place	Date	Hour	Summary of Events and Information	Remarks and references to Appendices
			Work in R.E. Store and workshops continued.	
			Forming dump of R.E. stores at AUCHONVILLERS continued.	
			Fitting up water piping in bath-house, MAILLY-MAILLET continued.	
			Additional supply of armoured Canadas carried u/s to mine tunnel B for use in blowing sap from end of tunnel to German front trench. Boring road metal to AUCHONVILLERS and constructing siding for turning motor wagons on MAILLY-MAILLET — AUCHONVILLERS road.	
			Strengthening dressing station roof at THURLES DUMP.	
			Experiments made by No 2. Section in blowing rapid by means of 3 ft. 3" dia. Canisters of ammonal buried 1 ft. deep in ground.	
			No. of Casualties during month :— 1 Officer wounded, 1 Driver wounded.	
			1 Sapper released for civil employment as munition worker.	
			The following reinforcements joined the Company :—	
			2nd Oct. 1st Lieut. S. J. HUNTER; S/Sgt. Major. R. MITCHELL. D.S.O.	

Capt.
Major, R.E. (T)
O.C. 1/2nd Highland Field Coy: R.E.

Army Form C. 2118.

WAR DIARY
INTELLIGENCE SUMMARY

1/2nd HIGHLAND FIELD Coy., R.E.

No. Vol. XXII
Date October 1916.

Place	Date	Hour	Summary of Events and Information	Remarks and references to Appendices
			No. of Officers then on leave during month:- Nil.	
			Roll of Officers with Company at 31-10-16. Captain W.P. Barron, M.C.; Captain W.C. Gegg; Lieut. T.J. Gordon; 2nd Lieut. A.G. Naismith, M.C.; C. Orrell; A.R. Fyffe; J.B. Ritchie ~ S.J. Hunter.	W.C.Y.

W.P. Barron
Major, R.E. (T)
O.C. 1/2nd Highland Field Coy. R.E.

Vol 22

51

1/2nd HIGHLAND
FIELD Coy., R. E.
No. —
Date 30/11/16

WAR DIARY
(WITH PLAN)
OF
1ST/2ND HIGHLAND FIELD COMPANY. R.E.T.
FOR
NOVEMBER
1916.

VOL: No XXIII

Army Form C. 2118.

WAR DIARY
or
INTELLIGENCE SUMMARY

(Erase heading not required.)

1/2nd HIGHLAND FIELD Coy., R. E.

No. Vol. XXIII.
Date. November 1915.

Instructions regarding War Diaries and Intelligence Summaries are contained in F. S. Regs., Part II. and the Staff Manual respectively. Title Pages will be prepared in manuscript.

Place	Date	Hour	Summary of Events and Information	Remarks and references to Appendices
FORCEVILLE	1st-6th		Work in R.E. Store. MAILLY-MAILLET continued; making Bangalore torpedoes, trench boards, sign boards, trench bridges and trench ladders. Carting timber from VARENNES to MAILLY store.	
			Nos. 1 & 3 sections assisting in work at store.	
			No. 2 section forming forward and intermediate R.E. dumps in trenches for use in attack.	W.E.W.
			Fitting up water piping in Sub-Sector MAILLY-MAILLET	
			No. 4 section constructing new shelter for spare ammunition for moving South sap between BRITISH & GERMAN front trenches (see War Diary for October). Moving ammunition to shelter. Strengthening regimental aid posts at THURLES and UXBRIDGE dumps. Cutting new trenches at night.	
			Carried out trial erection of alignment posts during darkness on North and Centre lines for use in attack. (see War Diary for October).	
			Nos. 1 & 4 sections marked with tapes in front trench distance	

O.C. 1/2nd Highland Field Coy. R.E.
Major, R.E. (T)

W.E.W.

W.J.Garner
Capt.

2449 Wt. W14957/M90 750,000 1/16 J.B.C. & A. Forms/C.2118/12.

Army Form C. 2118.

WAR DIARY
or
INTELLIGENCE SUMMARY

(Erase heading not required.)

1/2nd HIGHLAND FIELD Coy., R.E.

No. Vol. XXIII
Date NOVEMBER 1916

2.

Place	Date	Hour	Summary of Events and Information	Remarks and references to Appendices
			distance of 30 yds on North side, and 10 yds on South side of North sap, and 10 yds on North side and 30 yds on South side of South sap, with order to blow dangerous areas to be clear of infantry when saps were blown after attack. Fuzes prepared for removal taken for above sap.	
			No. 1 & 4 Sections in bivouacs billeted at FORCEVILLE.	
			No. 2 Section in bivouacs at MAILLY WOOD WEST.	
			No. 3 Section and details with attached infantry at R.E. store MAILLY-MAILLET.	
			2nd Lieut MACNEILL reconnoitred site for 12 NISSEN huts.	
			Work in R.E. Store MAILLY-MAILLET continued.	
			Party of No. 1 Section sent to clear tunnel A at front line (see War Diary for October). Ammonal for blowing sap from end of tunnel to front German trench was cleared to one side to give free	

O.G. 1/2nd Highland Field Coy: R.E.
Major, R.E. (T)

Army Form C. 2118.

WAR DIARY
or
INTELLIGENCE SUMMARY

(Erase heading not required.)

1/2nd HIGHLAND FIConfidentialELD Coy., R.E.
No. VOL. XXIII.
Date NOVEMBER 1916.

Place	Date	Hour	Summary of Events and Information	Remarks and references to Appendices
	8.		free passage in tunnel. No.2 section with working party of 100 infantry arranged to erect NISSEN huts at P.17.a.6.2. on FORCEVILLE - MAILLY MAILLET road, and to meet lorries with huts there at 9.15 a.m. Lorries did not arrive. Infantry party dismissed at noon. Proposed positions of huts marked out on ground. Work continued in R.E. Mine MAILLY-MAILLET. No.1 section constructing experimental trench bridge carried on sledge, suitable for mule traffic and to be carried overland by same. Nos. 2 + 4 sections erecting NISSEN huts on FORCEVILLE - MAILLY-MAILLET road.	v.b.y
	9.		No.3 section assisting in R.E. Mine MAILLY-MAILLET. Spare sappers clearing road in front of Militia FORCEVILLE. Work in R.E. Mine MAILLY-MAILLET continued.	v.b.y

W.J. Bonner
Capt
Major, R.E. (T)
O.C. 1/2nd Highland Field Coy: R.E.

WAR DIARY
or
INTELLIGENCE SUMMARY

(Erase heading not required.)

Army Form C. 2118.

1/2nd HIGHLAND FIELD Coy., R.E.

No. Vol. XXIII
Date. NOVEMBER 1916

Place	Date	Hour	Summary of Events and Information	Remarks and references to Appendices
	10		No. 3 Section assisting at store & repairing pumps.	
			Nos. 2 & 4 Sections erecting NISSEN huts as above.	
			No. 1. Section employed at R.E. store MAILLY-MAILLET, constructing Bowstring truss bridges and sledges for carrying same, improving billets at FORCEVILLE, and assisting with erection of NISSEN huts.	
			Timber carted from VARENNES to MAILLY-MAILLET store.	
			Volume of brickwork in two ruined buildings in FORCEVILLE measured for the purpose of purchase of same by town major for use in horse standings.	w.e.f.
			Well in FORCEVILLE being deepened.	
			Work in R.E. store MAILLY-MAILLET continued as above.	
			No. 1 section making truss bridges and sledges as above.	
			No. 3 section assisting in store.	
			No. 2 & 4 sections erecting huts in FORCEVILLE - MAILLY-MAILLET road.	

W.P.Lever
Major, R.E. (T)
O.C. 1/2nd Highland Field Coy: R.E.

WAR DIARY
or
INTELLIGENCE SUMMARY

(Erase heading not required.)

Army Form C. 2118.

1/2nd HIGHLAND FIELD Coy., R.E.

No. Vol. XXIII
Date NOVEMBER 1916

Place	Date	Hour	Summary of Events and Information	Remarks and references to Appendices
	11		No. 4 Section repairing well in FORCEVILLE, and making new drain down for same.	W.E.J.
			Work in R.E. store MAILLY-MAILLET continued.	
			Nos. 2 & 4 Sections erecting NISSEN huts as above, 9 huts partly completed.	
			No. 4 Section repairing well which and erecting bunks in billets at FORCEVILLE.	
			No. 3 Section filled in trench and laid corduroy road overrun for use of Tanks at Q.1.a.90.05.	W.E.J.
			Trench 15 yds south of same filling for same purpose.	
			Making 200 barbed wire goosberries in store.	
			No. 1 Section assisting in work at R.E. store, also constructing heavy trench bridges and sledges for pack mules.	
			Repairing wells. FORCEVILLE.	
	12		Work in R.E. store MAILLY-MAILLET continued.	

Major, R.E. ("T")
O.C. 1/2nd Highland Field Coy: R.E.

WAR DIARY
or
INTELLIGENCE SUMMARY

(Erase heading not required.)

Army Form C. 2118.

1/2nd HIGHLAND FIELD Coy., R.E.

No. Vol. XXIII
Date. NOVEMBER 1916.

O.C. 1/2nd Highland Field Coy: R.E.
Major, R.E. (T)
W.P. Bonnar (?)

Place	Date	Hour	Summary of Events and Information	Remarks and references to Appendices
	12		Nos. 1 & 4 Sections with party of 19 infantry joiners moved to bivouacs at MAILLY wood WEST.	
			Orders to Company by C.R.E. & O.C. Company in regard to work on saps, tunnels & alignment posts to be carried out on 13th Nov. before & after 51st Division's attack on BEAUMONT-HAMEL, attached.	W.O.1
			Work on NISSEN huts stopped.	
			2nd Lieut. FYFE with party of 15 sappers of No.1 Section and 1 Officer & 15 other ranks 1/8th Royal Scots proceeded at 10-30.p.m. from R.E. Store MAILLY-MAILLET to tunnel "A" to wait there until orders were sent to 2nd Lieut. FYFE from G.O.C. 153rd Infantry Brigade to break through tunnel to surface and blow sap to German front line.	
			Lieut. GORDON with party of 15 sappers of No. 3. Section and 15 men of 1/8th Royal Scots proceeded at 10-30.p.m. from R.E. Store MAILLY-MAILLET to tunnel "B" to wait there until front German trench was captured before blowing sap.	

WAR DIARY or INTELLIGENCE SUMMARY

Army Form C. 2118.

1/2nd HIGHLAND FIELD Coy., R.E.

No. Vol. XXIII
Date NOVEMBER 1916

Place	Date	Hour	Summary of Events and Information	Remarks and references to Appendices
	12		2ⁿᵈ Lieut HUNTER with party of 15 sappers of No. 2 Section and 15 men of 1/8ᵗʰ Royal Scots, proceeded at 10.30 p.m. from R.E. Store, MAILLY-MAILLET to trench "C" to wait there until front German trench was captured, before blowing saps.	
			1 N.C.O. and 3 sappers of No. 4 Section proceeded at 12 midnight to North line alignment posts, to erect same before daylight.	
			1 N.C.O. and 3 sappers of No. 4 Section proceeded as above to erect centre line alignment posts.	
			1 N.C.O. and 5 sappers of No. 2 Section, proceeded at 10 p.m. as above to erect South line alignment posts.	
			1 N.C.O. and 6 sappers of No. 1 & 3 Section and 1 Officer and 1 Platoon of 1/8ᵗʰ Royal Scots, proceeded at 12 midnight to site of North sap, which was to be blown after front German trench was captured.	
			1 N.C.O. and 6 sappers of No. 4 Section, proceeded at 10 p.m. to site of South sap, as above, and met 1 Officer and 1 Platoon of 1/8 Royal Scots at site	W.C.J.

O.C. 1/2nd Highland Field Coy: R.E.
W.P.Rainer Capt
Major, R.E. (T)

Army Form C. 2118.

WAR DIARY
or
INTELLIGENCE SUMMARY
(Erase heading not required.)

1/2nd HIGHLAND FIELD Coy., R.E.

No. ....
Date November 1916

Place	Date	Hour	Summary of Events and Information	Remarks and references to Appendices
	13.		Company headquarters and transport remained at FORCEVILLE and 2nd Lieut Ritchie, details and carrying party of 21 men remained at R.E. dump MAILLY-MAILLET.	W.G.
			51st Division attacked at 5.45 a.m.	
			The 3 sets of Alignment posts were successfully erected before daylight.	W.G.
			Tunnel "A" was broken through in evening, and sap between tunnel and German front line was blown except for 40 yds. for which there was not sufficient ammonal. 2nd Lieut FYFE was wounded on this work.	
			Tunnel "B" was broken through to surface before attack and sap as above, was blown in evening. Much trouble was experienced here from German minenwerfers and machine guns left in old German trenches.	
			Tunnel "C" was broken through about 10 a.m. & trench was dug

[signature] Lt Col
Major, R.E. (T)
O.C. 1/2nd Highland Field Coy: R.E.

Army Form C. 2118.

WAR DIARY
or
INTELLIGENCE SUMMARY
(Erase heading not required.)

1/2nd - HIGHLAND FIELD Coy., R.E.

No. Vol. XXIII
Date NOVEMBER 1916

Instructions regarding War Diaries and Intelligence Summaries are contained in F.S. Regs., Part II. and the Staff Manual respectively. Title Pages will be prepared in manuscript.

Place	Date	Hour	Summary of Events and Information	Remarks and references to Appendices
			dug to front German line. Ammonal was not used, owing to state of ground and number of wounded lying near.	
			Parties from tunnels "A" and "B" returned to billets at night.	
			Party from tunnel "C" returned on morning of 14th Nov.	
			North sap laid with ammonal tubes on 23rd Octr was found to be incorrectly sited, so a new trench was dug to German front line. Ammonal not being used by order of 1/8th Royal Scots officer in charge of work. Great trouble was experienced here from German machine guns and shelling.	
			Only six lengths of ammonal tubes laid on 23rd October in South sap collected, owing to wet. Spare supply of ammonal tubes was found to be buried by shell fire and trench to German front line was dug without flowing.	
			Work of unloading & issuing stores at R.E. S&P MAGXX MAILLET was continued	

W.R. [signature]
Major, R.E. (T)
O.C. 1/2nd Highland Field Coy. R.E.

WAR DIARY or INTELLIGENCE SUMMARY

Army Form C. 2118.

1/2nd HIGHLAND FIELD Coy, R.E.
No. Vol. XXIII
Date NOVEMBER 1916

Place	Date	Hour	Summary of Events and Information	Remarks and references to Appendices
	13		No 3. section moved to bivouacs at MAILLY WOOD WEST.	
			Suffered Casualties :- 3 wounded.	W.E.J.
			Divisional Ammunition Column wagons attached to Company placed at disposal of 1/1st Highland Field Co. R.E. for use in repairing roads.	
			Unloading of stores received and issue of same continued at R.E. Store.	W.E.J.
	14		MAILLY - MAILLET.	
			Work at store continued as above.	
	15		Capt BARRON, with Lieut GORDON reconnoitre near British line at night.	W.E.J.
			All No 4. section with 2nd Lieuts OKELL and HUNTER and infantry working party, dig new trench from LEAVE AVENUE to WAGON road east of BEAUMONT HAMEL as shown on attached plan.	
			Heavy shell fire experienced.	
	16		Work at R.E. Store continued as above.	

M.Barron
Major, R.E. (T)
O.C. 1/2nd Highland Field Coy. R.E.

Army Form C. 2118.

WAR DIARY
OR
INTELLIGENCE SUMMARY

(Erase heading not required.)

1/2nd HIGHLAND FIELD Coy., R.E.
No. Vol. XXIII
Date NOVEMBER 1916.

Place	Date	Hour	Summary of Events and Information	Remarks and references to Appendices
	17		All 4 sections engaged in improving new communication trench without infantry party.	w.c.h
			Nos. 1, 2, 3 & 4 Section & 19 infantry joiners move to R.E. Store.	w.c.h
			MAILLY-MAILLET for billets.	
			Work in R.E. Store, MAILLY-MAILLET continued as above.	
	18		Nos. 1, 2, 3 & 4 sections move from store, back to bivouacs at MAILLY wood WEST, as Division expected to be relieved by 32nd Division.	w.c.h
			Work at R.E. Store MAILLY-MAILLET continued as above.	
			Site for HARPER Stronghold - north of BEAUMONT HAMEL Reconnoitred and taped out at midnight. Arrangements made for section to work in relays on this strong point.	
			Part of No. 4 section with 2nd Lieut OKELL and infantry party engaged in dismounting German heavy trench mortar in BEAUMONT HAMEL, removing operating gear and firing off cap, taking off barrel and closing up buffer chamber, disconnecting sliding platform	w.c.h

W. Warren Capt.
Major, R.E. (T)
O.C. 1/2nd Highland Field Coy. R.E.

Army Form C. 2118.

WAR DIARY
INTELLIGENCE SUMMARY
(Erase heading not required.)

1/2nd HIGHLAND FIELD Coy, R.E.

No. Vol. XXIII
Date NOVEMBER 1916

Place	Date	Hour	Summary of Events and Information	Remarks and references to Appendices
	18		2nd Lieut HUNTER and 2 fitters from No. 2. Section inspected Electric Power Station South of BEAUMONT HAMEL Cross roads. A small brick arched cellar about 25' × 15' with 2 entrances was found. The dynamo, switch boards, pulleys etc were found to have been removed. The engine, of French manufacture, about 6-8 H.P. was almost intact. A drum of heavy lead covered cable and 3 gall. tin of petrol were found. At one end of the cellar a steep gallery had been started.	M.C.G.
	19		Work in R.E. Dump MAILLY-MAILLET continued as about. Officers and sappers who were at HARPER work, waited until 4.15 a.m. when first relief arrived, having been delayed on BEAUMONT-AUCHONVILLERS road by infantry relief. Lieut GORDON with No 3. Section, 1 section of 1/7/1st Highland Field Coy. R.E. and 1 company 1/8th Royal Scots carried on second shift of work on HARPER work at 5. a.m. but had to stop work after daylight owing to heavy shell fire. Communication trench leading to this	M.C.G.

O.C. 1/2nd Highland Field Coy: R.E.
Major, R.E. ("T")

Army Form C. 2118.

WAR DIARY
or
INTELLIGENCE SUMMARY

(Erase heading not required.)

1/2nd HIGHLAND FIELD Coy., R.E.

No. Vol. XXIII
Date NOVEMBER 1916

Place	Date	Hour	Summary of Events and Information	Remarks and references to Appendices
	20		works were improved.	
			Work in R.E. store MAILLY-MAILLET continued.	
			No 4. section with infantry working party constructing BURN Strong point at tunnel 'A', near old German front line. Material carried to site on extended trench railway. Work taped out. Forward portion of overhead work dug to average depth of 3ft. 6ins. Pickets erected for wire. Arrangements made for bringing up further wiring material to site.	
			No. 2 section and working party constructing CAMPBELL Strong point near old German trench. Overhead work taped out. Excavation started. Average depth of 2'-0" reached. Ground was very difficult to work being soft and slimy.	
	21		Work in R.E. Store MAILLY-MAILLET continued.	
			Excavation and wiring of BURN and CAMPBELL works continued.	
			M.G. emplacements commenced. Trenches & wiring of BURN work completed.	

Army Form C. 2118.

WAR DIARY
or
INTELLIGENCE SUMMARY

(Erase heading not required.)

1/2nd HIGHLAND FIELD Coy, R.E.
No. V24 XXIII
Date. NOVEMBER 1916

Instructions regarding War Diaries and Intelligence Summaries are contained in F. S. Regs., Part II. and the Staff Manual respectively. Title Pages will be prepared in manuscript.

Place	Date	Hour	Summary of Events and Information	Remarks and references to Appendices
	22		Work in R.E. Abri MAILLY-MAILLET continued. Company preparing to move on 23rd. Billets for company at VARENNES inspected. 2 attached D.A.C. wagons and team handed over to 2/2nd Highland Field Co. R.E.	
	23		Major Brand & running symical Company from Someville VARENNES. R.E. Abri MAILLY-MAILLET handed over to 7th Division. Attached Infantry returned to units. Details at R.E. Store & reinstatements at MAILLY W.C.J Wood WEST. Nos. 1, 2, 3, & 4 sections moved to VARENNES at 10 a.m. Company head-quarters moved to same at 11-30 a.m. Billets hired. Parties left behind to clean up billets and to obtain a certificate for clean state of same from Town Major. Tents and bivouac covers handed in to town major stores and receipts obtained at MAILLY Wood and FORCEVILLE respectively.	W.C.J
	24		Company moved to PUCHEVILLERS at 8.45 a.m. Arrived 1 p.m. Billeted	

A.J.Bonar Capt.
Major, R.E. (T.)
O.G. 1/2nd Highland Field Coy: R.E.

WAR DIARY
or
INTELLIGENCE SUMMARY

(Erase heading not required.)

Army Form C. 2118.

1/2nd HIGHLAND FIELD Coy., R.E.

No. Vol. XXIII

Date NOVEMBER 1916

Place	Date	Hour	Summary of Events and Information	Remarks and references to Appendices
	25.		these. Billets taken over from 1/1st Highland Field Co. R.E. One officer remained at VARENNES to hand over billets to 1/1st Highland Field Co. R.E. 2 attached D.A.C. wagons and teams returned to D.A.C. Lieut GORDON and RITCHIE with 16 sappers and transport of No 3 Section left PUCHEVILLERS at 9 a.m. and proceed to TARA VALLEY near ALBERT to take over work from 4th Canadian Division.	W.e.f. W.e.f.
	26.		Inspection of Company kit. Company moved at 11.30 a.m. to CROMWELL'S huts east of AVELUY. Arrived 7 p.m. Billeted there. Motor lorry attached for transport of kits.	W.e.f.
	27.		No 3 section, having been shown over divisional front by 4th Canadian Division, ordered to rejoin company. 2nd Lieut CLEGHORN joined company for duty.	
	28.		Company moved at 8-30 a.m. to huts near OVILLERS, X.14.6.2.9. Billeted in NISSEN huts. No 3 section rejoins company. Company transport billeted at CROMWELL'S huts near AVELUY.	

[signature]
Major, R.E. (T)
O.C. 1/2nd Highland Field Coy: R.E.

WAR DIARY or INTELLIGENCE SUMMARY

Army Form C. 2118.

1/2nd HIGHLAND FIELD Coy, R.E.
Vol. XXIII
Date NOVEMBER 1916

Place	Date	Hour	Summary of Events and Information	Remarks and references to Appendices
West of COURCELETTE	29		Lieuts OKELL & HUNTER reconnoitre site of overland track to be made west of COURCELETTE. Nos 2 & 4 sections with working party of 200 men commence construction of above track, with brushwood. 1 NISSEN hut erected at billets for use of company. Company cleaning ground and billets. 4 D.A.C. wagons attached to company for work.	
	30		Work on overland track continued as above. D.A.C. wagons used for conveying brushwood from POZIERES dump to site of track. Timber carted from BECOURT R.E. store to company's billets. Light railway from OVILLERS POST to CANADA POST, and branch line to POZIERES dump reconnoitred, to find if suitable for first locomotive traffic. Company engaged in improving billets. No. 2 Section and infantry working party continued laying of brushwood track as above by daylight. Over 700 yards of track	

Major, R.E. (T)
O.C. 1/2nd Highland Field Coy; R.E.

WAR DIARY
INTELLIGENCE SUMMARY

Army Form C. 2118.

1/2nd HIGHLAND FIELD Coy., R.E.

Vol. XXIII No. .... Date NOVEMBER 1916

Place	Date	Hour	Summary of Events and Information	Remarks and references to Appendices
			track constructed.	
			Pumping plant at SUGAR REFINERY near COURCELETTE surveyed by 2nd Lieut RITCHIE and found to consist of 15 H.P. oil engine, electric plant, and pump in good condition.	
			No. 1 section making beds and cookhouse for 154th Infantry Brigade Headquarters.	
			Carting timber from BECOURT R.E. S.15 to POZIERES dump.	
			Sorting out and preparing parts of NISSEN huts for erection.	
			Improving billets and cleaning up grounds.	
			No. of casualties during month :- 1 Officer, 1 Corpl., 1 2nd Corpl. + 3 Sappers wounded.	
			Sapper released for civil employment :- Nil.	
			Reinforcements joined company during month :- 1 Officer + 21 Other ranks.	
			No. of officers + men on leave during month :- 3 Sappers.	
			Roll of Officers with Company at 30/11/16 :- Captain W.P. BARRON M.C. Captain W.C. GLEGG, Lieut. T.J. GORDON, 2nd Lieuts MACNEILL M.C., C. OKELL, F.B. RITCHIE, S.J. HUNTER; and J.S. CLEGHORN.	

O.C. 1/2nd Highland Field Coy: R.E.
Major, R.E. (T)

Army Form C. 2118.

WAR DIARY
or
INTELLIGENCE SUMMARY

(Erase heading not required.)

1/2nd HIGHLAND FIELD Coy., R.E.

No. XXIII
Date NOVEMBER 1916.

Place	Date	Hour	Summary of Events and Information	Remarks and references to Appendices

Attached. Capt BARRON's orders to section Commanders & C.R.E.'s orders.

Appendices 2, 3 & 4 of C.R.E.'s report. Plans of BRITISH & GERMAN trenches at BEAUMONT shewing as far as FRANKFORT trench & trench at COURCELETTE.

W.E.H.

Capt
Major, R.E. (T)
O.C. 1/2nd Highland Field Coy: R.E.

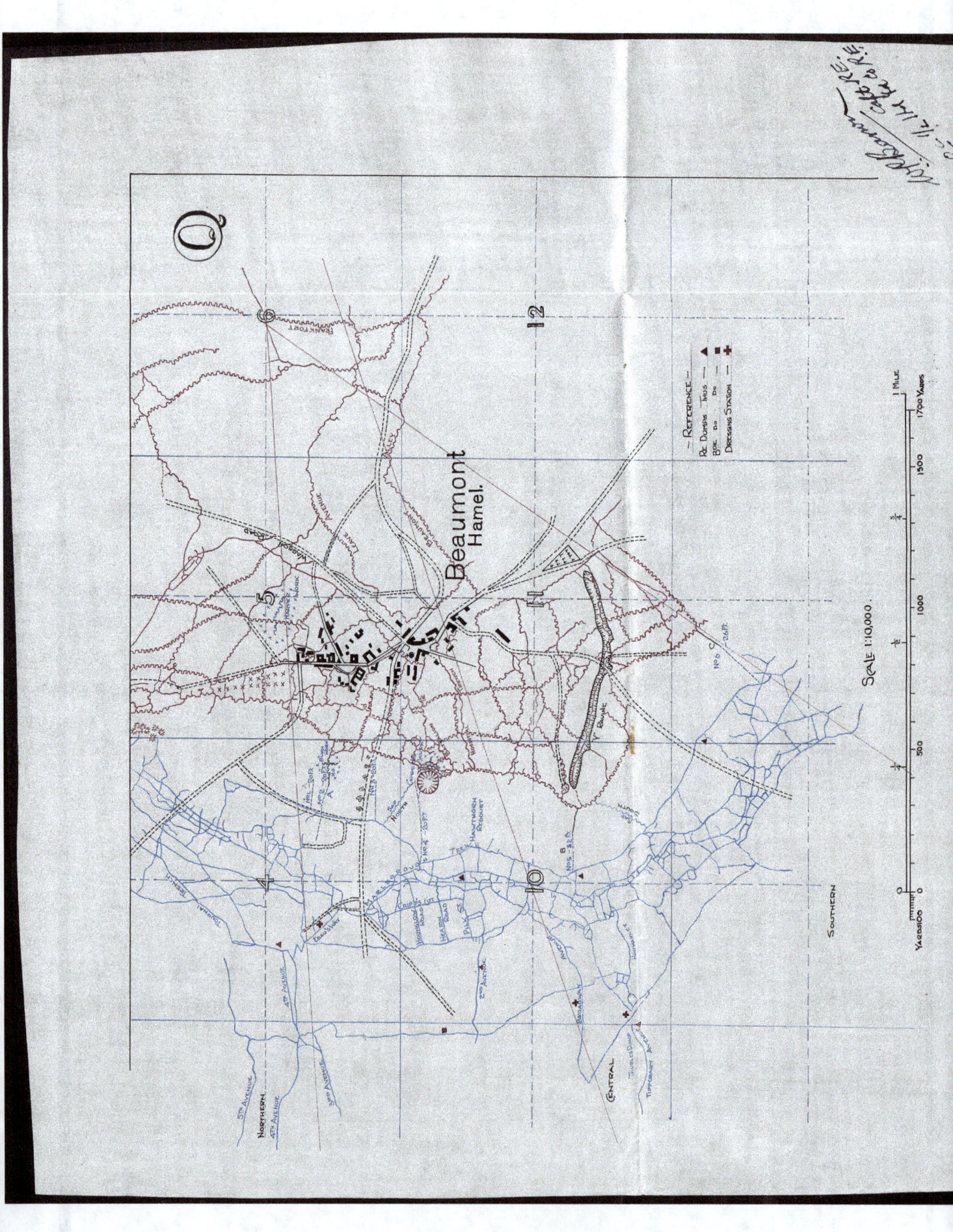

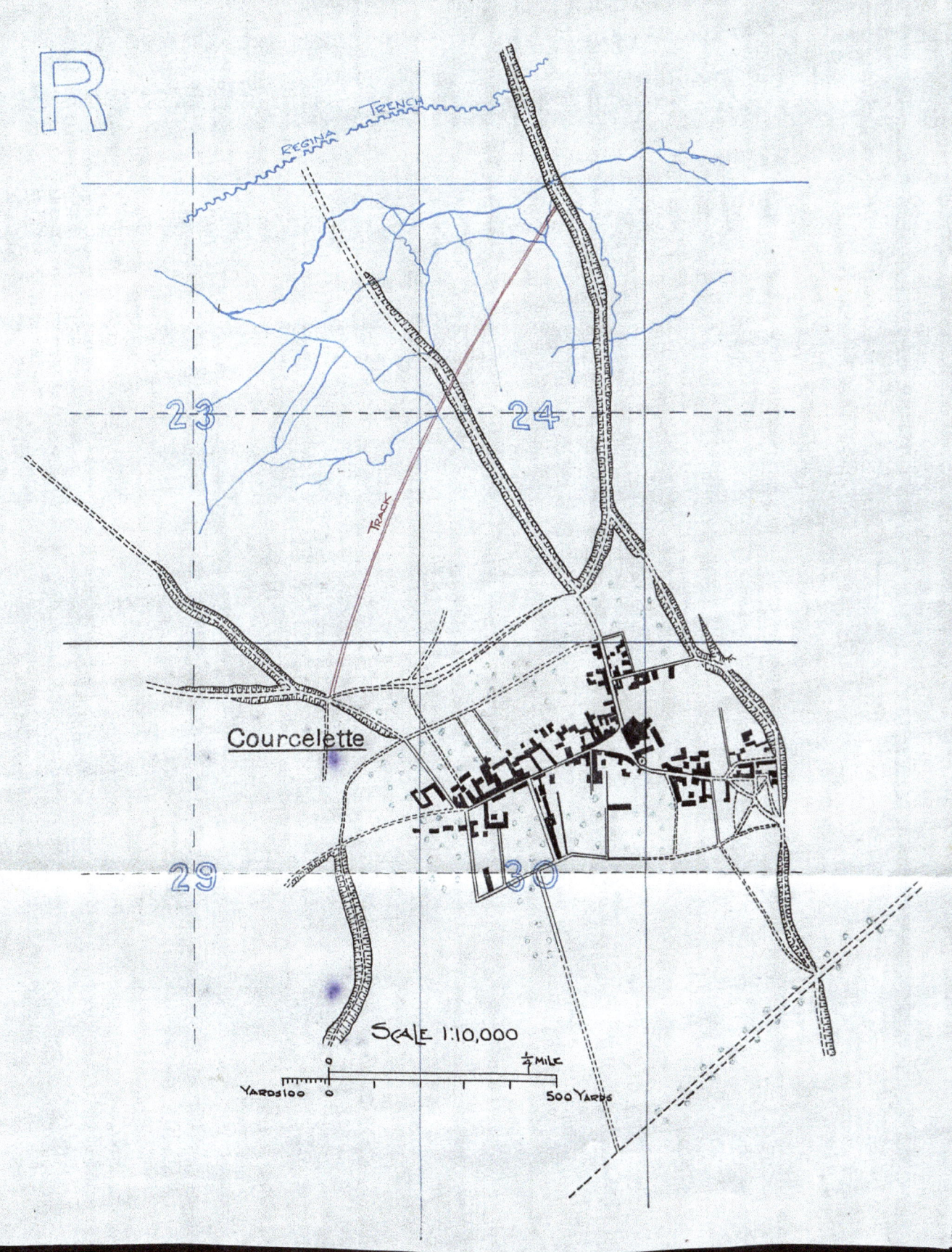

APPENDIX
"2"

The arrangements as regard the Tunnels and Saps are as follows:-

1. The Tunnels have been given identification letters as follows:-

  Tunnel "A" - from Q.4.d.2½.7.
       to Q.4.d.7.5.
  " "B" - from Q.10.d.1.6½.
       to Q.10.d.4½.7.
  " "C" - from Q.17.a.4.3.
       to Q.17.a.7.5½.

Communication Trenches will be blown and dug from the ends of these Tunnels to the German front Trench.

2. The saps to be blown and dug between our front line and the German line have been lettered as follows:-

  SAP. "R" from Q.4.d.40.05.
      to Q.10.b.65.85.
  SAP "S" from Q.10.d.40.15.
      to Q.10.d.60.55.

3. The work on trenches from Tunnels A.B.C. will be carried out by 3 Sections (less details) of 1/2nd Highland Field Coy. R.E. assisted by 1 Platoon 1/8th Royal Scots, who will report to O.C. 1/2nd Highland Field Coy. R.E. at MAILLY dump Q.7.c.9.8. at ZERO minus 7 o'clock.

O.C. 252nd Tunneling Coy R.E. will open B and C Tunnels to surface by ZERO hour.

Tunnel A will not be opened to surface until order is received from B.G.C. 152nd Infantry Brigade (vide S.G. 142/33.

An officer of 252nd Tunneling Coy. R.E. will be in charge "Underground" in "A", "B" and "C". An Officer of the 1/2nd Highland Field Coy. R.E. will be in charge of the "above ground" work at the end of each Tunnel.

Work will be commenced as soon as it is observed that our troops are established in the German Front line trench. After Communication trenches have been completed the troops detailed will return and report to their Company Headquarters.

4. Work on Saps "R" and "S" will be carried out by a party at each sap composed of 1 Platoon 1/8th Royal Scots and one Sergeant and 6 other ranks from 1st/2 Highland Field Coy R.E. Charges have already been laid at each sap for about 140 yards towards the German line.

The R.E. details acting under the orders of platoon Commander 1/8th Royal Scots will blow their charges at ZERO. In view of possible failure due to damp O.C. 1/2nd Highland Field Coy. R.E. will arrange to store in a protected site, close to each sap, sufficient Ammonal tubes to lay a fresh trench line. Work will be commenced immediately after ZERO to improve the trenches blown and to connect on to the German front trenches.

A mine will be blown at ZERO hour by 252nd Tunneling Coy. R.E. forming a Crater at Q.10.b.65.85. "R" Sap will be connected into this Crater and thence to the German trenches.

As soon as a satisfactory communication trench is through the troops will return and report to their Company Headquarters.

(signed) C.F. Rundall. R.E
C.R.E. 51st (H) Divn.

W.P.Barron
Capt.
Major, R.E. (T)
O.C. 1/2nd Highland Field Coy: R.E.

1/2nd HIGHLAND FIELD Coy., R.E.
No.
Date NOVEMBER 1916

APPENDIX "3"

Stores in R.E. Dumps reserved for "Z" day.

DESCRIPTION.	RESERVE DUMP	INTERMEDIATE DUMPS.			FORWARD DUMPS.			
	AUCHONVILLERS Q.8.c.5.0.	THURLES DUMP Q.10.c.00.25.	ESSEX DUMP Q.10.a.6.4.	SUNKEN ROAD Q.3.c.8.8.	SOUTH ALLEY Q.17.a.0.8.	TIPPERARY AV. Q.10.d.05.45.	2nd AVENUE Q.10.b.05.45.	4th AVENUE Q.4.c.5.9.
Screw Pickets (long)	1500	150	150	150	150	150	150	150
" " (short)	600	300	300	300	300	300	300	300
Barbed Wire (coils)	400	100	100	100	100	100	100	100
French Wire	230	20	20	20	20	20	20	20
Sandbags	69,250	5000	5000	5000	5000	5000	5000	5000
Shovels	800	500	500	500	500	500	500	500
Picks	1000	250	250	250	250	250	250	250
Plain Wire	35	5	5	5	5	5	5	5
Wire Cutters	–	10	10	10	–	–	–	–
Tracing Tapes	150	50	50	50	30	30	30	30
Mauls	30	10	10	10	5	5	5	5
Loophole Plates	45	10	10	10	10	10	10	10
3'6" Wood Pickets	400	200	200	200	100	100	100	100
Trench Bridges	20	10	10	10	20	20	20	20
Wire Netting (Rolls)	140	20	20	20	10	10	10	10
Nails 6" cwt	4	½	½	½	½	½	½	½
4" "	4							
3" "	4							
3" "	4							
Saws		10	10	10				
Hammers		10	10	10				
Axes felling		10	10	10				
Axes hand		10	10	10				
Canvas	18	–	–	–				
Spunyarn		1	1	1	1	1	1	1
Rope 2" fathoms		100	100	100				

1/2nd HIGHLAND FIELD Coy., R.E.
No. ✓
Date. NOVEMBER 1916

W.P. Barron
Capt.
Major, R.E. (T)
O.C. 1/2nd Highland Field Coy: R.E.

APPENDIX "4"

Instructions re Alignment Posts.

3 Sets of Alignment Posts as follows will be erected by you on night "Y"/"Z" by ZERO.

1. **Northern Alignment**
Alignment on square Q.6. central, two posts with triangular signs, flying triangular red and white flags below the signs. Erected in squares Q.3.d. and Q.4.c.

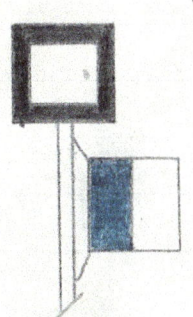

2. **Centre Alignment**
Aligned on Q.6.c.5.3. two posts with square signs, flying blue and white square flag under the sign. Erected in square Q.10.c.

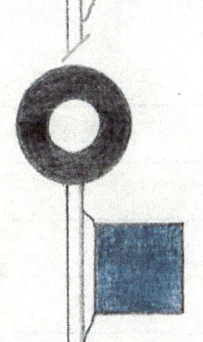

3. **Southern Alignment**
Aligned on Q.6.c.5.3. two posts with circular signs, flying a square blue flag under the sign. Erected in square Q.17.c.

4. These alignments are intended to serve as guides to 51st Division attack when surmounting the high ground East of BEAUMONT HAMEL. They will not be visible from the BEAUMONT HAMEL VALLEY.

5. The men detailed to erect posts will remain out till ZERO plus 3 hours, in order to erect spare posts if necessary.

(Sd) C.F. Rundall. R.E.
LT. COL.
C.R.E. 51st Divn.

1/2nd HIGHLAND
FIELD Coy., R.E.
No. ✓
Date NOVEMBER 1916

W.P. Barron Capt
Major, R.E. (T)
O.C. 1/2nd Highland Field Coy: R.E.

O.C. No 1. Section 1st/2nd Highland Field Co. R.E.

You will arrange to carry out the following work on Z day.

A communication trench will be blown and dug from the end of the Tunnel "A" to the German front Trench.

Tunnel "A" from Q.4.d. 25.70.
to Q.4.d. 70.50.

A proportion of 1 platoon 8th Royal Scots will assist you & these will report at MAILLY dump Q.7.c.9.8. at ZERO - 6 hours o'clock.

Tunnel "A" will not be opened to surface until order is received by Officer 252 Tunnelling Co. R.E. from B.G.C. 152 Infantry Brigade.

An Officer of 252 Tunnelling Co. R.E. will be in charge underground & you will be in charge "above ground" (Lt. Fyfe.)

After communication trench has been completed, the troops detailed will return to section billets & send a report to Company Headquarters.

Plan of tunnel herewith.

Detail 3 sappers to report to O.C. No. 3 Section at MAILLY on afternoon of day prior to ZERO to be attached to his party employed on "R" sap.

10 Notice boards TO TUNNEL "A" will be taken to site & placed in position by party on their return.

(Sgd) W.P. Barron. Capt R.E.T.

1/2nd HIGHLAND
FIELD Coy., R. E.

No. ...
Date NOVEMBER 1916

W.P. Barron
Capt
Major, R.E. (T)
O.C. 1/2nd Highland Field Coy: R.E.

O.C. No. 2. Section 1/2nd Highland Field Co. RE

You will arrange to carry out the following work on Z day.

1. A Communication trench will be blown & dug from the end of Tunnel "C" to the German Front Trench.

Tunnel C. from Q.17.a.4.3.
to Q.17.a.70.55.

A proportion of 1 platoon 8th Royal Scots will assist you & these will report at MAILLY Dump Q.7.c.9.8. at ZERO - 6 hours O'clock.

O.C. 252 Tunnelling Co. R.E. will open "C" Tunnel by surface by ZERO hour.

An officer of 252 Tunnelling Co. R.E. will be in charge "underground": An officer of 1st/2nd Highland Field Co.R.E. (Lt. HUNTER) will be in charge of the "above-ground" work at the end of the Tunnel.

Work will be commenced as soon as it is observed that our troops are <u>established</u> in the German front line trench.

After communication trench has been completed, the troops detailed will return to section billets and send a report to Company Headquarters.

Plan of tunnel herewith.

2. South Alignment Posts with circular discs will be erected at ZERO hour at sites already selected.

Sufficient men should be detailed to ensure that both posts are erected at the same time.

Arrangements should be made for the men detailed to have shelter on the site & all work to be done at ZERO should be reduced to a minimum by arrangements made prior to ZERO.

Men will remain until Z + 3 hours to ensure that posts remain in position.

1 Spare post will be on site.

Party will return to section billets & send on report to Company Headquarters.

Flags, plain blue for attachment to posts will be obtained at R.E. Store. MAILLY.

10 Notice boards TO TUNNEL "C" will be taken to site & placed in position in trenches by the party on their way back.

(Sgd) W P Banon Capt. R.E.

W P Banon
Capt.
Major, R.E. (T)
O.C. 1/2nd Highland Field Coy: R.E.

O.C. No. 3. Section 1/2nd Highland Field Co. R.E.

You will arrange to carry out the following work on 'Z' day.

1. A Communication trench will be blown & dug from the end of Tunnel "B" to the German front line.

Tunnel "B" from Q.10.d.10.65.
to Q.10.d.45.70.

A proportion of 1 platoon 8th Royal Scots will assist you & these will report at MAILLY Dump Q.7.c.9.8. at ZERO - 6 hours o'clock.

O.C. No. 3. section will allot parties from this platoon to O.C's No 1 & 2 Sections. 1/2nd Highland Field Co. R.E.

O.C. 252 Tunnelling Co. R.E. will open "B" Tunnel to surface by ZERO hour.

An officer of 252 Tunnelling Co. R.E. will be in charge "underground". An officer of 1/2nd Highland Field Co. R.E. (Lt. GORDON) will be in charge of the "above ground" work at the end of the tunnel.

Work will be commenced as soon as it is observed that our troops are established in the German front line Trench.

After communication Trench has been completed, the troops detailed will return to billets & send a report to Company Headquarters.

Plan of tunnel herewith.

2. A Sap will be blown & dug between our front line & German line.

Sap "R" from Q.4.d.40.05.
to Q.10.b.65.85.

1 Platoon 8th Royal Scots & 1 Sergt & 6 other ranks from the 1st/2nd Highland Field Co. R.E. are detailed for work at this sap.

Charges have already been laid for about 140 yards towards the German line.

The R.E. details acting under orders of Platoon Commanders 8th Royal Scots will blow their charges at ZERO.

In view of possible failure due to damp sufficient ammonal tubes to lay a fresh charge have been stored in a protected place near the site.

Work will be commenced immediately after ZERO to improve the trenches blown & to connect on to German front trenches.

A mine will be blown at ZERO hour by 252 Tunnelling Co. R.E. forming a crater at Q.10.b.65.85. "R" Sap will be connected into this crater & thence to German Trenches.

As soon as a satisfactory Communication trench is through, the troops will return to billets & send on report to Company Headquarters.

Further details will be sent with reference to meeting the 8th Royal Scots party for work on sap.

10 Notice boards | TO TUNNEL "A" |
& 10 Notice boards | TO SAP "R" |

will be taken to site & placed in position in the trenches by the parties on their way back.

(Sgd) W.P. Banon. Capt. R.E.

1/2nd HIGHLAND FIELD Coy. R.E.
No. ✓
Date: NOVEMBER 1916

W.P. Banon
Capt
Major, R.E. (T)
O.C. 1/2nd Highland Field Coy. R.E.

O.C. No. 4. Section. 1st/2nd Highland Field Co R.E.

You will arrange to carry out the following work on Z day.

1. Alignment posts (north) with triangular boards & △ flags red & white & alignment posts (centre) with square boards & square flags blue & white will be erected at ZERO hour at sites already selected.

Sufficient men should be detailed to ensure that all posts are erected at the same time.

Arrangements should be made for the men detailed to have shelters on the site & all works to be done at ZERO should be reduced to a minimum by arrangements made prior to ZERO. Flags for posts will be obtained at R.E. Store MAILLY.

Parties detailed will remain until Z+3 hours to ensure that posts remain in position. 1 spare post will be on site.

Parties will then return to section billets & send on report to Company Headquarters.

2. A sap will be blown & dug between our front line & the German line.

  Sap "S" from Q.10.d. 40.15.
    to Q.10.d. 60.55.

1 platoon 8th Royal Scots + 1 Sergt + 6 other ranks from 1/2nd Highland Field Co. R.E. are detailed for work at this sap.

Charges have already been laid for about 140 yds towards the German line.

The R.E. details acting under orders of Platoon Commander 8th Royal Scots will blow their charges at ZERO.

In view of possible failure due to damp, sufficient ammonal tubes to blow a fresh charge have been stored in a protected place near the site.

Further details will be sent re meeting party of 8th Royal Scots for work on sap.

Work will be commenced immediately after ZERO to improve the trenches blown & to connect on to German Front trenches.

As soon as a satisfactory communication trench is through, the troops will return to billets & send on a report to Company Headquarters.

10 Notice boards TO SAP "S" will be taken to the site by the party & will be placed in position in the trenches by the party on their way back.

(Sgd) W.P. Barron Capt. R.E.

1/2nd HIGHLAND FIELD Coy., R.E.
No.
Date: NOVEMBER 1915

W.P. Barron
Capt.
~~Major~~, R.E. (T)
O.C. 1/2nd Highland Field Coy: R.E.

Officer in charge.
R.E. Store. MAILLY.

On the day prior to Z day & on completion of work, you will instruct the 20 carpenters attached to you to report complete to the Company's billets at P.23.c.8.4. (MAILLY WOOD WEST)

They will there await orders as regards to continuing work under you at MAILLY.

The specialist sappers will rejoin the company & will report on afternoon of day prior to Z day.

The unloading party, Sergt Gilbert & Sapper Morrice will remain with you at MAILLY store.

(Sgd) W.P. Barron. Capt R.E.

W.P. Barron
Capt
Major, R.E. (T)
O.C. 1/2nd Highland Field Coy. R.E.

1/2nd HIGHLAND
FIELD Coy., R.E.
No.
Date: NOVEMBER 1916

Notes on attack.

1. Three sections R.E. were detailed for work in cutting communication trenches from points where 3 tunnels broke out in NO MAN'S LAND, to German front line. A working party of 45 men were detailed to assist sappers and this party was found to be too small to carry out the work expeditiously, only 15 men being available at each trench in addition to sappers.

2. Explosives were used on two of these trenches & the results obtained were satisfactory and justify their future use under similar conditions.

3. With reference to Forward R.E. Dumps, battalions should have more information as to the location of and stock of materials at these dumps.

4. It would be of great advantage, if each Field Coy. R.E. could have a party of 100 infantry attached for a period before and during operations.

The application for small working & carrying parties with the consequent loss of time in meeting same, and collecting tools & materials, would be avoided & these attached infantry would be comparatively _fresh_ men from whom better work could be obtained.

5. Instructions should be given to the Military Police not to consider small parties of R.E. as stragglers as time was lost by these parties being taken to Straggler's Posts.

(Sgd) W.P. Barron. Capt. R.E.T.

1/2nd HIGHLAND
FIELD Coy., R.E.

No.
Date. NOVEMBER 1916

W.P. Barron
Capt.
Major, R.E. (T)
O.C. 1/2nd Highland Field Coy: R.E.

CONFIDENTIAL.
No 21(A)
HIGHLAND DIVISION.

Vol 23

1/2nd HIGHLAND
FIELD Coy., R.E.
No............
Date 31/12/16

WAR DIARY
(WITH PLAN)
-OF-
1ST/2ND HIGHLAND FIELD COMPANY. R.E.(T)
-FOR-
DECEMBER
-1916.-

Vol: No. XXX

Army Form C. 2118.

WAR DIARY
INTELLIGENCE SUMMARY.
(Erase heading not required.)

1/2nd HIGHLAND FIELD Coy., R.E.
VOL XXIV
31st DECEMBER 1916

Instructions regarding War Diaries and Intelligence Summaries are contained in F. S. Regs., Part II. and the Staff Manual respectively. Title pages will be prepared in manuscript.

Place	Date	Hour	Summary of Events and Information	Remarks and references to Appendices
WOLFE HUTS OVILLERS LA BOISSELLE X.14.6.2.9.	1st to 4th		Constructing Corduroy brushwood track, wire netting overland track, French boards & fixing cross bears on trench-boards at POZIERES dump. Superintending infantry parties of 100 to 200 men, loading, unloading moving frames, trench boards, corrugated iron sheets and angle iron pickets at POZIERES dump, and unloading and carrying same from ALBERT-BAPAUME road to Headquarters. M.19.a.8.9. of infantry advancing battalion in front trenches; two trips made per night. Transporting wire netting and trench-boards by trench tramway from POZIERES dump to advanced brigade headquarters, working party of 50 infantry employed. No 2 Section, sitting constructing overland corduroy brushwood track from COURCELETTE road to EAST MIRAUMONT road as shown on attached plan. Working parties of 100 to 200 infantry employed on this work. Overhauling internal combustion engine and pumping plant in Sugar Refinery, COURCELETTE. R.36.a.6.7. Gap partly cleared from well pumping	N.C.B.

Capt.
Major, R.E. (T)
O.C. 1/2nd Highland Field Coy: R.E.

WAR DIARY
of
INTELLIGENCE SUMMARY.
(Erase heading not required.)

Army Form C. 2118.

1/2nd HIGHLAND FIELD Coy., R.E.
Vol. XXIV No. 2.
Date 31st DECEMBER 1916

Instructions regarding War Diaries and Intelligence Summaries are contained in F. S. Regs., Part II. and the Staff Manual respectively. Title pages will be prepared in manuscript.

Place	Date	Hour	Summary of Events and Information	Remarks and references to Appendices
			Pumping gear at foot of well connected up and intake pipe to pumps cleaned.	
			R.A.M.C. dugout at R.29.d.7.5. near COURCELETTE inspected for purpose of improving it.	
			Company and attached D.A.C. transport employed carting timber from BECOURT to POZIERES dumps, trench boards, screw pickets, barbed wire and mining frames from POZIERES dumps to posn on A-B road about Right battalion headquarters, and mining frames, trench boards, trench board trestles, screw pickets, barbed wire and sandbags from POZIERES dumps to R.29.d.7.8. near COURCELETTE.	
			Ground cleared for foundations and Nissen huts being erected, beside company billets, working parties of 50 infantry employed on this work.	
			Company billets improved. Cook houses, cupsules and chemins de-...	

O.C. 1/2nd Highland Field Coy: R.E.
Major, R.E. (T.)

Army Form C. 2118.

WAR DIARY
or
INTELLIGENCE SUMMARY
(Erase heading not required.)

1/2nd HIGHLAND FIELD Coy., R.E.
No. Vol XXIV
Date 31st DECEMBER 1916

Place	Date	Hour	Summary of Events and Information	Remarks and references to Appendices
			2nd Lieut-Mackinnel evacuated sick to 3rd Canadian Stationary Hospital.	W.E.J.
			4 Officers and 100 other ranks 1/5th Seaforth Highlanders attached to Company as coffin mates.	
	4		Site of IRONSIDE communication trench reconnoitred by Capt: Barron, and 2nd Lt OKELL with C.R.E.	W.E.J.
	5-9		Above work at POZIERES dump continued. R.E. Stores carted and carried to Right Battalion headquarters as above up to 6th December. From 7th December, mine frames and roofing timber carted and carried to C. dump; EAST MIRAUMONT road, French boards and trestles carted and carried to WEST MIRAUMONT road for use in IRONSIDE AVENUE. No. 2 Section constructing brushwood overland track to EAST – MIRAUMONT road with infantry working party. 1750 yards of track completed.	W.E.J.

W.J Barron
Capt.
Major, R.E. (T.)
O.C. 1/2nd Highland Field Coy: R.E.

Army Form C. 2118.

WAR DIARY
or
INTELLIGENCE SUMMARY.

(Erase heading not required.)

1/2nd HIGHLAND FIELD Coy., R.E.

Vol. XXIV
Date 31st DECEMBER 1916.

Place	Date	Hour	Summary of Events and Information	Remarks and references to Appendices
			Overhauling of pumping plant in Sugar Refinery COURCELETTE continued, magneto dismantled and repaired, inlet-valve reground, exhaust valve springs reset, broken piston ring removed, cylinder scraped, compression and timing of engine adjusted, pattern for new kicker starting spindle made and new kicker being made by Herbourdin.	
			Transport employed in carting R.E. Stores to points near Right battalion headquarters dump & EAST-WEST MIRAUMONT road dumps.	
			Erection of Nissen huts at company billets for accommodation of Sapping Motor continued.	
			7 huts erected. Parties of 50 infantry employed on this work.	
			New IRONSIDE C.T. commenced 300 yds of trench dug to 6 ft deep and 5 ft wide at top. Trench boards carried to trench. Working party of 400 infantry, sapping mates and two sections of Company employed on this work.	

Wilson Capt
Major, R.E. (T)
O.C. 1/2nd Highland Field Coy: R.E.

A 5834. Wt.W.4973/M687. 750,000 8/16 D, D, & L. Ltd. Forms/C.2118/13.

WAR DIARY
INTELLIGENCE SUMMARY.
(Erase heading not required.)

Army Form C. 2118.

1/2nd HIGHLAND FIELD Coy., R.E.

No. .... Vol XXIV
and 31st DECEMBER

Place	Date	Hour	Summary of Events and Information	Remarks and references to Appendices
	9.		Company horse standings being improved. Chalk carted and laid on standings. Shed for shoeing smith, harness and forage erected. 2nd/Lt. RITCHIE went on leave on 8th December.	W.E.Y.
			Company took over front line work from 1st/1st Highland Field Company R.E. and handed over work on overland brushwood track and new level of IRONSIDE AVENUE to 2nd/2nd Highland Field Co. R.E.	W.E.Y.
	9–16.		Work on forward end of IRONSIDE AVENUE commenced. Trench boards & trestles carried from WEST MIRAUMONT road dump and advance of brigade headquarters dump to site. Old trench dugout and widened to 8 ft at top. 35 sappers with 2 sections of company employed on this work, working party of 100 infantry obtained for work on 3 nights. 90 yds of trench completed, with trench boards laid from forward end; trestles 200 yards dugout – to 8 ft wide at top. Work on 10TH STREET commenced. Trench boards and trestles carried from EAST MIRAUMONT road to trench. New trench alongside old one,	W.E.Y.

Capt W. E. Yuner
Major, R.E. (T.)
O.C. 1/2nd Highland Field Coy., R.E.

WAR DIARY
of
INTELLIGENCE SUMMARY.
(Erase heading not required.)

Army Form C. 2118.

1/2nd HIGHLAND FIELD Coy., R.E.
Vol. XXIV No. ....
Date 31st December 1916

Place	Date	Hour	Summary of Events and Information	Remarks and references to Appendices
			Dugout to 6ft deep and 8ft wide at top, trench boards laid on trestles.	
			Working parties of 80 to 100 infantry obtained on 3 nights for this work.	
			2 Sections of Company and 30 to 40 Sappers/mates employed nightly.	
			300 yards of trench completed from forward end with trench boards	
			laid a further 50 yards dugout to 6ft deep and 8ft wide at top, and	
			further 100 yards partly dugout.	
			Company and attached D.A.C. Transport employed in carting curved	
			Corrugated iron sheets for shelters, flat corrugated iron sheets, angle iron	
			pickets, barbed wire, sandbags, nails, joiners tools, trench boards and	
			trestles from POZIERES dumps to D dump, R.29.d.7.8 near COURCELETTE.	
			4 Sappers and 10 infantry employed loading and unloading these stores.	
			Average amount carted per night 6000 sandbags, 80 sheets C.I. 50	
			Angle iron pickets, 100 trench boards & 200 trestles.	
			Overhauling of pumping plant, Sugar Refinery, COURCELETTE.	

W.J. Jones Capt.
Major, R.E. (T)
O.C. 1/2nd Highland Field Coy. R.E.

WAR DIARY or INTELLIGENCE SUMMARY

Army Form C. 2118.

1/2nd HIGHLAND FIELD Coy., R.E.
Vol. XXIV
Date: 31st DECEMBER 1916

Place	Date	Hour	Summary of Events and Information	Remarks and references to Appendices
	17		COURCELETTE continued. New boiler for starting apparatus of engine fitted. Electric cable in well repaired, exhaust and water circulation pipes altered and adjusted. Timing gear of engine overhauled. Ammeter voltmeter and starting switch connected to supply refitted, and fitted up on switchboard, wiring of same partly completed.	W.L.J.
			2nd Lieut. O'Neill went on leave on 15th December.	
			2nd Lieut. MacGregor joined Company for duty on 12th December.	
			Work on communication trenches stopped in favour of erection of trench shelters in front line. Working party of 100 infantry to meet a section of Company at POZIERES dump, and guides to be met at Left Battalion Headquarters to lead party to posts in front trench arranged for.	W.L.J.
			Working party arrived at rendezvous one hour & ten minutes late & only 40 strong. Infantry, sapping mats and sap線 were carried with six separate parties, and picked up corrugated iron, angle iron pickets and sandbags at D dump near COURCELETTE.	

O.C. 1/2nd Highland Field Coy: R.E.
Major, R.E. (T.)

WAR DIARY
or
INTELLIGENCE SUMMARY.

(Erase heading not required.)

Army Form C. 2118.

1/2nd HIGHLAND FIELD Coy., R.E.

No. Vol. XXIV
Date 31st December 1915.

Place	Date	Hour	Summary of Events and Information	Remarks and references to Appendices
	18		Infantry party were exhausted and carried stores to left Battalion Head-quarters only.	
			R.E. stores carted to D dump as on 16th.	
			Making 35 sign boards for dumps and overland tracks.	
			Overhauling of pumping plant. Sugar Refinery continued. Vaporiser dismantled and reassembled. Wiring of switch board continued.	M.C.H
			Transporting of stores to D. dump continued as above.	
			One turtle wagon working under orders of R.S.M. R.E. at AVELUY.	
			Similar arrangements made for working party and guide for erection of trench shelter to westward of Company net-working party of 80 infantry at advanced Brigade Head quarter. Guide failed to find posts in front trench and stores were dumped along front trench.	W.C.H
			Making 35 sign boards as above.	
			Overhauling of pumping plant. Sugar refinery continued. Making new spring for sparking apparatus of Engine.	

Major, R.E. (T.)
O.C. 1/2nd Highland Field Coy: R.E.

Army Form C. 2118.

WAR DIARY
or
INTELLIGENCE SUMMARY.
(Erase heading not required.)

1/2nd HIGHLAND FIELD Coy., R.E.
No. VI. XXIV.
Date 31st DECEMBER 1916

Place	Date	Hour	Summary of Events and Information	Remarks and references to Appendices
	19.		One trestle wagon employed in AVELUY as above.	
			12 rafters and 20 saffu mats carried french shelter store from C. dump EAST MIRAUMONT road to post near 10th STREET and erected.	
			6ft long shelter. Plan attached.	
			Difficulty was experienced in fitting circular corrugation sheet over large A frames as no small A frames were obtainable.	
			Carting of R.E. Store to D. dump continued as above. One trestle wagon employed in AVELUY as above.	
			Overhauling of pumping plant in sugar refinery continued. New spring fitted on sparking apparatus of engine. Wiring of switchboard continued.	
			Drying shed at company billets being constructed.	
			35 sign boards being made as above.	
			Sergeant Sutherland sent to CALAIS for two months duty as R.E. instructor.	

[Signed] W. L. Ramsay
Major, R.E. (T)
O.C. 1/2nd Highland Field Coy: R.E.

WAR DIARY
or
INTELLIGENCE SUMMARY.
(Erase heading not required.)

1/2nd HIGHLAND FIELD Coy., R.E.

No. Vol. XXIV

Date 20th December 1916

Army Form C. 2118.

Place	Date	Hour	Summary of Events and Information	Remarks and references to Appendices
	20		Instructor to drafts.	
			11 sappers and 38 sapper mates carried up stores from C. dump to post in front line near 10th STREET, and constructed trench shelter 7ft long with small A frame. Material for 7ft shelter only was found at C. dump.	
			Stores carted to D. dump as above. One trestle wagon employed.	W.E.
in AVELUY			as above.	
			Overhauling of pumping plant in sugar refinery continued. Switch board being wired and new belt to drive motor circulating pump fitted.	
			28 sign boards completed out of 35 as above.	
			Erection of drying shed at company billet completed.	
			Arrangements made for taking over work from 1/1st Highland Fd. Coy R.E. at OVILLERS' POST, Divisional Sawmill & R.E. Store.	
	21		Company moved to OVILLERS POST at 9 a.m. Billet here.	

Off. W. Roman

Major, R.E. (T)

O.C. 1/2nd Highland Field Coy: R.E.

WAR DIARY
OR
INTELLIGENCE SUMMARY.
(Erase heading not required.)

Army Form C. 2118.

1/2nd HIGHLAND FIELD COY. R.E.

No. VOL XXIV
Date 31st DECEMBER 1916

Place	Date	Hour	Summary of Events and Information	Remarks and references to Appendices
			About 200 divisional joiners, woodcutters, loading parties, cavalry pioneers and motor transport drivers taken over and rationed by Company.	
			Work in sawmill and store commenced. 90 trestles for truck bands, 50 truck bands and 40 mining frames made.	
			Company transport employed in carting stores from sawmill to POZIERES dump.	
			10 Raffin mats employed as loading party under Company N.C.O. in R.E. Store. 20 Raffin mats employed as loading party by R.S.M. R.E. at railway siding in AVELUY.	
			8 motor lorries in charge of Company transporting stores from AVELUY to sawmill. 45 infantry woodcutters employed in woodcutting and in constructing brushwood track in AVELUY wood. 170. 64th Brigade carried and sent to POZIERES dump. 8. G.S. wagons supplied by IV Corps for this work.	

O.C. 1/2nd Highland Field Coy: R.E.
Major, R.E. (?)
WJ Gamer (?) Capt.

Army Form C. 2118.

WAR DIARY
or
INTELLIGENCE SUMMARY.
(Erase heading not required.)

1/2nd HIGHLAND FIELD Coy., R.E.
Vol. XXIV No. 12.
Date 31st DECEMBER 1916

Instructions regarding War Diaries and Intelligence Summaries are contained in F. S. Regs., Part II. and the Staff Manual respectively. Title pages will be prepared in manuscript.

Place	Date	Hour	Summary of Events and Information	Remarks and references to Appendices
	22		1 N.C.O and 1 Sapper with working Party erecting Nissen huts for R.A.M.C. near OVILLERS. X.7.d.4.1.	
			8 Sappers working in two shifts rolling C.I. sheets for trench shelters. Average of 50 sheets rolled per day.	
			Proposed site for coal dump with loop road reconnoitred on BRICKFIELD W.E.M. road between ALBERT and BOUZINCOURT and report made thereon.	
			2 Sappers employed running steam pump at CRUCIFIX CORNER. W.11.d.8.1.	
			2 Sappers employed running petrol motor pump in ALBERT, for water supply to BOUZINCOURT.	
			Work in sawmill and store continued. 90 trestles, 70 trench boards & 56 mining frames made.	
			Transport employed as above.	
			Roading parties in store and in AVELUY employed as above.	

A.5834 Wt. W4973/M687 750,000 8/16 D. D. & L. Ltd. Forms/C.2118/13.

W.F.Bower Capt.
Major, R.E. (S)
O.C. 1/2nd Highland Field Coy: R.E.

WAR DIARY
OF
INTELLIGENCE SUMMARY.
(Erase heading not required.)

Army Form C. 2118.

1/2nd HIGHLAND FIELD Coy., R.E.
No. Vol. XXIV
Date 31st DECEMBER 1916
13.

Place	Date	Hour	Summary of Events and Information	Remarks and references to Appendices
	23.		25 Sappers, 40 saffin mats and 45 infantry employed in woodcutting as above. 128 mats made and carted to POZIERES dump.	W.C.J
			Erection of Nissen huts for R.A.M.C. continued as above.	
			Feedpipe of tank at CRUCIFIX CORNER covered.	
			Running of 2 power pumps continued as above.	
			2nd Lieut JAMESON joined company for duty.	
			Work in AUTHUILE and AVELUY continued. 100 trench boards, 180	W.C.J
			trestles, 56 mining frames, 16 A frames and 3 wooden bunk covers	
			for use at advanced dumps made.	
			Transport carting stores as above.	
			Roading stores at R.E. Sheet and AVELUY as above.	
			Woodcutting continued. 103 mats made.	
			Erection of Nissen huts for R.A.M.C. continued.	
			Corrugated iron roofing continued.	
			Running of 2 power pumps continued.	
			Proposed water supply for huts X.7.d.4.1. reconnoitred and reported on.	

W.P. Browne
Major, R.E. (T)
O.C. 1/2nd Highland Field Coy: R.E.

WAR DIARY
or
INTELLIGENCE SUMMARY.

(Erase heading not required.)

Army Form C. 2118.

1/2nd HIGHLAND FIELD Coy., R.E.
No. VOL XXIV
Date 31st DECEMBER 1916

Place	Date	Hour	Summary of Events and Information	Remarks and references to Appendices
	24		Centre line pegged out for new loop road at coal dumps on BRICKFIELD road.	
			Proposed water supply at R.A.M.C. Huts further reported on.	W.E.I.
			Erection of 2 Nissen huts to replace 2 damaged ones at BRUCE Camp W.16.a.3.1. commenced.	
			2nd LIEUT RITCHIE returned to Company from leave.	
			Work in Sawmill and R.E. Store continued; 100 trench boards, 110 trestles, 130 mining frames and 26 'A' frames made.	W.E.I.
			Carting stores by Company transport continued.	
			Loading stores continued as above.	
			Woodcutting continued; 120 mats made.	
			Erection of Nissen huts for R.A.M.C. continued.	
			Corrugated iron rolling continued.	
			Running of 2 power pumps continued.	

WBamer
Major, R.E. (G)
O.C. 1/2nd Highland Field Coy: R.E.

WAR DIARY
INTELLIGENCE SUMMARY

(Erase heading not required.)

Army Form C. 2118.

1/2nd HIGHLAND FIELD Coy., R.E.

No. VOL XXIV
date 31st DECEMBER 1916
15.

Place	Date	Hour	Summary of Events and Information	Remarks and references to Appendices
	25		Divisional trench shelter being erected at Divisional Headquarters.	
			Erection of 2 Nissen huts at BRUCE camp continued.	
			Arrangements made with A.S.C. for construction of loop road for coal dump on BRICKFIELD road.	W.E.W.
			Stables for sick horse being erected. Drain fields being improved.	
			Work in sawmill and R.E. store continued; 100 trench boards, 41 trench	
			100 trestles, 20 dugout frames, material for 4 trench shelters. Furniture	W.E.W.
			Tramway sleepers made and 50 pit-props cut to length. Furniture for C.R.E. constructed.	
			Carting of stores by company transport continued.	
			Roading store continued as above.	
			Corrugated iron rolling continued.	
			Running of 2 shower baths continued.	
			Design for drying shed made.	
			Erection of 2 Nissen huts at BRUCE camp continued.	

Capt.
Major, R.E. (T)
O.C. 1/2nd Highland Field Coy: R.E.

WAR DIARY
or
INTELLIGENCE SUMMARY.

Army Form C. 2118.

1/2nd HIGHLAND FIELD Coy., R.E.

No. Vol. XXIV
Date 31st DECEMBER 1916

16.

Place	Date	Hour	Summary of Events and Information	Remarks and references to Appendices
	26		Erection of Nissen huts for R.A.M.C. continued.	
			Pipe line for water supply to R.A.M.C huts X.7.d.4.1. set out.	
			Work in Sawmill and R.E. dump continued. 25 trench frames, 80 trestles, 12 dugout frames, 35 mining frames, 4 trench shelters (parts).	
			5 "A" frames with fire step made. 45 posts 4"x 2"x 20'. 25 ft long.	
			Prepared and painted, 6000 ft Timber sawn in mill daily.	
			Carting stores by Company transport continued.	
			Loading of stores continued as above.	
			Woodcutting continued. 120 mats made.	
			Erection of Nissen huts for R.A.M.C continued	
			Corrugated Iron rolling continued.	
			Erection of 2 Nissen huts at BRUCE camp completed.	
			Running of 4 hour pumps continued.	
			Erection of specimen trench shelter at Divisional Headquarters continued.	
			Selection of site for drying shed made at OVILLERS camp.	

O.C. 1/2nd Highland Field Coy: R.E.
Major, R.E. (T)

WAR DIARY
or
INTELLIGENCE SUMMARY.

(Erase heading not required.)

Army Form C. 2118.

1/2nd HIGHLAND FIELD Coy., R.E.

No. Vol XXIV
Date 31st DECEMBER 1916

17.

Place	Date	Hour	Summary of Events and Information	Remarks and references to Appendices
	27		2 loads of pit-props conveyed from AVELUY wood to loop road for coal dump, BRICKFIELD road. Power pumps at CRUCIFIX CORNER and ALBERT inspected. Alternative scheme for water supply to R.A.M.C. huts & 7.d.4.1. submitted to C.R.E.	W.e.f.
			Work in Sawmill and R.E. Store continued. 86 trench mats, 113 trestles, 20 dugout frames, 2 mining frames 16'9", frames ~3'9" frames with fire steps made. Carting of stores from Sawmill to POZIERES dump by Company Limber continued.	W.e.f.
			Loading of stores continued as above. Woodcutting continued. 110 mats made and 40 pit-props cut and despatched to loop road for coal dumps. Erection of Magor huts for R.A.M.C. continued. Running of 2 power pumps continued. Erection of chimney trench shelter and trench with fire step and	

W.P. Bonar
Capt
Major, R.E. (T)
O.C. 1/2nd Highland Field Coy, R.E.

WAR DIARY
or
INTELLIGENCE SUMMARY.

(Erase heading not required.)

Army Form C. 2118.

1/2nd HIGHLAND FIELD Coy., R.E.
Vol. XXIV No. ....
Date 31st DECEMBER 1916

Place	Date	Hour	Summary of Events and Information	Remarks and references to Appendices
	28		On "A" frames continued.	
			40 fil-props conveyed from AVELUY wood to loop road for corduroy.	
			Construction of loop road commenced.	
			160 yards of 1½" piping conveyed to site of water supply to R.A.M.C. huts	
			X.7.d.4.1.	
			Flexible rubber piping on water standards CRUCIFIX CORNER renewed.	W.E.R.
			Corrugated iron rolling continued.	
			5 Sappers sent to 51st D.A.C. near BOUZINCOURT to construct men's huts, 29 ft ×	
			treated with D.A.C.	
			Water supply at Divisional Headquarters USNA HILL inspected and report on defects sent to C.R.E.	
			Company horse standings being improved.	
			2nd Lieut MacNEILL rejoined company for duty.	
			Works in Sawmill and R.E. Store continued, 36 trench boards, 70 trestles, 52 mining frames, 30 "A" frames and 43 "A" frames with firestep made.	
			Transport sunlight casting doors as above.	

Call
Major, R.E. (T)
O.C. 1/2nd Highland Field Coy: R.E.

Army Form C. 2118.

WAR DIARY
or
INTELLIGENCE SUMMARY.
(Erase heading not required.)

1/2nd HIGHLAND FIELD Coy., R.E.

Vol. XXIV

Date 31 December 1916

Place	Date	Hour	Summary of Events and Information	Remarks and references to Appendices
	29		Loading of stones continued as above. Woodcutting continued; 110 mats made. Erection of Nissen huts for R.A.M.C. continued. Running of 2 power pumps continued. Plenum trench shelter and lengths of fire trench with "A" frames and drains completes at Divisional Headquarters. Material for drying sheds being prepared. 12 yds of road constructed at coaldump BRICKFIELD road. 16 ft of 1" water pipe fitted at pumping plant CRUCIFIX CORNER. 100 gall water tank erected on wooden stand and water taps fitted. Erection of Nissen huts for 51st D.A.C. continued. 4 Daffers sent to 255th Brigade R.F.A. wagon lines to erect Nissen huts for latter. Daffers filled with R.F.A. Corrugated iron rolling continued. Work in Sanctuel and R.E. Wd continued, 12 "A" frames, 10 trench boards, 130 "A" frames, 40 "A" frames, with five attifu	W.E.B. W.E.B

Lt Col
W.F. Jenkin
Major, R.E. (T)
O.C. 1/2nd Highland Field Coy: R.E.

Army Form C. 2118.

WAR DIARY
or
INTELLIGENCE SUMMARY.
(Erase heading not required.)

1/2nd HIGHLAND FIELD Coy., R.E.

No. Vol. XXIV .... 20.
Date 31st December 1916.

Place	Date	Hour	Summary of Events and Information	Remarks and references to Appendices

etc. 50 trench tramway slepers, 11 dugout frames, 500 direction boards 9"x 9" x 1", 120 lengths 9"x 1" x 2'-6" made.

Carting stores continued as above.

Woodcutting continued. 70 mats made and 26 hop/ropes sent to Corps road at coal dump.

Erection of Nissen huts for R.A.M.C. continued.

Running of 2 hour pumps continued.

Framework of drying shed at OVILLERS camp erected. Materials prepared for drying shed at WOLFE huts.

No working party available for works on loop road at coal dump.

2" water piping conveyed from sawmill to site of proposed water supply at R.A.M.C. huts X.7.d.4.1. 250 yards of piping already placed in position.

Erection of nissen huts for 51st D.A.C. continued.

Erection of nissen huts for 255th Brigade R.F.A. continued.

Corrugated iron roofing continued.

Water piping for supply at Divisional Headquarters being answered.

Making water circulating boiler and pipe system for drying shed.

O.C. 1/2nd Highland Field Coy: R.E.
Major, R.E. (T)

Army Form C. 2118.

WAR DIARY
or
~~INTELLIGENCE SUMMARY.~~
(Erase heading not required.)

1/2nd HIGHLAND FIELD Coy., R.E.
No. Vol XXIV 21.
Date 31st DECEMBER 1916

Place	Date	Hour	Summary of Events and Information	Remarks and references to Appendices
	30		Fitting silencer to motor of trench motor pump.	
			2nd Lieut. OKELL returned from leave.	
			Lieut. GORDON left Company on leave.	
			Work in SAUSAGE and R.E. Close continued; 35" trench bowels 70 trestles, 51 mining frames, 17 "A" frames, 150 steps as above, 16 p/h, 4"x2"x20ft long, made.	
			Carting of stores continued as above.	
			Woodcutting continued; 114 mats made.	
			4 wagon loads of fire wood sent from AVELUY wood to Corps dump.	
			Erection of Nissen huts for R.A.M.C. continued.	
			Running of 2 horse pumps continued.	
			Drying shed at OVILLERS camp completed except for stove.	
			Framework of drying shed at WOLFE huts continued.	
			Pumping plant for supplying water troughs near ALBERT investigated and found to have been taken in hand by ARMY TROOPS COY. R.E.	

W. Brown Cam
Major, R.E. (T)
O.C. 1/2nd Highland Field Coy: R.E.

Army Form C. 2118.

WAR DIARY
or
INTELLIGENCE SUMMARY.
(Erase heading not required.)

1/2nd HIGHLAND FIELD Coy, R.E.
No. Vol XXIV 22.
Date. 31st DECEMBER 1916.

Place	Date	Hour	Summary of Events and Information	Remarks and references to Appendices
	30		Well at CRUCIFIX CORNER being repaired.	
			Erection of Nissen huts for 57th D.A.C. and 255th Brigade. R.F.A. continued.	
			Corrugated how golling continued.	
			Water supply at Divisional Headquarters further investigated and report submitted to C.R.E. Large tank not in use, cut out of system.	W.E.S.
			Fitting up boiler and furnace for drying shed. Fitting silencer to trench motor pumps.	
			Stable being erected at company horse lines.	
	31		Work in Sawmill and R.E. store continued, 11 trench boards, 52 mining frames, 12 dugout frames, 16" 9" frames, 100 slipper as above, 15 huts 4" x 2" x 15ft long made.	W.E.S.
			Carting store continued as above.	
			Loading of stores continued as above.	
			Woodcutting continued, 98 mats made, and 11 wagon loads of fire-wood cut and sent to Corps dumps.	

O.C. 1/2nd Highland Field Coy. R.E.
Capt
Major, R.E. (T.)

WAR DIARY or INTELLIGENCE SUMMARY

Army Form C. 2118.

1/2nd HIGHLAND FIELD Coy., R.E.
No. VOL XXIV
Date 31st December 1916

Place	Date	Hour	Summary of Events and Information	Remarks and references to Appendices
			Erection of Nissen huts for R.A.M.C, 51st D.A.C. and 255th Brigade R.F.A. continued.	
			Running of two power pumps continued.	
			Stoves fitted in drying shed at OVILLERS camp. Drying shed at WOLFE huts completed.	W.E.H.
			Well at CRUCIFIX CORNER cleaned and recko repaired.	
			Corrugated iron rolling continued.	
			Fitting silencer to trench motor pumps.	
			Fitting up hot water circulating gear for drying shed.	
			N.C.O's men released for civil employment: — Nil	
			Reinforcements joined Company during month: — 2 Officers & 6 other ranks.	
			No. of Officers & men on leave during month: — 3 Officers & 7 other ranks.	
			Roll of Officers with Company at 31/12/16. Captain W.P.BARRON. M.C. CAPTAIN W.C.LEGG; Lieut. T.J.GORDON.M.C. 2/Lieuts. A.G.MACNEILL.M.C; C.O'KELLY; F.B.RITCHIE; S.J.HUNTER; J.S.CLEGHORN; J.L.MACGREGOR; D.JAMIESON.	
			Lt GORDON awarded the Military Cross in 7th December.	

W.P.Barron
Major, R.E. (T)
O.C. 1/2nd Highland Field Coy. R.E.

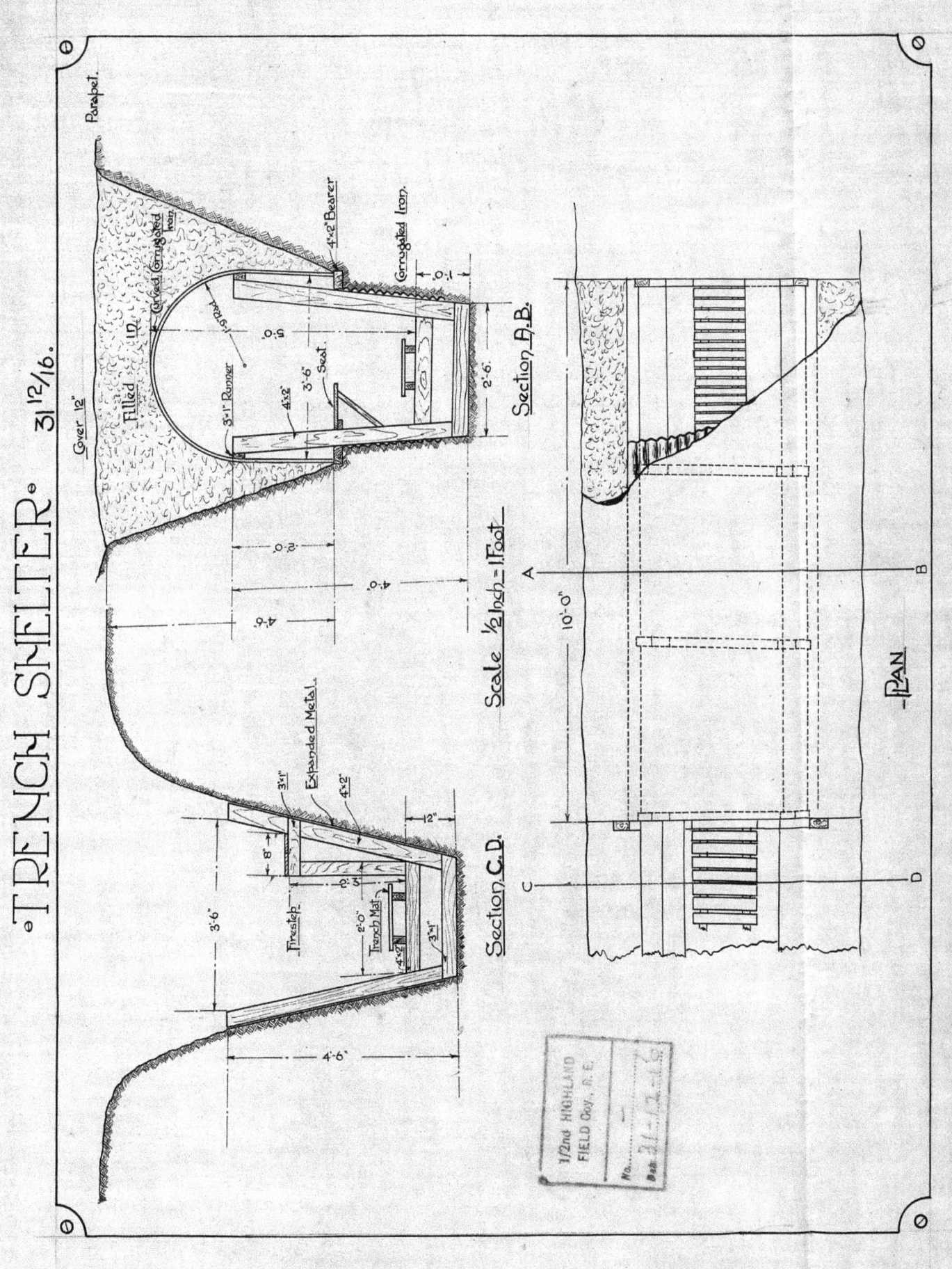

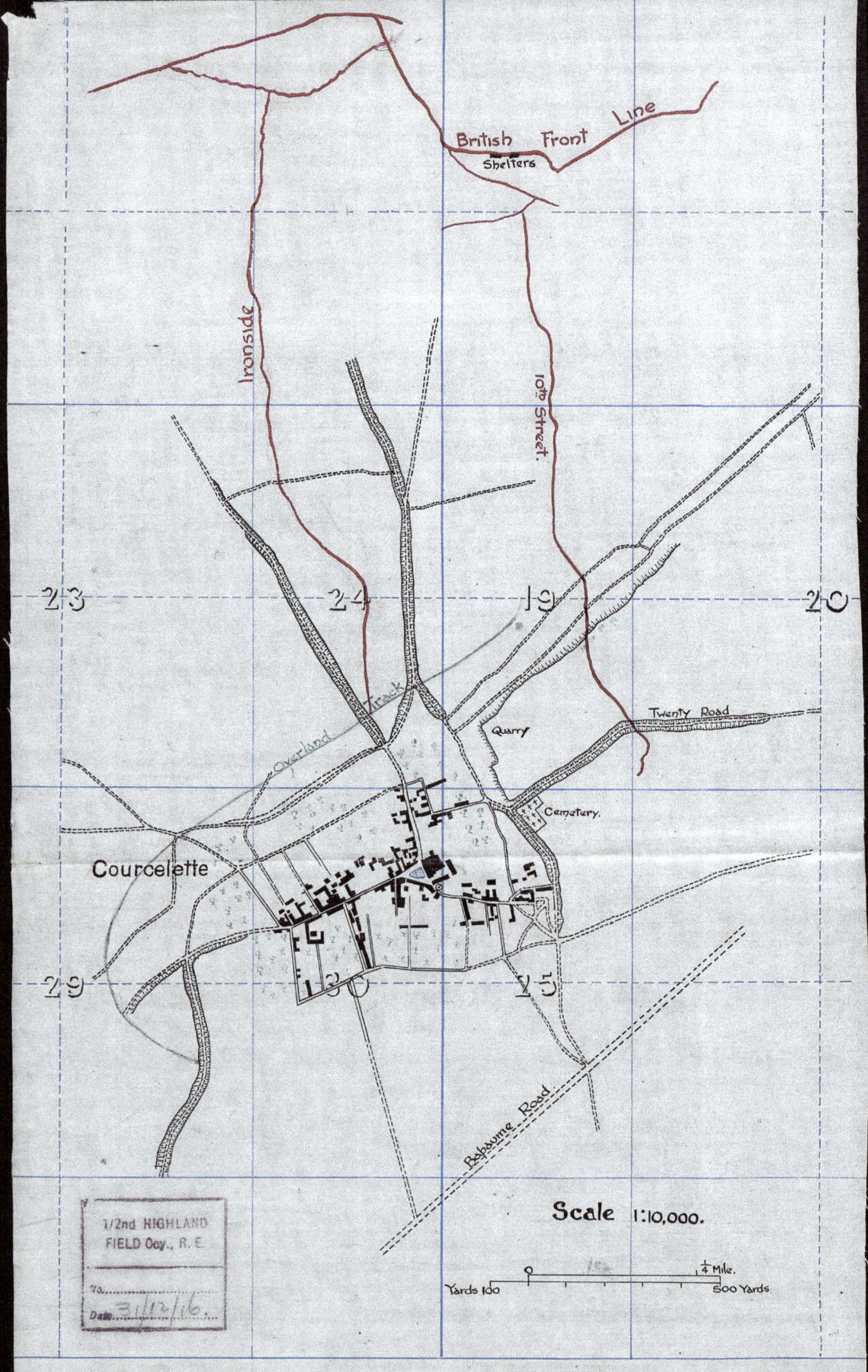

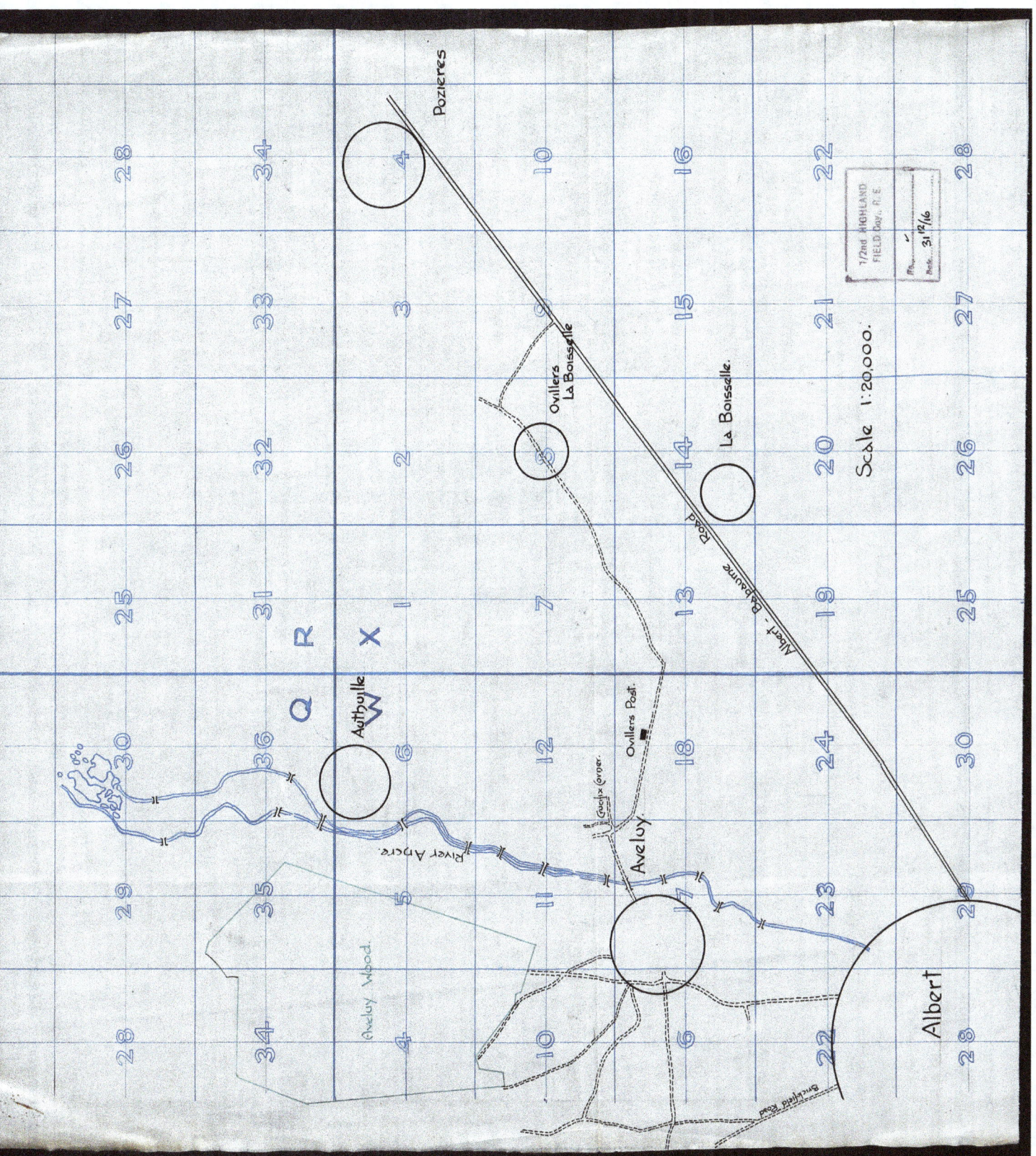

Vol 24

WAR DIARY
—OF—
401ST (HIGHLAND) FIELD COMPANY. R.E.
—FOR—
JANUARY
1917.

VOL: N°XXI

WAR DIARY
or
INTELLIGENCE SUMMARY.
(Erase heading not required.)

Army Form C. 2118.

404th (HIGHLAND) FIELD Coy., R.E.
Vol. XXV
31st JANUARY 1917.

Place	Date	Hour	Summary of Events and Information	Remarks and references to Appendices
OUILLERS POST	1.		Work in sawmill & R.E. store continued; trench boards, framing and dugout frames "A" frames and sleepers made.	
			Unloading, loading and carting stores from sawmill to POZIERES dump continued.	
			Woodcutting in AVELUY wood continued; 70 timbered mats made.	
			Wagons to convey firewood from AVELUY wood to Corps dump did not arrive at wood for loads.	
			Erection of Nissen huts for 51st D.R.C. BOUZINCOURT & newer huts for 255th Brigade R.F.A. near BOUZINCOURT continued.	
			Rolling of C.I. sheets continued, 50 sheets made.	
			Running of power pumps at CRUCIFIX CORNER and ALBERT continued.	
			Arrangements made for taking over work from 1st/1st Highland Field Co. R.E. at WOLFE huts, and for handing over work at sawmill to 2nd/2nd Highland Field Coy R.E.	
	2.		Company moved to WOLFE huts at 11. a.m.	

Major, R.E. (T)
O.C. 404th (Highland) Field Coy; R.E.

WAR DIARY or INTELLIGENCE SUMMARY

Army Form C. 2118.

400 (HIGHLAND) FIELD Coy., R.E.

No. Vol. XXV
Date 31st JANUARY 1917

Place	Date	Hour	Summary of Events and Information	Remarks and references to Appendices
			Men working at Nissen huts at BOUZINCOURT and men running pump at CRUCIFIX CORNER reported company.	W.E.H.
			Running of power pump in ALBERT continued.	
			6 sapper and 55 sapper mates working on new end of IRONSIDE AVENUE.	
			150 yds of berm cleared 3ft wide and trench cleared where fallen in.	
			Preparing material at POZIERES dump for overland route south.	
	3rd-6th		Arranging for transporting same forward.	
			Work at IRONSIDE AVENUE continued, 1 section R.E. 30 sapper mates and 75 men of infantry working party, clearing berm 3 ft, clearing out trench and widening & carrying up new timber material by night. Half section R.E. & 20 sapper mates employed revetting recent parts of trench with 'A' frames. Finishing out trench, digging sump holes, laying timber boards and clearing out trench by day. Mountainists party of 2 sapper and 2 sapper mates living near trench.	
			Work on overland route continued; brushwood tracks to 'A' New Dump	

O.C. .... Highland Field Coy: R.E.
Major, R.E. (T.)

WAR DIARY
or
INTELLIGENCE SUMMARY.
(Erase heading not required.)

Army Form C. 2118.

400th (HIGHLAND) FIELD Coy., R.E.
No. Vol. XXV
Date 31st January 1917

Place	Date	Hour	Summary of Events and Information	Remarks and references to Appendices
			New Dumps "B" and MANCHESTER dumps marked with official sign posts and plain cans and marked with official sign posts and trails towards "B" dump plant with transverse mats, and track from COURCELETTE road towards "C" dump being repaired. 2 Sections R.E. and working party of 75 infantry employed by night. 2 sappers and 5 infantry mats employed on maintenance by day. Pumping plant at Sugar Refinery, COURCELETTE being overhauled. Engine governor repaired, system received switchboard remade and refitted, voltmeter and ammeter repaired, hydraulic high pressure gauges dismounted and re-set. Plant got into running condition. Stores required for work on overland route and IRONSIDE AVENUE arranged and loaded at POZIERES dump. Jumper hole bores for IRONSIDE AVENUE being made at POZIERES dump. 15 boxes made per day. Stores for IRONSIDE AVENUE loaded + carted from POZIERES dump to "D" dump.	very

O.C. 400th (Highland) Field Coy: R.E.
R. Crawford Ch.
Major, R.E. (T)

Army Form C. 2118.

WAR DIARY
or
INTELLIGENCE SUMMARY.
(Erase heading not required.)

Instructions regarding War Diaries and Intelligence Summaries are contained in F.S. Regs., Part II. and the Staff Manual respectively. Title pages will be prepared in manuscript.

No. 401 (HIGHLAND) FIELD Coy., R.E.
No. Vol. XXV 4.
Date 31st JANUARY 1917

Place	Date	Hour	Summary of Events and Information	Remarks and references to Appendices
	7–8th		Trees near R.23.b.9.3 and MANCHESTER dumps demolished as they hindered ranging marks for the enemy. 2nd Lt MacGregor temporarily attached to 1st/1st Highland Field Coy RE. Interior pistoling went on as and as 5th Jany. Work on IRONSIDE AVENUE and overland track continued as above. 600 yds of beam cleared such as 405 y/k reverted with "9" frames in IRONSIDE AV. 590 yds of brushwood track relaid. Pumping plant began pumping. COURCELETTE tunnel exit the others continued. Water delivery 12 ft above ground level attained. Stove machinery moved from Major Ryneys and carted to aux overless POST.	K.Exp.
	9th		Construction of dugouts, horse-boxes, arranging of stores and carting of stores from POZIERES dumps continued. Brick road advanced beyond Headquarters continuous work progresses. 6 sappers were maintaining IRONSIDE AVENUE by repairing ruts in 6 inch mesh 6 inch wire.	

A.5834 Wt.W.4973/M687 750,000 8/16 D.D. & L. Ltd. Forms/C.2118/13.

N.S. McWhirter Colin
Major R.E. (T.)
O.C. 401st (Highland) Field Coy: R.E.

WAR DIARY or INTELLIGENCE SUMMARY.

Army Form C. 2118.

401st (HIGHLAND) FIELD Coy., R.E.
No. Vol. XXV
Date 31st JANUARY 1917
5.

O.C. 401st Highland Field Coy: R.E.
Major, R.E. (T)

Place	Date	Hour	Summary of Events and Information	Remarks and references to Appendices
			By day keeping out watercarts cleaning trench. Other work suspended on account of bombardment.	W.E.J
			Covered horse standings 160 ft long being erected at OUILLERS POST. 2 sections R.E. and 40 Coy men employed.	W.E.J
			Capt. Barron goes to O.C. 1st Coy. R.E. Course at G.H.Q. Maintaining IRONSIDE AVENUE as above. Construction of stables continued.	
	10			
	11		Covered horse standings 160 ft long, completed. Acceded sapper men returned to sections. Two coffee runner horse plough in ALBERT, returned by R.T. Coy. R.E. and returned to company. 1 officer and 9 N.C.O's of 5th Field Coy. R.E. arrived to take over work of company. Order received that company will be temporarily attached to 61st Division while in rest area.	W.E.J
	12		Company engaged in packing wagons, greasing wagon wheels, loading pontoons and trestle equipment and in cleaning billets.	

Army Form C. 2118.

WAR DIARY
or
INTELLIGENCE SUMMARY.
(Erase heading not required.)

404 (HIGHLAND) FIELD Coy., R.E.
No. Vol. XXV
Date 31st JANUARY 1917.

Place	Date	Hour	Summary of Events and Information	Remarks and references to Appendices
			Officer of 8th Field Coy R.E. shown over front area, and given report of work in hand, with plan.	w.e.y.
	13		Lieut. T.J. Gordon returned from leave. 2nd Lieut. A.J. Macaulay proceeded to VAL-DE-MAISON to arrange billets. Company arrived at 7-30 a.m. to VAL-DE-MAISON. Billets here. Time of arrival 3-30 p.m.	w.e.y.
	14		2nd Lieut. J.S. Hunter temporarily attached for duty to 10th/11th Highland Field Coy R.E. Company moved at 12 noon to GORGES in 154th Infantry Brigade group. Billets here. Time of arrival 7 p.m.	w.e.y.
	15		2nd Lieut. F.B. Ritchie left Company for duty at 5TH ARMY Headquarters. Company moved at 10 a.m. to NEUVILLE in 154th Infantry Brigade group. Billets here. Time of arrival 4-30 p.m. Order received at midnight 15th/16th inst. Came under orders of 61st Division at midnight. 15th/16th inst.	w.e.y.
	16		Company moved at 10 a.m. to MARCHEVILLE. Billets here. Time of arrival. 1 p.m.	w.e.y.

O.C. 404 Highland Field Coy: R.E
C.M.
Major, R.E. (T.)

Army Form C. 2118.

WAR DIARY
of
INTELLIGENCE SUMMARY.
(Erase heading not required.)

400th (HIGHLAND) FIELD Coy., R.E.
No. 10. XXV
Date 31st JANUARY 1917

Place	Date	Hour	Summary of Events and Information	Remarks and references to Appendices
	17		Sections inspected. Company engaged in our workshop equipment. Events for Officers submitted.	W.E.B
	18		Sets for 3 Nissen huts received at 61st Divisional headquarters BRAILLY. Company engaged in erecting drill and overhauling equipment. 3 wagons sent to AUXI-LE-CHATEAU for R.E. store. No store obtained.	W.E.B
	19		Major Barron and Lieuts. Hitchings returned to company. Sappers standing by to erect Nissen huts at BRAILLY. Huts were not supplied. Part of company moved billets from one area of village into another. 75 allows for accommodation of 2/7th Batt Worcester Regiment. 2nd Lieut. A.G. Macneil went on leave.	W.E.B
	20		Sappers engaged in cleaning equipment and billets. Crews cleaning harness. Timber and Corrugated iron drawn from dump LE PLESSIEL.	W.E.B
	21		Sections inspected. Cook-houses built. Mounted section cleaning harness.	W.E.B
	22		Programme of training commenced. Physical exercise 7.30 a.m. drill without arms & saluting. Hours of training 9 a.m. to 1 p.m. and 2 p.m. to 4 p.m. Company inspection by O.C Company. Mounted section squad drill, driving drill and harness cleaning.	W.E.B

S. Carmichael
Major, R.E. (T.)
O.C. 400th (Highland) Field Coy: R.E.

WAR DIARY or INTELLIGENCE SUMMARY.

(Erase heading not required.)

Army Form C. 2118.

1/1st (Highland) Field Coy. R.E.
Vol. XXV
Date 31st JANUARY 1917

Place	Date	Hour	Summary of Events and Information	Remarks and references to Appendices
	23		Training continued; 2 sections physical exercise, lecture drill without arms, rifle exercises, knotting and lashing. 2 sections pontooning and use of wire cattle.	W.C.H
			Mounted section; squad drill, driving drill and harness cleaning. Indent for deficiencies in trenching equipment submitted.	
	24		Training continued as for 23rd inst. sections reversed. Mounted section training as above.	W.C.H
			3 Sappers engaged in enlarging bath-house at ARGENTVILLERS. Indent for deficiencies in tool cart equipment submitted.	
	25		Training continued; 2 sections physical exercise, pontooning, rebuilding of cavalry trestle. Knotting and lashing. 2 sections pontooning and use of cavalry trestle.	W.C.H
			Mounted section training continued. Harness being cleaned. Bath-house at ARGENTVILLERS being repaired. Pumps at BRAILLY being repaired.	
	26		Company training continued as for 25th inst., sections reversed. Mounted section training and harness cleaning continued.	W.C.H

O.C. 1/1st Highland Field Coy: R.E.
Major, R.E. (T)

WAR DIARY
or
INTELLIGENCE SUMMARY.
(Erase heading not required.)

Army Form C. 2118.

400th (HIGHLAND) FIELD Coy., R.E.
No. Vol. XXV.
Date 31st January 1917.

O.C. 400th (Highland) Field Coy: R.E.
Major; R.E. (T.)

Place	Date	Hour	Summary of Events and Information	Remarks and references to Appendices
	27		Bath-house being repaired as above at ARGENVILLERS. Repairs necessary to	
			bath-house, CANCHY investigated.	
			Company transport being washed.	
			No 4 section erecting Nissen huts at 61st Divisional Headquarters, BRAILLY.	
			R: T.J. Gordon surveying system of practice trenches between GAPENNES —	
			ST. RIQUIER road and YVRENCHEUX - ONSUN road.	
			Company training continued. 2 sections afternoon anti-gas	
			instruction, other drill instruction, communicating drill. Practice lashing	
			1 section pontooning and use of welding torches.	
			Company transport washed.	
			Horses inspection in morning. Drivers cleaning harness.	
			Bath-house at CANCHY repaired.	
			Pump at BRAILLY repaired.	
			Survey of practice trenches continued.	
			Supervising erection of Nissen huts at BRAILLY.	

WAR DIARY or INTELLIGENCE SUMMARY

Army Form C. 2118.

404th (HIGHLAND) FIELD Coy., R.E.
Vol. XXV No. 10
Date 31st JANUARY 1917

Place	Date	Hour	Summary of Events and Information	Remarks and references to Appendices
	28		(Sunday) No Training. Army of Practice Trenches continued.	W.E.J.
	29		Improving erection of Wiremetic into BRAILLY continued. Company engaged in fitting up equipment, cleaning horses and transport wagons and in cleaning billets. Army of Practice trenches put TTM.	
	30		Improving erection of wiremetic into BRAILLY continued. Dismounted party of Company moved by motor lorry at 11.30 a.m. to ARRAS. Time of arrival 6.30 p.m. Billeted there. Mounted section under Lt. J.J. Gordon moved to BONNIÈRES, billeted there.	
	31		Dismounted party moved at 5.30 p.m. to AVESNES, billeted there. Mounted section moved to LATTRE—ST QUENTIN, billeted there. For map references see December war diary. 1 C.O⁵ given relaxed for work employment - nil. Reinforcements joined Company during month :- 12 other ranks.	

O.O. 404th (Highland) Field Coy: R.E.
Major, R.E. (T)

WAR DIARY
or
INTELLIGENCE SUMMARY.

(Erase heading not required.)

Army Form C. 2118.

400th (HIGHLAND) FIELD Coy., R.E.
Vol. XXV No. 11
Date 31st JANUARY 1917

Place	Date	Hour	Summary of Events and Information	Remarks and references to Appendices
			No. of Officers taken on leave during month:— 1 Officer + 17 other ranks	
			Roll of Officers with Company at 31/1/17:— MAJOR W.P. BARTON M.C., CAPTAIN W.C. GLEGG, LIEUT. T.F. GORDON M.C., 2LIEUTS. R.G. MACNEILL M.C., C. OKELL, F.B. RITCHIE, S.T. HUNTER, J.S. CLEGHORN, J.T. MACGREGOR, O.C. TM SSON.	

W. Erskine-Hill
Major, R.E. (T)
O.C. 400th (Highland) Field Coy: R.E.

War Diary
— of —
401st (Highland) Field Company. R.E.
— for —
February
1917.

Vol: No XXVI

401st (HIGHLAND) FIELD COMPANY, R.E.
No. ....
Date 28/2/17

Army Form C. 2118.

WAR DIARY
or
INTELLIGENCE SUMMARY.
(Erase heading not required.)

401st (HIGHLAND) FIELD COMPANY, R.E.
No. VOL XXVI
Date 28 February 1917

O.C. 401st Highland Field Coy: R.E.
Major, R.E. (T)

Place	Date	Hour	Summary of Events and Information	Remarks and references to Appendices
ANZIN ST AUBIN	1.		Mounted section moved from LATTRE – ST. QUENTIN to MAROEUIL.	
	2-11		Company engaged in improving billets.	
			Company working under orders of 9th Division.	
			2 Sections engaged constructing covered C.T. shelters, mining dugouts and digging approach trenches, at advanced divisional headquarters, MAROEUIL.	
			1 section employed improving and widening MADAGASCAR Avenue "out" trench through ECURIE, to permit of passage of stretchers.	
			1 section excavating site for sub-stores at A.29.c.60.95. THURSDAY AVENUE, A.29.a.2.6. RIPPERT AVENUE, and A.28.b.60.55. CHEMIN CREUX.	
			2 sections employed in patrolling trench water supply system,	
			1 section employed as storemen at advanced company store, FERME MODELE (2 dumps).	
			Painting and making trench notice boards etc at company store, ANZIN.	
			Driving tunnel under LILLE – ARRAS road at A.28.c.4.7.	

Army Form C. 2118.

WAR DIARY
or
INTELLIGENCE SUMMARY.

(Erase heading not required.)

401ST (HIGHLAND) FIELD COMPANY, R.E.
No. XXVI. 2.
Date 23rd FEBRUARY 17.

Place	Date	Hour	Summary of Events and Information	Remarks and references to Appendices
	12-13		Major Borrow went on leave on 4th Feb.	
			3 Officers and 100 other ranks from 1st Batt. R.H. attached to company as Infantry water.	
			Work continued on :-	
			Advanced Divisional Headquarters, MAROEUIL.	
			Trench under LILLE road discontinued	W.E.H.
			Improvement of "OUT" trenches. VILLAGE ST and SOLE AVENUE revised for shelters.	
			Bomb-stops at THURSDAY AVENUE, RIPPERT AVENUE and CHEMIN CREUX. Excavation completed and frames erected.	
			Water pipe patrol.	
			1 Section and attached infantry employed in clearing and erecting "A" frames. GRAND COLLECTEUR TRENCH near VILLEROAD, CHARLES AVENUE, BOOT AVENUE "G" AVENUE and "A" AVENUE.	
			1 Section working under Battalion orders in front line area employed.	

B. Brandfgg
Major, R.E. (T)
O/C 401st Highland Field Coy: R.E.

WAR DIARY or INTELLIGENCE SUMMARY.

(Erase heading not required.)

Army Form C. 2118.

401st (HIGHLAND) FIELD COMPANY, R.E.
No. V2. XXVI 3
Date 28th FEBRUARY

Place	Date	Hour	Summary of Events and Information	Remarks and references to Appendices
	28/2/18		employed in improving THURSDAY AVENUE, SEAFORTH AVENUE & SINNAL Company transport and attached D.F.C. wagons employed in carting R.E. stores from MAROEUIL to ANZIN DUMP and thence as required to "G" Dump. FLATIERS AVENUE deepened at lower end and fresh boards laid. 40 c.m. railway cleared between BETHUNE ROAD and "G" Dump and also from ROCLINCOURT forwards. Work commenced on roof of Dressing Station at MADAGASCAR. Reconnaissance of trenches completed, and number of boards prepared & placed as required. Water supply system:- Old water pipe taken up between 4" main and FANTOME N°1. TANKS. New 2" pipe line laid and branch in place of old one. New connection made between 4" and 2" pipe. Several lengths of pipe between FANTOME N°1 and N°2. TANKS taken up and renewed. 50 gal. tank and stand fitted at FANTOME N°1 tanks.	O.C. 401st Highland Field Coy. R.E. McLean Lt Major, R.E. (T)

Army Form C. 2118.

WAR DIARY
or
INTELLIGENCE SUMMARY.
(Erase heading not required.)

401st (HIGHLAND) FIELD COMPANY, R.E.
Vol. XXVI
Date 28th FEBRUARY 1917

Place	Date	Hour	Summary of Events and Information	Remarks and references to Appendices
			Reconnaissance of accommodation for additional motor lorries in trenches and of dugout accommodation in right sub-sector of divisional area made.	
			Work on dressing station MADAGASCAR handed over to R.A.M.C.	
			Dressing station on LILLE ROAD refixed & improved.	
			Artillery bridge built over ANZIN and GENIE trenches on ST. CATHERINE - ECURIE road.	O.K.
			Section working under battalion orders employed in clearing, deepening and revetting THURSDAY AVENUE from COLLECTEUR forwards. TRENCH BONNAL left of SAP 125B and SEAFORTH TRENCH.	
			Work commenced on new boot-store ANZIN. Buildings opened cases for boots to accommodate 4,000 pairs of boots.	
			Revetting of GRAND COLLECTEUR trench continued.	
			Work continued on Bomb store.	
			THURSDAY AVENUE:- Frames fitted and ary work with brick revetting cross completed. Sandbag wall built in front of store.	

O.C. 401st Highland Field Coy: R.E.

B Connolly
Major, R.E. (T)

WAR DIARY
or
INTELLIGENCE SUMMARY.
(Erase heading not required.)

Army Form C. 2118.

401ST (HIGHLAND) FIELD COMPANY, R.E.
No. Vol. XXVI
Date 28th February 1917

Place	Date	Hour	Summary of Events and Information	Remarks and references to Appendices
			RIPPERT AVENUE :- Frames fitted and roof with bricks brushing course completed. Sand bag wall built in front of store.	
			CHENIN CREUX. Work continued on roof & sandbag wall built in front of store.	
			Part of WEDNESDAY AVENUE which had fallen in cleared and re-revetted.	
			Forward R.E. store formed at ROCLINCOURT. Stores carried from G dump to new dump.	
			Whore engaged in erection of notice boards erected in trenches throughout divisional area.	
			Section employed in erection of Nissen Huts at MAROEUIL. 5 huts embodied and 2 huts erected on 28th inst.	
			1 Officer and 50 additional infantry from 154th Infy Brigade attached to Company on 22nd Feby.	
			Trench map of divisional sector attached.	
			No. of officers & men detailed for special duty during month :- 2 other ranks.	

O.C. 401st Highland Field Coy: R.E.
Major, R.E. (T)

Army Form C. 2118.

WAR DIARY
of
INTELLIGENCE SUMMARY.
(Erase heading not required.)

Instructions regarding War Diaries and Intelligence Summaries are contained in F. S. Regs., Part II. and the Staff Manual respectively. Title pages will be prepared in manuscript.

401ST (HIGHLAND) FIELD COMPANY. R.E.
No. ....
Date 28TH FEBRUARY.17.

O.O. 401st Highland Field Coy: R.E.
Major, R.E. (T)

Place	Date	Hour	Summary of Events and Information	Remarks and references to Appendices
			No. of Officers men on leave during month :- 1 officer.	W.E.J
			Roll of Officers with Company at 28/2/17 :- Major. W.D.BARRON. M.C. CAPTAIN. W.C.	
			GLEGG., LIEUT. T.J.GORDON. M.C. 11 LIEUTS. A.G. MACNIELL. M.C. C. OKELL, F.B. RITCHIE,	
			S.J. HUNTER, J.S. CLEGHORN, J.L. MACGREGOR, D. JAMIESON.	

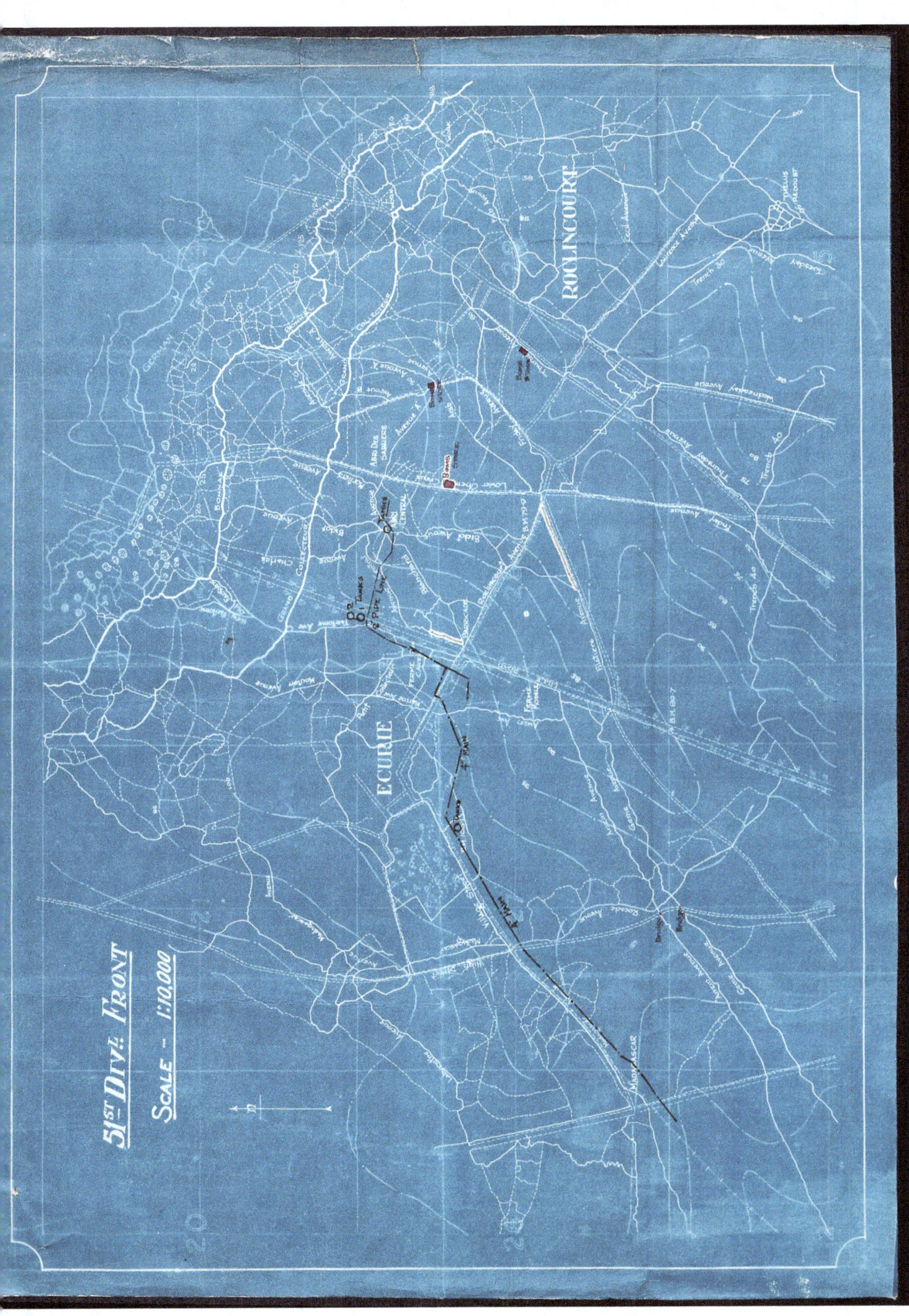

War Diary

of

401st (Highland) Field Company. R.E.

for

March 1917.

Vol. No XXVII

Army Form C. 2118.

WAR DIARY
or
INTELLIGENCE SUMMARY

(Erase heading not required.)

401st (HIGHLAND) FIELD COMPANY, R.E.
No. VOL. XXVII
Date 31st MARCH 1917

O.C. 401st (Highland) Field Coy. R.E.
Major, R.E.
[signature]

Place	Date	Hour	Summary of Events and Information	Remarks and references to Appendices
ANZIN – ST AUBIN.	1st to 6th		Digging out and revetting of GRAND COLLECTEUR trench continued from Avenue A towards right. One section and attached infantry employed on this work. Digging out and revetting of THURSDAY Avenue continued between GRAND COLLECTEUR trench and BONNAL trench. One section and attached infantry employed. Strengthening of dressing station dugout at LILLE road GENIE Avenue completed. New frames constructed and erected. Work in Company R.E. store ANZIN continued. Notice boards painted, timber ripped in sawmill. Latrine seats & stands for water tanks made & trunks erected in billets. Transport employed in carting stores to ANZIN & to trenches. Construction of divisional gum boot store, ANZIN. Continued. Racks for drying boots erected in two rooms, stove fitted and roof repaired. Construction of three brigade bomb stores at CHEMIN CREUX,	[signature]

WAR DIARY
INTELLIGENCE SUMMARY
(Erase heading not required.)

Army Form C. 2118.

401st (HIGHLAND) FIELD COMPANY, R.E.
No. Vol. XXVII
Date 31st MARCH 1917

Place	Date	Hour	Summary of Events and Information	Remarks and references to Appendices
			RIPPERT Avenue and THURSDAY Avenue completed. Erection of Nissen huts at MAROEUIL continued. 11 huts completed and 2 partly completed. Work on divisional trench store dugout at FERME MODELE, LILLE road commenced. Entrance stairway and front chamber 9'/15 ft. Repairs to and extension of trench water supply system continued. Shelter for water tanks at AERI CENTRAL being erected. Additional water tanks fitted in position and connected to supply system at HIGH STREET, ECURIE and FANTOME avenue tanks No 1. 30 yards of new 2" pipe laid between 4" water main and FANTOME avenue tanks. Forward company R.E. store moved from FERME MODELE to ROCLINCOURT.	
		6-14	2 sappers employed as patrol on trench water supply system. Work on GRAND COLLECTEUR trench and THURSDAY avenue continued.	

A.H. Kerr
Major, R.B.
O.C. 401st (Highland) Field Coy, R.E.

WAR DIARY
or
INTELLIGENCE SUMMARY

Army Form C. 2118.

401st (HIGHLAND) FIELD COMPANY, R.E.
Vol. XXVII
Date 31st MARCH 1917

O.O. 401st (Highland) Field Coy. R.B.

Place	Date	Hour	Summary of Events and Information	Remarks and references to Appendices
			Work in Company stores, ANZIN, continued as above. Repairing company wagons, making chevaux de frise, dugout frames, ringlet ironwork for stop cocks on water mains, fitting bolts to hold water cans on wagons & preparing timber for work in trenches.	
			Construction of divisional gun boot store ANZIN, complete. Laying racks for 4,000 pairs of boots erected, racks for 8,000 pairs of boots erected; 6 Canada stoves fitted, and shed for collecting and sorting boots received, erected.	W.E.S.
			19 Nissen huts erected at MARŒUIL, and stoves fitted. Construction of trout store dugout at LILLE road continued. Excavation and framing of stairways completed. Stairway at the dugout completed. Excavation of chamber commenced. Passage between foot of stairways driven and temporarily strutted. Frames for chamber prepared. Pithead cut and fitted with angle iron cleats. Ground sills checked and chocks for R.S. legs. Steel bays tried on this work in continuous shifts.	
			One section R.E. and attached infantry employed on this work in continuous shifts.	

Major, R.E.

Army Form C. 2118.

WAR DIARY
or
INTELLIGENCE SUMMARY
(Erase heading not required.)

401st (HIGHLAND) FIELD COMPANY, R.E.
No. ......XXVI........
Date 31st MARCH 1917

Place	Date	Hour	Summary of Events and Information	Remarks and references to Appendices
	14th to 31st		Work on trench water supply system continued. Munfifu line laid between FANTOME Avenue, ABRI CENTRAL and SABLIERE. Shelter and additional tanks erected at, and branch line completed to ABRI CENTRAL. Additional tanks fitted at SABLIERE and sandbag walls built. Bridges laid to carry 5/fifts line across MOUTON, BLANCHARD & BIDOT trenches and CHEMIN CREUX. Trenches deepened and revetted at these points. Trench revetted at junction of 2" and 4" fifts. Additional tanks fitted & connected at HIGH STREET, ECURIE, fitted at VILLAGE STREET ECURIE and fitted and connected by new 2" fifts to 4" main at MADAGASCAR. 2 Sappers employed as water patrol. Stores for forward right brigade dump carried to ROCLINCOURT. Major Barrow returned from leave on 10th March. 2nd Lieut- MacNeill struck off strength of company on 8th March. Digging out and revetting of GRAND COLLECTEUR trench continued between Avenue "A" and THURSDAY Avenue. Work much delayed by shell fire.	

Major, R.B.
O.C. 401st (Highland) Field Coy. R.E.

Army Form C. 2118.

WAR DIARY
of
INTELLIGENCE SUMMARY
(Erase heading not required.)

401st (HIGHLAND) FIELD COMPANY, R.E.
No. VOL. XXVII 5.
Date 31st MARCH 1917

Instructions regarding War Diaries and Intelligence Summaries are contained in F. S. Regs., Part II. and the Staff Manual respectively. Title Pages will be prepared in manuscript.

Place	Date	Hour	Summary of Events and Information	Remarks and references to Appendices
			Digging out and revetting of THURSDAY Avenue continued. Trench revetted with "A" frames from GRAND COLLECTEUR to within 10 yards of BONNAL trench. Avenue frequently damaged by shell fire.	
			Work in company R.E. yard, ANZIN continued.	
			Notice boards painted; chevaux de frise; ablution benches latrines seats, stands for water tanks, dugout frames, handles for unculoverlids and fittings to take valves and ball cocks of water tanks made.	
			Company wagons & lyddite repaired. Tools overhauled. Trench pumps repaired, clips for X.P.M. gabions made.	
			Company drying shed, ANZIN erected.	
			Stores carted from dumps through MAROEUIL to ANZIN, and from ANZIN to ROCLIN COURT.	
			Control of electric power station, ANZIN, taken over by company.	
			Divisional bomb store dug out at LILLE road completed. Chambers excavated 30ft × 8ft × 6ft and framed. 2 sandbag partitions built in chamber.	
			Work on trench water supply system continued. 2" lifts connected from	

Major R.E.
O.C. 401st (Highland) Field Coy, R.E.

2449 Wt. W14957/Mgo 750,000 1/16 J.B.C. & A. Forms/C.2118/12.

Army Form C. 2118.

WAR DIARY
of
INTELLIGENCE SUMMARY

(Erase heading not required.)

401st (HIGHLAND) FIELD COMPANY, R.E.

No. Vol. XXVII
Date 31st March 1917

Instructions regarding War Diaries and Intelligence Summaries are contained in F.S. Regs., Part II. and the Staff Manual respectively. Title Pages will be prepared in manuscript.

Place	Date	Hour	Summary of Events and Information	Remarks and references to Appendices
			From 4" mains across ECURIE road to HIGH STREET. Fittings made to take ball cocks at tanks, VILLAGE STREET and at SABLIERE and fitted. Short lengths of pipe cut and screwed and fitted at SABLIERE tanks. Stop cocks fitted on 2" pipe line and marked with notice boards. Flexible hose connected to feed tanks where no ball-cocks were fitted. Recess excavated for tanks at RIPPERT Avenue and 2" pipe line laid & buried from CHEMIN CREUX to this point. Taps fitted to tanks. Damaged tank connections and damaged lengths of pipe repaired. Old pipe line near SUGAR REFINERY cut and plugged to prevent leakage. 4 recesses for 50 gall. tanks excavated and framed in old mine shaft in BONNAL trench & tanks placed in position. Pump & platform for same erected in shaft, and pipe connected to tanks. Winch barrel and frame, bucket, chain and rope made for well at ECURIE making winch formed for second well. Right brigade reserve dump being formed near THURSDAY Avenue. Following stores carried from ROCHINCOURT to this dump:— 6000 sand bags; 200 coils barbed wire; 100 posts angle iron long; 350 posts screw long; 700 posts screw short revetting; 10 coils plain wire; 10	

O.C. 401st (Highland) Field Coy. R.E.
Major, R.E.

WAR DIARY of INTELLIGENCE SUMMARY

Army Form C. 2118.

10 loophole plates; 50 trench ladders; 50 trench bridges.

Further strengthening of dressing station dugout at LILLE road, GENIE

Avenue commenced. Frames being prepared.

Digging out and resetting of Avenue "A" between RIPPERT Avenue and GRAND COLLECTEUR commenced.

Tunnel No. L.21A, near Avenue G, turning from BONVAL trench to German front line, reconnoitred with a view to being connected to German trenches in the event of British advance.

Improving old dugouts and making new shelters in ECURIE for use of Company during operations.

One officer and 50 men of 154th Infy. Brigade attached to Company transferred to 400th Field Coy. R.E. on 31st March.

Casualties during month:- 4 other ranks WOUNDED.

No. of officers + other details for General duty during month :- 1 other rank.

Roll of Officers with Company at 31/3/17 :- MAJOR. W.P.BARRON. M.C., CAPTAIN. W.C. GLEGG, LIEUT. T.J.GORDON. M.C., ii LIEUTS. C.OKELL, F.B.RITCHIE, S.J.HUNTER, J.S.CLEGHORN, J.L.MACGREGOR, D.JAMIESON.

W.P.Barron
Major, R.E.
O.C. 401st (Highland) Field Coy, R.E.

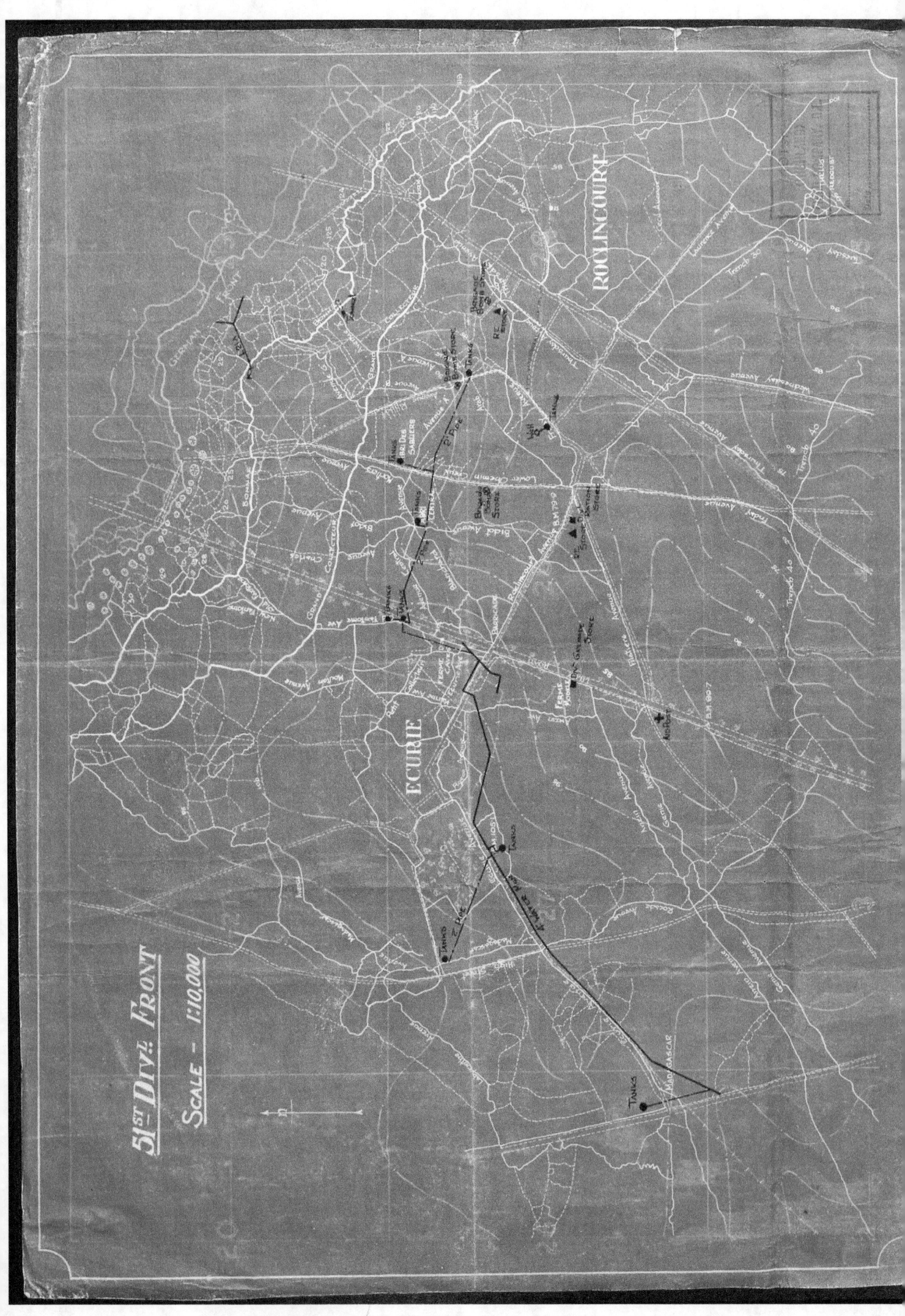

401ST
(HIGHLAND)
FIELD COMPANY, R.E.

No.

Date

Vol 27

WAR DIARY
—OF—
401ST (HIGHLAND) FIELD COMPANY. R.E.
—FOR—
APRIL 1917.

Vol: No XXVIII

WAR DIARY or INTELLIGENCE SUMMARY

Army Form C. 2118.

401st (HIGHLAND) FIELD COMPANY, R.E.

No. Vol. XXVIII / 1.
Date 30th April

Place	Date	Hour	Summary of Events and Information	Remarks and references to Appendices
ANZIN-ST.AUBIN	1st to 8th		Clearing and revetting GRAND COLLECTEUR trench, where damaged by shell-fire between ARAB AVENUE and "L" work, continued. Revetting material carried from ROCLINCOURT R.E. Store to trench. Day and night parties employed. Digging out and revetting of WEDNESDAY AVENUE, where damaged by shell-fire, continued from FISH AVENUE to BONNAL trench; parapets heightened to give cover from view. Digging out and revetting of THURSDAY AVENUE with "A" frames completed from GRAND COLLECTEUR trench to BONNAL trench. Avenue repaired when damaged by shell-fire. Parapets heightened to give more cover from view. Day and night parties employed. Revetting material carried from ROCLINCOURT R.E. Store to trench. Shelters and muddy portions of Avenue A between RIPPERT Avenue and GRAND COLLECTEUR trench dug out and revetted with angle iron pickets and expanded metal; gabion revetment experimental work on two French 5 sappers and 6 attached infantry employed at ECURIE in neighbourhood of south end of HIGH STREET in enlarging old dugouts, and in constructing shelters for accommodation for fire section R.E., 50 attached infantry, and seven officers for use during operations. Dugout on "L" work repaired after having been blown in by shell-fire	W.C.Y.

W.P. Simms
Major, R.E.
O.C. 401st (Highland) Field Coy. R.E.

WAR DIARY or INTELLIGENCE SUMMARY

Army Form C. 2118.

401st (HIGHLAND) FIELD COMPANY, R.E.

No. Vol. XXVIII 2
Date 30th APRIL

Place	Date	Hour	Summary of Events and Information	Remarks and references to Appendices
			Frames and roof strengthened and revetment resetted.	
			Inspection made of dug-outs driven by infantry into sides of FISH TUNNEL.	
			Framing and roofing of dug-outs found to be very weak. Strong shoring of same carried out.	
			Repair and extension of trench water supply continued. 2" pipe 2,000 feet laid. 3,100 gal. Tanks fitted in position. Pipes cut, screwed, and shells for tanks erected to tanks. Water taps fitted to tanks. Tanks connected by flexible hose to tanks.	
			Defective length of 1½" pipe near LILLE ROAD in FANTOME Avenue to ABRI CENTRAL line replaced. Leakage on pipe line through wood ECURIE, between VILLAGE STREET and HIGH STREET located and new length fitted.	
			Winch with bucket and rope erected at ANZIN and carted to and installed at well in ECURIE. Second well in ECURIE repaired. Shore type, bars and lengths of 2" pipe, cut and screwed, stored in water patrol dugout, for use in emergency.	
			2 sappers employed on water patrol duties.	
			One sapper employed assisting Signal Company R.E. in constructing dug-out and shelter at MADAGASCAR.	
			Damage to bridge on BETHUNE road, over ANZIN Avenue investigated and repaired.	

A.W. Bonnar
Major, R.E.
O.C. 401st (Highland) Field Coy, R.E.

WAR DIARY
INTELLIGENCE SUMMARY

Army Form C. 2118.

401st (HIGHLAND) FIELD COMPANY, R.E.
No. Vol. XXVIII
Date 30th APRIL

Place	Date	Hour	Summary of Events and Information	Remarks and references to Appendices

Repair of dressing station dugout, LILLE road, GENIE Avenue, continued. 12 old caps with replaced by 5"x 3" R.S. joists cut to length and fitted with angle iron cleats against uprights. Floor joists fitted and 100 sq ft of sheeting renewed.

14 sappers (working in 2 shifts) employed in mining and framing a chamber 6 feet by 4 feet at foot of one entrance to dugout of 152nd Infantry Brigade Headquarters in THURSDAY Avenue.

Right Brigade reserve dump formed near THURSDAY Avenue Infantry sortie carted to ROCLINCOURT dump and carried thence to Brigade dump :—
50, sheets corrugated iron; 25, bundles French wire with staples; 250, picks; 250, shovels; 15 c/f
10, crowbars; 5, billhooks; 10, axes-hand; 10, saws hand; 10, hammers hand; 1 cwt, nails 3", 4" and 6"; 50, tracing tapes; 5, balls sphagnum.

Work in company R.E. store continued
ANZIN

Notice boards painted. Complete bench for sell in ECURIE, sweating trough, clips for X.P.M. gabions, timber covers for exposed portions of trench mat'ls type "A", ends and handles for muck scoops made. Tools overhauled, company waggons repaired and painted. Timber shifted on sawmill.

Stores carted from Divisional dump MAROEUIL to ANZIN and from carrying dump ANZIN to advanced dump, ROCLINCOURT. 1 sapper and 1 attached infantry

WAR DIARY
or
INTELLIGENCE SUMMARY.

Army Form C. 2118.

401st (HIGHLAND) FIELD COMPANY, R.E.
No. 24 XXVIII
Date 30th APRIL

Place	Date	Hour	Summary of Events and Information	Remarks and references to Appendices
			men employed as stretcher at advanced company also ROCLINCOURT. 3 sappers employed running electric power station, ANZIN. Cables damaged by shell-fire repaired. Damaged electric light leads ANZIN. repaired.	
			Company have lines MARŒUIL, also billets en 1st inst. and went to outskirts of village in consequence. 1 officer and 2 hours movement 3 officers and 100 men 1/6th Black Watch attached to Company returned to regiment on 6 inst.	
			1 officer and 23 men, 17th Argyll and Sutherland Highlanders, and 1 officer and 25 men 1/8th Argyll and Sutherland Highlanders attached to company on 8th inst. for use as working parties during operations.	p.e.y
			Lt Gordon proceeded to 154th Infantry Brigade Advanced Headquarters on SABLIERE on evening of 8th inst, to act as liaison officer between C.R.E. and 154th Infantry Brigade during operations.	
			2nd Lt Hunter and number 1 section, with 1 officer and attached infantry party of 1/4th Argyll and Sutherland Highlanders proceeded at 9 p.m. on 8th inst. to Cruxwell L. 21.a. (A.23.C.3.d). To await opportunity of connecting tunnel	

Major, R.E.
O.C. 401st (Highland) Field Coy. R.E.

Army Form C. 2118.

WAR DIARY
or
INTELLIGENCE SUMMARY.
(Erase heading not required.)

401st (HIGHLAND) FIELD COMPANY, R.E.
Vol. XXVIII
Date 30th APRIL

Place	Date	Hour	Summary of Events and Information	Remarks and references to Appendices
			to front German Trench after capture of latter. Instructions by Major Barron in regard to this work attached.	W.e.f.
			Major Barron, 2nd Lieuts. O'Kell, MacGregor, and parties and numbers 2, 3, and 4 sections with 1 officer and party of attached 1/3rd A.Cyl. and Sutherland Highlanders proceeded to dugouts in ECURIE at our night 8th/9th and Headquarters details of company remained stationed at ANZIN. Company taught under 2nd Lt. Isleghorn remained stationed at MAROEUIL.	
	9th		51st Division attacked German lines & battered end of VIMY ridge at 5.30am. End of tunnel L.21.a ticked through to surface of ground at 10 a.m., and communication trench dug by No. 1 Section was established up early half at 12 noon from end of tunnel to German front trench. Work carried on at Askm. No casualties occurred. Party returned to company & others billeted in ECURIE. 4 men of French Mortar Battery attached to company were killed or wounded in the afternoon, company received orders to construct a strong point at B.19.d.55.95 on ZEHNER WEG Trench, and of the three slung points previously arranged to be constructed when the objective had been captured. Major Barron and 2/Lt O'Kell reconnoitred all on early evening but found that the third objective POINT DUJOUR-FARBUS LINE had not been captured and	W.e.f

Major R.B.
D.G. 401st (Highland) Field Coy., R.M.

Army Form C. 2118.

WAR DIARY
or
INTELLIGENCE SUMMARY.
(Erase heading not required.)

401st (HIGHLAND) FIELD COMPANY, R.E. No. 6.
Vol. XXVIII Date 30th APRIL.

Place	Date	Hour	Summary of Events and Information	Remarks and references to Appendices
	10th		that the REGIMENTS W.E.G. trench formed the British front line. A civilian strongpoint was occupied by and a field out further back at B.19.c.9.4.cm. the ZEHNER WEG trench.	p.e.if.
			No. 2 Bomb section went attached party of 1/6 Argyll and Sutherland Highlanders coming 2nd/13 Machguns arrived at aula at 5 p.m. and dug out civil strongpoint by 3 am on 10th inst. No casualties occurred.	p.e.if
			Company engaged in digging ECURIE, strath line trench with heavy enemy fire.	
			Three lorries of pontoons carried from MAROEUIL to ROCLINCOURT by company transport. 36 Pontoons bridges, footway, trench and overland tracks were and further Company returned to ANZIN at noon. Lorry has been relieved by 5th Field Company R.E. 2nd Division. Orders received to arrange for billeting of company in ST NICHOLAS, but same accommodation was available. This company received permission to remain billeted in ANZIN.	w.e.if
	11th		Parties of 17th and 18th Argyll and Sutherland Highlanders attached to company returned to their respective Regts and the employed on	w.e.
			Company received orders to become XVII corps troops and to be employed on the repair of roads East of ARRAS.	
	12th		Necessary reconn to road at ST LAURENT—BLANGY along old firing	

A.5834 Wt. W4973/M687 750,000 8/16 D. D. & L. Ltd. Forms/C.2118/13.

O.C. 401st (Highland) Field Coy. R.E.
Major, R.E.
[signature]

WAR DIARY or INTELLIGENCE SUMMARY

Army Form C. 2118.

401st (Highland) Field Company, R.E.
Vol. XXVIII
Date 30th APRIL

Place	Date	Hour	Summary of Events and Information	Remarks and references to Appendices
	13th		Front extends from G.15.c.5.4. to River SCARPE, inclusive, held by Majors Bisset and 2/Lt Ohel. Control of electric power station ANZIN handed over to 423rd Field Coy R.E. between ROCLINCOURT and 2 new intelaces worked to railway. Reps of about 200 traversed. Employed making front line fire bays and mak. Channels cut through old German front work on east side of bank and wire entanglement. Restore of road allowed to cross away Two foot bridges cut from flooded area over G.17.d and in 18.a. & west SCARPE and over Zwingstraat. Road cleared of debris, German horse entanglement, holes filled in, and part stones said. Road repair from front towards Bricard between this road and river.	W.e.y.
	14.15th		ST. NICHOLAS — ST. LAURENT — BLANGY. Road repaired. Road landed. Surface of bottom laid in excellent state, chalk and broken bricks collected and laid. Damaged parts of front heard, third front cell collected from buildings. Fortification, as far as possible, and laid, infantry escorts and recovery machine-gun emplacements, dugout, traps and other defences worked on including clearing of otherwise demolished road ballast, earth cleared. Front Maria Joseph and shells removed from roadway. 2 companies of pioneers working to right	W.e.y. W.e.y.

O.C. 401st (Highland) Field Coy R.B.
Major, R.B.

WAR DIARY or INTELLIGENCE SUMMARY

Army Form C. 2118.

(Erase heading not required.)

401st (Highland) Field Company, R.E.
Vol. XXVIII
30th April

Place	Date	Hour	Summary of Events and Information	Remarks and references to Appendices
River SCARPE	16th to 20th		and in repair of sand across island between LOCK and main channel of river SCARPE. Company transport employed carting tools etc. from MARCEUIL XVII corps dump to site of work at BLANGY. Repair of above road completed between ST NICHOLAS – ST LAURENT – BLANGY road and bridge over LOCK. Levelling and installing and slipping of hard sets where available, continuation of sand across island continued by pioneer battalions supervised by company. Work of dismantling and rebuilding five span masonry arch bridge over main channel of river SCARPE on the above road at BLANGY G.24 a.8.6. commenced. The old masonry bridge consisted of five arches, the centre one being 23'-6" span and the other four 20'-6" span each, from centre to centre of piers, the roadway being carried on 9"×6" R.S. joists placed across the bridge at 4'-3" intervals filled between with brick arching carrying the pavement 3'-6" beyond the edge of the masonry and giving a roadway of 16'-0" wide. The centre and two north spans, with the two north piers had been badly damaged by shell-fire and the masonry of these arches and piers had been completely	W.E.S.

O.B. 40181 Field Coy., R.E.
Major, R.E.

WAR DIARY
INTELLIGENCE SUMMARY
(Erase heading not required.)

Army Form C. 2118.

401st (HIGHLAND) FIELD COMPANY, R.E.
No. Vol. XXVIII 9
Date 30th APRIL.

Place	Date	Hour	Summary of Events and Information	Remarks and references to Appendices
			collapsed into the river diverting the stream entirely through the second arch from the south end, and leaving a bristol waggon halfway between the last intact pier and the northern abutment of the old bridge. Only the pavement and balustrade of the west side of the bridge remained in a damaged condition suggesting a possible breakdown. It was decided to block the bridge damaged masonry arch by chess girder bridges and prepare the two damaged piers by two Long tom 65 trestles on concrete foundations. Debris of damaged arches and foundations of old piers uncovered to permit building of new piers. Abutment of concrete built up against scarp of west pier from old abutment at north end of bridge supplied with concrete curtey 0/c. Suitable gardens 12" × 6" and 10" × 5" collected from old railway of new bridge. Building and yard ready to take late. Company transport employed in carrying tools and stores	Well

O.C. 401st (Highland) Field Coy, R.E.
Major, R.E.

Army Form C. 2118.

WAR DIARY
or
INTELLIGENCE SUMMARY.
(Erase heading not required.)

Instructions regarding War Diaries and Intelligence Summaries are contained in F. S. Regs., Part II. and the Staff Manual respectively. Title pages will be prepared in manuscript.

401st (HIGHLAND) FIELD COMPANY, R.E.
No. W.d. XXVIII 10.
Date 30th APRIL.

Place	Date	Hour	Summary of Events and Information	Remarks and references to Appendices
			From Corps dump MAROEUIL to site of work, BLANGY.	
			Numbers 2 and 4 sections with 2nd/Kents. O'Kell and Jemison moved to BLANGY on 17th inst. Billeted then in old German dugouts.	
			Numbers 1 and 3 sections moved to BLANGY on 20th inst. Billeted then in old German dugouts.	
			Company Headquarters remained stationed in ANZIN.	

W. E. G.

W. E. Grover
Major, R.E.
O.C. 401st (Highland) Field Coy. R.E.

Army Form C. 2118.

WAR DIARY
or
INTELLIGENCE SUMMARY.
(Erase heading not required.)

401st (HIGHLAND) FIELD COMPANY, R.E.
No. Vol. XXVIII
Date 30th APRIL 1917

Place	Date	Hour	Summary of Events and Information	Remarks and references to Appendices
	21st to 26th		Repairs to road from road junction at G.23.b.7.4. across river SCARPE to junction at G.18.c.5.4.; to road from G.17.c.5.6. through ST LAURENT-BLANGY to LE POINT DU JOUR, H.3.d.3.1.; and to awn bridge at H.8.c.a.o being carried out by other units, supervised by Company; a large amount of work in clearing entanglements and in dealing with trenches was required on first part of road, between G.23.b.7.4. and SCARPE. Construction of bridge at BLANGY continued. Concrete work of pier of second pier from south end completely finished, being set in concrete to hold 12"x12" timber bearer for girder bridge. As other main girders of span resting on piers, lay beyond masonry of bridge, 12"x12" timber upright resting on concrete footing of pier will have outside masonry of pier supporting 12"x12" timber bearer and were bolted to both footing and bearer. Second pier from north end of bridge built of concrete and old masonry footing 2'-6" wide by 21'-0" long pier being built on concrete to hold 12"x12" timber trestle carrying girder bridges. Two 12"x12" timber trestles 3'-7" high	W.E.G.

Major, R.E.
O.C. 401st (Highland) Field Coy., R.E.

Army Form C. 2118.

WAR DIARY
or
INTELLIGENCE SUMMARY.
(Erase heading not required.)

401st (HIGHLAND) FIELD COMPANY, R.E.
No. Vol. XXVIII
Date 30TH APRIL 1917

Place	Date	Hour	Summary of Events and Information	Remarks and references to Appendices
	27th to 30		with six uprights and 9"x 3" diagonal bracing erected on the pier trestles being bolted together. Excavations being carried out for foundations of foot pier on north end of bridge. Materials for bridge spans being prepared. Two 21'-6" clear span bridges to be used for double width roadway over longest span transported from Corps dumps MAROEUIL to BLANGY. Company transport used to convey part of this. Right footbridge on two-legged trestles erected alongside main bridge to carry foot traffic during erection of bridge. 40'-6" span between R.E. and R.S. girders and spikes cepts fastened along verges. Bridges carrying an extra girder and spike caps fastened to the 5 stringer lengthwise of traffic. Two pontoon wagons with pontoon wagons handed over to 400th Field Coy R.E. on 21st inst. Two pontoon wagons with saddle beams of pontoons received from 400th Field Co. R.E. on 26th inst. Repairs to road from road junction at G.23.6.7 to accd over SCARPE	W.C.y

O.C. 401st (Highland) Field Coy, R.E.
Major, R.E.

Army Form C. 2118.

WAR DIARY
or
INTELLIGENCE SUMMARY.
(Erase heading not required.)

401st (HIGHLAND) FIELD COMPANY, R.E.

No. XXVIII.

Date 30th APRIL 1917

13.

O.C. 401st (Highland) Field Coy., R.E.
Major, R.E.

Place	Date	Hour	Summary of Events and Information	Remarks and references to Appendices
			To junction at G.18.c.5.4. almost completed. Work supervised by Company. Erection of bridge over river SCARPE continued. First-four piers northward of bridge cleared to foundations, built up with concrete, 1'-0" wide by 2'-0" long, with line set in concrete to hold 12"x12" timber trestle - same design as for second pier - erected on concrete to carry girder bridge. Next superstructure of 21'-6" clear span bridge erected in position. This bridge consisted of frame work for two bridges each 9'-0" wide, giving a double width of 18'-0". Each bridge consisted of two main girders, 18'x7", with four cross girders meeting on bond flanging means girders and bolted to latter by means of angle irons, the length of the span being thus divided into three panels each cross braced by 7x2 ties bolted to upper flange of cross-girder. Two girders 8"x6" were carried the length of the span on the cross-girder, the upper flange being flush with the upper flanges of the main girders. 10"x6" × 2" run cant pieces were nailed along centre of bridge, abutting on cross-girders and packed up flush with top of ebon, longitudinal stringers. 10"x6" timber stringers bolted to the four longitudinal girders carried the 9"x4" timber decking which was spiked to stringers.	W.C.f

WAR DIARY or INTELLIGENCE SUMMARY

Army Form C. 2118.

401st (HIGHLAND) FIELD COMPANY, R.E.
No. Vol. XXVIII
Date 30th APRIL 1917

Place	Date	Hour	Summary of Events and Information	Remarks and references to Appendices
			Outside main girders tied back to old girders of masonry arched bridge, by four flat steel straps. Heavy timber cleat bolted to underside of main girders against timber trestle pier. Part of 9"x4" timber decking spiked down. Old pavements on masonry arches reduced by 1'-0" to allow of 18'-0" roadway, stone curb replaced, and 1'-0" channel iron laid along extremes on top of cross girders in order to support roadway. Packing pieces fitted between girders on one half of double timber pier and packing pieces fitted on other half to bring roadway on 7.12.x 6" girders to same level of rest span, 14'-6" in the clear. To level of top roadway on first span. Packing pieces prepared to make up difference of sizes of girders to be placed on East pier (with north end of bridge). Following units worked under direction of Company on roads near ST. LAURENT-BLANGY— 289th Army Troops Coy R.E., 152nd Field Coy R.E., 1 section 184th Tunnelling Coy. R.E., battalions West Yorks pioneers, 18th Northumberland Fusiliers pioneers, 8th Royal Scots pioneers, 6th Seaforth pioneers 7th Italian Yorks, 1 Kanoo pioneers. Company transport moved from MAROEUIL to ANZIN on 30th inst.	D.C.B.

W.J. Boisson
Major, R.E.
O.C. 401st (Highland) Field Coy, R.E.

Army Form C. 2118.

WAR DIARY
or
INTELLIGENCE SUMMARY.
(Erase heading not required.)

401st (HIGHLAND) FIELD COMPANY, R.E. Vol. XXVIII No. 15.
30th APRIL 1917.

O.O. 401st (Highland) Field Coy., R.E.
Major, R.E.

Place	Date	Hour	Summary of Events and Information	Remarks and references to Appendices
Billeted Area			Company Transport employed carting stores and tools from Corps dump MAROEUIL to site of works at BLANGY. Company wagons being repaired and repainted. Notice boards made and painted. Plans showing trench systems and position of water in ROCLINCOURT sector. Captured German trench systems and site of strong point on ZEHNER WEG and roads and bridge being repaired in ST. LAURENT — BLANGY area, attached. Casualties during month:- 5 other ranks — wounded. Reinforcements received during month:- 7 other ranks. Transfers during month:- 4 other ranks transferred to 408th (Highland) Bn Res Coy R.E Roll of Officers with Company at:- 30/4/17:- MAJOR W.P.BARTON, M.C., CAPTAIN W.C.GLEGG, LIEUT. T.J.GORDON, M.C., 2ndLIEUTS. C.OKELL, F.B.RITCHIE, S.J.HUNTER, J.S.CLEGHORN, J.L.MACGREGOR, O.JAMIESON. Detailed plan showing reconstruction of bridge over river SCARPE at BLANGY, will accompany War Diary for next month.	

Officer i/c. No I Section.
401st (Highland) Field Co. R.E.

The following work will be carried out by No. 1. Section. R.E. along with sappers mates, who will report for duty by noon on Y day; the number of sappers mates will be notified to you later.

Making a communication trench by digging from the Tunnel L.21.a. (A.23.C.3.8) to the German lines.

Accommodation in the tunnel during the night Y/Z will be allotted by 154 Inf. Bde.

The party will proceed to the tunnel on Y day arriving there by 12 midnight Y/Z.

Rations will be carried for consumption on Z day.

Tools will be drawn from R.E. Store. ROCLINCOURT.

12 notice boards "POSER WEG" and 5 boards "TUNNEL" are at R.E. store. ROCLINCOURT. & will be taken up to tunnel by party.

The boards will be placed in position on completion of work to show infantry the entrance.

The R.E. Officer will decide when situation permits of work being commenced.

He will report completion of work to HdQrs 154 Inf Bde (at SABLIERE in CHEMIN CREUX) and by wire to the C.R.E. after which failing receipt of other orders, the parties will return to Coy HdQrs. in HIGH ST., ECURIE.

401st (HIGHLAND) FIELD COMPANY, R.E.
No.
Date 6-4-17

W P Barron
O.C. 401st (Highland) Field Coy. R.E.
Major, R.E.

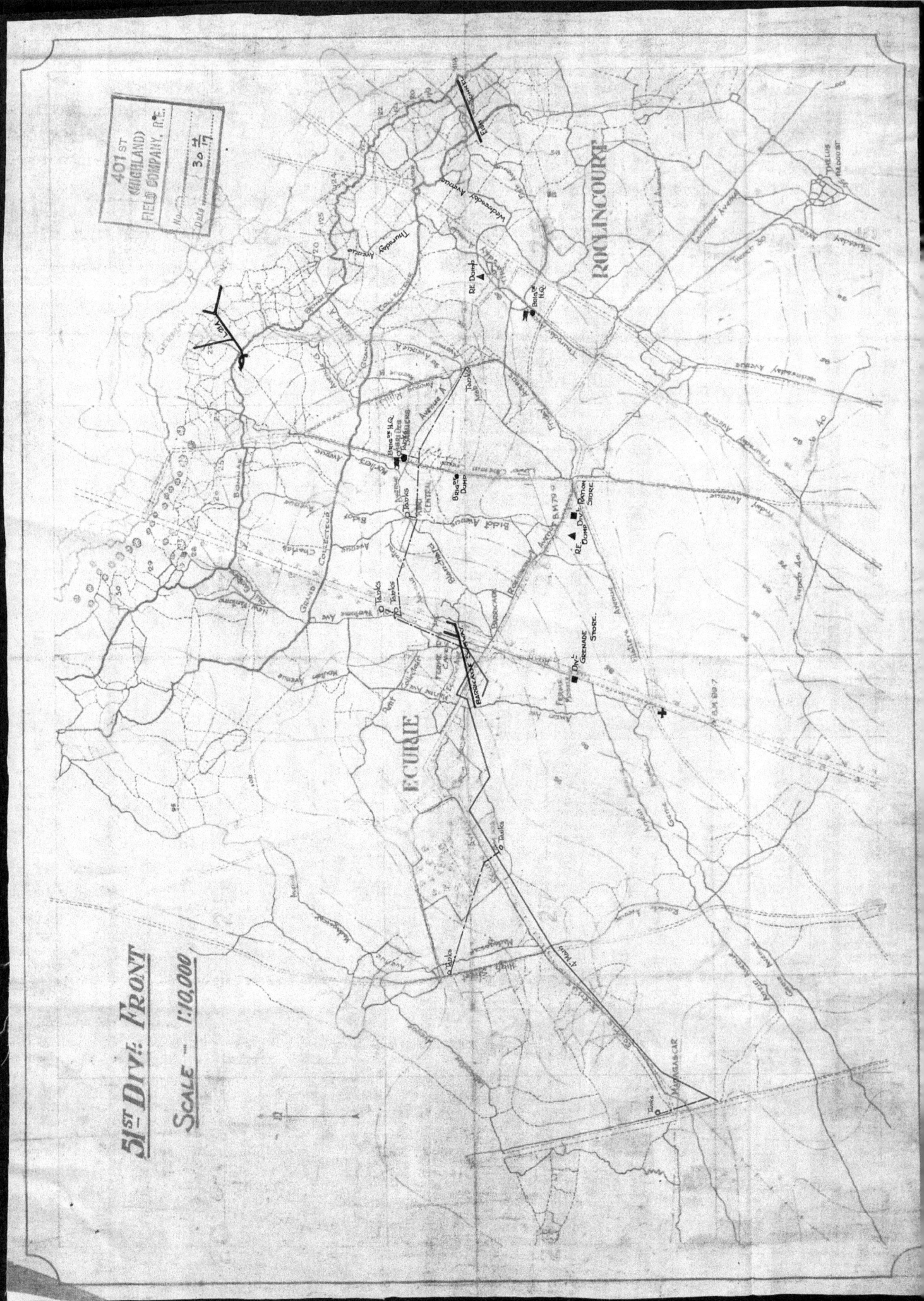

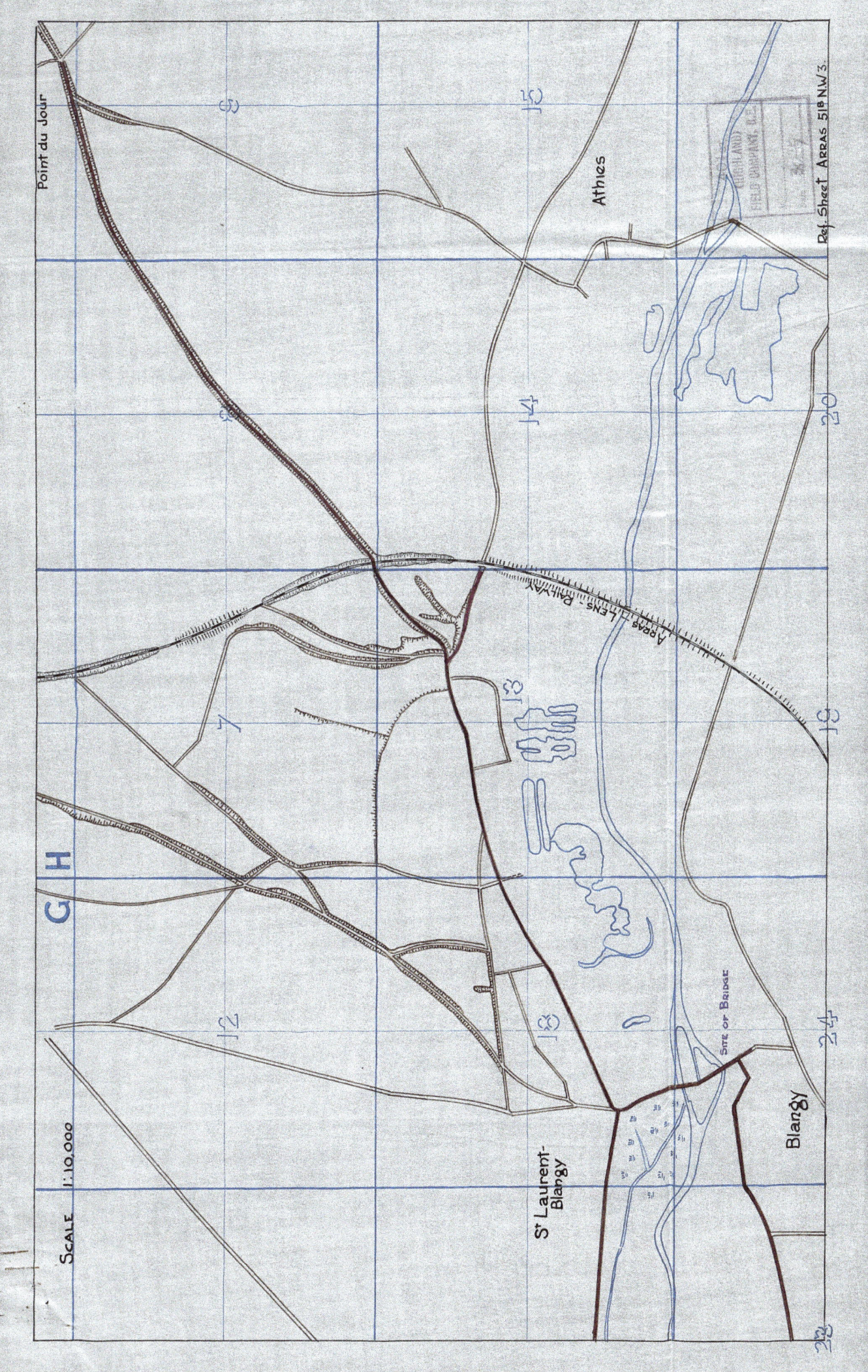

WAR DIARY
— OF —
401st (HIGHLAND) FIELD COMPANY. R.E.
— FOR —
MAY
1917

Vol: No XXIX

Army Form C. 2118.

401st
(HIGHLAND)
FIELD COMPANY, R.E.

No. ...VOL XXIX...
Date ...31st MAY 1917...

WAR DIARY
or
INTELLIGENCE SUMMARY.
(Erase heading not required.)

Instructions regarding War Diaries and Intelligence Summaries are contained in F. S. Regs., Part II. and the Staff Manual respectively. Title pages will be prepared in manuscript.

Place	Date	Hour	Summary of Events and Information	Remarks and references to Appendices
ANZIN - ST AUBIN	1st to 4th		Company working under orders of XVIITH Corps. Reconstruction of bridge over River SCARPE at BLANGY WEIR, G.24.a. 8.6 continued. Trestle on north end piers erected. This consisted of a 12"x12" sill with six uprights and 9"x3" bracing similar to those on second pier. Trestle assembled with 1" drift bolts. Seven I girders, 12"x6", erected on second span. Stringers of two 9"x3" laid together, bolted to top of girders and decking of 9"x4" spiked down to stringers similar to other span. Packing pieces of 2 timbers placed on north end trestle to take the eight 10"x5" girders, other end of same resting on concrete foundation on north bank. Stringers of two 9"x3" similar to second span and decking 9"x4" spiked down. All decking laid so as to allow traffic over bridge at earliest date. Instructs L.G. Hutchings went on leave on 5TH.	
	5TH to 10TH		Completing bridge over River SCARPE. All decking spiked down, curb and hand-rails erected. Checking pieces bolted on to 12"x6", 10"x5"	

C^{dt} ....
Major, R.E.
O.C. 401st (Highland) Field Coy. R.E.

Army Form C. 2118.

WAR DIARY
or
INTELLIGENCE SUMMARY.
(Erase heading not required.)

401st (HIGHLAND) FIELD COMPANY, R.E.
No. Vol. XXIX 2
Date 31ST MAY 1917.

Instructions regarding War Diaries and Intelligence Summaries are contained in F. S. Regs., Part II. and the Staff Manual respectively. Title pages will be prepared in manuscript.

Place	Date	Hour	Summary of Events and Information	Remarks and references to Appendices
	5TH to 10TH		girders against side of trials. Brickwork completed between girders on north end abutment. Light steel girders bolted under ends of decking on second span from north end to transmit cantilever load on to casts. Above northern free roll girders bolted apart by 9"×3" pieces and outside clamps bolted through 12"×12" trestle.	
	11TH and 12TH		Pointing of existing stone arches carried out. Drawings of bridge attached. Commencement made of clearing debris under bridge to allow maximum waterway and also upstream to temporary weir. Bollards placed on north end of bridge to guide traffic and part raised for 10yards north and south of bridge and also western portion of road between two bridges.	
	13TH		Huts erected for Divisional Headquarters at ST NICHOLAS and approaches improved. Work on debris and weir continued at bridge. Erection of huts continued, furniture made, latrines erected, stables	

A.E. Murray? Lt
Major, R.E.
O.C. 401st (Highland) Field Coy, R.E.

WAR DIARY
or
INTELLIGENCE SUMMARY.
(Erase heading not required.)

Army Form C. 2118.

401st (HIGHLAND) FIELD COMPANY. R.E.
No. Vol. XXIX 3
Date 31st May 1917

Place	Date	Hour	Summary of Events and Information	Remarks and references to Appendices
	13th		and footbridges, seats and shelves erected in Divisional Bath-house. Lieut. CLEGHORN and 2 N.C.O's proceeded to gas school at FREVIN	
CAPELLE	14th		for course of instruction. Work on debris and roads completed. Company H.Q. moved to dug-outs and cellars in BLANGY (G.24.a.) Transport lines moved to St NICHOLAS.	
	15th to 19th		Company came under Divisional orders. Work at Divisional Headquarters continued. Work on roads at BLANGY handed over to 4th Division. Interpreter Hutchings returned from leave 15th inst. Work at Divisional Headquarters continued. 13 huts erected, stable for 60 horses completed. Work on stays for Divisional etc. made for same. table and tables, chairs Theatre commenced. On 17th Sec/Lieut. CLEGHORN and 2 N.C.O's return from FREVIN/CAPELLE Front trench system reconnoitred.	Major R.E. O.C. 401st (Highland) Field Coy, R.E.

Army Form C. 2118.

WAR DIARY
or
INTELLIGENCE SUMMARY.
(Erase heading not required.)

401ST (HIGHLAND) FIELD COMPANY, R.E.
No. Vol. XXIX
Date 21st MAY 1917

Place	Date	Hour	Summary of Events and Information	Remarks and references to Appendices
	18th		Work on Divisional Headquarters - Living huts, filling shell holes, making trestles for stage of Divisional Theatre. One section working under 400th Army clearing 400 yards of canal towpath at FAMPOUX.	W.C.V.
	19th to 20th		Repairs to R.A.M.C. Dressing Station, L'ABBAYETTE. Work at Divisional Headquarters and stables, canal bank, and dressing station continued. Cutting front bench through Railway Embankment, I.13.c. 6.1. 70 yards wide. Work at 153 Brigade Headquarters commenced, erecting two English shelters and two O.P.s at H.16.d.2.7.	W.C.V.

A.C.Griffiths
Major, R.E.
O.C. 401st (Highland) Field Coy, R.E.

Army Form C. 2118.

401ST
(HIGHLAND)
FIELD COMPANY, R.E.
No. .... Vol. XXIX.
Date 30TH MAY 1917.

WAR DIARY
INTELLIGENCE SUMMARY.
(Erase heading not required.)

Place	Date	Hour	Summary of Events and Information	Remarks and references to Appendices
	21		Work on stage for theatre, dressing station, English shelters continued. New front trench cut across railway at I.13.b.8.2. - 30 yards. 1 man killed & 5 wounded while proving CHEMICAL WORKS. Erecting open air bathhouse & shelter at Railway Embankment. Screening of ATHIES-FAMPOUX road at H.16.c. and H.16.d. from enemy observation commenced.	
	22		Twenty 50 gall. tanks taken up to quarry at I.13.a.1.2. 430 picks & 360 shovels dumped at H.18.a.4.2. east of FAMPOUX. Major W.P. Barron M.C., evacuated sick to C.C.S. Work at divisional theatre completed. Work on dressing station L'ABBAYETTE, English shelters at 153 Brigade H.Qrs, screens on road H.16.c. x H.16.d. continued. 1 Lieut MacGregor assisting infantry in establishing Lewis gun post on SUNKEN ROAD. I.14.c.4.7.	
	23-26		Clearing main road east of FAMPOUX, H.18.a. & filling shell holes also.	

WAR DIARY or INTELLIGENCE SUMMARY

Army Form C. 2118.

401st (HIGHLAND) FIELD COMPANY, R.E.
No. Vol XXIX
Date 31st MAY 1917

Place	Date	Hour	Summary of Events and Information	Remarks and references to Appendices
	23-26		also repairing road from FANFOUX towards Batt. H.Bn. H.18.c. and H.18.d. Repairs to dressing station L'ABBAYETTE continued; forming and lining entrance tray repaired. At 153 Brigade H.Bn., excavation & erection of Engineer Shelter continued. Scrernung of Road at H.16.c. and H.16.d. Coy's line at H.16.d. H.17.22.3. completing mine, clearing trench & cutting fire steps. Tanks in Quarry at I.13.a.1.2. erected & Sandbag protective built round them. 6 tables provided by shell splinters repaired under frights. Old German dug-out in Quarry repaired. Assisting Brigade in supervision of working parties in CROW TRENCH. On 23rd Sec Lieut S.J. HUNTER went on leave.	W.E.H.
	27-29		Work at Quarry I.13.a.1.2., FANFOUX road H.18.b., Dressing station, L'ABBAYETTE, Coy's line, Scrernung of ATHIES-FANFOUX Road continued. Sample shelter & firestep cut in CROW. I.13.6.6.4. Rails across trenches cut by explosive on railway I.13.6.8.2. and I.13.6.6.1. – 37 cuts.	

Major R.E.
O.C. 401st (Highland) Field Coy, R.E.

WAR DIARY or INTELLIGENCE SUMMARY

Army Form C. 2118.

401st (HIGHLAND) FIELD COMPANY. R.E.
No. Vol. XXIX
Date 31st MAY 1917.

Place	Date	Hour	Summary of Events and Information	Remarks and references to Appendices
	27-29		Making sample hurdles for trench camouflage & erecting same in disused trench at H.14.a.7.6. Hurdles consist of 2"x1" timber frame, 6ft by 3ft, covered with wire netting, filled in centre and edges of painted canvas, to give empty appearance when placed over occupied trench, as seen by aeroplane. Photographs taken of above camouflage by aeroplane at 4.45 p.m. on 29th. Sun flares lighted to indicate position of camouflage trench across railway at I.13.b.8.2. defined & trench cut across road at I.13.b.6.3. — CROW TRENCH.	W.E.J.
	30		Work on dressing station L'ABBAYETTE continued. Dugout chamber with double roof completed, passages damaged by shell fire, repaired & new ramp entrance to dugout constructed. Improvement of Corps defence line at H.22.b. continued, hurdles made for trench camouflage. Report made on wells and pumps in east-side of FAMPOUX, also main BIACHE road. One officer and 9.O.R. of 90th Field Coy. R.E. 9th Division, took over work	W.E.J.

Army Form C. 2118.

WAR DIARY
or
INTELLIGENCE SUMMARY

(Erase heading not required.)

401ST (HIGHLAND) FIELD COMPANY, R.E.
No. XXIX
Vol.
Date 31st MAY 1917.

Place	Date	Hour	Summary of Events and Information	Remarks and references to Appendices
	30		O/Company and now billeted with it. 2/Lt. Garrison went on leave.	M.E.S.
	31		Company transport employed during month in carting stores to front line area and in carting stores at XVII Corps R.E. dump. Company equipment loaded on transport by 7 a.m. Billets cleaned and handed over to 90th Coy R.E. Company transport & cyclists left at 7.30 a.m. and proceeded by road to BAILLEUL-AUX-CORNEILLES under Lt. GORDON. Dismounted personnel marched at 1 p.m. to G.20.a.9.8. west of ARRAS, and proceeded by motor lorries at 5 p.m. to BAILLEUL-AUX-CORNEILLES. Arrived 7 p.m. Billeted there. Plans of bridge over river SCARPE, BLANGY WEIR roads at BLANGY and divisional trench system attached. Reference Maps, sheet 51B N.W. Edition 6.A. 1:20,000. Casualties during month :- 2 other ranks killed & 6 wounded. Reinforcements received during month :- 1 C.S.M. 10 other ranks. No of Officers taken on leave during month :- 2 officers, 5 other ranks.	M.E.S.

A. Willing
Major, R.E.
O.C. 401st (Highland) Field Coy, R.E.

Army Form C. 2118.

WAR DIARY
INTELLIGENCE SUMMARY.
(Erase heading not required.)

401st (HIGHLAND) FIELD COMPANY, R.E.
No. Vol. XXIX
Date 31st MAY 1917.

Place	Date	Hour	Summary of Events and Information	Remarks and references to Appendices
			Roll of Officers with Company at 31/5/17 :- Major. W.P.Barron. M.C., Captain W.C.Glegg., Lieut. T.J.Gordon. M.C., ii Lieuts. C.Okell, F.B.Ritchie, S.O.Hunter, J.S.Cleghorn, J.L.MacGregor, D.Jamieson.	W.P.B.

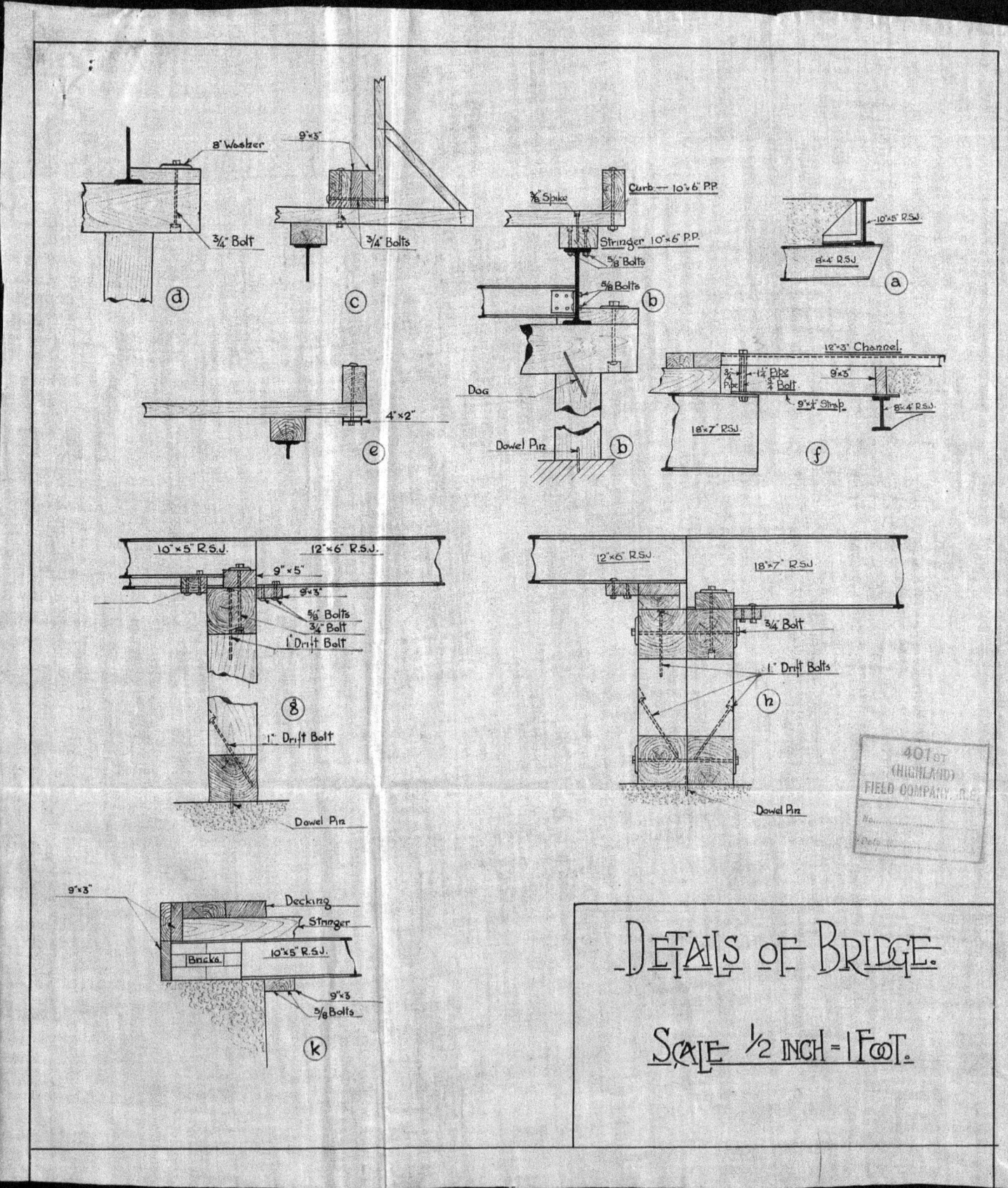

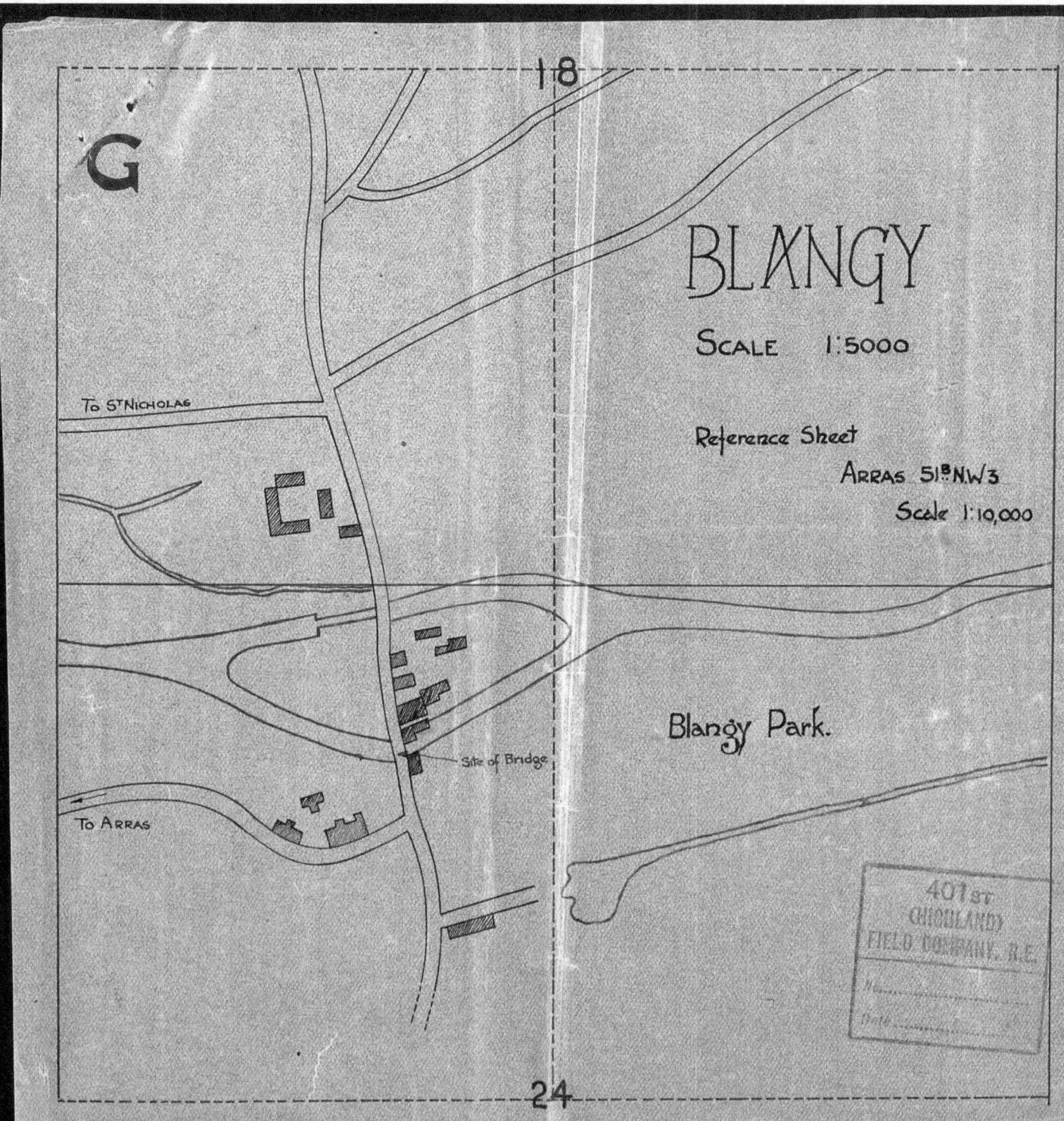

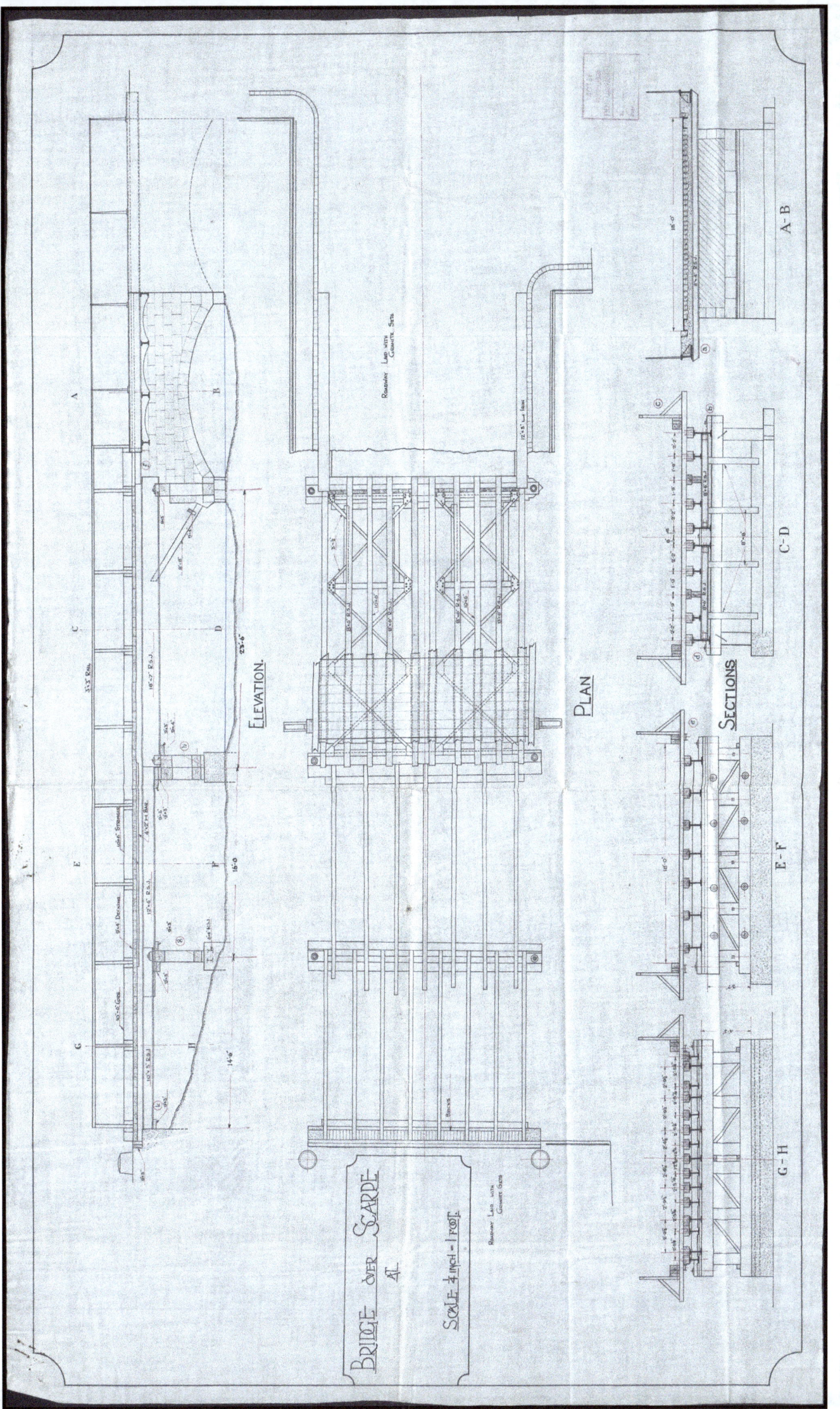

War Diary

of

401st (Highland) Field Company R.E.

for

June

1917.

Vol: No XXX

Army Form C. 2118.

WAR DIARY
or
INTELLIGENCE SUMMARY.
(Erase heading not required.)

401st (HIGHLAND) FIELD COMPANY, R.E.
Vol XXX No. 1.
Date 30th JUNE 1917

Place	Date	Hour	Summary of Events and Information	Remarks and references to Appendices
BAILLEUL-AUX-CORNAILLES	June 1.		Company engaged in cleaning up equipment and billets. Company inspected. Made short route march in morning for training. Received 2 new tool carts.	
	2.			
	3.		Company bathed at TINCQUES bath-house. Returned 2 old G.S. tool carts to railhead. Timber purchased and pontoon wagon repaired. Transport passed ready for moving.	
ANTIN.	4.		Marched at 6 A.M. to ANTIN. Arrived 8-30 a.m. Billeted here.	
	5.		Marched at 8-30 a.m. to HEZECQUES. Arrived 4-30 p.m. Billeted there.	
HEZECQUES	6.		Company Transport moved at 8 a.m. to WIZERNES. Billeted there. Dismounted personnel remained at HEZECQUES. Programme of training submitted to C.R.E.	
	7.		Dismounted personnel moved at 7 a.m. by motor bus to CLERCQUES. Arrived 2 p.m. Billeted here. Company Transport moved from WIZERNES to CLERCQUES.	
CLERCQUES.	8,12		2nd Lieut. S.J. HUNTER returned from leave. Company training commenced. Company inspected. Squad drills, musketry exercises, triangle of error, practice in hoisting guards, pontoon bridging, use of Weldon	

Army Form C. 2118.

WAR DIARY
or
INTELLIGENCE SUMMARY.
(Erase heading not required.)

401st (HIGHLAND) FIELD COMPANY, R.E.
Vol. XXX
Date 30th JUNE 1917.

Place	Date	Hour	Summary of Events and Information	Remarks and references to Appendices
CERCQUES	11th & 12th		Walker trestles, lectures on demolitions, map reading, use of prismatic compass, and musketry. R.E. dump established at NORDAUSQUE for 154th Infantry Brigade area. One sapper detailed as storeman. Company billets improved & transport overhauled. Bayonet assault courses erected at 154th Infantry Brigade battalion. 2nd Lieut D. JAMIESON returned from leave on 12th inst.	
	13		Company training discontinued. Orders received to be ready to move at 12 hours notice. Bridging equipment packed in wagons and wagons cleaned. C.S.M. F. THOM rejoins company for duty.	
	14		Captain J.R. WARREN, M.C. takes Command of the company. AUTHORITY:- A.G.N.P.A/2238/630. Orders received to be prepared to move to forward area on 15th.	
	15	3-30 A.M.	Receive orders to move. Dismounted, sighs, water cart, proceed by train from WATTEN at mid-day after a march of 11 miles; and detrain at HOPOUTRE near POPERINGHE. Thence by road to Camp at A.29.b.6.0. By Map Belgium Sheet 28.N.W./20000	

WAR DIARY
or
INTELLIGENCE SUMMARY.

Army Form C. 2118.

401st (HIGHLAND) FIELD COMPANY, R.E.
VOL. XXX
Date 30th JUNE 1917.

Place	Date	Hour	Summary of Events and Information	Remarks and references to Appendices
CLERQUES	15		Transport 30 miles by road to HERZEELE & halt for night.	
CAMP AT A.29.b.6.0.	16		Transport rejoins company arriving in the afternoon.	
	17		Capt Warren with C.R.E. to canal bank abt C.25.a.7.7. Billets and work found for 2 Sections. Lts OKELL, HUNTER, CLEGHORN & JAMIESON reconnoitre canal banks & routes thereto. Capt WARREN with Lts HUNTER & CLEGHORN and Sections 1 and 2 move into billets on West Bank of Canal at C.25.a.7.6.	
CANAL BANK	18		Commence improving & extending billets. No 4 Causeway taken over by 2/Lieut CLEGHORN — an earthwork roadway, just commenced, to cross Canal at C.25.a.6.9. Chief problem, a culvert through causeway to take flow of Canal: material available, sleepers and spikes. Maintenance of Bridge 3B, a light pontoon bridge, and 4, a heavy trestle bridge, taken over by 2/Lieut HUNTER.	
	19-20		Small shelters started on West Bank over roofs of existing Chillin Bridge. 3.B repaired — pier set up over own sunk pontoons. Capt CLEGG & 1 O.R. on leave on 20th. Section 3 came up daily to work.	

Army Form C. 2118.

WAR DIARY
or
INTELLIGENCE SUMMARY.
(Erase heading not required.)

401st (HIGHLAND) FIELD COMPANY, R.E.
Vol. XXX
Date 30th JUNE 1917.

Instructions regarding War Diaries and Intelligence Summaries are contained in F. S. Regs., Part II. and the Staff Manual respectively. Title pages will be prepared in manuscript.

Place	Date	Hour	Summary of Events and Information	Remarks and references to Appendices
CANAL BANK	21-22		2nd LIEUT. MACGREGOR with Section 3 moves to Canal bank to stay. All work carried on.	
	23-24		Working party of 100 Infantry on high level shelter. 2nd LIEUT. JAMIESON attached to 400th Coy. Another pontoon sunk on Bridge 3B; another pier erected, 19 small shelters completed and occupied by 100 Pioneers who carry on work on these. 2. O.R's wounded on 24th.	
	25		Capt WARREN with MAJOR ALLAN of 400th Coy to reconnoitre line, and later with Lts OKELL & MACGREGOR. Working parties arranged for work on left half of front line, and on a dressing station about C.20.a.6.7. on HEADINGLY LANE. LT. MACGREGOR wounded while in charge of party carrying to front line. 2 LT OKELL with Section 4 relieve 2 LT. HUNTER and Section 2.	
	26-27		Work commenced on very low and badly enfiladed front of front line. Parapet to be raised, trench to be dug out and trench boards and traverses to be made. Also on Dressing Station. 6 large steel shelters to be dug in and covered. Two	

O.C. 401st (Highland) Field Coy. R.E.
Major, R.E.

WAR DIARY or INTELLIGENCE SUMMARY.

(Erase heading not required.)

Army Form C. 2118.

401st (HIGHLAND) FIELD COMPANY R.E.
Vol. XXX
Date 30th JUNE 1917

Place	Date	Hour	Summary of Events and Information	Remarks and references to Appendices
CANAL BANK	26-27		To be deepened & large camouflage screens to be made to hide excavations. Lt JAMIESON rejoins company on 27th.	[initials]
	28		All work carried on. 2 more pontoons sunk on Bridge 3B and 2 more piers erected by Section 1. Canal Banks heavily shelled. Company transport bringing up R.E. stores at night caught in barrage. Lt HORNE killed & 1 wounded. 1 O.R. wounded, 1 shell shock. No 402108 2nd Corpl G. YULE does very good work in attempting to bring up stores during heavy shelling before & after casualties are incurred.	[initials]
	29-30		Bridges on Canal Bank continue to be shelled. Section 1 complete culvert. Front line made easily passable in daylight which it had not been. Trench boards and parados still require in the front portion. Section 2 relieves section 3 on this work. Section 3 to hindlines. Excavation for Dressing Station shelter commenced. Camouflage of wire netting on large frames, with strips of green canvas to imitate grass laid over pit by day.	[initials]

Major R.E.
O.C. 401st (Highland) Field Coy, R.E.

Army Form C. 2118.

WAR DIARY
or
INTELLIGENCE SUMMARY.
(Erase heading not required.)

401st (HIGHLAND) FIELD COMPANY, R.E.
No. Vol.: XXX
Date 30th JUNE 1917

Instructions regarding War Diaries and Intelligence Summaries are contained in F. S. Regs., Part II. and the Staff Manual respectively. Title pages will be prepared in manuscript.

Place	Date	Hour	Summary of Events and Information	Remarks and references to Appendices
	15-30		Sections in rest at A.29.6.6.0. employed in improving Camp & Horse Lines in repairing pontoons, in digging a well, and in making camouflage screens. Company transport employed in carting R.E. stores from Corps R.E. dump at PESELHOEK to RAILWAY COTTAGE dump and MARENGO HOUSE dump near CANAL BANK.	
			Casualties during month:– 1 Officer & 3 other ranks.	
			Reinforcements received during month:– 4 other ranks.	
			No. of Officers & men on leave during month:– 1 Officer & 6 other ranks.	
			Transfers during month:– 2 other ranks transferred to 408 (Highland) Reserve Field Co. R.E. – Candidates for Commissions.	
			Roll of Officers with company at 30/6/17. – Major J.R. WARREN, M.C., CAPTAIN W.C. GLEW. Lieut. T.J. GORDON, M.C., 11 Lieuts. C. ORELL, S.J. HUNTER, J.S. CLEGHORN, D. JAMIESON. 2 Lieut. F.B. RITCHIE transferred to 17/11 Black A.T.C., R.E. Authority A.G.T.P.A/2/1977 A/4-2-17.	

CONFIDENTIAL
No 21(A) Vol 30
HIGHLAND
DIVISION.

401st (HIGHLAND) FIELD COMPANY. R.E.
No. —
Date 31/7/17.

WAR DIARY

OF

401ST (HIGHLAND) FIELD COY R.E.

— FOR —
— JULY —
— 1917 —

VOL: XXXI

Army Form C. 2118.

WAR DIARY
or
INTELLIGENCE SUMMARY.
(Erase heading not required.)

401st (HIGHLAND) FIELD COMPANY, R.E.
No. XXXI Vol...
Date 31st July 1917.

Place	Date	Hour	Summary of Events and Information	Remarks and references to Appendices
	1-5		Major Warren, 2/Lt Orr, 2/Lt Hunter & 2/Lt Cleghorn revise Sections 4, 2 and 1 on Canal Bank. Section 4 working by night on Dressing Station in support line. Excavation commenced 20' long x 2' wide, and revetted. 1 span required by a shell and has to be dug out. Work regularly shelled. Section 2 working on front line, digging a control trench about 5 ft. behind fire trench between traverses, raising parapet & making firesteps for fire trench, deepening fire trench & laying trench boards in fire trench & control trench. Night parties — 1 carrying party of 50 and 1 digging party of 50. Day parties — 2 parties of 7. Section 1 improving cover and improving Coy and other billets on Canal Bank. Day party of 20. Billets occasionally heavily shelled — notably on 2nd when 2 Coy billets were rendered uninhabitable. Capt. Gregg returns from leave on 4th. 2/Lt Cleghorn & Section 1 relieved by 2/Lt Jameson and section 3 on 5th.	
	6		Pioneers trouble under shelling at Dressing Station. 2 man dugouts	

Major, R.E.

O.O. 401st (Highland) Field Coy. R.E.

Army Form C. 2118.

WAR DIARY
or
INTELLIGENCE SUMMARY.
(Erase heading not required.)

401ST (HIGHLAND) FIELD COMPANY, R.E.
No. V.O.S.: XXXI
Date 31st JULY 1917.

Instructions regarding War Diaries and Intelligence Summaries are contained in F. S. Regs., Part II. and the Staff Manual respectively. Title pages will be prepared in manuscript.

Place	Date	Hour	Summary of Events and Information	Remarks and references to Appendices
			Flagshifts commenced on excavation, but Headingly Lane was shelled and screen knocked off. Towards dusk work was again shelled, 200 S.9's being reported as landing in the neighbourhood & trench destroyed. Excavation possibly observed from the air whilst screens were off. Work suspended & new site chosen on old trench at C.20.a.9.7.	Apl.
	7-9		Section 3rd interchange work. Section 3 take dressing station, section 4 take shelter on Canal Bank. Better progress made with Dressing Station in spite of regular barrage a short distance in front. R.A.M.C. party increased to 35. Other work as usual. No work on front line on night 7/8th owing to Boster relief.	Apl.
	10		11/Lt Jamieson killed on morning of 9th while at Dressing Station some distance Conference of O.C.'s R.E. & Pioneers at R.E. Headquarters to discuss general arrangements of R.E. & Pioneers on operations. 3 sections 400 & 401 Coys to be on Canal Bank. 404 Coy to be divnl. reserve on intermediate filler. 2 sections of Coy to be detailed for strong points work 152 Brigade on	Apl.

Major, R.B.
O/C 401st (Highland) Field Coy, R.E.

Army Form C. 2118.

WAR DIARY
or
INTELLIGENCE SUMMARY.
(Erase heading not required.)

Instructions regarding War Diaries and Intelligence Summaries are contained in F. S. Regs., Part II. and the Staff Manual respectively. Title pages will be prepared in manuscript.

401st (HIGHLAND) FIELD COMPANY, R.E.
Vol. XXXI
No. 3
Date 31st July 1917.

Place	Date	Hour	Summary of Events and Information	Remarks and references to Appendices
	12		In Regtl. Int. sector) 1 section to maintain & repair footbridges over canal, 1 section to be in reserve in intermediate pillbox. Work carried on without casualties. 152nd Brigade relieve 154 Brigade. Section 1 relieve section H.	W.
	13		3 Field Coys to move from Canal Bank to CHATEAU DES TROIS TOURS. Night work much impeded by 1) Barrage 2) Batt'n relief 3) Gas alarm. Front line parties failed to get up. Three parties attend to & party of 40 carrying and 2 of 40 each digging. Sapper STYLES killed in front line during day. 1 O.R. wounded in Canal Bank.	W.
	14		Section 1 commence construction of shelter at TROIS TOURS and dug out here. Arrange to hand over Dressing Station to 57th Field Coy on night 14/15. 1 Sensation by 33rd Brigade. 11th Division retro take over survey parties for night of 16 only. Section 1 continue at TROIS TOURS. Other work as usual. 152nd Brigade relieved. Arrangements made to move remaining 2 sections to TROIS TOURS.	W.

J.P. [signature]
Major, R.E.
O/C 401st (Highland) Field Coy, R.E.

Army Form C. 2118.

WAR DIARY
or
INTELLIGENCE SUMMARY.
(Erase heading not required.)

401st (HIGHLAND) FIELD COMPANY, R.E.
Vol. XXI No. 4.
Date 31st July 1917.

Place	Date	Hour	Summary of Events and Information	Remarks and references to Appendices
	14		Captain Glegg to Canal Bank, Major Warren to Transport lines. Section 4 relieve section 2. Section 1 continue erection of shelters at TROIS TOURS CHATEAU.	Nil.
	15		Day work continued as above. No work carried out at night owing to no working parties were available. No 1 and 3 sections move to TROIS TOURS at night. No 4 section proceeds direct here from transport lines.	Nil.
	16		No 1 Section continue work at TROIS TOURS. No 3 and 4 sections carry on work on front line as before. Morning and day provided for to-night only by permanently by 33rd Inf Brigade. Night party provided for to-night only by 33rd Brigade.	Nil.
	17		Work as above continued. Night working parties obtained from 8 East Yorks (morning) Nil.	
	18		Work as above, continued. One company 1/7" Argyll & Sutherland High. allotted to Company for night working parties. Work at front lines much disrupted by gas shelling. — No 2 section commence construction of NISSEN huts at E. Camp, A.30. central.	Nil.
	19		Work as above, continued. No 1 section commence construction of brick piers at	Nil.

Major, R.B.
O.C. 401st (Highland) Field Coy. R.E.

Army Form C. 2118.

WAR DIARY
or
INTELLIGENCE SUMMARY.
(Erase heading not required.)

401st (HIGHLAND) FIELD COMPANY, R.E.

No. Vol. XXI
Date 31st JULY 1917

Instructions regarding War Diaries and Intelligence Summaries are contained in F. S. Regs., Part II. and the Staff Manual respectively. Title pages will be prepared in manuscript.

Place	Date	Hour	Summary of Events and Information	Remarks and references to Appendices
	19		Piers for spans bridges for CANAL. Work at front line delayed by gas shelling. No 2 section continue erection of NISSEN huts.	
	20-24th		Captain Gagg to transport lines, Major Mearns to TROIS TOURS on 20th. Section 1 on preparation of 2 barrel-pier footbridges to take infantry in single file. These are to be moved in canal ready for rafting out on assembly if necessary. Sections 2 and 3 on front line. A large amount of maintenance work is now necessary, both in front line and in communication trenches owing to shelling. Work is much impeded by shelling, and particularly by gas shells. Some of a new type. The area behind the canal banks also fairly heavily shelled at times, causing casualties. Our bombardment in full swing, in vicinity of TROIS TOURS.	
	25		Conference at R.E. Headquarters. New front instructions given by C.R.E., M.R.E. Liaison officer to be at 159 Brigade Hd. Qrs. in LANCASHIRE FARM to keep in touch with the situation and assist work when sections may move up to sites of bridges 2 to be the 28th.	

Major, R.E.
O.C. 401st (HIGHLAND) FIELD COY., R.E.

Army Form C. 2118.

WAR DIARY
or
INTELLIGENCE SUMMARY.
(Erase heading not required.)

401st (HIGHLAND) FIELD COMPANY. R.E.
No. Vol. XXXI
Date 31st July 1917.

Place	Date	Hour	Summary of Events and Information	Remarks and references to Appendices
	25		Action & start furnishing of 153 Brigade Headquarters and 3 Battn Headquarters. 2/Lt. HUNTER wounded.	Afk.
	26		2 Platoons 3 days. Rain. Increasing amount of maintenance required on trenches. 33rd Brigade Battn unable to cope with this. FUSILIER & ELGIN Avenue in Afk.	Afk.
	27		Enemy reported withdrawn from front system. 33rd Brigade sent forward patrols which however do not get much beyond front line and have to come back after some losses.	
	28		Work on front lines, bridges and Brigade & Battn Headquarters, large number supplied by members of troops living in these abbatis & tunnels. Expediting Crossing of Rbn. 2/Lt. STEEL 1/5th Royal Scots reports to take place of 2/Lt HOOPER. 153 Brigade relieve 33rd Brigade in evening. A low wire fence erected behind front line as extreme left for forming up on. Much maintenance work.	Afk.
	29		1, 2 & 3 Sections move to Canal Bank, leaving Headquarters and 4th Coy. Section 4 remains at TROIS TOURS. 3 days rations sent up.	Afk.

Major, R.B.
O.C. 401st (Highland) Field Coy, R.E.

Army Form C. 2118.

WAR DIARY
or
INTELLIGENCE SUMMARY.
(Erase heading not required.)

401st (HIGHLAND) FIELD COMPANY, R.E.
No. Vol. XXI
Date 31st July 1917

Place	Date	Hour	Summary of Events and Information	Remarks and references to Appendices
	29		Section 2 commence souring trees in front of Canal, obstructing for C/255 Batty. Evro Blankets fitted in Brigade & Batt. Headquarters — 7 in all. Other work in progress. Brig. Gen. GORDON, wounded & Brig. Maj. 153 Brigade, killed. 2 Platoons of 7th Arg. H. & Sutherland Hd. rafting mat. are attached & sent to live at TROIS TOURS.	Apb.
	30		Section 2 recorts our front line, completing friendstrips to be used for steps out of trench. Sections 2 and 3 clear & hunge out FUSILIER TRENCH for tanks coming up to front line. Section 1 complete arrangements for repair of bridges — bring up approach materials and have a tank assembly of barrel pier bridges. Parts of sections 1 & 2 fell to trees already cause through to Enable Battery to fire.	Apb.
	31		Zero hour 3·50 a.m. Word from liaison officer, Lieut ALLAN, 4ou Coy, about 10 a.m. that all objectives have been taken & that strong points may be proceeded with.	Apb.

Major, R.E.
O.C. 401st (Highland) Field Coy, R.E.

WAR DIARY
or
INTELLIGENCE SUMMARY.

(Erase heading not required.)

Army Form C. 2118.

401st (HIGHLAND) FIELD COMPANY, R.E.
Vol. XXI
Date 31st July 1917

Place	Date	Hour	Summary of Events and Information	Remarks and references to Appendices
	31		Major WARREN & 11 Lt STEEL with 1 NCO & 3 sappers forward to reconnoitre. Call at 152 Brigade Headquarters and are instructed by Brig. Gen'l BURN that only forward Strong Point will be required. 1 Corporal sent back to bring forward Section 2 and 1 platoon sappers mates. 2 hours later to BELLE ALLIANCE dump. Reconnoitring party forward to VON WERDER HOUSE in front of which 1 platoon & 2 Vickers gun teams are established. Arrangements made with platoon commander & M.G. officer to make strong point here & have it manned on completion. Cavalry now advancing to STEENBECK about 1.30 p.m. They came under M.G. fire some hundreds of yards behind the STEENBECK, but continued to advance & disappear into the hollow. Major WARREN sends guide back to BELLE ALLIANCE dump & sends forward Section 2 & sappers mates who took tools & sandbags. 11 Lt STEEL remains at VON WERDER HOUSE on arrival of party successfully complete Strong Point. Owing to smallness of Party and of garrison, a simple type is made, as our sketch.	

```
         →
  ┌──┐ ┌────┐
  │  │ │    │
  │12'│ │10' │  MG.
  │  │ │    │
  └──┘ └────┘
  MG.     →
```

O.C. 401st (Highland) Field Coy. R.E.
Major, R.E.

Army Form C. 2118.

WAR DIARY
or
INTELLIGENCE SUMMARY
(Erase heading not required.)

401st (HIGHLAND) FIELD COMPANY, R.E.
No. Vol. XXXI
Date 31st May 1917.

Place	Date	Hour	Summary of Events and Information	Remarks and references to Appendices
			This was covered by a thin hedge about 50' in front and has a fair field of German wire about 40' in front. During construction enemy attempted 2 counter attacks & strong point had to be manned. M.G's got on to enemy who never got within 600' of position. Section 3 + 1 platoon supplies unarmed were kept for emergency work but were not required. I have practically no repair work to do on bridges and frames piers bridges were not required. During the month the Coy was engaged in preparing for the offensive. Work was fairly uneventful, but working strength of sections was low owing to numbers of men on leave, and numbers detached for special work. Front line work was perhaps done too thoroughly on parts, and other parts rather neglected in consequence, but this was partly due to great amount of maintenance work which had to be done in the latter part of the month. Work was much hampered by gas shelling. On Z day arrangements were found to be adequate.	

Major, R.E.
O.C. 401st (Highland) Field Coy. R.E.

2353 Wt. W2544/1454 700,000 5/15 D. D. & L. A.D.S.S. Forms/C. 2118.

Instructions regarding War Diaries and Intelligence Summaries are contained in F. S. Regs., Part II. and the Staff Manual respectively. Title pages will be prepared in manuscript.

Army Form C. 2118.

WAR DIARY
or
INTELLIGENCE SUMMARY.
(Erase heading not required.)

401st (HIGHLAND) FIELD COMPANY, R.E.
No. V.24.; XXXI
Date 31st JULY 1917.

Place	Date	Hour	Summary of Events and Information	Remarks and references to Appendices

Casualties during month :- 1 Officer & 1 O.R. Killed; 1 Officer & 2 O.R's wounded.
Reinforcements received during month :- 6 O.R's
No. of Officers & men on leave during month :- 1 Officer, 31 other ranks.
Transfers to other units during month :- 4 Drivers to No. 6. R.E. Reinforcement Co'y
Transfers from other units during month :- 207442 Sapper G.H. R.E. (other rank); 1/8 Aberdeen Bn. 10R.
Roll of Officers with Company at 31/7/17 :- MAJOR. J.R. WARREN M.C., CAPTAIN. W.C. GLENN.
LIEUT. T.J. GORDON, M.C., 11/LIEUTS. C. OKELL, J.S. CLEGHORN.

JRW.

Major, R.E.
O.C. 401st (Highland) Field Coy. R.E.

Secret

Da 9
  3rd Echelon, Base.

Herewith Copy Report on Operations
July 31st to Augt 1st 1917 — to be filed
with August War Diary. This report
was not forwarded sooner, owing to
official report not being received in this
Office until a few days ago.

[Stamp: 401ST (HIGHLAND) FIELD COMPANY, R.E. 15-10-17]

R. ___ Capt
for O.C. 401st (Highland) Field Coy. R.E.

Report on the Operations of the 51st (Highland) Division N.E of Ypres July 31st to August 1st 1917

INDEX

Section I.   The Preparations   Pages 1 to 5

		Pages
	Terrain	1
	Objectives	2
	Dispositions	2 & 3
	Barrage	3 & 4
	Cavalry	4
	Engineers, Tanks & Aeroplanes	5
	Assembly	5

Section II.   The Battle

First Phase: to the BLUE OUTPOST LINE

General		1
Bn. Narratives	1/5th Seaforth Highrs	1 & 2
	1/8th A & S.H	2
	1/7th Gor. Highrs	3
	1/7th Blk. Watch	4

Position at 5.15 a.m. — 4

Second Phase: THE BLACK & BLACK OUTPOST LINES

General		5
Bn. Narratives	1/6th Gor. Highrs	5 to 7
	1/6th Sea. Highrs	7 & 8
	1/6 Blk. Watch	8 & 9
	1/5th Gor. Highrs	9 & 10

Position at 7-30 a.m. — 10 & 11

Third Phase: The GREEN LINE & TRANS STEENBEEK POSTS

Bn. Narratives	1/6th Gor. Highrs	12
	1/6th Sea. Highrs	12 to 14
	1/6th Blk. Watch	14 & 15
	1/5th Gor. Highrs	16

Situation at Nightfall — 17
The Relief — 18
Casualties — 19

Tanks — 5, 6, 7, 8, 13 & 18
Cavalry Action — 13
Artillery (see also pages 3 & 4 Section I) — 4 & 10 & 17
Engineers (see also page 5 Section I) — 11 & 17

Preliminary Summary.

Before describing in detail the part played by the 51st (Highland) Division in the battle N.E of YPRES on the 31st of July 1917, the results obtained on the Divisional front may be briefly summarised:—

The enemy front over a width of over 1400 yards was pushed back from 2600 yards on the right to 3200 yards on the left. The front, support and reserve lines of the first system, the STOTZPUNKT line and the fortified places between that and the STEENBEEK were captured and the enemy definitely driven back to the LANGEMARCK LINE covered by outpost positions.

Between the 1st and 4th August a complete line of posts on East Bank covering the crossings of the STEENBEEK was established by the 154th Infantry Brigade.

Prisoners numbered 15 officers and 624 Other Ranks; 2 field guns 4 trench mortars and 29 machine guns (many destroyed in addition were taken.

Previous to the battle each Infantry Brigade had a tour of duty in the line, and thus acquainted with the conditions withdrew to practice the attack over a full sized taped out course at ST. MOMELIN.

The artillery began the preliminary bombardment and wire cutting on the 16th July, firing daily approximately 3500 rounds from 18-pdrs, 1000 from 4.5" hows, and 400 from trench mortars. The difficulties were considerable – the HIGH COMMAND REDOUBT just behind the enemy front line opposite the centre of the Division front, overlooked every battery position in our lines and prevented observation by us of any part of the enemy's trench system excepting the front line.

The various objectives boundaries between Divisions and Brigades are shewn on Map No 1.

The terrain over which the Division had to attack was remarkable for the fact that, with the exception of the enemy front line no portion of the ground could be seen and consequently the bombardment of the enemy wire and trenches was dependant entirely on aerial observation.

What was known as the HIGH COMMAND REDOUBT in the German front line to a great extent looked down on our communication trenches and a considerable portion of the ground immediately in the rear of our front line.

Although some of the numerous concrete erections which the enemy had constructed had escaped detection on the air photographs and came as a surprise to our attack, it is noteworthy that the wire on the BLACK LINE had been thoroughly destroyed before ZERO day. This may be taken as one of the few instances of strong wire being completely delt with without ground observation.

From HIGH COMMAND REDOUBT to the STEENBEEK, the ground falls gradually with no pronounced irregularities.

The RIVER STEENBEEK was fordable on the day of the battle. There were 5 Bridges capable of taking field guns and numerous light infantry bridges on the Divisional Front.

A good deal of rain fell during the week preceding the attack and the ground shell torn as it was was in a bad state all the way and especially in the German front line system at the BLACK LINE & near the STEENBEEK.

The

2.

The Main Objective — The main objective of the Division was — a line immediately South of the STEENBEEK, known as the GREEN LINE — after the capture of which two companies were to push across the stream and hold two posts

Four Stages of Attack — The Attack was divided into four stages

1st Objective — The BLUE LINE: the enemy's front line system — firing line, support and reserve trenches with some fortified farms and blockhouses

2nd Objective — The BLACK LINE: The enemy's 2nd (KITCHENER) System — a deeply wired line of trenches 800 yards beyond the BLUE LINE supported in front and rear by many fortified farms and strong points

3rd Objective — The GREEN LINE — a line to be made South-West of the STEENBEEK, commanding the crossings

4th Objective — One company post at MON du RASTA on rising ground 200 yards beyond the STEENBEEK on the right front and one company post on the MILITARY ROAD, a similar distance beyond the stream on the left front.

Main Infantry Dispositions — The division attacked on a front of two Brigades 152nd Infantry Brigade (Brigadier-General H.P. BURN D.S.O Commanding) on the right and the 153rd Infantry Brigade (Lieut-Colonel H.G. HYSLOP D.S.O., 1/7th Bn A.&S.H Commanding) on the left: the 154th Brigade (Brigadier-General J.G.H. HAMILTON D.S.O Commanding) being held in reserve. Each Brigade attacked on a two battalion front, employing two Battalions to capture up to and including the BLUE DOTTED LINE and the remaining 2 battalions to continue the attack as far as the GREEN LINE. (Map N°5).

On the 29th July Brigadier General A.I. Gordon C.M.G D.S.O., Commanding 153rd Infantry Brigade was mortally wounded and Captain H.H. McLEAN M.C. his Brigade Major killed by a shell whilst inspecting the front line trenches

Enemy's Trench System & Dispositions — Opposite the Divisional front the enemy were holding the line on a front extending to about 400 yards to our Right and 100 yards to our left with the 392nd I Rgt. 23rd (Res) Saxon Division. This division was in process of being relieved by the 3rd Guards Division on the morning of our attack; the WILHELM STELLUNG (LANGEMARCK LINE) and the ALBRECHT STELLUNG (BLACK LINE) had been relieved on the nights of the 28th and 29th July and the front line system was in course of changing hands at ZERO

The enemy's front line system was from 300 to 500 yards deep; the BLACK LINE was 1100 to 1500 yards from the firing line; and the LANGEMARCK LINE about 1500 yards beyond the STEENBEEK.

Thos

The two regiments of the Division had one battalion in front, one at the BLACK LINE, and one in the LANGEMARCK line, the 3rd regt being held in reserve (Map No 4)

Artillery

Six Brigades of Artillery supported the Division in the attack:—
255th & 256th Brigades R.F.A. (51st Divisional Artillery) East of the CANAL; range to front line 2000 yards
58th & 59th Brigades R.F.A. (11th Divisional Artillery) West of CANAL; range to front line 3000 yards
77th & 282nd Army Brigades R.F.A. West of Canal; range to front line 3500 yards

They formed two equal groups each covering an Infantry Brigade. The front was divided into four lanes corresponding to the frontages of the four attacking battalions. Each battalion front was covered by one Brigade and in addition one Brigade was superimposed on each Infantry Brigade front; thus:—

153rd Infantry Brigade		152nd Infantry Brigade	
Battn Front	Battn Front	Battn Front	Battn Front
59th Brigade R.F.A.	255th Brigade R.F.A.	58th Brigade R.F.A.	256th Brigade R.F.A.
77th Brigade R.F.A.		282nd Brigade A.F.A.	
Left Group Lt. Col. M.M. Duncan C.M.G. comdg.		Right Group Lt Col. L.M. DYSON D.S.O comdg.	
255th Brigade R.F.A.		256th Brigade R.F.A.	
59th Brigade R.F.A		58th Brigade R.F.A	
77th Army Brigade R.F.A		282nd Army Brigade R.F.A	

This gave one 18-pdr for every 12½ yards of the front.

18 pdrs of four Brigades formed the creeping barrage; time shrapnel, one in four to burst on ground

18-pdrs

4.

18 pounders of two Brigades formed the Standing and Searching barrage; all 4.5" howitzers were in this barrage, but never firing nearer than 200 yards beyond the creeping barrage

Beyond this 6" howitzers and 60-pdrs put down another barrage

The barrage came down on the German front line at ZERO (3.50 A.M.) and lifted off it 6 minutes later. Thence it advanced at the general rate of 100 yards in 4 minutes; owing to the differences in dept to be penetrated by the infantry it progressed much more slowly at certain parts while swinging up at normal rate on the flank. (See barrage Map N° 3)

After reaching the objective the barrage "became Protective" for an interval — getting slower and slower though not altogether ceasing to advance, and then, as a warning to the Infantry, quickening up before resuming its advance at normal rate. Such protective barrages were put down 200 yards in front of the BLUE and BLACK outpost lines, in front of the GREEN line and again in front of the outpost line across the STEENBEEK

Immediately the barrage lifted in front of the BLUE outpost line the 77th and 282nd Army Brigades began to move forward, the first battery coming into action near our old front line in time (7-45 a.m.) to join in the GREEN barrage. Next, the 58th & 59th Brigades moved to positions in NO MAN'S LAND

Machine Guns
Of the 112 machine guns available — 64 of the 51st Division and 48 of the 11th Division — 64 were allocated to three successive barrages, covering the ground in front of the BLUE, BLACK & GREEN LINES, the two latter designed also to prevent the enemy from withdrawing guns across the STEENBEEK; 16 for consolidation under orders of the Brigadier-Generals Commanding and 32 were in reserve

Stokes Guns
Seven Stokes guns fired 277 rounds at ZERO on strong points in the enemy first system — 10 were moved forward with the Infantry at successive stages of the attack — 2 at the BLUE LINE, 7 at the BLACK LINE and 1 at the GREEN LINE.

Burning Oil and Thermite
206 Bombs filled with oil were thrown from Mortars at ZERO — 150 on enemy's support and reserve lines on the 152nd Infantry Brigade front and the remainder on the reserve line on the adjoining part of the 39th Divisional front. To assist in demoralizing the enemy just before the infantry attack, 150 shells filled with thermite were thrown in three minutes after ZERO at FORT CALEDONIA in the reserve line

Cavalry
One Squadron of the 1st King Edward's Horse was attached for the purpose of sending out patrols after establishing itself under cover of infantry posts beyond the STEENBEEK.

Tanks

5.

Tanks

Eight Tanks of XXI Co. "G" Battalion Heavy Branch Machine Gun Corps plus one supply Tank, crossed the CANAL BANK on X/Y night and at ZERO set off from a spot behind the centre of our support line in 2 echelons - the first, to mop up the BLUE and BLACK LINES and then to advance with the Infantry to the GREEN LINE and cover the crossing of the STEENBEEK; the second, to cross the Stream and cover the consolidation of the bridge heads.

Aeroplanes

Contact aeroplanes were provided by the 7th Squadron R.F.C. and picked up infantry flares on the BLACK & GREEN LINES.

Engineers & Pioneers

At Zero the C.R.E. had at his disposal the 400th 401st and 404th Field Co RE., 3 companies of the 1/8th Royal Scots (Pioneers) and a detachment of the 179th Tunnelling Company. Their tasks were to make four strong points; continue a main track and a road into the captured ground, complete the forward water supply and if necessary to throw 3 Field Artillery bridges across the STEENBEEK.

Headquarters

Divisional Headquarters	X Camp A.16.c.1.6.
Advanced Div Report Centre	CANAL BANK C.25.a.7.2.
152nd Inf. Bde. Headquarters	FOCH FARM C.20.d.05.95.
153rd Inf. Bde. Headquarters	LANCASHIRE FARM C.13.d.95.45

No 2 Map shows position of troops at ZERO hour.

The Assembly

On the night of the 28/29th July 152nd and 153rd Infantry Brigades took over with four companies each their own battle fronts, the remainder of the troops moving up Y/Z night. Hostile Artillery was exceptionally quiet on the night Y/Z and the assembly of the troops was carried out without incident. About half an hour before ZERO some shells fell in rear of 153 Brigade front line where 6th Black Watch were assembled and caused some casualties.

All men had a hot meal before starting for the line and a hot drink was issued from hot food containers on arrival in the trenches. In addition each man was issued with a special breakfast ration and chocolate from Divisional Funds.

II

The Battle

First Phase — UP TO THE BLUE OUTPOST LINE

A

152nd Infantry Brigade
1/5th Sea. Highrs - Right
1/8th A & S.H - Right Centre

153 Inf Bde
1/7 Gordon Highrs left
1/7 Black Watch Centre Left

The Division attacked at 3.50 a.m.

The morning was cloudy and the light still obscure at that hour, but the burning oil thrown on the enemy lines by our trench mortars at ZERO lit up the whole front.

An instant after the barrage opened the men of the first wave on the right were pouring through the numerous gaps in the wire, with the second wave getting over the parapet hard on their heels; on the left the first wave had been waiting beyond the wire.

There was no difficulty in getting to within 40 yards of the barrage — the distance generally observed — excepting that of getting round the many water-filled shell holes quickly enough without losing the proper extension and direction; the state of the ground made going heavy. Few enemy shells fell in No MAN'S LAND, and the first wave was almost on the objective before machine gun fire, and that at first of a very feeble kind, was encountered. The reply to our barrage did not come for nearly ten minutes and then fell on and in rear of the old front line.

The 5th Seaforth Highrs
Right
(Lt Col. J.M Scott D.S.O Commanding)

On the right (from C.15.d.25.75 to C.16.a.65.13) the 5th Seaforth Highlanders met with little resistance. "A" Company entered the enemy's battered front and support lines when the barrage lifted at ZERO plus 6 minutes, these were almost unrecognisable as trenches and few Germans were found in them. "B" Company passing through at once easily disposed of the reserve trench and switch lines which together formed the BLUE LINE; a few dugouts had to be bombed — one Lance Corporal unaided clearing two shelters and taking 5 prisoners. Next came two platoons of "C" company, which captured SANDOWN & WELSH FARMS without any resistance. One machine-gun falling to them and the few Germans who got away having a Lewis Gun turned on them sixty prisoners in all were captured

Consolidation was at once undertaken and was well advanced when the Protective Barrage lifted in front of the BLUE OUTPOST LINE. On the line of the two farms, the two platoons dug their part of the BLUE OUTPOST LINE but later were withdrawn

2

Owing to heavy shelling and dug in near "B" Company. which held the BLUE LINE; A Company at 9am. was withdrawn to old British front Line

Casualties:— 1 officer wounded
Other Ranks - Killed 23
Wounded 118
Missing 9

1/8th A.&S.H.
— Right Centre
(Lt Col R. CAMPBELL
D.S.O Commanding)

Meantime on the Right Centre (C.15a.65.13 to C.14b.80.23.) the 1/8th Argyll & Sutherland Highlanders, in three waves had taken their three objectives immediately on the lift of the barrage. Three platoons of "B" Company dealt with what was left of the front trench, and one platoon of "A" Company preceding "B" Company on the left in the rush cleared the ruined support line. Some casualties were caused by the wave getting too close to the barrage.

Passing through the first wave, 2 platoons of "A" Company on the Right and 3 platoons of "D" company on the left, captured CALEDONIA Reserve trench with little opposition. Beyond them one platoon of "D" Company took the ruins of BELOW FARM disposing en route of a party in a concrete shelter; and one platoon of "A" Company killed or captured the dozen men who were all that was left of the garrison of FORT CALEDONIA when it was reached by them.

MULLER COTTAGE, just beyond the reserve line had been so effectively levelled that it could not be discerned until full daylight revealed the scattered bricks which marked the site.

In all cases the waves, as instructed cleared the shell holes for 50 yards beyond their objective. The prisoners numbered 28.

Although the assaulting waves did not undergo as severe a test as their training prepared them for, there was still some scope for individual gallantry and for the exercise of initiative by the N.C.O's only five officers being left in the three companies. For example a sergeant carrying on when his platoon commander was wounded, himself killed two and captured three of the enemy, sited his outpost position excellently and maintained himself there under heavy shell fire later. One Lance Corporal rushed an isolated building himself; another tackled and killed 2 snipers

Casualties :- Officers — Killed 1
Wounded 4 (2 died of wounds)
Other Ranks Killed 14
Wounded 98
Missing 3

153rd Infantry Brigade.

3.

153rd Inf Bde.
1/7 Gordon Highrs
— Left Centre

(Lt Col I.A. de L. Long
Commanding)

On the Left centre and Left also, the advance was "going like clockwork". The two battalions concerned had half as far, again as the right battalions, to go and sent over four waves for the work.

On the Left Centre (from C.14.b.80.23 to C.14.b.1.1.) the 1/7th Gordon Highlanders advanced on a front of two companies each, on a front of two platoons. Their first wave, two platoons of "A" company on right and two platoons of "D" company on left, occupied the enemy front line without any difficulty; and their second wave similarly composed, after capturing beyond the front line a few Germans who had been throwing sling bombs, and some more in a machine gun emplacement, easily entered CALEDONIA SUPPORT to CAKE RESERVE.

Practically no opposition was encountered by the third wave (two platoons of "B" company on the right; two platoons of "C" company on the left) in taking NEW CALEDONIA trench.

The fourth wave (two platoons of "B" company and two platoons of "C" company), however, on the way to CALEDONIA RESERVE were troubled by snipers and a machine gun at HINDENBURG FARM and had a sharp tussle, in which rifle grenades and bombs played the chief part, before the farm was occupied; at least 10 Germans were killed and wounded and an officer and 22 other ranks were captured. On the right of the line too, a machine gun and some prisoners were captured. This formed the battalion's part of the BLUE LINE and from there a party was thrown out to make the BLUE OUTPOST LINE.

All objectives were taken by 5.5 a.m.

Battalion Headquarters advanced to HINDENBURG FARM at 11.15 a.m.

Casualties

Officers	Wounded	3
Other Ranks	Killed	7.
	Wounded	70.
	Missing	13.

1/7th Black Watch

4

**1/7th Black Watch
Left
(Lt. Col H.H. Sutherland)
D.S.O. Commanding**

On the Left (C.14.b.1.1. to C.14.a.40.25.) the 1/7th Black Watch, which had the greatest dept of German front to traverse, to reach the BLUE OUTPOST LINE, had the first wave formed up in NO MANS LAND about 2.35 a.m. Little opposition was encountered, and only slight casualties suffered in taking the first objectives, CAKE TRENCH & CAKE SUPPORT, and KRUPP & ESSEN FARMS a little way beyond were found to be nearly non-existent.

The second wave had a strong point in front of it in CAKE RESERVE but the machine-guns there were speedily silenced by a hail of rifle grenades backed by rifle fire, N.C.O's and men showing great promptitude and skill in tackling the situation. Here at 5 CHEMINS ESTAMINET, the pre-arranged meeting place touch was established with the 10th Welsh Regiment (38th Division)

Some resistance was offered to the third wave at HINDENBURG SWITCH, but here the Lewis gun and rifle grenades came into play, and over twenty prisoners were taken. Otherwise little trouble was found in occupying the BLUE LINE — the objective.

No great difficulty presented itself to the forth wave in advancing to the BLUE OUTPOST LINE where a strong point was established on the forward slopes of 23 METRE HILL.

Casualties:— Officers Wounded   2
Other Ranks Killed   14
             Wounded 105
             Missing   8

**Position at
5.15 a.m.**

Thus as planned, all objectives were taken, the BLUE LINE over half its length was well advanced in consolidation and many of the platoons in the OUTPOST LINE had dug good cover before the Protective Barrage lifted (5.13 a.m. on right, 5.9 a.m. on left) and resumed its forward movement at the rate of 100 yards per four minutes.

Meanwhile the waves for the BLACK LINE had come up and extended behind the barrage for the advance, and orders were given at 5.15 a.m. for the gun-limbers of two batteries to go forward, and for wagons to start getting ammunition ahead to new gun positions.

Consolidation of the captured area was carried out in depth, and landmarks such as trenches and farms were avoided, not for more than two hours after the BLUE and BLUE OUTPOST LINES were taken did any hostile shelling occur. Snipers however troubled platoons in the OUTPOST LINE during the first half hour after positions were taken up.

5.

B.   Second Phase   The Black & Black Outpost Line

152nd Inf Bde.
1/6 Gordon Highrs - Right
1/6 Seaforth Highrs
    Right Centre

On the advance to the BLACK LINE the character of the fighting changed. Until then the attacks had been directed against a system of closely linked trenches which, though affording by their position great possibilities of obstinate defence, were found to be very badly damaged and thinly held. Now while the ground was more strongly and stubbornly held, the fighting resolved itself into a series of struggles against isolated farms, blockhouses strongly built of concrete with double walls cellars, and wide machine gun loopholes.

152 Inf Bde.
1/6 Black Watch - Left
1/5 Gordon Highrs
    Left Centre

This was the only form of defence that withstood the bombardment.

The BLACK LINE (known at different portions of its length as CANNON, CANNISTER and CAKE TRENCH) was, it is true, before the bombardment a strong trench, deeply wired with several subsidiary trenches and communications to the front trench system; but it had been so badly smashed as not to present in itself a serious obstacle to the assaulting waves. On the other hand the concreted farms and blockhouses had suffered little damage. This had been foreseen, however. Every such separate objective had a platoon or two sections detailed to deal with it and the training given to the men in the methods of attacking strong points enabled them effectively and in most cases promptly to carry out their tasks. Rifle grenades, as the O.C., 1/6th Seaforth Highrs. reported, "saved the situation again and again."

Tanks in several of these actions hastened the surrender of the garrisons. The condition of the ground, to which one Battalion Commander applied the word "indescribable", badly hampered their movements; the infantry themselves found it fatiguing work merely to push ahead.

1/6 Gordon Highrs - Right
(Lt Col. Hon N Fraser M.C.
    Commanding)

On the right rapid progress was made by the 1/6th Gordon Highlanders, who "leap frogged" over the 1/5th Seaforth Highrs holding the BLUE OUTPOST LINE.

"A" and "D" Companies detailed for the capture of the BLACK and its OUTPOST LINE had began their advance at 4.20am. from NO MANS LAND (into which they moved at 4.10am when the old British front line was knocked about by enemy artillery). At the same time 2 platoons of "B" company detailed for VON WERDER HOUSE and ADAM'S FARM - beyond the BLACK OUTPOST LINE, but covered by the Protective Barrage - had set out from HARDY'S TRENCH overtaking "A" and "D" Companies on the BLUE LINE

The whole

The whole at 5.13 a.m., went steadily forward behind the barrage towards the BLACK LINE. There was only one skirmish of any consequence on the way. ASCOT COTTAGE, GATWICK HOUSE, NEWSON'S HOUSE and MINTY'S FARM were occupied without resistance; but an active machine gun between ASCOT COTTAGE and the line gave an opportunity for combined action by infantry and a tank. Engaging the gun with rifle grenades, the Gordons signalled "Tank Wanted" to Tank G43 (Gordons). The Tank fired, the infantry advanced and the gun quickly silenced about 12 of the enemy being killed or captured.

The BLACK LINE was occupied at 5.25 a.m. Most of the work had still to be done however. To the left of the battalion frontage, where there was considerable trouble, the BLACK LINE was not then occupied. A platoon of "D" Company pushed off to get in touch with 1/6th Seaforth Highrs on the left and captured a machine gun in this part of the line. Further along in the centre of the divisional frontage McDONALD'S FARM and MACDONALD'S WOOD were giving considerable trouble and this platoon on the fight at the Wood with flanking fire.

2 platoons of "A" Company had before this passed through the BLACK LINE — one towards HURST WOOD, the other to BOCHCASTLE and then on to KITCHENER'S HOUSE. On the northern edge of HURST WOOD, which was on the left of the battalion frontage, 2 machine guns were active; and here two platoons of "B" Company, whose destination was VON WERDER HOUSE further ahead, joined the "A" Company platoons in firing rifle grenades and working round the flanks. The fight was still in progress, the machine-guns being strongly posted in concrete emplacements, when Tank G44 came up. On its arrival the guns ceased firing and the infantry rushed in, 2 officers and 30 men being captured. This fight resulted in a loss of direction by all excepting one section of the 1½ platoons of "B" Company destined for VON WERDER HOUSE. Pushing on, the platoon and a section arrived at FRANCOIS FARM on the 1/6 Black Watch front where they took part in the fighting before finding their way to VON WERDER HOUSE.

The "A" Company platoon going to BOCHCASTLE and KITCHENER'S HOUSE, took its first objection and passed on to the HOUSE. Here there was a stiff little fight resulting in the capture of one officer and 12 other ranks and two light trench mortars. This post was then and for some time afterwards the most advanced on the front. It proved of great value in covering the consolidation of the BLACK OUTPOST LINE and so enabling the waves on the GREEN LINE to form up and get off right up to programme time.

Similar service

7.

Similar service was performed by the ½ platoon of "B" Company sent to ADAM'S FARM which was close up to the Protective Barrage and formed the extreme right of the OUTPOST LINE. The farm itself was occupied without resistance but a machine gun ahead gave trouble. The sergeant in charge, by skilfully getting his Lewis gun round the flank, while bringing fire to bear in front caused the Germans to abandon their gun and inflicted several casualties on them as they ran away.

To their left a section of "B" Company had been working towards VON WERDER HOUSE, also a very advanced post. Here they began consolidating and were later joined by the ½ platoons who had turned left and become involved in the fight at FRANCOIS FARM.

In the meantime the Company detailed for the GREEN LINE "C", which had left HARDY'S TRENCH at 4.50 a.m., had undertaken a fight not in its programme while on the way between the BLUE & BLACK LINES. Touch not having been obtained with the Battalion on the right (the 16th Rifle Brigade) the Company's right flank was pushed out over the Divisional boundary as far as RACECOURSE FARM. Finding a machine gun active between the Farm and KITCHENER'S WOOD, the Company knocked it out before proceeding up to the BLACK LINE Protective barrage, to re-organise for the advance on the GREEN LINE.

1/6th Seaforth Highrs
Right Centre.
Lt Col. S. McDonald DSO
Commanding

More opposition than that experienced by the 1/6th Gordon Highrs., was encountered on the Right Centre by the 1/6th Seaforth Highrs. after passing through the 1/8 Arg. & Suth. Highrs.

Of the two Companies detailed for the BLACK and BLACK OUTPOST LINE, one platoon captured FYSH FARM before the BLUE OUTPOST LINE Protective Barrage lifted: the remaining seven platoons were waiting in readiness when the barrage lifted forward. BRITTANIA FARM contained a strong undestroyed emplacement from which two machine guns played, and these offered the only obstacle before the assault on the BLACK LINE. Again the Lewis gun was got to work in front rifle grenadiers and riflemen working round to the rear and the two guns were rushed and 25 prisoners taken.

The BLACK LINE was reached under the barrage, a Tank close at hand labouring over the broken ground. Men of the 3rd Guards Division were here instead of the Saxons hitherto encountered, and, as was to be expected they put up a stiffer fight.

On the right of the frontage, where most of the trench was destroyed, the fight did not last long; the Guardsmen came out of half destroyed when the barrage lifted and opened machine gun and rifle fire but after several had been killed a great many surrendered and that part of the line was occupied.

It was

8

It was on the left, where the line enclosed the strong point of McDONALD'S FARM, backed 100 yards further on by McDONALD'S WOOD, that the sharpest struggle took place and where a good example of Tank and Infantry Co-operation was shown. The two platoons detailed for the BLACK OUTPOST LINE (which was to cover the northern edge of the wood) were the first to grapple with the Farm. A platoon of the 1/6th Gordon Highrs. aided with fire against the wood and Tank G 50 which had by its mere appearance on the scene, helped to reduce the line on the right joined in the fray. The Tanks put 6 shells into the Farm and this with the showers of rifle grenades and the rifle fire, brought out the Germans of whom a great many had been killed; more than 70 were taken prisoners and a 4.2" howitzer and 2 machine guns were captured here.

The Tank "GORDON" helped considerably in the consolidation of the BLACK OUTPOST LINE placing his Lewis Guns in position in the BLACK LINE under heavy fire.

There was much scattered fighting on the ground between woods in the Outpost area, and there were many displays of individual gallantry and initiative; as for instance, when a private advancing with another man, got a machine gun causing heavy loss to his platoon, he himself shooting 6 and capturing 4 Germans. A lance-corporal his party being hindered in consolidating on the BLACK LINE by hostile machine gun fire, led 4 men to a position enfilading the machine gun and with two of them rushed and captured it.

All this had taken place while the Proctective Outpost Barrage was resting its 1½ hours in front; and now the seven platoons for the GREEN LINE and MON DU RASTA who had come up from HARDY'S TRENCH formed up for the further advance.

Black Watch-Left Centre
(Lt.Col. T.M. BOOTH D.S.O. Commanding)

On the Left Centre the 1/6th Black Watch after passing through the 1/7th Gordon Highrs had severe fighting to clear the BLACK & BLACK OUTPOST LINES. Of the battalions engaged on the Divisional front, it incurred most casualties - 9 Officers, 292 other ranks.

The battalion suffered considerable in the half hour before ZERO while lying assembled immediately behind the old British front line and while waiting in front of the BLUE OUTPOST LINE to advance found that machine gun fire was being directed along the front of GOURNIER FARM, 400 yards ahead of the OUTPOST LINE, and about 100 yards in front of the BLACK LINE.

When the barrage

9.

When the barrage lifted No 1 platoon tackled this farm which by working round the flanks from shell hole to shell hole, it took at 5.27 a.m. with 20 prisoners and two machine guns — a lance corporal taking one of them and killing the two Germans in charge of it. This platoon further on captured a field gun.

Considerable fighting followed in and immediately beyond the BLACK LINE. Before 6 o'clock "B" Company had dealt with the dugouts — a private clearing three and killing 6 Germans himself — and occupied the line on the centre of the Battalion front

On the flanks heavy machine gun fire made progress slower. On the right the line (CANISTER TRENCH) took a right-angle turn continuing for 200 yards in a line perpendicular to the advance; this part of it was cleared by a platoon of the 1/6th Seaforth Highlanders working by half platoons from each end. At the northern end of it the machine guns of McDONALD'S FARM and McDONALD'S WOOD interrupted progress across the BLACK LINE to the OUTPOST LINE.

By 6.40 a.m. however, all the BLACK LINE on the Battalion front was occupied — confronted on the centre by machine gun fire from CANE WOOD — by "B","C", and "D" Companies and at about 7 a.m. touch was established with the 1/6th Seaforth Highlanders on the right.

About this time the Adjutant Lieut. J. ROTHERFORD while forward on a reconnaissance. Observing that a strong point in the BLACK LINE, 100 yards to the left of the Battalion front (at C.9.a.7.3.) was still holding out, organised the troops at hand, both Black Watch and Gordon Highrs, and supported by a Stokes mortar joined in the assault. About 100 prisoners were taken in this fight.

The ground to the BLACK OUTPOST LINE was being gradually cleared up and at 7.45 a.m. "B" Company took CANE WOOD including a strong point at the N.W. corner which yielded 12 prisoners

By this time the protective barrage has lifted towards the GREEN LINE and the depleted Battalion was pressing onwards

1/5 Gordon Highrs
Left
Lt Col. M.F. McTAGGART
D.S.O (Commanding)

On the left the 1/5th Gordon Highrs who passed through the 1/7th Black Watch encountered no defended farms up to the BLACK LINE, but machine guns posted ahead of the line in strong concrete emplacements undestroyed by the bombardment, put up a stout resistance.

These were vigorously assailed by "C" and "D" Companies who advanced first in extended waves, with "A" and "B" Companies in close support in artillery formation

A conspicuous

10.

A conspicuous example of gallantry was early given by 2nd Lieut Maitland Commanding "C" Company. Without waiting to organise a platoon attack he advanced single-handed on a machine gun which was firing from a shell hole just behind an emplacement. Jumping from shell hole to shell hole he worked round its flanks, rushed in, shot 2 of the team with his rifle, clubbed the third and captured the crew — Soon after this he was wounded.

Prolonged fighting took place in front of the line, rifle grenades being largely used to dislodge the gun teams. "C" and "D" Companies kept up the attack in front while 2 platoons of "B" Company joined with one of "D" in working round the German left flank; this was where the 1/6th Black Watch also attacked, and a Stokes gun lent effective aid. A Tank was signalled for but it unfortunately stuck in the mud and was unable to assist. A stubborn stand with machine guns, rifles and bombs was made, but by taking advantage of every shell hole the platoons managed to get ahead. The trench was entered simultaneously along the front, it was found to be filled with enemy dead mostly killed by rifle fire. The 100 prisoners included 2 infantry officers and an Army Doctor.

By this time the protective barrage was lifting and "A" and "B" Companies who had to establish the GREEN LINE, pushed forward at once.

Position at 7·30 a.m.

While the Infantry on the right were awaiting the lift of the barrage, for the advance on the GREEN LINE, and on the left were pushing on beyond the BLACK LINE closely behind it, the artillery had already gone forward in new positions between TURCO and LANCASHIRE FARMS just behind our old front line; the first battery there was in action by 7.45 a.m.

Machine guns and Stokes guns had been hurried forward as soon as the BLUE LINE was reported captured. Stokes mortars, on it being found that they were not needed in the BLUE LINE, were got forward to the BLACK LINE in time, as has shown in the Battalion narratives to take part effectively in the fighting there.

Machine Guns

Machine guns for "B" barrage on the ground between the BLACK and GREEN LINES were not able, owing to the heavy state of the ground, to reach in time their positions on the high ground at the extreme right of the BLUE OUTPOST LINE, but of the 16 guns for consolidation under the orders of the Brigadier-Generals commanding half were on their way to pre-arranged positions on the Black Line. Pack animals were bringing up ammunition to the guns an hour after they had reached positions. Carrying parties — the "Yukon Pack" was found very useful in this connection — were threading their way through the BLUE LINE, and half companies of the 1/8th Royal Scots had began work on a tracks and a road across No Man's Land while the Engineers were out reconnoitring at 23 METRE HILL for a strong point —

12.

Third Phase — Capture of The Green Line.
Trans-Steenbeek Posts
Counter Attacks

Advance from Black Outpost Line
152nd Inf. Bde.
1/6th Gor. Highrs. Right
1/6th Seaforth Hrs.
Right Centre

On the right, before the advance to the GREEN LINE was undertaken, the 1/6th Gordon Highrs. had firmly established themselves close under the protective barrage and "C" Coy. had thus, an excellent start forward from the BLACK OUTPOST LINE. Its progress was uninterrupted. There were no farms in the way and FLEMING'S WOOD, a half way mark, harboured no opposition. The GREEN LINE was reached at 7.50 am. and consolidation was begun about 250 yards S.W of the STEENBEEK.

Hostile aeroplanes flying low, watched the work. As soon as they retired the front line was moved forward 100 yards and the support line withdrawn an equal distance. The company commander soon afterwards had the satisfaction of seeing his original lines thoroughly shelled while his new positions escaped. (This Company had only 2 killed and 19 wounded when withdrawn at ZERO plus 1 day.

An exploit by Pte G.I. McIntosh is worthy of mention. Machine guns 60 yards beyond the STEENBEEK were playing on the Company front. Without any orders Pte McIntosh crossed the stream alone under fire, armed with a revolver and a bomb. Working round to the rear he threw a Mills Grenade into the emplacement, killing 2 Germans and wounding a third. He found two light machine guns which he brought back with him.

The 1/6th Gordon Highrs. in their advance from the BLUE OUTPOST LINE to the GREEN LINE, captured 4 officers and 130 Other Ranks. They took 3 machine guns (in addition 6 were destroyed) two trench mortars (not removed) and two anti tank guns (removed by some other unit). The casualties numbered 6 officers, 130 Other Ranks.

Advanced Battalion Headquarters —
Minty's Farm

1/6th Seaforth Highrs
Right Centre

On the right centre the 1/6th Seaforth Hdrs were allotted the task of establishing a post beyond the STEENBEEK at MON DU RASTA after capturing the GREEN LINE. One Company was detailed for the post, three platoons for the line. They passed through the BLACK OUTPOST area while fighting was proceeding at McDONALD'S WOOD on their left flank and lent a hand to its reduction.

Beyond the

Beyond the BLACK OUTPOST LINE half platoons occupied VANACKERT and PALACE FARMS without resistance; but at FERDINAND FARM, on the GREEN LINE 200 yards from the STEENBEEK, machine guns supported by machine gun and rifle fire from across the stream had to be fought. Lewis Guns were trained to sweep all vantage points on the further bank; Tank G.43 (GORDON) signalled for came up and silenced one machine gun in the enclosure, while the infantry accounted for the other and occupied the position. Under cover of their Lewis Guns the GREEN LINE Platoons then set to work to dig posts and get in touch on the flanks.

The Company for MON DU RASTA finding all the bridges and the river banks swept by hostile machine gun fire, dug in 100 yards from the stream and awaited an opportunity to cross.

Cavalry dig in near STEENBEEK.

While they were there, about noon, the Squadron of the 1st King Edward's Horse detailed to send out patrols under cover of infantry posts beyond the STEENBEEK, advanced from GOURNIER FARM, on receiving a message that the 1/6th Black Watch had crossed. They deployed in front of PALACE FARM but on reaching a line about 150 yards from the STEENBEEK came under heavy machine gun fire, suffering losses in men and horses, and dismounted. Half an hour later, under orders from the O.C. 1/6 Seaforth Highrs they dug in with their Hotchkiss guns near FERDINAND FARM in a position covering the MON DU RASTA remaining there until withdrawn next morning.

It was at this time that Sergt A. Edwards of the 1/6th Seaforths gave one of his many striking examples of courage during the battle. On the way forward he had led his men against a machine gun at McDONALD'S WOOD, wiping out the team and had alone stalked, and though wounded in the arm killed a sniper; when Major Swan of the Squadron fell wounded, he went out under heavy fire, dressed the Officer's wounds in a shell hole and helped him to the trench. Sergt Edwards was wounded next day in the leg, but refused to leave his platoon.

For some time the situation in front of the STEENBEEK remained stationary. Consolidation went steadily on under shell fire, machine gun and rifle fire. The Tank Gordon offered Lewis guns assistance but was not required and after waiting two hours, went back. Tank G.44 moved up and down the line until it received orders to return. Two machine guns intended for consolidation of MON DU RASTA took their place in the GREEN LINE; they fired altogether about 1000 rounds reserving their fire for good targets.

Then between

Then between three and four o'clock the enemy were seen on the left flank coming down the gentle slope on the opposite side of the STEEN BEEK, while a heavy barrage was put down in front of the BLACK OUTPOST LINE. This attempted counter attack failed; the combined fire from machine guns, Lewis guns and the men's rifles dispersed the attacking parties and sent them running back with heavy casualties.

Crossing the STEEN BEEK.

Taking advantage of this check to the enemy the trans-STEEN BEEK Company (which had been reinforced by 2 platoons from "C" Company 1/8th Argyll and Sutherland Highlanders) pushed parties across the stream, seized the bridge-heads opposite FERDINAND FARM, and rushed MON DU RASTA driving out the Germans and killing several and taking two in the process. Other parties were then pushed over and positions dug. At MON BULGARE a strong point was constructed with good post on either flank. Here a mortar of the 152nd Trench Mortar Battery was placed and with 30 rounds from it parties of the enemy were dispersed on the road in front running past MONDU RASTA. As however the enemy was in considerable force on the flanks and the STEEN-BEEK was becoming a torrent owing to heavy rain there was some danger of the detachment across the stream being cut off. It was therefore withdrawn with orders to hold the bridges.

The battalion took 2 officers and 276 other ranks prisoners, and captured a 4.2" howitzer and 9 machine guns. The casualties were:- Officers killed 3, wounded 7. Other Ranks killed 38 wounded 174 missing 21.

Advanced Battalion Headquarters BRITANNIA FARM.

153 Inf Bde.
1/6 Black Watch-Left Centre
1/5 Gordon His-Left

On the left centre and left the advance from the BLACK LINE towards the STEEN-BEEK was more gradual than on the right centre and right. It consisted of a series of attacks on the numerous farms that dotted the ground and the consolidation of successive small lines. The two battalions at this stage worked in close association, without meticulous regard for the demarcation line between the fronts.

1/6th Black Watch

When the BLACK protective barrage lifted forward at 7.14 am the 1/6th Black Watch were occupied with clearing out the nests of Germans with machine guns in the BLACK OUTPOST Area. "B" Company after taking at 7.45 am. a strong point at the west corner of CANE WOOD, in company with No 2 platoon of the 1/5 Gordon Highs pushed on to RODOLPHE FARM, which at 7.55 am yielded about 70 prisoners. Their next move was in conjunction with No 1 platoon of 1/5th Gordon Highs., the reduction, easily effected of a block-house 100 yards N.W. of the CEMETERY beside FRANCOIS FARM while the farm itself was being assailed by four Gordon platoons.

There at 8.40 am

There at 8.40 a.m. "B" Company, with a strength of 50 rifles was digging in on a line covering the farm. Meanwhile "C" and "D" Companies, much depleted, were pushing forward to the GREEN LINE. In front of CANE TRENCH (BLACK LINE) 40 men of "A" Coy. were consolidating, assisted by all spare men from Headquarters personnel; at 9.20 a.m. a company of the 1/7th Gordon Highrs. was sent off to assist in this consolidation taking up a position on their arrival on the right "A" Company, and in touch with the 1/6th Seaforth Highrs.

At 10.30 a.m. the O.C. Battalion made a reconnaissance of the GREEN LINE. Collecting 30 to 40 men of "D" Coy. at the gun pits on the road running parallel to the stream along the front from FERDINAND FARM, he took them with a few casualties across the STEEN-BEEK by the bridge N.W. of the MILITARY ROAD BRIDGE, and four posts were established on the rising ground a little North of the road.

The positions of the battalion when this operation was concluded were:— Remainder of "D" Coy - trans-STEEN-BEEK posts; "C" Company on FERDINAND FARM road; "B" Company on FRANCOIS FARM line; and "A" on BLACK LINE. A message was sent back to the Cavalry at GOURNIER FARM that the posts were across the stream.

These posts well dug in during the afternoon, had a severe ordeal. Three counter attacks - at 3.45 p.m. 4.0 p.m. and at 4.30 p.m. - were beaten off, at a low estimate 80 Germans being killed and wounded by Lewis Gun and rifle fire. A fourth counter attack was made at 6.5 p.m. after a heavy bombardment with gas and other shells, and owing to heavy casualties and the withdrawal of troops on the left, the parties were forced to return across the STEEN-BEEK to the Gun Pit Line. Here a strong point line commanding the stream was consolidated and standing patrols put out in front. Two platoons of the 1/7th Black Watch, which came up at 9.0 p.m. were placed in position N.W. of FERDINAND FARM, and at PALACE FARM.

The Battalion's casualties were:- Officers killed 2, wounded 7; Other Ranks killed 45, wounded 231, missing 116.

Advance Battalion Headquarters GOURNIER FARM.

1/5 Gordons

1/5th Gordon Hdrs-Left

On the left, "C", "D" and two platoons of "B" Coys of the 1/5th Gordon Hdrs had taken the BLACK LINE and "A" Coy and 2 platoons of "B" undertook the advance to the GREEN LINE.

No 2 platoon joined with the 1/6th Black Watch while Nos 3, 4, 7 and 8 Platoons, attacked the Farm from which 5 machine guns were firing. Here, as elsewhere, "dribbling" - the advance of small parties moving in twos from shell hole to shell hole - brought success; the defenders finding themselves unable to stop the advance, surrendered when the assailants were 50 yards away, the prisoners numbering 4 officers and 40 other ranks.

VARNA FARM, which also was found to be defended with three machine guns, was tackled by No 7 and 8 platoons in conjunction with troops of the 38 (Welsh) Division, whose right flank was close to the farm. Again the shell hole advance resulted in the surrender of the teams before a final rush could take place. About 20 prisoners were taken and a great many enemy dead were left in the position.

It was now 8.15 am. An outpost line was taken up running from VARNA FARM across the battalion front in a S.E. direction. At about 9.30 am. the front was established without opposition on the line of the INGS — COMEDY FARM, 250 to 300 yards from the STEENBEEK. Outposts were sent out to the stream and these later took up a position on the enemy side. They were withdrawn to the near side with the 1/6th Black Watch parties in the evening.

The battalion captured 7 officers and 160 other ranks (excluding wounded), and 10 machine guns.

The casualties were :— Officers killed 1, wounded 7; other ranks killed 49; died of wounds 9, wounded 171, missing 7.

Advanced Battalion Headquarters CANE TRENCH

C.9.a.70.15.

17

Situation at Nightfall

Each phase in the operations was closely followed up by other arms and services in accordance with pre-arranged plans and before nightfall the whole of the captured area had been powerfully organised (MAP No 6)

The first Battery of Artillery to go forward – "A" of 282nd Brigade A.F.A. – was in action at 7.45 am in a position just behind our old front line, and the next "B" of the 77th Brigade A.F.A. – in less than an hour afterwards. At 9.0 am the D's.L. 58 & 59th Brigades R.F.A. set out to reconnoitre for new positions and "A" Battery of the 59th Brigade was moving forward to the OLD NO MAN'S LAND at 11.40 am and "C" Battery of the 58th Brigade at 11.50 am.

The machine gun protective barrage of 18 guns was able to answer an S.O.S. signal in the afternoon from new positions near the BLACK LINE, and the 16 consolidation guns were all fired during the day, with 4 near FERDINAND FARM, 6 at FRANCOIS FARM, 2 at VON WERDER HOUSE, 2 at McDONALDS WOOD and 2 at CANE AVENUE

The 152nd Machine Gun Coy's barrage guns fired about 20,000 rounds on one S.O.S. call; the consolidation guns had not the same supply of ammunition, and reserved their fire for good targets. Two guns were knocked out.

The Engineers had constructed strong points at 23 METRE HILL, CANE AVENUE and VON WERDER HOUSE, by the afternoon; PILCKEM ROAD up to 5 CHEMINS ESTAMINET, a track across NO MAN'S LAND to join the old road beyond BELOW FARM, and boundary road up to KEMPTON PARK were put in condition, and the water supply point at LANCASHIRE FARM, with a track to the nearest road forward was completed.

Next days rations for the troops were at the BLACK LINE by 7.0 pm. – a fact which provides one illustration of the remarkable work done by the Pack Train, with its 328 mules. This first loads of S.A.A. were on their way three hours after ZERO to dumps at HORST PARK and GOURNIER FARM on the BLACK LINE; from then onwards S.A.A., Sandbags, Lewis Gun drums Very lights water and rations were carried up in a constant stream while daylight lasted. Only one mule was killed – an instance of the advantage of beginning quickly and in daylight during the comparatively undisturbed hours behind the fighting line that follow an attack

Telephone wires were out early to advanced battalion headquarters and no trouble was experienced about communications. In the early stages, pigeons were found a useful adjunct to the other means of communication; two were sent with each battalion to each line, and valuable information was brought back by this means. A dog sent from the GREEN LINE reached its destination 2 days later, minus collar and message

The Relief.

The Relief

Rain fell heavily during the night of 31st July/1st August and during the morning; from many a trench the men were flooded out and over the whole captured area movement was a matter of the utmost difficulty. The enemy suffering from a like disability, was quiet; and our men's spirit was shown by a message from a Company Commander in the GREEN LINE: "Water two feet deep but spirits very high!"

The Brigades were relieved during the afternoon and evening of 1st August by the 154th Inf Bde. To men who had fought a severe battle, endured the extremity of discomfort in the disused trenches and been without sleep for 60 hours, this relief was very welcome; but an incident on the "homeward" route showed how well their spirits had sustained the strain. Into one of the pool-like shell holes in a track a man stumbled, head under water. Nothing daunted, he proceeded to "quack" loudly and with a chorus of "quacks" his laughing comrades livened the whole of the march back to Camp.

Tanks Summary

8 Tanks plus one Cable laying were situated on the Divisional front as follows:-

G.49 — Stuck in BLUE LINE
G.41 — Stuck 200 yards beyond BLUE LINE
G.51 — Got to KITCHENER WOOD
G.45 — Silenced several machine guns en route to STEENBEEK where it supported infantry for several hours
G.50 — Up to VARNA FARM several fights on way
G.44 — Up to STEENBEEK VIA HORST PARK where it fought several machine guns
G.52 — Patrolled GREEN LINE
G.42 — Worked along BLACK LINE

G.12 (Cable) — Took signal gear to station between SANDOWN and HORST PARK.

19

Casualties.

The 152nd and 153rd Infantry Brigades went into action each with the approximate strength of 80 officers and 2,700 Other Ranks. Their casualties totalled 52 Officers (32.5%) and 1,516 Other Ranks (28.07%) made up as follows:

	Officers	O.R's	Officers	O.R.
152 Infantry Bde				
1/5th Seaforth Highrs	2	151		
1/6 Seaforth Highrs	10	240		
1/6 Gordon Highrs	6	174		
1/8 A. and S.H.	5	117		
152nd M. Gun Coy	2	16		
152nd T.M. Battery	1	4		
	26	702	26	702
153rd Infantry Brigade				
1/6th Black Watch	9	292		
1/7th Black Watch	2	129		
1/5th Gordon Highrs	8	236		
1/7th Gordon Highrs	3	124		
153rd M. Gun Coy	1	19		
153rd T.M. Battery	1	13		
153rd Bde H.Q.	2	1		
	26	814	26	814
		TOTAL	52	1,516
51st Div Artillery	0	12		

Vol 31

War Diary
of
401st Highland Field Co. R.E.
for
August
1917

Vol XXXI

Army Form C. 2118.

WAR DIARY
or
INTELLIGENCE SUMMARY

(Erase heading not required.)

Instructions regarding War Diaries and Intelligence Summaries are contained in F. S. Regs., Part II. and the Staff Manual respectively. Title pages will be prepared in manuscript.

401ST (HIGHLAND) FIELD COMPANY, R.E.
Vol. XXVII
31st Aug 1917

Place	Date	Hour	Summary of Events and Information	Remarks and references to Appendices
CANAL BANK 1000 yds N. of YPRES	1.		Weather breaks down. Major Mearns to 152 Brigade A.Q. and 6th Gordon H.Q. to find out what is required. It is decided to start an infantry track from GATWICK Cor. forward, and to divert some weather proof shelters for infantry near MINTY FM. Section I to commence the track, using casual bundles, &c. Section IV out just for 40 men in CALENDAR Tr. Who wanting huts, dugouts &c are sorting wagons, and layout (repair) &c dugouts &c has been made.	
	2		154 Brigade relieve 152 and 153 Brigades. Section II and II move dugouts materials nearer the track & begin the left side of MINTY FM. Weather bad and track much shelled. One sapper wounded. Lieut ORR gone on leave. Major Mearns and Lieut Clayton Jn reconnoitre STEENBEEK, found to be practically unfordable, but 3 large bridges and 9 footbridges needed in fairly good condition in	Major R.E. O.C. 401st (Highland) Field Coy. R.E.

WAR DIARY or INTELLIGENCE SUMMARY

(Erase heading not required.)

Army Form C. 2118.

401ST (HIGHLAND) FIELD COMPANY, R.E.
Vol. XXXII
Date 31st Aug 17

Place	Date	Hour	Summary of Events and Information	Remarks and references to Appendices
	2/3		On right half of Divl. Sector. Section I & 2 continue track towards HOPST BOSCH. Supplies which arrived on carrying party. Roads very bad and transport difficult in getting forward period. Impossible to dig trenches. No. 3 Sec. SCOTLAND attacked from 4.0-4.12 Coy.	
	3		Sections I and II continue track towards VON WERDER HO. work with Australians. Mats not available and material can not be placed. Second reclaiming enemy station. Additional accommodation opened up in MAIN Rd. Three dugout shelters in VON WESPER Ho prepared and extra shelter put in well buildings being dug out. Weather improves.	
	4/5		Brigade decide that present big trench may be passed to STEENBECK. Major Bowen and Walter Scotland forward to arrange for digging this. Infantry all found to have gone back to zone in front of STEENBECK. on right of Divl. Sector.	

Army Form C. 2118.

WAR DIARY
or
INTELLIGENCE SUMMARY.
(Erase heading not required.)

Instructions regarding War Diaries and Intelligence Summaries are contained in F. S. Regs., Part II. and the Staff Manual respectively. Title pages will be prepared in manuscript.

401st (HIGHLAND) FIELD COMPANY, R.E.
No. VOL.XXII.
Date 31st Aug 17

Place	Date	Hour	Summary of Events and Information	Remarks and references to Appendices
A.27.b.3.S.	5.		Section III continue track towards VON WERDER Ho. along park enclosure He. Section I clears some trees from Von Werder Ho. to the Mon D. Rajta bridge.	
Hq Huts BELGIUM SHEET 28 N.W.	6		Mon Steenbeck. Section IV (Cinys. than bogs) for infantry E. of Steenbeck. Orders received to work on the 7th by the 86 Field Coy. Acquiring trenches will not be required by the 154th Brigade. O.C. 86th Field Coy shown round ample. Section III continues track. Section I to advance Bhase road Steenbeck for advance on wheels. 11th Divn relieves 51st Divn.	Yes. Yes. Yes.
	6/7 7		Iron now track ready for advancing to make new Hd. Qrs. for O.C.E. Bullets in Canal bank Square area pt 8846.	
			Section moves return to Hutments. Section I continue work on New Hd Qrs. Remaining section was inspected for advance in morning & W. section bathed in afternoon.	Yes. Yes.

O.C. 401st (Highland) Field Coy., R.E.
Major R.E.

Army Form C. 2118.

WAR DIARY
or
INTELLIGENCE SUMMARY.
(Erase heading not required.)

401ST (HIGHLAND) FIELD COMPANY, R.E.
No. ....
Date 31st Aug 17.

Instructions regarding War Diaries and Intelligence Summaries are contained in F. S. Regs., Part II. and the Staff Manual respectively. Title pages will be prepared in manuscript.

Place	Date	Hour	Summary of Events and Information	Remarks and references to Appendices
	9.		Major WARREN on leave to PARIS. Company parade at 9AM. Squad drill and practice in use of gas respirator. Camp improved and wagons repaired. Sgt Brew joining from Army list at CRE=L.	W.E.J.
	10		Company parade at 9AM. Squad drill without arms, and rifle exercises. Camp improved and wagons and pontoons being repaired. Hut being erected at CRE. Lieut Barlow goes on leave.	W.E.J.
	11—13		Company employed as above.	W.E.J.
	14		Company employed as above. Three days course practised in equitation.	W.E.J.
	15		Company parade at 9AM. Company drill, Squad drill & (?) trench and communication drill.	
	16		Wagons and pontoons repaired. Major WARREN returned from leave. Company parade as usual. Squad drill and rifle exercises. Wagons and pontoons repaired.	Major, R.E. O.C. 401st (Highland) Field Coy, R.E. W.E.J.

WAR DIARY or INTELLIGENCE SUMMARY

Army Form C. 2118.

401st (HIGHLAND) FIELD COMPANY R.E.
Vol. XXI
From 1st Aug '17

Place	Date	Hour	Summary of Events and Information	Remarks and references to Appendices
	17		Section at Aqueduct drill and fire drill in the morning. Mounted section at riding drill. Lt Clifford with Signals XVIII Corps reconnoitre site for [illegible] with Hunt Tn. Received orders to relieve 400th Coy. Others are working for troops in forward area. Major WARREN proceeded to 400th & 413th & Maj MARENGO Divnl 2nd Army RE. Lieut OKELL returned from leave.	
B.24.d.7.7 at Mal BELGIUM SHEET 28 NW 1/40,000	18		To reconnoitre 400 Coy's work 13 — Maintenance and improvement of old track from KEMPTON PARK to HURST PARK and construction of new road phase to ROCHCASTEL EST. New work to be made of Duck boards. 6' 9" wide to be got away first. And Lieut Shaw and River to write 12th to 13th with Standing Orders. Storn [?] etrand by Company transport to 4 forward REs compd. from RAILWAY COT to HURST PARK. Section T proceeded to MINTY FM and met Major [?]. Major WARREN 2/Lt OKELL and 2 STEEL Shook shelter to took Coy while work commenced, 2 section worked from 5.30 AM to 11.30 AM. See 3 Section from 11.30 AM to 5.30 P.M.	
	19			

Major R.E.
O.C. 401st (Highland) Field Coy. R.E.

Army Form C. 2118.

WAR DIARY
or
INTELLIGENCE SUMMARY.
(Erase heading not required.)

Instructions regarding War Diaries and Intelligence Summaries are contained in F. S. Regs., Part II. and the Staff Manual respectively. Title pages will be prepared in manuscript.

401st (HIGHLAND) FIELD COMPANY, R.E.
Vol. XXIII.
31st Aug '17

Place	Date	Hour	Summary of Events and Information	Remarks and references to Appendices
	19.(cont)		Two Officer reinforcements report — 2nd Lt G.B. HARDEN M.C. from a London Company & 69th Division and 2nd Lt A.T. HALL from a unit training in England.	
	20		2nd Lt CLEGHORN proceeds to IV Army Rest Camp.	
			2nd Lt OKELL goes sick. 2nd Lt HARDEN relieves 2nd Lt OKELL who returns to Transport lines to be in charge of mounted section.	
	21		2nd Lt REID transferred from 401 to 2nd	
	22		Same section proceeded in lorry buses Eastern siding to railway cut. Three reinforcements report from No 11 Entrenching Bn.	
	23		2nd Lt HALL relieves 2nd Lt STEELE who returns to the Transport lines	
	24		Sections 1 and 4 & works at POPERINGHE. Sections 2 and 5 on water cart detail	
	25		Sections 2 and 3 to huts. Night — 2nd Lt HALL with Sections in first shift. 2nd Lt HARDEN with No 2 Co. about shift. 2nd Lt HARDEN to transport. 2nd Lt Col. CLEGG proceed. 2nd Lt REID rejoins 2nd Lt HARDEN.	
	26		Work on huts. No casualty. Sections proceeded in first shift. Lieut Smith in command shift.	

Army Form C. 2118.

WAR DIARY
or
INTELLIGENCE SUMMARY.
(Erase heading not required.)

401st (HIGHLAND) FIELD COMPANY, R.E.

Place	Date	Hour	Summary of Events and Information	Remarks and references to Appendices
	26		Officer reconnaissance report — Capt NIVEN & Capt PEEBLES from AOR 5 Coy.	N.A.
	27		Receive warning order to relieve the 115 Field R.E. on the 29th, and to take over duties on the 29th N.O.B. at about Noon. 1123 and 12 works from 10:30pm till 3am. 2nd Lt PEEBLES attached to 4/5 Roy.	N.A.
	28		10th Capt NIVEN to see work of B/115 Field Coy. and duties of 1st Lt R.E. Work in the Canal Bank. Work consists of maintaining track near HURST PARK to VON DE ROSIA, which is to be continued to the LANGEMARCK Road, and to improve track by breech from HURST PARK to FERDINAND F.M. Belts found near Dugouts; 150 sandbags mud, and 50 sandbags dirt to day. Last day of work; 170 yards of new formation has been constructed and beech slabbing laid on on side. 80 yards of metal road of no use. Prepared for soldering with slabbing, twinned ... Marine cut off and side slipped and new layer at the Affair. 100 Sandbags mud from the four Ratton J. At 154 Brigade Hut Group the Wooden with and 15 Room, Benj, Brace and Lav and are liable for to-night. Work on hand as above.	N.A.

2353 Wt. W2514/1454 700,000 5/15 D. D. & L. A.D.S.S. Forms/C. 2118.

WAR DIARY or INTELLIGENCE SUMMARY

Army Form C. 2118.

401st (HIGHLAND) FIELD COY R.E.
No. Vol. XXI
Date 31 Aug 17

Place	Date	Hour	Summary of Events and Information	Remarks and references to Appendices
CANAL BANK YPRES	29	10.00 p.m.	Ladies move from Camp near MARENGO Dump to new billets on Canal Bank. Major WARREN Capt. NIVEN and 2nd/Lt. HADDEN to Canal Bank. Nothing to report. Lines to be carried out.	
N. of YPRES			4 infantry officers passed purified water exam to Canal Bank. 2nd/Lt REED reconnoitred for day party the sides and two hundred dumps to be visited.	yes
	29/30		Party No III went to Canal Bank for mile groundwork. 4 G.S. loads of Timber and Tools issued for A.G.C. wagon to HURST PARK 1 gallon water container. 5/6 Division Adv. HY Divsn. 152 Brigade. No two aeroplane over enemy engaged	yes
	30		Air observation since the 6th. Other activities noted and Major LARREN, Brigade, Hd Qs. C.R.F. decided to camp 1st May to Infantry Street. Bridges on right of Dug 2nd to be repaired and maintained a considerable amount of sentry and construction work done B + C	yes yes
	31		Siting of Arks Section II early established of HURST PARK Section I siting 5 foot bridges over STEENBECK and subsidiary streams	yes yes

Major R.B.

O.C. 401st (Highland) Field Coy R.E.

Army Form C. 2118.

WAR DIARY
or
INTELLIGENCE SUMMARY.
(Erase heading not required.)

Instructions regarding War Diaries and Intelligence Summaries are contained in F.S. Regs., Part II. and the Staff Manual respectively. Title pages will be prepared in manuscript.

Place	Date	Hour	Summary of Events and Information	Remarks and references to Appendices
	31		Action, slow and lined approaches to the MON DU RASTA. Sector II contained the Alemand track from Boer Farm with LANGEMARCK Road. Sector III digging out about behind the YPRES Road this could as mine its place. The line of the YPRES - ROULES industries to Food Allies. Sector IV About 400 yards to the westward track starting from WEST PARK. The march divides itself into 4 periods:— ① Operations after the advance on 31st July were very much hindered by the rain. Digging trenches was useless. Parties simple of (?) the great amount of labour expended on them were very bad and roads were extremely difficult to get forward. For this reason tracks progressed slowly. There might have been done this way of achieving forward and slipped general shells. ② Period of rest. ③ Work on roads. Main construction mile - Pilcher Bapy Boesinghe Duck Board C? ④ Period of. Attendance for Second area 7 miles on the road made not being? The scheme of having expert units attached to divisions may prove useful.	

2353 Wt. W2544/1454 700,000 5/15 D. D. & L. A.D.S.S. Forms/C. 2118.

WAR DIARY
INTELLIGENCE SUMMARY

Army Form C. 2118.

401st (Highland) Field Company, R.E.
Vol. XXVI No. 10
Date: 31st Aug 17

Place	Date	Hour	Summary of Events and Information	Remarks and references to Appendices

...indeed, but the bodies of the new Thunder..... in the meantime much below the average. Even so, they are for shell accounts..... non.... the ordinary working party.

Casualties during night — nil.
Casualties during day — one wounded.
Reinforcements received during night — 4 officers, 11 OR.
No of horses and mules — limit — 2 officers; A.3.2
Transport to the works during month — 400 Mtd Off 102, 4054 Reserve Field 102, 302.
Transport from Off'd... to ... Other ... my..... 2 o/r.Rgt — 40 o/r Field 102.
Roll of officers with the company at 31/8/17: Major J.R. Warren M.C., Capt W.C. Gegg, Capt Runnen, 2/Lieut C. O'Kell, 2/Lieut J. Gleghorn, 2/Lieut G.B. Harden M.C., 2/Lieut A.E. Hall, 2/Lieut J. Peebles, 2/Lieut A.P. Reid.

Warren
Major, R.E.
O.C. 401st (Highland) Field C—

CONFIDENTIAL
No 21 (A)
HIGHLAND DIVISION.

Vol 32

401st (HIGHLAND) FIELD COMPANY, R.E.
No.
Date 30/9/17.

War Diary
of
401st Highland Field Coy. R.E.
For
September
1917.

Vol: XXXIII

Army Form C. 2118.

401ST (HIGHLAND) FIELD COMPANY, R.E.
Vol: XXXIII
No.
Date 30/9/17

WAR DIARY or INTELLIGENCE SUMMARY.
(Erase heading not required.)

Place	Date	Hour	Summary of Events and Information	Remarks and references to Appendices
YSER CANAL C.25.a.3.8.	September 1		Section I and Sapper mates repair bridges over STEENBEEK. Section III continued work on overflow from YPERLEE to CANAL and improvement to billets in CANAL BANK. Section II and Sapper mates relay double trenchboard track from HURST PARK forward. 320 trench boards laid. Trenchboards carried from HURST PARK to MON DU RASTABRIDGE. Carrying party 50 infantry. Section II and Sapper mates continue trenchboard track towards LANGEMARK RD. by night. Company transport lines moved from A.27.b.4.5 SHEET 29 N.W. to Camp at TESELHOEK — covered horse standings and huts.	w.y
	2		Section I and Sapper mates carry timber to STEENBEEK for emergency repair of bridge. Material also salved from old German collection. Double trench board track from HURST PARK continued. Trench boards carted from RAILWAY COTTAGE dump to HURST PARK. Trench board track to LANGEMARK ROAD continued. Bridge across STEENBEEK completed, other work as on 1ST continued.	w.y

2353 Wt. W3544/1454 700,000 5/15 D. D. & L. A.D.S.S. Forms/C. 2118.

O.C. 401st (Highland) Field Coy. R.E.
Major, R.E.

Army Form C. 2118.

WAR DIARY
or
INTELLIGENCE SUMMARY.

(Erase heading not required.)

401st (HIGHLAND) FIELD COMPANY, R.E.
No. ....
Vol. XXXII
Date 3.-9.-17

Place	Date	Hour	Summary of Events and Information	Remarks and references to Appendices
	3.		Section I erecting shelters at VONWERDER HOUSE. No III Section double track at STEENBEEK. No IV Section, double track from HURST PARK forwards. No II Section continue track to LANGEMARK ROAD by night. Salving old German concrete shelters East of STEENBEEK commenced by night.	w.a.g.
	4		As above. 2/Lt. CLEGHORN returns from Rest Camp. 2/Lt. REID to Transport lines, sick.	w.a.g
	5		Tenth board track from HURST PARK forwards, continued. Work on old German concrete shelters continued. LANGEMARK ROAD, continued. Reconnaissance made for artillery.	w.a.g.
	6		2/Lt. CLEGHORN to CANAL BANK. Artillery bridge over STEENBEEK being built by No II Sect at C.4.6.9.9. Above work continued.	w.a.g.

Major, R.E.
O.C. 401st (Highland) Field Coy, R.E.

Army Form C. 2118.

WAR DIARY
or
INTELLIGENCE SUMMARY.
(Erase heading not required.)

401st (HIGHLAND) FIELD COMPANY, R.E.
No. of ... XXXIII
Date ... 30-7-17

Instructions regarding War Diaries and Intelligence Summaries are contained in F. S. Regs., Part II. and the Staff Manual respectively. Title pages will be prepared in manuscript.

Place	Date	Hour	Summary of Events and Information	Remarks and references to Appendices
	7		As above. Also hit on MILITARY ROAD, bridged by No1 Section.	W.D.
	8		As above. 2/Lts. HARDEN M.C. and REID evacuated sick.	W.D.
	9		As above. Certain other bridges over STEENBEEK repaired.	W.D.
	10, 11th		As above.	W.D.
	12		As above. Erection of elephant troughing shelters at C.5.C.4.9 East of STEENBEEK commenced by No1 Section. Artillery bridge over STEENBEEK at C.4.b.9.9 completed. Taping and levelling branch track from C.5.a.95.05 to C.5.b.55.00 — very hard ground.	W.D.
	13		Making of concrete shelters East of STEENBEEK continued. Small party of men in reserve. Can do approaches only by night. Elephant shelter proceded with. Preparation of artillery areas. Trench board track from HURST PARK forwards continued. R.E dump started to be formed by night at LANGEMARK ROAD. C.5.b.80.70 Erecting artillery areas at C.10.a.9.8.	W.D.
	14			W.D.

Major, R.E.
O.C. 401st (Highland) Field Coy., R.E.

Army Form C. 2118.

WAR DIARY
or
INTELLIGENCE SUMMARY.
(Erase heading not required.)

401st (HIGHLAND) FIELD COMPANY, R.E.
No. 104. V.XXIII
Date 30 – 7 – 17.

Instructions regarding War Diaries and Intelligence Summaries are contained in F. S. Regs., Part II. and the Staff Manual respectively. Title pages will be prepared in manuscript.

Place	Date	Hour	Summary of Events and Information	Remarks and references to Appendices
	14		Trench board track continued as above. Elephant shelter erected with rotating of corrugated shelters continued. 2/Lt CLEGHORN to transport lines.	W. Ely
	15		Work as above continued. Clearing STEENBEEK of obstacles. 2/Lt CLEGHORN to ST OMER on leave.	W. Elg
	16		Work as above continued. 2/Lt OKELL reconnoitres POELCAPELLE ROAD for details. Stores for forward dumps carted to HURST PARK. Repair of track near STEENBEEK & MONBULGAR. 2/Lt CLEGHORN returned to CANAL BANK.	W. Elg
	17		As above Dressing station at MON DU RASTA strengthened by sandbag work.	W. Elg
	18		As above. POELCAPELLE ROAD cleared of obstacles at night. Fifteen trees removed. Trench board track continued East of LANGEMARK ROAD. Dressing station at MON DU RASTA. Sandbag wall in front built up to 6 ft. in height; brackets erected to accommodate 6 stretchers. 10 old German concrete shelters now valued.	W. Elg

Major, R.E.
for O.C. 401st (Highland) Field Coy., R.E.

WAR DIARY
INTELLIGENCE SUMMARY

401st (HIGHLAND) FIELD COMPANY, R.E.
Vol. XXXIII
Date 30-9-17

Place	Date	Hour	Summary of Events and Information	Remarks and references to Appendices
	18		6 Elephant shelters now complete at MON DU RASTA. 1 shelter built at MON BULGAR.	W/ly
	19		Forward R.E. dump formed at C.5.6.5.7. and camouflaged. Prepared notice boards carried to dump. 250 yards artillery revmens completed. Trench board tracks from HURST PARK forwards:- 110 yards of track laid East of LANGEMARCK ROAD. 20 French tracks taken to BULOW FARM for flooring. Total completed single track to C.6.a.2.6 and C.5.b.35.05. Double track to C.5.b.25.45. Concrete shelter at U.30.c.88.16. debris cleared, door and windows received, temporary floor laid, furniture arrived. Company moved from CANAL BANK to bivouacs at FUSILIER FARM. One mounted N.C.O. and two rep horse teams with drivers for two horse wagons stationed at CANAL BANK.	W/ly
	20		at 5.40 a.m. the Division attacked on a 1200 yard front and advanced approx 1000 yds. The following work was carried out by the various sections :-	W/ly

Army Form C. 2118.

WAR DIARY
or
INTELLIGENCE SUMMARY.
(Erase heading not required.)

Instructions regarding War Diaries and Intelligence Summaries are contained in F. S. Regs., Part II. and the Staff Manual respectively. Title pages will be prepared in manuscript.

401st (HIGHLAND) FIELD COMPANY, R.E.
No. Vol. XXXVII
Date 30-9-17

Place	Date	Hour	Summary of Events and Information	Remarks and references to Appendices
	20		Section I. Reconnaissance and consolidation of Strong point at BAVAROISE HOUSE, in view of the captured line. Owing to observation by the enemy and heavy shelling this section was unable to work until dusk. Section II Repaired duckboard track between STEENBEEK and LANGEMARCK ROAD. Tail about 300 yds of track forward from LANGEMARCK ROAD by VON BULOW HOUSE. Heavy shell fire continued most of the day. Section III Cleared STROMBEEK of any obstructions and counted four small footbridges. Section IV Cleared POELCAPELLE ROAD from junction with LANGEMARCK ROAD near the Bridge over LEKKER BOTTERBEEK. The vicinity of this Bridge was shelled and also was under M.G. fire. A reconnaissance of the bridge was made which was found intact. 2/Lt CLEGHORN to transport lines, sick. Repairing tracks from HORST PARK forwards, where damaged by shellfire.	M.G.
	21			

O.C. 401st (Highland) Field Coy. R.E.
Major, R.E.

WAR DIARY
INTELLIGENCE SUMMARY.
(Erase heading not required.)

Army Form C. 2118.

Place	Date	Hour	Summary of Events and Information	Remarks and references to Appendices
	21		Tracks laid nearly to POELCAPELLE ROAD. 700 yds of track completed from LANGEMARCK ROAD forward.	
	22		300 yards of tracks forwards from MON DU RASTA repaired. Laying 120 yards double track on pole plates, C.5.6.20 to C.5.6.6. — Forward dumps of 151 French bombs and 159 sole plates formed. 100 French bombs and 50 sole plates carried to dumps at C.5.6.35.25. Trench board track at C.6.5.0.8 repaired for 100 yards. 9 Concrete blocks houses numbered.	
	23		Staircase into dug out at FOCH FARM repaired out line damaged by shell fire. 50 trench boards carried by rail from HURST PARK to near MON DU RASTA.	
	24		120 yds track doubled, 50 yards of single track plated or pole plates between C.5.6.6.6. and C.6.a.1.7. Clearing BÜLOW FARM. Company hands over tracks to 80 th Field Coy RE 11 th Division.	

Army Form C. 2118.

WAR DIARY
or
INTELLIGENCE SUMMARY.
(Erase heading not required.)

401ST (HIGHLAND) FIELD COMPANY, R.E. Vol. XXXIII. Dates 30-9-17

Place	Date	Hour	Summary of Events and Information	Remarks and references to Appendices
	24		and return to transport lines at PESELHOEK. Billeted there. Bivouacs erected and camp improved. Major WARREN proceeds on leave.	S.C.J.
PESELHOEK	25		Company paraded at 9 a.m. for Kit-inspection. Fatigue Parade 10.15 improving and cleaning camp and for loading wagons.	
	26		Company parade at 9 a.m. and 2 p.m. Company refitting.	S.C.J.
	27		Company parade at 9 a.m. and 2 p.m. Squad drill.	S.C.J.
	28		Company parade at 9 a.m. and 2 p.m. Preparing to move on 29th.	S.C.J.
	29		Company transport moved off at 7 a.m. to HOPOUTRE Station to entrain. Sappers and Staffs paraded at 8 a.m. and marched to HOPOUTRE to entrain. Train left at 11.25 a.m. Arrived BAPAUME MAIN Station at 6.30 p.m. Detrained and marched to camp at COURCELLES - LE - COMTE. Arrived 11.30 p.m.	S.C.J.
	30		Company employed improving camp. Casualties during month :- 4 O.R. Killed; 11 O.R. Wounded. Reinforcements received during month - 7 other ranks.	W.C.J.

O.C. 401st (Highland) Field Coy. R.E.
Major, R.E.

Army Form C. 2118.

WAR DIARY
or
INTELLIGENCE SUMMARY.

(Erase heading not required.)

401ST (HIGHLAND) FIELD COMPANY R.E.
No. Vol. XXXIII 9.
Date 30-9-17.

Place	Date	Hour	Summary of Events and Information	Remarks and references to Appendices
			Number of Officers & other ranks on leave during month:- 1 Officer; 48 other ranks. Transfers to other units during month:- I.O.R – 407th (Highland) Field Coy. R.E. Number of other ranks to Army Rest Camps:- 8 other ranks. Casualties during month (Sapper Motes) 2.O.R. Killed; 8.O.R. Wounded. Roll of Officers with company at 30-9-17:- Major T.R.WARREN. M.C. CAPTAIN W.C.GLEGG; CAPTAIN R.O.NIVEN; LIEUTS:- COXELL; T.S.CLEGHORN; A.E.HALL; J.PEEBLES.	

Major, R.E.
O.C. 401st (Highland) Field Coy, R.E.

Army Form W.3091.

Cover for Documents.

CONFIDENTIAL
No 81 (A)
HIGHLAND DIVISION.

Nature of Enclosures.

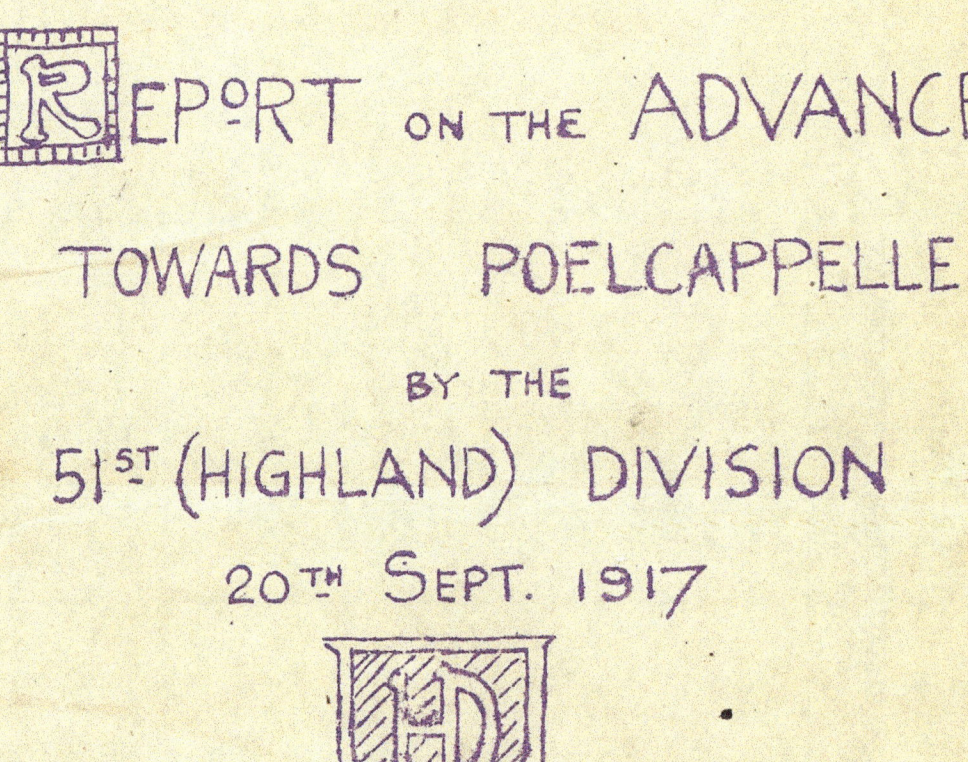

Report on the Advance towards Poelcappelle by the 51st (Highland) Division 20th Sept. 1917

Notes, or Letters written.

INDEX.

SECTION I. Preparations and Dispositions.

	Pages.
Infantry Dispositions	1.
Enemy Dispositions.	2.
Artillery Barrage.	2-4
The Ground.	4
Assembly.	4
Communications.	4
Headquarters.	5

SECTION II. The Battle.

First Phase.	To Dotted Blue Line.	5a-7
	1/9th Royal Scots.	5a-6
	1/4th Seaforth Highrs.	6-7
Second Phase.	To Blue Line.	7-8
	1/7th A. & S. H.	7-8
	1/4th Gordon Highrs.	8
Third Phase.	The Counter Attacks.	8-11

Position on 21st.	11
Holding the line	
21st/22nd - 24th - 25th.	11
Prisoners & Material captured.	12
Casualties.	12

MAPS.

No.1. Brigade & Battalion Boundaries; British Dispositions at ZERO; Enemy Dispositions during 20th September.

No.2. Artillery Barrage.

No.3. Dispositions on 21st September.

-o-o-o-o-o-o-o-o-o-o-

REFERENCE MAP : POELCAPPELLE, 1/10,000

SECTION I.

PREPARATIONS AND DISPOSITIONS.

TWO FACTORS IN THE ADVANCE.

The attack of the 51st (Highland) Division East of LANGEMARCK towards POELCAPPELLE on the 20th September, 1917, resulted in the gain of roughly 1,000 yards in depth; thus securing positions for the Artillery in the Valley of the STEENBEEK and providing an advantageous jumping-off ground for an advance on POELCAPPELLE itself.

Two factors must be borne in mind for a clear comprehension of the narrative of the days' fighting which follows:—

(a) Owing to the enemy retaining ground beyond the Division's left boundary, the two battalions touching that boundary had each to form a defensive flank of roughly 500 yards and thus correspondingly weaken the front line.

(b) The enemy — resolved to prevent us from reaching POELCAPPELLE, and perhaps not anticipating the British advance further South — threw the main weight of his counter attack that evening on the XVIII Corps front, and chiefly against the 51st Division. Of the 10 battalions massed on the Corps front, 7 were directed at the 51st Division's lines; the Artillery of the HOUTHULST, POELCAPPELLE and PASSCHENDAELE groups concentrated their fire in an extremely heavy barrage on and behind the high ground at PHEASANT FARM on our left, and beyond the LEKKERBOTERBEEK on our right.

Distinguishing features of the attack were the depth and weight of the barrage, the vigorous and incessant use of the rifle, and the success of the methods employed to overcome the system of defence in depth by concrete "pill-boxes" and shell-hole posts.

INFANTRY DISPOSITIONS.

The attack was made by the 154th Infantry Brigade (Brigadier-General J. G. H. HAMILTON, D.S.O., Commanding) on a two-company front by each of the two battalions taking up to the BLUE DOTTED LINE, and on a three-company front (one company in reserve) by each of the two battalions going to the BLUE LINE, where the front (barely 1,500 yards at the jumping-off line) widened to about 1,900 yards. Every known strong point and concrete emplacement had a separate unit told off for

/its

its capture, and special parties were detailed from the battalions taking up to the DOTTED BLUE LINE to go forward to counter any counter attacks. Two battalions of the 152nd Infantry Brigade were held in instant readiness to help, the 1/8th Argyll & Sutherland Highlanders, which was all in by the evening, being distributed in the morning from VARNA FARM to CANE TRENCH, and the 1/5th Seaforth Highlanders being held at the CANAL BANK. (Map No.1)

The three Brigades of the Division had each had a turn in the line and the 154th Infantry Brigade had spent five days on a taped-out course practising the attack before the advance.

ENEMY DISPOSITIONS.

Facing the 154th Infantry Brigade was the 36th Division (175th I.R., 128th I.R., and 5th Grenadiers) whose boundary overlapped the front of the 58th Division on our right; on our left the edge of the 185th I.R. (208th Division) touched our front. For the main counter attack the 234th Division was brought up; the 452nd and 451st I.R. being identified from prisoners; while the 5th Grenadiers (a fresh battalion) remained — prisoners from all three battalions of this regiment being taken.

After the main counter attack, the 371st I.R. (10th Ersatz Division) replaced the 452nd I.R. (Map No.1).

Though "pill-boxes" and shell-hole posts came very largely into the scheme of defence, there were still two well-defined trench lines — PHEASANT TRENCH and NEW TRENCH, right across our front about 150 yards from our old front line, most stubbornly defended; and KANGAROO TRENCH and BEER TRENCH running across our front, roughly about the BLUE LINE.

THE ARTILLERY BARRAGE.

To meet the new conditions opposed to the advance — concrete "pill-boxes" and strong points placed irregularly in depth, and posts in small groups of shell-holes — the Artillery barrage (Map No.2) was organised in depth in four Zones; as follows:—

(i) The Main Creeping Barrage.

By the 18-pdr. batteries of the 255th 256th, 58th and 59th Brigades, with the 18-pdr. batteries of the 34th and 282nd Brigades 100 yards beyond. Rate of advance:— 50 yards every 2 minutes for the first 200 yards; 50 yards every three minutes up to the DOTTED BLUE LINE, then in every four minutes up to the BLUE LINE.

The Protective Barrage pause was for 1 hour, during which No.3 guns of the batteries fired smoke bombs. (Enemy observed putting on gas helmets when smoke bombs came).

(ii) **The Combing Barrage.**

By the 18-pdr. batteries of the 65th A.F.A. Brigade, 200 yards beyond the main creeping barrage; by all the 4.5" howitzer batteries 300 yards beyond. Special task -- to dwell on strong points and work up communication trenches.

(iii) **Neutralising Barrage.**

By 6" Hows. and 60-pdrs. Task -- to search beyond Combing barrage.

(iv) **Standing Barrage.**

By Heavy Howitzers and 60-pdrs. Task -- searching out any formed bodies of enemy troops massed for counter attack.

Altogether the attack was supported by 22 18-pdr. batteries (approximately 67,000 rounds from noon on the 19th to noon 20th and 67,000 from noon to noon 20th - 21st); 6 4.5" Howitzer batteries (approximately 14,000 rounds from noon on 19th to noon 20th, and 14,000 from noon 20th to noon 21st); 12 batteries 6" Howitzers (5551 rounds -- 5.30 a.m. to 9.53 a.m. on 20th September); One battery 6" Mk VII (114 rounds); One battery 8" Hows; one battery 9.2" guns (49 rounds); 3 batteries 9.2" Hows. (685 rounds); and one 15" How. (30 rounds). In addition there were the 60-pdr. batteries and 16 Trench Mortars (152nd and 153rd Trench Mortar Batteries). The latter fired 2,700 rounds. Captured enemy N.C.Os. reported that it was the heaviest trench mortar bombardment that they had experienced and that their officers ran away from it.

Before the attack barrage opened, the enemy's positions had been subjected to 24 hours' intense bombardment.

A special feature during the 24 hours' bombardment was a "Draw Net" barrage of H.E. It started 1500 yards behind the German front line and moved back slowly towards his front line, pausing here for 10 minutes and then commencing with shrapnel as if for attack. This was carried out at 7.30 a.m. on 19th September, again at 4.30 p.m. and finally repeated immediately before ZERO. All evidence proves that this "draw net" barrage was most demoralizing to the enemy and caused many casualties.

MACHINE GUNS.

Fire from 32 machine guns was opened at ZERO round suspected strong points, lifting with the advance of the Infantry to the Protective S.O.S. Barrage Lines running from WINCHESTER

/FARM

(4)

FARM (650 yards beyond QUEBEC FARM, final objective on the right) to FERDAN HOUSE (800 yards beyond ROSE HOUSE on the left).

Sixteen guns assisted in the consolidation of the ground captured and four more were drawn from the reserve in the course of the main counter attack.

TANKS.

Of 12 Tanks (No. 12 Co., "D" Battalion) allotted for work on the Divisional front, one only, which did excellent service in an advanced position, was able effectively to assist the attack.

THE GROUND.

Divisional and Battalion boundaries are shewn on Map No.1. On the area over which the advance was made the gradual rise from the STEENBEEK is continued on the right and left, with, down the centre, a depression marking the course of the LEKKERBOTERBEEK (about 2 feet deep and 6 feet broad, with banks about 5 feet high). On the left the highest ground is reached in a slight ridge above PHEASANT FARM, from which close observation of POEL-CAPPELLE is obtained, and which covers the STEENBEEK Valley. On the right the ground is cut across the middle by the tiny STROOMBEEK, beyond which a slight ridge on the QUEBEC FARM line commands a stretch of about 300 yards to another slight ridge; from which also the surroundings of POELCAPPELLE can be surveyed. This ground was broken with swamp and pond at the part from which the attack was made, but was drier and firmer as the higher ground was reached.

THE ASSEMBLY.

Despite the necessity of moving in the open over badly ploughed-up land, and across a heavily shelled area, the assembly of the Brigade was effected quietly and in ample time, with the light total casualties of 2 officers and 25 other ranks. Rain fell heavily for two hours during the night and considerably aggravated the difficulties in the area where the ground was a mass of water-filled shell-holes when not pond and swamp.

COMMUNICATIONS.

Pigeons proved an invaluable means of communication, especially during the earlier stages of operations. Forty were taken up by the Infantry (with 20 more at mid-day and 30 in the evening), 20 by the Tanks, and 4 by the Artillery.

/HEADQUARTERS

(5)

HEADQUARTERS.

Divisional - BORDER CAMP A.30.b.2.3.

154th Inf. Bde. CANE POST C.9.a.6.3.

1/9th Royal Scots)
1/7th A. & S. H.   ) BULOW FARM.

1/4th Sea. Highrs.)...DOG HOUSES.
1/4th Gor. Highrs.)...U.29.d.67.50.

(5A)

SECTION II - THE BATTLE.

First Phase: Up to the DOTTED BLUE LINE.

Right Sector -

1/9th Royal Scots.
1/7th A. & S. H.

Left Sector -

1/4th Sea. Highrs.
1/4th Gor. Highrs.

The 154th Infantry Brigade attacked at 5.40 a.m. in the half-light of a clear morning. The men, well acquainted by their training with their objectives, and thoroughly imbued with the necessity of keeping up to the barrage, went off briskly and steadily the moment the barrage opened. The going was heavy, but the most swampy patches were known and avoided.

In the first phase it was found that the opposition came almost entirely from PHEASANT TRENCH, where the garrison, heavily though it had been punished by the barrage and the preceding 24 hours intense bombardment, was still strong enough to put up a stubborn fight with machine gun and rifle. When occupied, the trench was found in some parts to be literally choked with dead; one stretch of about 200 yards on the left Sector was heaped with 150 of the enemy, slain by shell, bullet, bomb and bayonet.

The barrage in depth was found to be very effective in dealing with the shell-hole groups, judging from the number of enemy dead found.

The enemy barrage came down five minutes after the attack opened and was heavy on the area between our original front line and the LANGEMARCK road, thinning out to the STEENBEEK.

Right:
1/9th Royal Scots.
(Lt.Col. W. GREEN, D.S.O. Commanding).

Barrage:
Off PHEASANT TRENCH.

Left Z + 3
Right Z + 5

Off DOTTED LINE.

Left Z + 14
Right Z + 23

On the Right Sector the 1/9th Royal Scots at first met with varying fortune.

On the right, "A" Company, which led off, was assisted by "C" Company (destined for the DOTTED BLUE LINE) in the fight for PHEASANT TRENCH. Against the machine guns which swept their front the men advanced in twos from shell-hole to shell-hole, pouring in a steady rifle and rifle grenade fire.

Five machine guns were put out, the trench and adjacent strong points occupied, the dug-outs cleared by bombing, and the line was in process of consolidation by 6.45 a.m.

/Protective

Protective in front of
DOTTED LINE.

Left Z + 26 to
       Z + 1.33
Right Z + 35 to
       Z + 1.33

On the left, where "B" Company led off followed by "D" Company, the attacking waves suffered severely before PHEASANT TRENCH was taken, particularly in the part from the POELCAPPELLE road to the LEKKERBOTERBEEK. The centre of the trench was first occupied. On the left two platoons of "B" Company, after getting up to the trench, were stopped by heavy machine gun fire, and returned to our lines. There, on very difficult ground, a splendid piece of work was accomplished by the O.C. Company, the Battalion Intelligence Officer, and the Artillery Liaison Officer, in rapidly reorganizing and leading the men (who now included some of the 1/7th A. & S. H.) forward again. Meanwhile a platoon of "B" Company in the centre of the trench worked outwards and greatly assisted the reorganized platoons in occupying their objective; another platoon worked to the right and took over a part which "D" Company had occupied

Only slight opposition was met in the advance from PHEASANT and NEW TRENCHES to the STROOMBEEK (the DOTTED BLUE LINE). "C" Company on the right, after killing the 15 Germans who defended FLORA COTT. in posts to the right and left, came under enfilade fire from HUBNER FARM (300 yards to the South beyond the Divisional boundary). Two Lewis Guns and two Rifle Sections with grenades were pushed out, and after a twenty-minutes' fight, during which heavy execution was effected among the Germans, the 2/8th London Regiment, which was attacking from the front, was able to occupy the farm. "C" Company established a post in touch with the Londoners about 100 yards beyond the boundary. "D" Company, on the left, taking a machine gun at NEW HOUSES on the way, got easily to the STROOMBEEK, but owing to heavy casualties in the vicinity of PHEASANT TRENCH was unable to supply two platoons detailed to support the 1/7th A. & S. H. beyond the STROOMBEEK. By 8.10 a.m. the Battalion was established on the line of the STROOMBEEK.

Left:
    1/4th Sea. Highrs.
  (Lt.Col. J. S. UNTHANK,
     Commanding).

On the Left Sector the 1/4th Seaforth Highlanders found the opposition stiffest on their Centre and Right.

On the Left, where No.4 Company operated, WHITE HOUSE was occupied ~~without resu~~

/without

without resistance, and Posts at Point 48 and in shell-holes up to DELTA HUTS were quickly cleared. In front of Points 48 to 85 there was a harder tussle; three machine guns firing from PHEASANT TRENCH and a "Pill-Box" West of it were captured, about 30 Germans being killed round the farm after putting up a good fight. But it was along PHEASANT TRENCH from Point 85 to the LEKKERBOTERBEEK that the real struggle took place. Here the trench was very strongly held, with newly constructed posts in front, some as much as 40 yards in advance; machine gun fire came from top of blockhouses and bombs and rifle fire from the trench. In this part the advance culminated in hand-to-hand fighting, No. 4 Coy. coming round on the flank to the aid of No. 3 Company, which was in front. Four machine guns were taken, and the trench, when entered was found heaped with German dead: of those who escaped from the trench most were killed when running away, by rifle fire and bombs, which were largely used in the attack. Beyond the trench no difficulty was encountered in getting to the DOTTED BLUE LINE. At 6.28 a.m. all objectives were captured and consolidation was proceeding on line from Point 82 by PHEASANT FARM to WHITE HOUSE.

So much S.A.A. had been expended that a further supply of 12,000 rounds was sent up to consolidating parties soon after 7 a.m.

Second Phase: To the BLUE LINE.

In the next stage of the advance, though the enemy had no continuous line strongly held, as in the case of PHEASANT TRENCH, there was much hard fighting, chiefly from the POELCAPPELLE ROAD to the Left Boundary, where fire from the enemy on the flank added considerably to the difficulties.

Right Sector:
  1/7th A. & S. H.
  (Lt.Col. E.C.HILL-
   WHITSON, Commanding)

Left Sector:
  1/4th Gordon Highrs.
  (Lt.Col. J. ROWBOTHAM,
   M.C., Commanding.)
  - - - -

Protective Barrage in front of DOTTED LINE lifts -
  Z plus 1.33

Barrage off BLUE LINE -
  Z plus 2.1

On the Right Sector, the 1/7th A. & S. H. on a three-company frontage, "D", "A" and "C", had moved off at Zero plus 5 minutes to get clear of the hostile barrage (which caused heavy casualties to "D" Company), and had on the left joined in the fight for PHEASANT TRENCH, leaving a few men there to help to mop up. They passed the DOTTED BLUE LINE in good time, and when the Protective Barrage lifted, advanced rapidly and without check, though not without brisk fighting, to the BLUE LINE. A machine gun over the STROOMBEEK in front of FLORA COTT. was captured by means of rifle grenades, and turned on the enemy with good results.

/ At ...

(8)

At QUEBEC FARM, on the extreme right, a light machine gun and 2 officers and 22 O.R. were taken; and at BAVAROISE HOUSE 2 light machine guns were put out of action.

Consolidation quickly proceeded along the BLUE LINE, joint posts being established with the 2/5th Bn. London Regiment on the right and the 1/4th Gordons on the left. The 1/9th Royal Scots were unable to supply two platoons as a reserve East of the STROOMBEEK, as planned; and two platoons of the 1/8th Arg. & Suth. Highrs. (152nd Infantry Brigade) came forward in their place — only about 30 O.R. reaching the front line, however, owing to the heavy casualties suffered in passing through the hostile barrage.

Left:
1/4th Gordon Highrs.

On the Left Sector the 1/4th Gordon Highlanders, advancing at ZERO plus 10 to PHEASANT TRENCH, suffered considerably from machine gun and rifle fire before reaching the Protective Barrage; 5 officers were casualties before the attack proper began, fighting having taken place near WHITE HOUSE with parties of the enemy firing from the other side of the Divisional boundary.

The first fight after the Protective Barrage lifted took place at the North of the PHEASANT FARM CEMETERY; a Lance Corporal was responsible for taking 2 machine guns and 28 prisoners there. MALTA HOUSE, ROSE HOUSE and DELTA HOUSE were taken in succession after stiff fighting, seven machine guns being destroyed. Gallant work was done by Captain D. M. JACKSON, 1/4th Seaforth Highrs., who, already wounded in the attack, was immediately behind the front battalion; seeing some Gordons without officers he led them to the capture of a Post at Point 25 beyond the BLUE LINE. By this time the 1/4th Gordon Highrs., had only three officers with 6 platoons of about 10 men each in the front line; two more officers and the remainder of the reserve company were brought up. The line was then formed along CHURCH TRENCH (touching with the 1/7th A. & S. H.) by DELTA HOUSE and ROSE HOUSE, thence running to U.24.d.0.3., with two platoons of the reserve company forming there a defensive flank.

Third Phase: The Counter Attacks.

First Counter Attack
11.45 a.m.

Intermittent fighting continued

/along

along the front when the BLUE LINE had been taken, and consolidation had not been long in progress before that series of enemy counter attacks began which culminated in the late afternoon and early evening in a most determined assault, backed by very heavy masses.

Throughout our attack the ground from our old front line to the STEENBEEK was heavily shelled; when the BLUE LINE was taken the area steadily pounded extended up to the PHEASANT FARM ridge and over the STROOMBEEK. This entailed many casualties to reinforcements and to machine gun teams coming forward to join in consolidation, and, through heavy losses in runners, made communication difficult.

It was at 11.45 a.m. that the first counter attack was made on the left of the 1/4th Gordon's front; it was slight and easily repelled. At 12.30 p.m. on the same part of the front the enemy came on again in greater numbers; this attack also was beaten off. Meanwhile, "A" Company of the 1/8th A. & S. H. (152nd Infantry Brigade) came up as reinforcements: three platoons took up a line in front of DELTA HUTS through the CEMETERY towards the POELCAPPELLE Road, and one was placed in STROOM TRENCH on the other side of the road. Tank D.44 had reached a point on the POELCAPPELLE Road at V.25.a.15.65; it was utilized as a Company Headquarters. One Lewis Gun from it was sent forward to DELTA HOUSE to replace one knocked out there; two were sent to reinforce the two already in BEER TRENCH, and one was retained in the tank; 300 rounds S.A.A. per man were distributed from it to the garrison of BEER TRENCH (held by about 40 men); and a Corporal was detailed to work the 6-pdr. gun it contained.

Machine Guns had been pushed steadily forward all the morning. On the Left Sector two on the right and two on the left of PHEASANT FARM CEMETERY came into action soon after the DOTTED BLUE LINE was captured; two were at MALTA HOUSE and one at ROSE HOUSE. On the right two were at BAVAROISE HOUSE, 2 - 100 yards in front of FLORA COTT. and 2 at V.25.c.1.2.

This was the position during the afternoon — the BLUE LINE held

/along

along its length up to ROSE HOUSE, where it bent back along the defensive flank formed on the left by the 1/4th Gordons and the 1/4th Seaforths until touch was obtained with the Division on the left — while from the direction of POELCAPPELLE and on the right, parties of the enemy were gradually creeping up, and farther back larger masses were gathering for the counter attack. Throughout this period heavy casualties were inflicted on the enemy by our artillery fire and machine and Lewis guns, and rifles were turned on every target that offered; all but 6 rounds for the 6-pdr. gun in Tank D.44 were fired.

THE MAIN COUNTER ATTACK.

At 5 p.m. the enemy counter attack was fairly launched to the accompaniment of a barrage of unusual intensity — it has already been pointed out that in this the HOUTHULST, POELCAPPELLE and PASSCHENDAELE groups co-operated. On the Right Sector the enemy came on between YORK FARM and TWEED HOUSE, but the BLUE LINE was not reached here; although the attack was pressed until about 7 p.m. it was completely broken by our artillery, rifle and machine gun fire, the artillery in particular inflicting very heavy losses.

On the Left Sector the enemy was held from DELTA HOUSE to the LEKKERBOTERBEEK until the S.A.A., of which there had been an extraordinary expenditure, was exhausted. ROSE HOUSE held out but was isolated. The three platoons of the 1/8th A. & S. H. stretching from the left flank along the N. of the CEMETERY towards the LEKKERBOTERBEEK held firm, and severely punished the enemy; but the small party in BEER TRENCH withdrew — all the 1/4th Gordon Officers who had gone into the attack in the morning were casualties by this time — MALTA HOUSE was overwhelmed, the platoon garrisoning STROOM TRENCH gave way, and in the V formed by the POELCAPPELLE road and the LEKKERBOTERBEEK there was a general withdrawal about 6.30 p.m.

Meanwhile defensive flanks were formed on the right by "C" Company 1/7th Arg. & Suth. Highrs., 2 platoons of the 1/8th A. & S. H. and "D" Company 1/9th Royal Scots, and on the left by the 1/8th A. & S. H. and 1/4th Seaforth Highlanders; and from these heavy

/enfilade

(11)

enfilade fire was poured on the advancing enemy. The troops who had withdrawn were promptly rallied, and, collecting ammunition from the wounded, were led forward from PHEASANT TRENCH. At the same time "C" Company, 1/8th A. & S. H., who had been earlier sent forward from COMEDY FARM, was brought up, and also launched in a counter attack from the same trench. The enemy was thrown back and when darkness came was left with his farthest point of penetration near Point 82 on the POELCAPPELLE Road, behind which he had fixed a machine gun post.

The front line on the left was then re-organised to run from U.24.d.1.4. to the Northern end of the CEMETERY, thence curving round Point 82 until touch was obtained across the LEKKERBOTERBEEK with the 1/8th A. & S. H. East of the STROOMBEEK. The line was continued along the South side of the LEKKERBOTERBEEK until it joined the original BLUE LINE. During the evening "D" Company, 1/8th A. & S. H., was brought up to reinforce the left Sector, and consolidation went on steadily during the night, (Map No.3).

Position on 21st September.

During the 21st September the position remained stationary, and the line, when the 152nd Brigade relieved the 154th Brigade on the night 21st/22nd September was substantially the same as at the end of the enemy counter attack.

While the 152nd Brigade were in the line (night 21/22nd to night 24th/25th September) a hostile counter attack was beaten back with heavy loss to the enemy. This attack, preceded for some hours by a very heavy barrage all along the Brigade front, was made just after 7 p.m. on the 23rd September; coming from the right towards the centre. Advancing in Artillery formation, the enemy were caught by our artillery barrage while extending to the right and rear of MALTA HOUSE, and under our shell, Lewis gun and rifle fire were seen "to waver and melt away"; in no place did they get near our lines, and next morning heaps of their dead were seen to the right of MALTA HOUSE.

The right battalion (1/6th Seaforth Highlanders) played a most effective part; one Company had five Lewis guns turned on the enemy and one of these fired 28 drums of ammunition during the attack.

/The

The Brigade had other opportunities, promptly seized, of punishing the enemy. On one occasion, in the early morning, the Left Battalion (the 1/5th Seaforth Highrs.) practically wiped out a platoon 40 strong, caught at close range in marching order; on another, the same battalion inflicted such heavy loss by enfilade fire on a Sturm trupp endeavouring to raid the 12th K.R.R. on the Brigade left that the survivors, 23 in number, ran towards the K.R.R's with their hands up and surrendered.

PRISONERS & MATERIAL CAPTURED.

The number of unwounded prisoners passed to the Divisional Cage from the morning of the 20th September to noon of the 21st September was 6 officers and 235 other ranks — from the 1st Bn. 185th I.R.; the 2nd and 3rd Bns., 5th Grenadiers; all 3 Bns. of 175th I.R.; and all three Bns. of 128th I.R.

The material taken totalled 23 machine guns, 1 small Trench Mortar, 2 Minenwerfers, 3 Granatenwerfers, 1 Message Rocket Thrower and 1 Light Gun.

CASUALTIES. - 20th to 21st September.

UNIT	Officers			Other Ranks			Total	
	K.	W.	M.	K.	W.	M.	Off.	O.R.
154th Inf. Bde.								
1/9th R. Scots.	3	4	-	31	161	28	7	220
1/4th Sea. Highrs	4	4	-	41	153	15	8	209
1/4th Gor. Highrs	3	8	1	39	149	40	12	228
1/7th A. & S. H.	-	2	-	22	150	12	2	184
154th M. G. Co.	2	-	1	9	30	5	3	44
154th T. M. Batt.	-	-	-	2	4	-	-	6
Total	12	18	2	144	647	100	32	891
152nd Inf. Bde.								
1/5th Sea. Highrs	-	2	-	14	30	-	2	44
1/8th A. & S. H.	1	4	2	14	94	9	7	117
152nd M. G. Co.	-	-	-	-	5	-	-	5
Total	1	6	2	28	129	9	9	166
153rd Inf. Bde.								
153rd M. G. Co.	-	1	-	2	9	-	1	11
153rd T. M. Batt.	-	-	-	-	2	-	-	2
Total	-	1	-	2	11	-	1	13
Divl. Troops.								
Art. (Inc. Att.)	-	1	-	3	18	-	1	21
232nd M. G. Co.	-	1	-	2	4	-	1	6
1/8th R. Scots (Pns)	-	1	-	-	3	-	1	3
Fld. Cos. R.E.	-	-	-	1	4	2	-	7
Field Ambs.	-	-	-	-	3	-	-	3
Total	-	3	-	6	32	2	3	40
Grand Total	13	28	4	180	819	111	45	1110

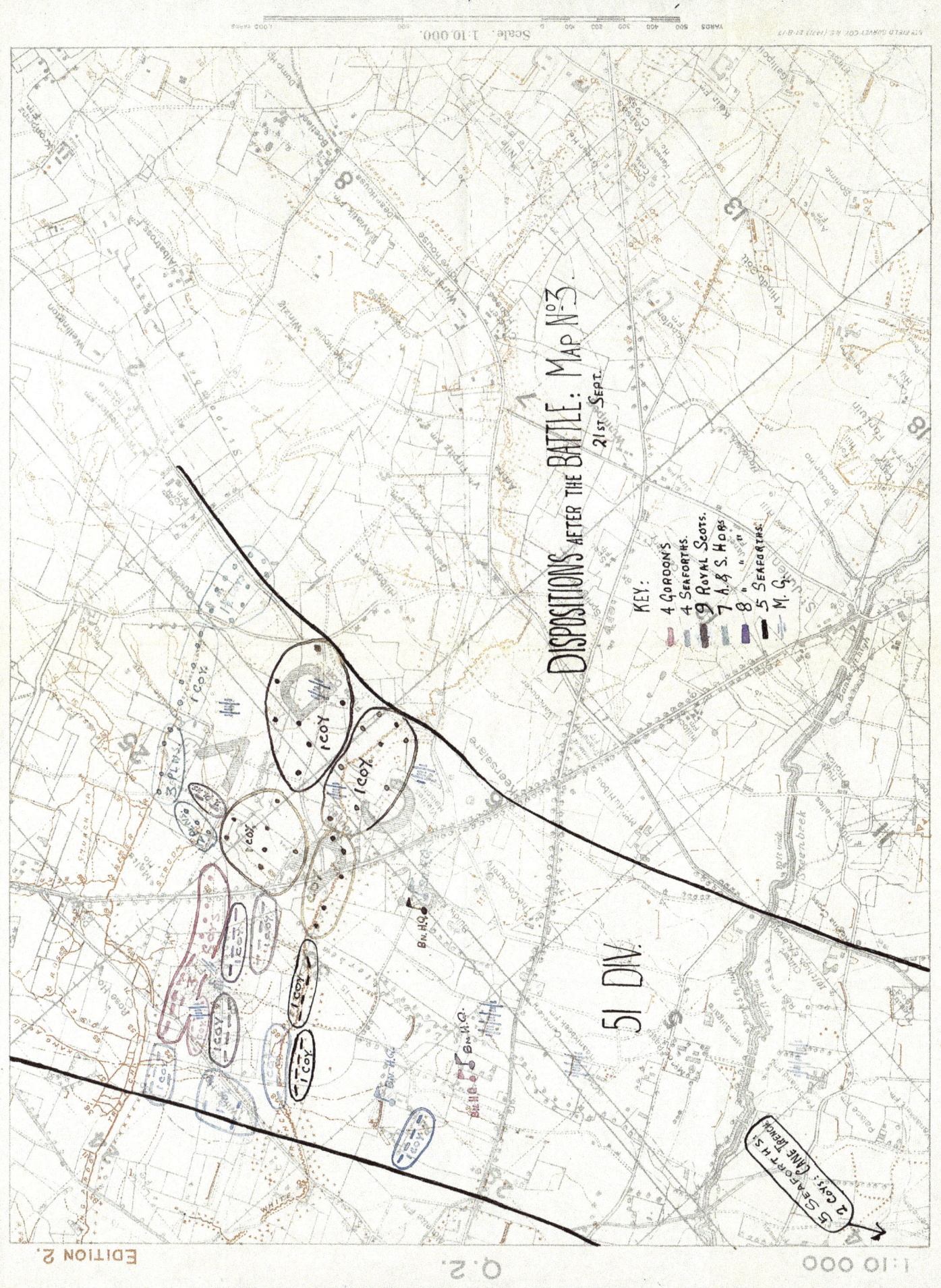

Map No 3.

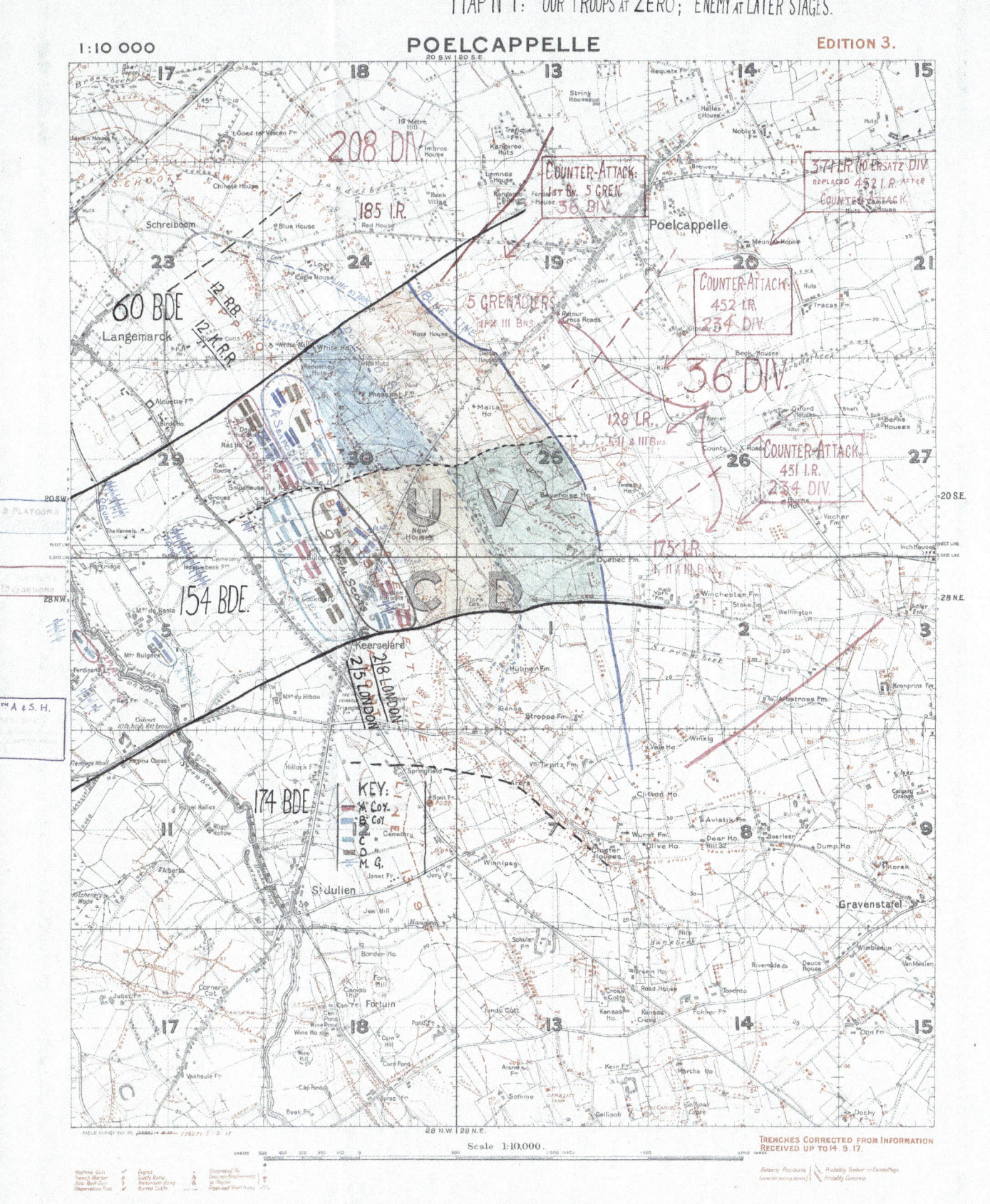

MAP Nº 1.

Map No. 2. Barrage Lines.
Superimpose on Sheet Q2.

Standing Barrage

Protective Barrage

2·15 — End
9·2·15

30

61

Z+2·1
Z+1·57—Z+2·1
Z+1·53—Z+1·57
Z+1·49—Z+1·53
Z+1·45—Z+1·49
Z+1·41—Z+1·45
Z+1·37—Z+1·41
Z+1·33—Z+1·37
Z+1·26—Z+1·33
Z+·23—Z+·26
Z+·20—Z+·23
Z+·17—Z+·20
Z+·14—Z+·17
Z+·11—Z+·14
Z+·9—Z+·11
Z+·7—Z+·9
Z+·5—Z+·7
Z+·3—Z+·6
Zero—Z+·3

MAP Nº 2

War Diary

of

401st (Highland) Field Company. R.E.

for

October 1917.

Vol: XXXIV.

Army Form C. 2118.

WAR DIARY
or
INTELLIGENCE SUMMARY.
(Erase heading not required.)

401st (HIGHLAND) FIELD COMPANY, R.E.
No. XXXIV
Date 31/10/17

Place	Date	Hour	Summary of Events and Information	Remarks and references to Appendices
COURCELLES LE COMTE	1.		Company parade at 9 a.m. Squad drill. Parade 2. p.m. Squad drill. Troops inspected.	
	2.		Company parade, drill as above. Capt CLEGG and 2 N.C.O's to 447th Field Coy. R.E. BOIRY BECQUERELLE, to take over work. Left sector of left brigade, 50th Division, reconnoitred.	
	3.		Company parade as above. Capt CLEGG to 447th Field Coy R.E. Right sector, left brigade, 50th Division reconnoitred.	
	4.		Company parade as above. Company prepare to move.	
	5.		Company parade 8-30. a.m. Move to BOIRY BECQUERELLE. Billeted Hors in Nissen hut camp. Nos 1 and 4 sections move to forward billets near HENINEL in afternoon.	
BOIRY - BECQUERELLE.	6		Work commenced in forward area, COJEUL Valley. No 1 Section working in left sector, improving front line posts, revetting and trench boarding support line. Sewing MARLIERE - GUÉMAPPE roads, & mining two exits from MARLIERE Caves. No 4 Section working in right sector, improving posts in front line, constructing "cubby holes", revetting and trench boarding support line, constructing post in GANNET Trench, overhauling pumps in PANTHER WELL, altering artillery O.P. in	

Major R.E.

2353 Wt. W2544/1454 700,000 5/15 D. D. & I. A.D.S.S. Forms/C. 2118.

Army Form C. 2118.

WAR DIARY
or
INTELLIGENCE SUMMARY.
(Erase heading not required.)

Instructions regarding War Diaries and Intelligence Summaries are contained in F.S. Regs., Part II. and the Staff Manual respectively. Title pages will be prepared in manuscript.

401ST (HIGHLAND) FIELD COMPANY, R.E. Vol. XXXIV No ...... 2.
Date 31/10/17.

Place	Date	Hour	Summary of Events and Information	Remarks and references to Appendices
	7		in LION trench, improving cover and entrance to water point in SHIKAR Avenue. Sites for proposed rifle ranges and bayonet assault courses reconnoitred near MERCATEL and NEUVILLE VITASSE. Company horse lines improved.	yes.
	8		Above work continued. No 3 Section to forward billets. Improvement of 154th Inf. Bde. H.Q. commenced.	yes.
	9		Above work continued. No 2 Section to forward billets. Major WARREN returns from leave. Major WARREN to left sector with Capt. CLEGG.	
	10		Work continued as above. All supplies matter billeted in WAN COURT. Major WARREN to right sector with Capt. CLEGG. Inspection work of ?? ???? in left battalion area. Also various work by No 3 Section, providing new right battalion area. No 1 Section employed on new works. MARLIERS sewer. 154th Inf. Bde. H.Q. roofing across COJEUL valley. One exit from MAYNARD CROSS completed, flooring of cross continued. Lt. HALL to forward billets. Section 2 take over all work behind the trenches; erection of screens covering approaches to trenches; bunting & cutting new exits to MARLIERE Camp, work at Brigade H.Q. Company billets.	yes.

W. Green
Major, R.E.
O.C. 401st (Highland) Field Coy., R.E.

Army Form C. 2118.

WAR DIARY
or
INTELLIGENCE SUMMARY

(Erase heading not required.)

401st (HIGHLAND) FIELD COMPANY. R.E. No. Vol. XXXV 3 Date 31/1/9/17

Place	Date	Hour	Summary of Events and Information	Remarks and references to Appendices
	10-13		Company with 154th Brigade who have 2 battns in the line and half Section 3 in Right Battn Sector constructing support line shelters in parapet of front line and support. Also working on water supply and a stel O.P. (enemy material) Lt CLEGHORN with Section 1 and half Section 3 in similar work with left battn. Sappers made with infantry ration. Works proceed as above. Water supply on right (consisting of well, small petrol driven pump, lifting about 16 ft. pipe line rising about 75 feet and 3 long gal. tanks) not satisfactory. Pumps not sufficiently powerful to deliver. Proposed to fit a small auxiliary rotary pump on pipe line about 40 ft above 1st pump. Major WARREN to forward details on 11th. Capt FLEGG to transport lines, over to 400th Field Coy. R.E. on 13th to take command — Major DIXON leaving for England on 15th.	Yes. Yes.
	14		It is decided by C.R.E. that the Field Coys shall work on front line posts. Arrangements made to start about 6 posts on each battn front, getting working parties from the garrisons. An 8 hours bombardment by the Bosh. on the left culminated	Yes.

Major, R.E.
O.C. 401st (Highland) Field Coy., R.E.

Army Form C. 2118.

WAR DIARY
or
INTELLIGENCE SUMMARY.
(Erase heading not required.)

401st (HIGHLAND) FIELD COMPANY, R.E.
No. Vol. XXXIV
Date. 31/12/17

Instructions regarding War Diaries and Intelligence Summaries are contained in F. S. Regs., Part II. and the Staff Manual respectively. Title pages will be prepared in manuscript.

Place	Date	Hour	Summary of Events and Information	Remarks and references to Appendices
			Estimates ins a raid at 4-4.5 p.m. Between 60 + 70 prisoners are taken. 2Lt GIBSON reports as a reinforcement. 2Lt ROOM, 9th Royal Scots returns from leave. Gallantry cards received for Lt HALL, Sgt HAY, Cpl MIDDLETON, Spr CAMPBELL and Cpl MITCHELL, 147th A.S. Hts.	
	15-19		Work as usual. 2Lt KEPPIE, 9th Royal Scots, back to Bttn on 16th. 2/Lt GIBSON takes over from Lt CLEGHORN on the 17th. Lt CLEGHORN to England on 18th for home service. Instructions from Divn to start more posts.	yes.
	20-23		Work done on 20 posts; 11 on right, 9 on left. Pumps obtained for Ripple Brown supply after some trouble. Engine House completed, and pump installed. Pipe line broken by shell fire on the 22nd. Conference of Field Coy Commanders & Brigade Majors with C.S.O. + at C.R.E.'s Hd Qrs on the 23rd — It was decided that fewer posts should be worked on and that all garrisons should have stretches of proposed work. (already done)	yes.
	24-26		Lt BRUCE 1/4th Gordons from leave on 23rd. Number of posts worked on reduced to 6 on each sector. Sapphire + Sapphire wants	yes.

H. Clair
Major, R.E.
O/C. 401st (Highland) Field Coy R.E.

Army Form C. 2118.

WAR DIARY
or
INTELLIGENCE SUMMARY.
(Erase heading not required.)

Instructions regarding War Diaries and Intelligence Summaries are contained in F.S. Regs., Part II. and the Staff Manual respectively. Title pages will be prepared in manuscript.

401st (HIGHLAND) FIELD COMPANY, R.E.
Vol. XXXIV
No. 5
Date 31/10/17

O.C. 401st (Highland) Field Coy., R.E.
[signature]
Major, R.E.

Place	Date	Hour	Summary of Events and Information	Remarks and references to Appendices
	27-28		Water worked in 2 shifts, 9-30 a.m. to 3-30 p.m. & 3-30 p.m. to 9-30 p.m. Sappers supposed to work 2 men for 2 hours at a time, continuously. 2/Lt LAW, 1/7 A.I.S. this reports from 174 Tunnelling Coy. 2/Lt PURVES to Tunnelling Coy in his place. — 3 posts completed in each batn front. — Pipe line on Right. rehal & pumps tried. Original pump out of order. Capt GRESS returned from 400th Cy R.E. on 28th. Work as usual. Tanks for Right Batn water supply filled. One pump being tried for Left Batn supply but found unsatisfactory. 154 Brigade relieved on 28th by the 12th Brigade.	*[initials]*
	29		Orders received to move sappers back to transport lines on 29th; other move uncertain. Orders received to move to BEAULENCOURT on the 30th and YPRES on the 1st. Sappers move back to the transport lines, leaving Lt OKELL & 9 O.R's to hand over work and forward billets to the 208th Field Coy. The Sapper mates return to their battalions, who have gone to the IZEL-LES-HAMEAUX area.	*[initials]*
BEAULENCOURT	30		Capt NIVEN with 5 O.R's to BEAULENCOURT to billet. Wagons packed. The company leaves for BEAULENCOURT — 10½ miles — about 8 a.m., and billets in F Camp.	*[initials]*

Army Form C. 2118.

WAR DIARY
or
INTELLIGENCE SUMMARY.
(Erase heading not required.)

401ST (HIGHLAND) FIELD COMPANY, R.E.
Vol. XXXIV No. 6
Date 31/10/17

Place	Date	Hour	Summary of Events and Information	Remarks and references to Appendices
	31.		2 Sections of the 404th Field Coy attached for men and rations	Nil
			Capt. NIVEN & 5 O.R's to billet in YPRES.	
			Reinforcements received during month :- 1 Officer 24 other ranks.	
			Number of men on leave during month :- 24 other ranks.	
			Number of men to 3rd Army Rest Camp during month - 6 other ranks.	
			Transfers during month :- 1 O.R. to Depot Field Survey Coy. 2 NCO's to England. Candidates for Commissions.	
			Roll of Officers with Company at 31/10/17 :- MAJOR J.R. WARREN M.C., CAPT W.C. GLASS, CAPTAIN R.O. NIVEN, LIEUTS:- C. OKELL, A.E. HALL, J. PEEBLES, 11/Lts J.D. GIBSON.	Nil
			Report on the advance towards POELCAPPELLE by the 51st (Highland) Division on 20th September 1917, attached. (To be filed with September War Diary.)	

Major R.E.
O/C 401st (Highland) Field Coy, R.E.

CONFIDENTIAL
No. 31 (A)
HIGHLAND
DIVISION

Vol 34

401st (HIGHLAND) FIELD COMPANY, R.E.
Date 30-11-17

WAR DIARY
of
401st (HIGHLAND) FIELD COY. R.E.
for
NOVEMBER 1917

Vol: XXXV

WAR DIARY
or
INTELLIGENCE SUMMARY.
(Erase heading not required.)

Army Form C. 2118.

401st (HIGHLAND) FIELD COMPANY, R.E.
Vol. XXXV
Date 30-11-17

Place	Date	Hour	Summary of Events and Information	Remarks and references to Appendices
YTRES.	1st		Company marched to YTRES with 2 Section of the 404 Coy. and billets in huts. Conference with C.R.E. in evening, at H.Q. of 9/18th Royal Scots. Informed that preparations are to be made for a surprise offensive. HAVRINCOURT WOOD to be reconnoitred on 2nd with a view to accommodating large numbers of troops. 400 Coy. to take the right, 401 the left.	H.
	2nd		5 officers to reconnoitre wood. Existing camps allotted numbers from 1 to 20, deep dugouts from 21 to 30, near camps to be numbers from 31 upwards. Arranged at Conference with C.R.E. to commence constructing shelters at various points in the wood, and to move the sappers forward shortly. Also that 1 section of 404 be attached to 400 Coy. Lieut. ALLAN re-maining with 401.	H.
	3-5		At HALL Commence repair of old dugouts at Q.1.c.40.25 — Camp 31. Lt. ORELL with 2 sections erection of elephants in old cutting at Q.13.6.0.0 — Camp 32. Lt. ALLAN with 2 sections commence conversion of old stables at Q.3.a.0.0 — Camp 33. Ground on West side of wood reconnoitred for shelter but not found suitable. On 5th Lt. HALL meets O.C. 44 H.A.C. and reconnoitres site for H.A.C. Hrs. Qrs. in VERU	H.

Army Form C. 2118.

WAR DIARY
or
INTELLIGENCE SUMMARY.

(Erase heading not required.)

401ST (HIGHLAND) FIELD COMPANY, R.E.
Vol. XXXV
No. 11-17
Dec 30-11-17

Instructions regarding War Diaries and Intelligence Summaries are contained in F. S. Regs., Part II. and the Staff Manual respectively. Title pages will be prepared in manuscript.

Place	Date	Hour	Summary of Events and Information	Remarks and references to Appendices
	6-8th		Sapper worked on 5th. Capt NIVEN and Lt GIBSON with sections 3 and 1 to live in Camp 32. Part of section 2 commence HA & MG Bns at VELU, 2 Iron Huts, 2 elephants, and furnishing 2 deep dugouts. On the 8th Lt OKELL with section 4 moves to Camp 32, and Lt ALLAN after cleaning out some old dugouts at Q.13.d.2.7 - Cup No 6 - moves into them at night.	Nb.
	9-10th		Capt NIVEN commences Camp No 34 at P.12.d 6.0 on 9th. Lt OKELL to 4th Army Infantry School. Lt PEEBLES opens Coy, takes over Section 4, and commences Camp 35 at P.18.b.1.4. Part of Section 2 commence Camp 36 at P.18.b.0.2. Major WARREN with CRE's 51 & 62 to wood. Camps and approach for 62nd Div. 51st Div. to have right half of the wood. Major WARREN to stay in forward billets.	Nb. Nb.
HAVRINCOURT WOOD	11th			Nb.
	12/16th		Regiments of 62 Div now attached to the Billets for 3 battns. The new Camps will provide accommodation as follows :- 32, 1 Coy; 33, 5 Coys; 34, 1 Coy; 35, 1 Coy; and 6 (old camp enlarged) 1 Coy. Balance will be accommodated in presently existing accommodation.	Nb.

Major, R.E.
O.C. 401st (Highland) Field Coy. R.E.

Army Form C. 2118.

WAR DIARY
or
INTELLIGENCE SUMMARY.
(Erase heading not required.)

401st (HIGHLAND) FIELD COMPANY, R.E.
Vol. XXXV
Date 30-11-17.

Place	Date	Hour	Summary of Events and Information	Remarks and references to Appendices
	17/19th		All camps completed, with latrines, and 3 battns. to Bn on 16th. Transport lines move to NEUVILLE on the 15th. — Camps for 350 commenced on right half of the wood on the 16th. Conference at C.R.E.; IV Corps to attack on the 20th with tanks in front of the infantry. 51st Division to advance through FLESQUIERES. Company rail 2 Section of the 400 Coy and the 1/8th Royal Scots to repair the road from TRESCAULT to FLESQUIERES. 20 G.S. wagons to be obtained in METZ to supply materials. R.E. dump to be in METZ and TRESCAULT. Forward billets moved to Q.14.b.2.8. on 17th. Camps for 350 completed on the 18th at ALLAIN and section of 400 Coy joins their Coy at NEUVILLE. Footwear washed by all officers. 154 Brigade supplies mats upon the Coy on the 18th. — On 19th previous made for 4 stretchers, 2 limbers, and teams at forward billets. Finish arrangements made for 20th. 3-4 hours relief to be worked, nos. 1 + 4 to go out first followed by nos 2-3, and then 2 sections of the 400 Coy, all with rations. Section 1 + 4 to take stretchers and limbers which will be handed over to the other relief.	

Major R.E.
O.C. 401st (Highland) Field Coy, R.E.

WAR DIARY or INTELLIGENCE SUMMARY

Army Form C. 2118.

401st (HIGHLAND) FIELD COMPANY, R.E.
No. Vol. XXXV
Date 3a – 11 – 17.

Place	Date	Hour	Summary of Events and Information	Remarks and references to Appendices
	20		T.G.S. wagons at METZ to be ready to convoy material forward. The IV Corps attacks at 6.40 a.m. — Tanks leading the infantry. At PEEBLES and reconnoitring party go out at zero hour, and useful messages are received. At 8.30 a.m. Lt GIBSON, with half of the first shift go out, followed by the remainder at 9 a.m. under Lt HALL. — Our troops are on the outskirts of FLESQUIERES. The second and third shifts go out together at 1 p.m. The road is found to be impassable for 1000 yds and a cross country diversion is made. Trouble are bridged, filled in and all obstacles are cleared by dusk, but men starting at 2 p.m. makes the diversion very soft, and guns and other transport speedily cut it up. The days fighting has been very successful. GRAINCOURT is reported to be taken, but FLESQUIERES still holds out.	
	21		The company is held in reserve by the C.R.E. — weather conditions making the road impassable. FLESQUIERES is taken, and 4 sections are ordered forward with tool carts, about 12-15 p.m. They arrive in FLESQUIERES about 4 p.m.	

Army Form C. 2118.

WAR DIARY
or
INTELLIGENCE SUMMARY.
(Erase heading not required.)

O.C. 401st (Highland) Field Coy. R.E.
Major, R.B.

401st (HIGHLAND) FIELD COMPANY, R.E.
Vol. XXXV
30-11-17

Place	Date	Hour	Summary of Events and Information	Remarks and references to Appendices
FLESQUI-ERES.	22		The work on the defence of FLESQUIERES and it is decided to billet here. After len a line of 15 posts is dug North East of the village. CANTAING is taken. Enemy dumps is taken over. Billets are put in order and kits arrive. Defences are completed in afternoon and work is commenced on the CANTAING road. FONTAINE is taken and lost.	W.L.
	23		Extra transports brought to forward billets. All extra work on the CANTAING road. The Division attacks FONTAINE which is again taken and lost. A dump of wiring material is formed at LA JUSTICE. The lighting set on the catacombs of FLESQUIERE is taken in hand. H.Qm Transport to the rear.	W.L.
	24		Division relieved by the Guards. Orders received to proceed to DERNANCOURT. Dismounted by train, transport by road. Company concentrate at the narrow gauge leaves for BEAULENCOURT. Sappers & sapper mates entrain at YTRES, but the company is detained and the sappers detrain and billet at YTRES.	W.L.
	25		Major WARREN to HAVRINCOURT to report to C.R.E. 40th Div. to return the company is attached and to reconnoitre for billets in HAVRINCOURT. Transport returns to YTRES.	W.L.

Army Form C. 2118.

WAR DIARY
or
INTELLIGENCE SUMMARY.

(Erase heading not required.)

401st (HIGHLAND) FIELD COMPANY, R.E.
No. Vol. XXV
Date 3 - 11 - 17

Instructions regarding War Diaries and Intelligence Summaries are contained in F.S. Regs., Part II. and the Staff Manual respectively. Title pages will be prepared in manuscript.

Place	Date	Hour	Summary of Events and Information	Remarks and references to Appendices
WOOD.	26		Jaffres to HAVRINCOURT and work on billets in ruins. Transport to HAVRINCOURT	do.
	27		Work commenced on Infantry Track between HAVRINCOURT & GRAINCOURT to be used in emergency.	do.
	28		Track made passable.	do.
	29		Track complete and alternative tracks started. 1 officer reinforcement received Lt. L.R. MACKNESS.	do.
	30		Orders received to march to "ROCQUIGNY". The company concentrate at the transport lines, and marches to Reinforcement Camp, ROCQUIGNY. Reinforcements received during month :- 1 Officer, 10 other ranks. Number of men on leave during month :- 1 Officer, 8 other ranks. Roll of officers with company at 30-11-17. MAJOR. J.R. WARREN. M.C., CAPT W.C.GLESS., Capt R.O.NIVEN., LIEUTS:- C.OKELL, A.E. HALL., J. PEEBLES, J.D. GIBSON, L.R. MACKNESS.	do.

O.C. 401st (Highland) Field Coy., R.E.
Major, R.E.

CONFIDENTIAL
No. 21(A)
HIGHLAND DIVISION.

401st (HIGHLAND) FIELD COMPANY R.E.
31·12·17

War Diary

of

401st (Highland) Field Co. R.E.

For

December 1917

Vol. XXXVI

Army Form C. 2118.

WAR DIARY
or
INTELLIGENCE SUMMARY.

(Erase heading not required.)

401st (HIGHLAND) FIELD COMPANY, R.E. No. Vol. XXXVI
Date 31.12.17

Place	Date	Hour	Summary of Events and Information	Remarks and references to Appendices
BERTINCOURT	1.		The company marched with 154 Brigade from ROCQUIGNY to BERTINCOURT. 2 battalions go into line in front of MOEUVRES.	
	2		Orders received to take over from 213 Field Coy. R.E. on 3rd. Major Morrey to 213 Coy. at FREMICOURT. Work consists of posts behind TADPOLE COPSE. He arranged to take over their forward billets at BOURSIES and former rear billets at LEBUCQUIERE. Lieut HALL to Bridging Source. Major KIGGELL acting C.R.E.	
	3		The sappers march to BOURSIES. Major WARREN and Lieuts GIBSON and MACKNESS (sunward) Transport to LEBUCQUIERE Dump at BEUGNY taken over. At night the 4 sections put out 1600' of light wire in front of line of posts to right and left of TADPOLE COPSE.	
BOURSIES	4		2 Brigades are in the line. 154 on the right, 153 on the left. On the left we are in the original front line of November. On the right we have advanced about 2000 yards. At night the 4 sections put up 650' of double apron fence in front of old line on the right of ROBIN ALLEY D 22.c.0.4.	
	5		During the night the whole Divisional front is withdrawn to the original front line of November 19th and the 152 Brigade takes it over. 2 Sections thicken wire put out on the 4th.	

Major, R.E.
O.C. 401st (Highland) Field Coy. R.E.

Army Form C. 2118.

WAR DIARY
or
INTELLIGENCE SUMMARY.

(Erase heading not required.)

401st (HIGHLAND) FIELD COMPANY, R.E. Vol. XXXVI. Date 31.12.17. 2.

Place	Date	Hour	Summary of Events and Information	Remarks and references to Appendices
DOIGNIES	6.		Transport moves to FREMICOURT. It is arranged that 401st Coy. and 2 sections 400th Coy. work with 152 Brigade in lieu O.C. 401st Coy. The Company takes over 5 deep dug-outs at J.16.b.83 near DOIGNIES from the 100th Coy. BOURSES being too near the line. Lieut. MACKNESS, Sergt. MIDDLETON and 1 sapper are wounded. At night 400' of new support line are dug from ROBIN ALLEY East until 640 Infantry at PEEBLES pivoted on the 7th. The trench system is very poor and requires all-round reconstruction. A sap is to be made with a wide support line with 31 sides, traverses giving a change of direction of only 45°, and frequent deep dug-outs. ROBIN SUPPORT is dug 900' long and 300' are much traversed and two deep dug-outs are commenced. 200' of STURGEON SUPPORT are dug from STURGEON AVENUE J.6.d.1.3. to the left.	ML
	7th-10th		On the 7th 6 sappers are sent locating on a left dug-out at J.7.c.9.1 with T.M. Party working funny. On the same day 2nd Lieutenant ALLAN and sappers CAMPBELL and LABURN are killed by a shell.	ML

Nilsson
Major, R.E.
O.C. 401st (Highland) Field Coy., R.E.

Army Form C. 2118.

WAR DIARY
or
INTELLIGENCE SUMMARY.
(Erase heading not required.)

401st (Highland) Field Company, R.E.
Vol. XXXVI
31.12.17

Place	Date	Hour	Summary of Events and Information	Remarks and references to Appendices
	11.12.16		The Transport moves to BEUGNY. 153 Brigade relieves the 152 on the night 10th/11th. Beside the dug-outs in the support line, posts are to be made, consisting of fire bays, with ladders to the firestep, wired ammunition recesses, sump pans and rifle racks. The dug-outs are to be roofed, furnished, whitewashed, and fitted with handrails, gas gongs and gas curtains. Also 2 latrines and a washing are to be made. The work of completing ROBIN SUPPORT over Mill Posts is handed over to the 400th Coy. STURGEON SUPPORT is carried on to BISHOPGATE 450x and Trench boards. SHARK SUPPORT is dug 50x North from FISH AVENUE and FISH SUPPORT is dug 550x Southwards from FISH AVENUE to the edge of BOURSIES. Capt Gray returns from leave on the 15th and Lt. H.J. RICHARDSON reports for duty.	
	17th -22nd		The 154 Brigade relieves the 153 Engineers are re-arranged. 401st Coy takes charge of the Griffith sector as far as FISH AVENUE inclusive. The 401st Coy take the right. Mined "Bubby Holes" 4' wide × 3' high and 6'6" long to be made in the	

Army Form C. 2118.

WAR DIARY
or
INTELLIGENCE SUMMARY.
(Erase heading not required.)

401st (HIGHLAND) FIELD COMPANY. R.E.
No. Vol. XXXVI
Date 31.12.17. 4

Place	Date	Hour	Summary of Events and Information	Remarks and references to Appendices
	23rd – 26th		Front line slits are reconnoitred on the right of STURGEON AVENUE, frames are brought up, and 6 are completed. FISH SUPPORT is extended 70ˣ southwards and trench boarding commenced. STURGEON SUPPORT is trench boarded and forts commenced. The dug-out at J.7.c.9.1. is handed over to the 404th Coy. and slits are started at J.6.c.6.4. and J.R.a.2.8. where there are unfinished entrances. A tunnel is also commenced under the (AMBRAI ROAD where STURGEON SUPPORT crosses it. The DOIGNIES – DEMICOURT Road is screened for 800ˣ and a start is made with the DOIGNIES – BEAUMETZ road. On the 18th Capt Nivers goes on leave. Lieut HALL returns from Brittany School on the 19th. The 154 Brigade is relieved by the 152 and the 153. The 152 Brigade taking 2/3 of the line on the right. It is arranged that the 401st and 2 sections of 404th Coy will work with the 152 Brigade under O.C. 401st Coy. on the same lines as before. 6 more "Subby holes" are made	

Army Form C. 2118.

WAR DIARY
or
INTELLIGENCE SUMMARY.

(Erase heading not required.)

Instructions regarding War Diaries and Intelligence Summaries are contained in F. S. Regs., Part II. and the Staff Manual respectively. Title pages will be prepared in manuscript.

401st (HIGHLAND) FIELD COMPANY, R.E.
Vol. XXVI
31.12.17.
5.

Place	Date	Hour	Summary of Events and Information	Remarks and references to Appendices.
	27th – 30th		SHARK SUPPORT is dug through from FISH AVENUE to old SHARK SUPPORT. Dug-outs are commenced on SHARK and FISH and also on STURGEON. Posts with latrines and cookhouses are commenced on SHARK and STURGEON. Lt HALL goes on leave on the 23rd. The 152 Brigade handover to the L.H. of RABBIT ALLEY to the 153 Brigade and take over new line as far as BETTY AVENUE from the 5th Brigade, 2nd Division. Lt GIBSON to Transport Lines on the 27th. Sgt GLEGG goes to III Army Infantry School on the 28th. The new line taken over is found to be very bad and 430ˣ of new support are dug from BETTY to the right, on the 28th. STURGEON AVENUE is continued 160ˣ to the right of STURGEON AVENUE. Posts are carried on on SHARK,(2) FISH, and STURGEON.(2)	yes yes yes 25
	31st		SHARK, FISH, and STURGEON supports have been "King" covered. "Cubby holes" have been made. In the day-out at J.6.c.6.4. and J.12.a.2.8. the passages have been journeyed and chambers commenced	yes

Major, R.E.
O.C. 401st (Highland) Field Coy., R.E.

Army Form C. 2118.

WAR DIARY
OF
INTELLIGENCE SUMMARY.

(Erase heading not required.)

Instructions regarding War Diaries and Intelligence Summaries are contained in F. S. Regs., Part II. and the Staff Manual respectively. Title pages will be prepared in manuscript.

401st (HIGHLAND) FIELD COMPANY, R.E.
No. Vol: XXXVI 6.
Date 31.12.17

Place	Date	Hour	Summary of Events and Information	Remarks and references to Appendices
			The month has been spent in working hard to make a trench system. Hard frost nearly all month has hindered this work, but the sector has been very quiet. Reinforcements received during month:- 1 Officer and 9 other ranks Number of men on leave during month:- 2 Officers and 11 O.R's Number of men to Divisional Rest Camp during month:- 8 O.R's Transfers during month:- Lt. G. OKELL Transferred to Zone Training Centre Roll of officers with Company at 31.12.17:- MAJOR J.R.WARREN, CAPT W.C.GLEGG, CAPT R.O.NIVEN, LIEUTS:- A.E.HALL, J. PEEBLES, J.D.GIBSON, and A.J.RICHARDSON.	

WA 36

WAR DIARY

OF

401st (HIGHLAND) FIELD COMPANY R.E.

FOR

JANUARY 1918

VOL XXXVII

401st (HIGHLAND) FIELD COMPANY, R.E.
No.
Date 31.1.18

Army Form C. 2118.

WAR DIARY
or
INTELLIGENCE SUMMARY.
(Erase heading not required.)

401st (HIGHLAND) FIELD COMPANY, R.E.
No. VOL XXX VII
Date ....

Place	Date	Hour	Summary of Events and Information	Remarks and references to Appendices
DOIGNIES	1918 JAN. 1		The Officers Have a Holiday & spent at personal billets where they have a good dinner.	Nil.
	2-7		All work is returned. Continuous work is started on the tunnel under the CAMBRAI Road, and arrangements are made to extend TURGEON SUPPORT nightly to the Right. Lt PAULIN is attached from the 4th to the 7th as part of the TT Coff course. Capt NINIAN returned from leave on the 4th, and issued T.R. would billets on the 5th. Lt PEEBLES transferred Leave on the 6th and on the 7th. The 1st Rgld relieved the 154 Rgde on the nights 7/8th. 200 ft of TURGEON Support have been dug and filled sandbag shelters have also been constructed to Ind. obsposit, and the numbers of annual front line shelters have been increased to 34. The covering of the BEAUMETZ-DOIGNIES road has been completed, and that of the DEMICOURT-GRAINCOURT road started. The 1st Rgde have continued WALSH SUPPORT about 500 yards to the left, without RE supervision, but it is not advanced.	Nil.
	8-15		Work is continued with the 152 Brigade. Lt WALL returns from leave	Nil.

2353 Wt. W2514/1454 700,000 5/15 D.D.&L. A.D.S.S.Forms/C 2118.

WAR DIARY or INTELLIGENCE SUMMARY

Army Form C. 2118.

Place	Date	Hour	Summary of Events and Information	Remarks and references to Appendices
DOIGNIES	1918 JAN 8-15		On the 13th, and party to forward billets in the Barastre Befarts, within the 152 Brigade. The tunnel under the CAMBRAI - BAPAUME road has been completed (51'). The East chamber of the dug-out at V.C.6.4. and V.12.a.2.8. are in progress. The number of mined shelters in front has been increased to 42. The recovery of the DEMICOURT - GRAINCOURT road has been nearly completed, as far as PHILIP ALLEY. About 400' of fire-trench between STURGEON and SHARK, RABBIT supports have been completed, and a start has been made on 400' of trench between STURGEON and FISH SUPPORTS. Altimate traverses and front have been started. The weather turned severely, but neither while they have tried nor any snow lately any further work could have effected. Both have crumbled. Rifled trench are had. On the 11th No. 402188 Spr. J.W. FRASER is severely wounded, and later dies.	AL.

2353 Wt. W3544/1454 700,000 5/15 D.D.&L.   A.D.S.S. Forms/C.2118.

Army Form C. 2118.

WAR DIARY
or
INTELLIGENCE SUMMARY.
(Erase heading not required.)

Instructions regarding War Diaries and Intelligence Summaries are contained in F.S. Regs., Part II and the Staff Manual respectively. Title pages will be prepared in manuscript.

Place	Date	Hour	Summary of Events and Information	Remarks and references to Appendices
	JAN.			
DOIGNIES	16&17		154th Bde. whom 152nd Bde. on night of 15th/16th. Work continued with 154th Bde. Very wet weather set in and much work done & to then clearing trenches of falen. Major WARREN to transfer some on 17th.	BM
	18th		Major WARREN & R.E. Training School, BLENDESQUES. Company returned by 4.55 P.M. (West Riding) Field Coy R.E. Enemy Trench Company STURGEON+FISH SUPPORTS practically completed. Number of Mined Shelter in front line increased to 51. Dugout T.6.C.6.4. 2.18 Chamber completed + bunked 1.10 Chamber completed but bunks started. Dugout T.12.a.2.8 completed + bunked 1.10 Chamber completed mt bunked started. Dugout T.12.a.2.8 2.18 Chamber completed + bunked 1.10 Chamber completed 2nd bunked Scenery of DOIGNIES — DEMICOURT RD in DOIGNIE'S nijunan about 1/2 completed by 4 huts in BEVANY, 150 to Bn. viewed 7/41 - Bn.	BM
BEVANY	19th		Company Trans with 154th Bde. Camp & COURCELLES-le-COMTÉ.	BM
COURCELLES	20th		Company move with 154th Bde. Camp & RAMSART & thence independently & BOISLEUL-MONT	BM
BOISLEULMONT	21st		Company & much in R.E. Camp BAILLEULMONT. Training started on 23rd & Lieut. J.	BM
	25th		PEEBLES return from leave on the 24th.	
	26th		A Platoon numbering 1 Officer + 20 O.R. is attached to The Company from 1/5 T.T. S.H. Lieut MCLAREN in Command), they went on Sapper Trans. Company move to ABLAINZEVILLE and is accommodated in the Camp there.	

Army Form C. 2118.

WAR DIARY
or
INTELLIGENCE SUMMARY.
(Erase heading not required.)

Instructions regarding War Diaries and Intelligence Summaries are contained in F. S. Regs., Part II. and the Staff Manual respectively. Title pages will be prepared in manuscript.

Place	Date	Hour	Summary of Events and Information	Remarks and references to Appendices
ABLAINZEVELLE	27th		Company employed in making Latrines Cookhouses etc for 2 new Camps	
	28th		2 Sections erect 5 Nissen huts and 2 Section work on Camps and estates improvements.	
	29th		Company erect 10 Nissen huts for R.A.M.C. Camp.	
	30th		R.A.M.C. Camp completed & 2 huts Latrines attached Lignum Vitae Cottages.	
	31st		Work on Company Camp and estates.	
			Reinforcements received during month — 12 other ranks	
			Number of officers & men on leave during month 1 officer 15 other ranks	
			All 8 Officers with Company on 31.1.18 — Major J.R. WARREN M.C., Capt. H.C. CLEGG, Capt. R.O. NIVEN, Lieuts — A.E. HALL, J. PEEBLES, J.D. GIBSON, H.J. RICHARDSON	

WH 37

401st (HIGHLAND) FIELD COMPANY, R.E.
2/3/18

WAR DIARY

OF

401ST (HIGHLAND) FIELD COY. R.E.

FOR

FEBRUARY 1918.

Vol XXXVIII.

Army Form C. 2118.

WAR DIARY
or
INTELLIGENCE SUMMARY.
(Erase heading not required.)

Instructions regarding War Diaries and Intelligence Summaries are contained in F. S. Regs., Part II. and the Staff Manual respectively. Title pages will be prepared in manuscript.

Place	Date	Hour	Summary of Events and Information	Remarks and references to Appendices
ABLAINZEVILLE	Feb. 1st		Company paraded in Infantry drill, musketry etc.	
	2nd		154th Infantry Bde arrives and the whole Company is put on to Cookhouse, ablution sheds, and latrines for the Brigade Gp's Camp at LOGEAST WOOD, in conjunction with 11th Battalion	
	3rd		Company continues work in LOGEAST WOOD Camp. A Church Parade is held.	
	4th		2 Section resumes Infantry Training and 2 Section remains at work at LOGEAST WOOD Camp. Major CLEGG returns from Course at VII Corps Infantry School.	
	5th		Lieut RICHARDSON and 2 N.C.O's & Cadre of instruction to Bgdes proceed to VII Corps School. Training and work on LOGEAST Camp carried on as to 4th inst.	
	6th & 7th		Company received in Infantry Training, Exercises Drill etc. 2 Section at Work on Camp.	
	8th		Company took over Camp. Grounded ans for a Shirt musketry course from P.E. Training School.	
	9th		Training and work on Camp continues. Major WARREN goes on leave. BLENDECQUES.	

Army Form C. 2118.

WAR DIARY
or
INTELLIGENCE SUMMARY.
(Erase heading not required.)

Instructions regarding War Diaries and Intelligence Summaries are contained in F. S. Regs., Part II. and the Staff Manual respectively. Title pages will be prepared in manuscript.

Place	Date	Hour	Summary of Events and Information	Remarks and references to Appendices
HEBUTERNE	FEB 10th		Work on Camp continued. A start is made with section of stables for Battalion Transport.	
	11th		Rehearsal of movements for Infantry Inspection. Full parade of mounted orderlies mounted with horses, vehicles etc.	
	12th		Inspection of whole Company by C.R.E. Lieut PEEBLES + HALL proceed to LEBUCQUIERE to take over work and billets from 509th (London) Field Coy R.E.	
	13th		Work and billets at LOREAST WOOD CAMP are handed over to 130th Field C.R.E. Company moves to billets evacuated by 509th Field Coy R.E. at LEBUCQUIERE.	
LEBUCQUIERE	14th		Capt. A. LEGG is attached by C.R.E. to be in charge of the IVth Corps Defence line in 51st Divisional Sector. Sectors 3 + 4 start work in Infantry trades. Capt CLEGG assisted by Pt. WILSON R.E. IInd Corps and by Sgt OATES + 12 O.R. of R.A.R.E. who are also billeted with our Company. Sections 1 + 2 undertake HALL STAFF work on Infantry trenches in 258, 253rd + 293rd Reb. R.F.A. at PEEBLES + 154th Bde. Lewis Gun Course.	

Major, R.E.

WAR DIARY
or
INTELLIGENCE SUMMARY.
(Erase heading not required.)

Army Form C. 2118.

O.C. 101st (Highland) Field Coy. R.E.

Place	Date	Hour	Summary of Events and Information	Remarks and references to Appendices
LEBUCQUIÈRE	15th		8 Augts. fm R.A. under construction by Secs 1 & 2. Drilling working parties supplied. Work on Cope Lens Gnoats & wiring, thickening wire, laying knife rests. Listening and clearing old french, wiring, firesteps and cutting fireshops also digging new trench and spitlocking & CR:TR. line. Working parties of 2 & 90. Infantry	
	16th		11 Augts. and under supervision of Secs 1 & 2. Work as before as before. Lt. RICHARDSON, Corpl. MILNE (No 3 Secn), 2nd Cpl. ROCKETT (No 2 Secn) return from GAS Course.	
	17th		Work continued as on 15th & 16th. Lt. PEEBLES return from Leave. Gnoac once taken over temporarily. The RICHARDSON section. No work on Cope line.	
	18th		Work continued as before. Lt. RICHARDSON & 154 Btn Lewis Gun Course. Work as on MIDGSON & COSTING O.P.s	
	19th		12 Drilling Augts. and under company supervision. Secn 3 & 4 work on Cope line. Sent two infantry working parties on craters as 19th 20th & 21st. A. GIBSON return from leave.	
	20th		Work on 12 Augts. and I.O.R. Riveting firestep, laying thickening wire & Cope line.	

Army Form C. 2118.

WAR DIARY
or
INTELLIGENCE SUMMARY.
(Erase heading not required.)

B.B. 401st (Highland) Field Coy, R.E.

Major, R.E.

Place	Date	Hour	Summary of Events and Information	Remarks and references to Appendices
LEBUCQUIERE	Feby			
	21st		Work on 11 dugouts and 3 O.P.s by Secs 1 & 2. Corps dmn worked on Secs 3 & 4. Supplying a few men to working party available	R.E.
	22nd		13 dugouts and 3 O.P.s under construction by Secs 1 + 2. Supplying a few men to working party. 1 dugout and 1 Gas Point under construction with infantry working party. Secs 3 + 4 dug with 340 Infantry work on O.P.s in Lt. RICHARDSON finished. Lieut Enn Course.	
	23rd		Lieut Enn Course	23/4
	24th		Work continued as before.	24/2
	25th		do	25/2
	26th		do	26/2
	27th		do	
	28th		Lt PEEBLES to CRE's office. Preparations made for change in position of Infantry Brummel Front. By the morning of the 2nd 2nd Div will be two Brigades holding the line, the 154 Bgde in the night, 2 Batteries will now be housed with the Brigade. 1 section with E and one Capt PEEBLES	R.E.

WAR DIARY
or
INTELLIGENCE SUMMARY

Army Form C. 2118.

Place	Date	Hour	Summary of Events and Information	Remarks and references to Appendices
BRONFAY	Feb 28		Party with 1 Cpl 404 Coy for work on the Rifle Range with 293 (Army) Bgde RFA affiliating 184 Bgde. Lts GIBSON and RICHARDSON with R.E Stores & mp/s & mounted orderlies at J.17.a.8.7 marched by 404 Coy. and others the new 184 Bgde lines in trenches over F.T.O 450 and 404 Coy. C.S.M OGDEN hospital.	NC
				Rh
			Recce parties received during march 25 17 No. of Officers incl. O.R. in Recce 10	Nbs

O.C. 401st (Highland) Field Coy. R.E.

Major. R.E.

51st Divisional Engineers.

WAR DIARY

401st FIELD COMPANY R.E.

MARCH 1918

WAR DIARY.

401st (Highland) Field Coy. R.E.

MARCH - 1918

W.L. Buckingham
Major R.E.
29/4/18

WAR DIARY
or
INTELLIGENCE SUMMARY.
(Erase heading not required.)

Army Form C. 2118.

Place	Date	Hour	Summary of Events and Information	Remarks and references to Appendices
LEBUQUIERE	1918 MARCH 1-4		Unit commenced to forward certain Lectures 1 on Sept 15th Regt. front making reconnaissance preparing to defend and reserve lines and maintaining and emptying STURGEON GRAYLING SUPPORTS. Lecture 2 on night working reconnaissance most fire positions, also on A.D.S., we reserve line, and maintaining and emptying WALSH SUPPORT. Lecture 2 con- tinued work on 3 R.E. dugouts and one O.P. dugout in 29.3 Army By as R.F.A. and also work in relief of men of the R.E. at J.23.6. Lect. 4 with Capt FLEES on Reg. Lines. Filling gas cleared sandbags in for- ward unit. Transfer work by the Batt. front opposite to the infested 2 listening work by night. Lt. TELFORD and ALLAN re-enter of kilts issued by Lectures 1+3. Yth. S.E. MOSS returned for duty on 1st.	Yes.
	5-8		Work as above continued, all definite objective on Feb 28th Lt PEERLES returned from L.E.H.Q. and Lt MOSS returned to the 2nd C.S. from above the level lines. The forward lectures are continued to stand to in PEACH. There was night wind mornings.	Yes.

WAR DIARY
or
INTELLIGENCE SUMMARY.

Army Form C. 2118.

Place	Date	Hour	Summary of Events and Information	Remarks and references to Appendices
LERUCQUETZ	1919 MARCH 9-13		Took on tours. Informed the Division of the DELICOURT – GRAY COURT road as compared to reform 3, and small armed patrols are sent out in the front line by gets 2 on the Coys. This is a period of normal vigilance, and on the 13th the forward patrols are ordered to stand to at 4 am and the remainder of the Coys at 5 am. There is no attack. On the 13th gets 2 + 4 return above.	App.
		M-12	pre orders 7 + 3. pre forces to be directed in acct to Gpl. Hutty to further exploit the advance Park. It is decided however to try a antonion thrust thirty from the Lft. Capt GLEGG put in Resne ag the 14th Batt. 3 is relieved from rest in the Coys. Lazy in the 19th. G.O.C Division has been w/km/ted G.O.C. II Corps. (Lt. Ben Sin G.M. HARPER)	
	19		The reserve line is out 3' deep for 800 x from the Rft, and this now depts are ennumed in it, at R.12 a.8.6 + R12 b.11	App.

WAR DIARY or INTELLIGENCE SUMMARY

Army Form C. 2118.

Place	Date	Hour	Summary of Events and Information	Remarks and references to Appendices
TRENCH J.19.C.3. 57.C.N.W.	21st March 1918		Enemy start heavy bombardment at 5 A.M. — Major WARREN & Lt PEEBLES SON wounded by shell splinter at "SNIPPER" C.H.I.P. The two forward sections were Lt PEEBLES are heavily shelled by H.E. & 5.9" shells there two sections stood to in their field positions in "ROACH TRENCH" from 5.30 A.M. till 7.30 A.M. so no attack was developed they return to their dugouts at about 10.30 A.M. the enemy attack on their right flank, sections return to their battle positions. CAPT McCRONE 403 & 404 Regt & rest Coy. E. takes temporary command of the Coy. at 12 noon. Two sections 401 Coy & two sections 404 Coy are ordered to Shelled K53b89. 1 E.R.E. 404 Coy under CAPT RHE & 401 Coy under CAPT McCRONE workers to Front of HEBUTERNE 401 Coy on the left 404 on the right. Sections heavily shelled before reaching their positions. northern observation posts ask O.C. McCrone (CAPT McCrone) progress to report & 152 Bde say in order B.G.C. 152 Bd Bngs orders two sections to improve the works in front of HEBUTERNE NORGNIES LINE, while the line carries the DOMONS CRIMSON TOP C.P.E. dead bodies were carried to the SOUPSITCHEN at TYNES enemy were dug in on thorns hills of one wire pickets scheme vehicles... to make the carrying of HEBUCOURNE the 152 Bde Bngs orders men are still on Sunday then move into a very nice day hot from there ... ... carrying out with Holiday hot I day ... trench

WAR DIARY
or
INTELLIGENCE SUMMARY.
(Erase heading not required.)

Army Form C. 2118.

Place	Date	Hour	Summary of Events and Information	Remarks and references to Appendices
TRENCH T.19.C.31. 57.C.S.W.	21st March	10.15	Coy. start(?) my the position to Lookeon on shown on sketch ③. Coy. formed under CAPT NIVEN march from SAPPER CAMP to new work on BAPAUME PERONNE Rd. at N.4.b.4.3.	
	22nd March		The two forward sections made HYPES BLUES numbers poles to represent that position & return to BDE. 134 Inf.Brig. at 3.30pm to form extra ordered to rejoin their own front line & R.V.S. camp on BAPAUME PERONNE Rd. Section in front of LEBOEUFSIERE found a new 2 point morning informs third Division Inf-team attack the SEM-MEIZ MORCHIES LINE that have been very [illegible], as our unreadable finds all the above attacks were repulsed about 5pm [illegible] the BRANCH line N. of VAULENCOURT, I come to a point the north of the road, there is not a battalion, [illegible] a battalion state with the three companies but...	

(A7092) Wt. W12859/M1293. 750,000. 1/17. D. D. & L., Ltd. Forms/C.2118/14.

WAR DIARY
or
INTELLIGENCE SUMMARY.

Army Form C. 2118.

Place	Date	Hour	Summary of Events and Information	Remarks and references to Appendices
TRENCH J19.C.37. 57C.N.W.	22nd March 1918		the BAPAUME RD to hang on BEAUMETZ and during the night the Bn [illegible] back to [illegible] ... The Bn left [illegible] ready to go in the SOUP KITCHEN at 8.30. The Bn moved up to [illegible] ... and took up [illegible] Btn hg 401 5 men [illegible] ... GREVILLERS & IRLES [illegible]	
	23rd March		Enemy attacked the [illegible] ... CAMBRAI RD [illegible] ... the range to the valley [illegible] ... east of the village [illegible] ... We withdrew at 10.30 am [illegible] ... at LEBUCQUIERE [illegible] ... the village	

WAR DIARY or INTELLIGENCE SUMMARY

Army Form C. 2118.

(Erase heading not required.)

Place	Date	Hour	Summary of Events and Information	Remarks and references to Appendices
M.V.S. CAMP AT N.4,B,4,3. SHEET 57.C.	23rd March		We leave the railway embankment about 12 noon. I got instructions from Col SCOTT 1/5th SEAFORTHS to fall back to the GREEN LINE in front of HAPLINCOURT. Take up a position on the GREEN LINE about 1 P.M. – 117th started an engagement from Reserves to the GREEN LINE about 5 P.M. US Bde Artillery the GREEN LINE passing to 1st 5th Div to support at BANCOURT. Seaforth moved back right up the Road until 154 I of Bde went BAPAUME when in turn they were asked to fall back. At 11 P.M. sectors at REAR H.Q. parallel to PEEBLES are ordered at 11 P.M. to make POSTS East of BANCOURT, I/k the POSTS and simulate action in the shape to hold them.	
	24th March		Sections 401 & 404 come under orders of the 154 Inf Bde. The infantry running through the village of BEAULENCOURT, the action was to have retired. Fort Mowton is on the crest of a hill running from W.11.C.8.3. The 1st 5 Inf Bdes take over the position of the Seaforths by 8 a.m. and are now holding a hill East of CAPE LINE TRENCH. I wrote and no further actions occurred about 1 P.M. the infantry to retain forward about 1 BEAULENCOURT up and advance and dig in along a cemetery running from N.11.C.8.5. to W.11.B.5.2. at 3 P.M. the 152 Inf Bdg take over the position of the Seaforths By I P.M. Guns in action along the other side of the BAPAUME TRONCHE RD.	

(A7092) Wt. W1859/M1293. 75,000. 1/17. D. D. & L., Ltd. Forms/C2118/14

Army Form C. 2118.

WAR DIARY
or
INTELLIGENCE SUMMARY.
(Erase heading not required.)

Instructions regarding War Diaries and Intelligence Summaries are contained in F. S. Regs., Part II. and the Staff Manual respectively. Title pages will be prepared in manuscript.

Place	Date	Hour	Summary of Events and Information	Remarks and references to Appendices
LOUPART WOOD. 3 miles W of BAPAUME LENS 11 & 57C.SW.	24th March		Showed me a copy of the orders; they were as follows. The returns following the line through BEAULENCOURT were to put out to be strongly entrenched & will fall back on our frontier. The 45 Bde were to fall back on the vicinity of ROCQUIGNY, — ours C were ordered to LE BARQUE & N11C.3S. to reinforce the hospital at BARQUES, two platoons from Barque. Sergt Mackay 404 ACoy 2 platoons with Lieut ————— were ordered to Le Taylor tp to be taken by the Company Miller and on the spot I took C Coy on the left about 500 yards & left CO out on my left about SSam. Everything was very quiet as there were no troops about. The sitten withd in good order. Had a a men fired to any fire 500 yds so as to enfilade the trench at about ferst occupd of bay at N10c85 a 10th man from trench at N07.d43 (as he hung back we thought everything I saw them turned had retired at N.Cp.b.b.g. The Byg Anny 154th & A Boys not moved to battle with my men at LOUPART WOOD. I had instructions to report to 68th of Brig 153 Ind Brig reported me. Then Sergt Mackay 404 ACoy reported as at LETHEROY & reporter held the fort had been set on fire. No could see them sending to the distance. The two sections under LT PEEBLES forced a fairly quick movement in front of BANCOURT They withheld started in the afternoon.	

(A7092) Wt. W12839/M1293. 750,000. 1/17. D. D. & L., Ltd. Forms/C.2118/14.

Army Form C. 2118.

WAR DIARY
or
INTELLIGENCE SUMMARY.
(*Erase heading not required.*)

Instructions regarding War Diaries and Intelligence Summaries are contained in F. S. Regs., Part II. and the Staff Manual respectively. Title pages will be prepared in manuscript.

Place	Date	Hour	Summary of Events and Information	Remarks and references to Appendices
	1918.			
LOUPART WOOD	24th	March	retired and make the position untenable for the sappers. LT PEEBLES falls back to LE TILLOY and receives instructions there to report at LOUPART WOOD.	
3 miles W of BAPAUME.	25th	March.	I got in touch with LT PEEBLES & his two sections about 12.30 AM. The sappers come under the orders of 153 Inf Brig which is detailed to hold the left of the Div sector. Officers from the 51st Div Staff meet the troops and arrange them in their [illegible] positions for the following day. The sappers are put in support about 250 yds in rear of LOUPART WOOD. The party under my command is now about 80 strong, consisting of about 45 OR 401st Coy under LT PEEBLES [illegible] GIBSON 25 OR 404th Coy under LT ROBERTSON & 10 OR 400th Coy under LT PEEBLES. The sappers hold a length of 400 yds. The men are evenly divided among the officers each officer holding 100 yds. LT PEEBLES on the right, then LT HAIG, LT GIBSON & LT ROBERTSON. The infantry on our right flank were very shaky and required to be rallied & put back in their positions before the enemy really made a determined attack. About 12.30 P.M. the enemy attack the position in force, the main attack being [illegible] on our flanks. As the trench [illegible] from the centre of our section to the crest of the hill behind, I decided that although our flanks were [illegible] [illegible] we could hold on for some time, [illegible] [illegible] this trench without suffering heavy casualties [illegible] at the same time bring heavy fire on the enemy from the trench. The infantry on our right flank were driven in. LT GIBSON [illegible]	

(A7092). Wt. W12839/M1293. 750,000. 1/17. D. D. & L., Ltd. Forms/C.2118/14.

Instructions regarding War Diaries and Intelligence Summaries are contained in F. S. Regs., Part II. and the Staff Manual respectively. Title pages will be prepared in manuscript.

WAR DIARY
or
INTELLIGENCE SUMMARY.

(Erase heading not required.)

Army Form C. 2118.

Place	Date	Hour	Summary of Events and Information	Remarks and references to Appendices
FONQUEVILLERS. 10 miles N.W. of BAPAUME LENS 11.	1918 25th March		section and [illegible] the right flank, the other three sections keeping up a heavy fire on the centre of the wood, it was here that Lt GIBSON was shot through the head, I deeply regret the loss of this gallant officer, he was a splendid type of British manhood. I then gave the order to withdraw up the trench. LT ROBERTSON 404th Coy was killed just as he was withdrawing his section, LT HALL with his section were the last to withdraw, LT HALL being wounded in the leg. On leaving the trench at the top of the crest the men came under very heavy rifle & MG fire, it was crossing this stretch of open to towards IRLES that most of our casualties were sustained. The remnants of the men then held a line of shell holes in front of IRLES, the enemy made no attempt to advance there for about an hour. [illegible] were finally withdrawn to a line along the crest behind IRLES. LT PEEBLES with a party of sappers was attached by the 153 Bde to [illegible]. This line eventually withdrew to about 400 yds behind IRLES [illegible] trench on the reverse slope of the hill. We then received orders that the 51st Div was to rejoin their HQ. LT PEEBLES & myself with as many sappers as we could collect marched to PUISIEUX-AU-MONT [illegible] to FONQUEVILLERS, where we rejoined our transport. The total casualties of 400 Coy from the beginning of operations was 6 officers 70 O.R.	

(A7092). Wt. W12839/M1293. 750,000. 1/17. D. D. & L., Ltd. Forms/C.2118/14.

Army Form C. 2118.

WAR DIARY
or
INTELLIGENCE SUMMARY.
(Erase heading not required.)

Instructions regarding War Diaries and Intelligence Summaries are contained in F. S. Regs., Part II. and the Staff Manual respectively. Title pages will be prepared in manuscript.

Place	Date	Hour	Summary of Events and Information	Remarks and references to Appendices
TRANSHET. 3 mile NW of DOUULENS LENS.II.				

WAR DIARY
or
INTELLIGENCE SUMMARY.

Army Form C. 2118.

Place	Date	Hour	Summary of Events and Information	Remarks and references to Appendices
TANSART	28/3/18		A/Major W.E. BUCKINGHAM M.C. rejoined the Company from 66th Divi. to take over Command. S.C. MOSS R.E. temp. attached to company from 400th Fld. Coy. R.E. - Capt. McCRONE rejoined 400th Fld Coy RE. Company marched to FREVENT where it entrained for LA FUGNOY arriving at latter place at about 9.30 a.m. next day, and marched into billets at GONNEHEM.	
	29/3/18			
	30/3/18			
	31/3/18		In rest billets GONNEHEM. Casualties suffered during active operations from 21/3/18 - 25/3/18 were as follows.	
	21/3/18		A/Major J.R. WARREN R.E (T) wounded) by same shell in billet at LEBUCQUIÈRE	
	"		Lieut H.J. RICHARDSON R.E.(T) ")	
	25/3/18		Lieut E J.D. GIBSON R.E (T) killed in action	
	"		A.E. HALL R.E.(T) wounded	
			5 O.R. killed	
			17 O.R. wounded	
			16 O.R. missing.	
			Also the following casualties among O.R.s	
			Strength on 31/3/18 — 4 officers +1 attached officer	
			174 O.R.	

29/4/18

W.G. Buckingham
Major RE
O.C. 401st (W.R.) Fld. Cy. RE

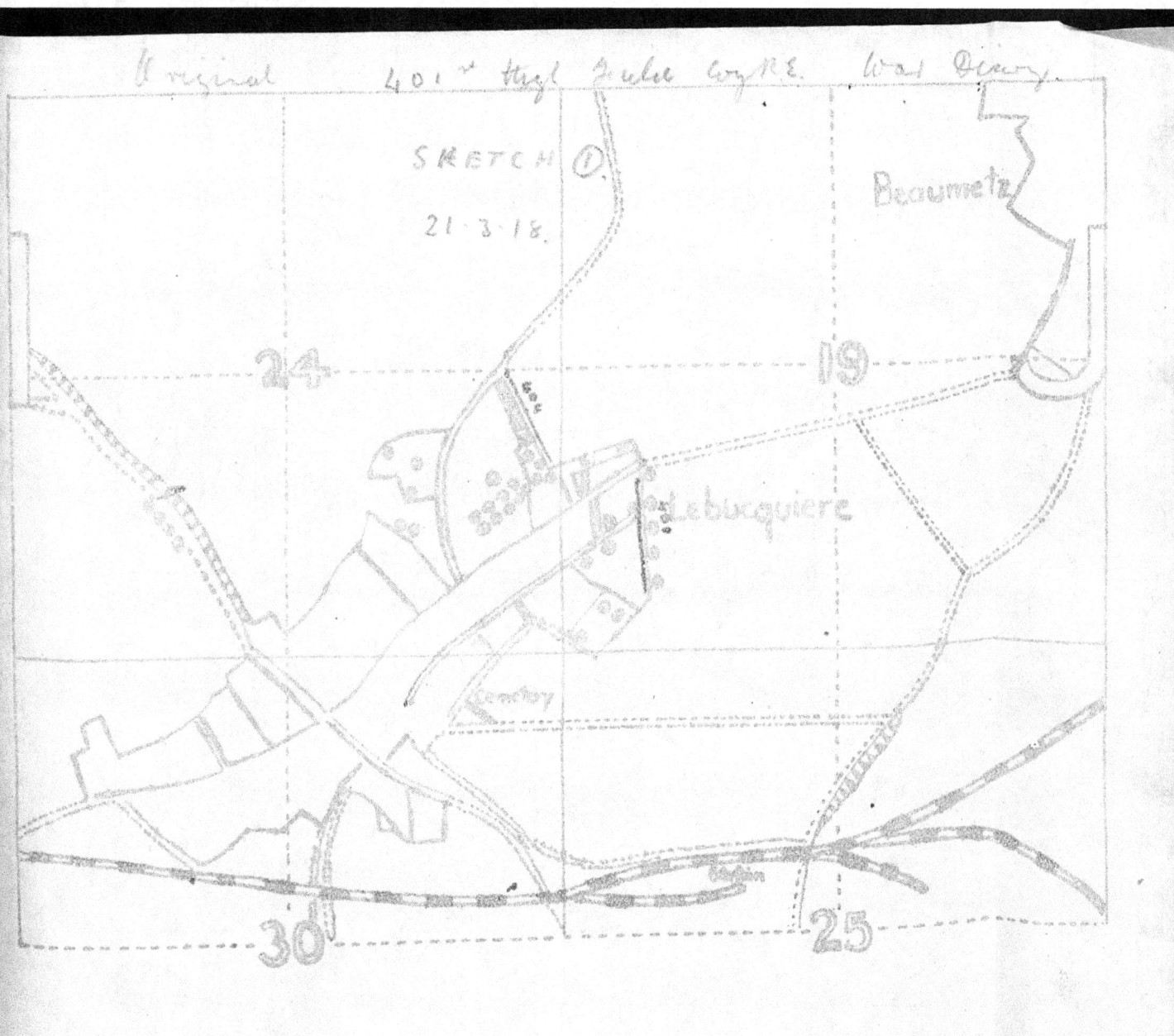

Part of Sheet 57c.

Original British Line to 21-3-18 ———
Line at 22-3-18 - - - - - -

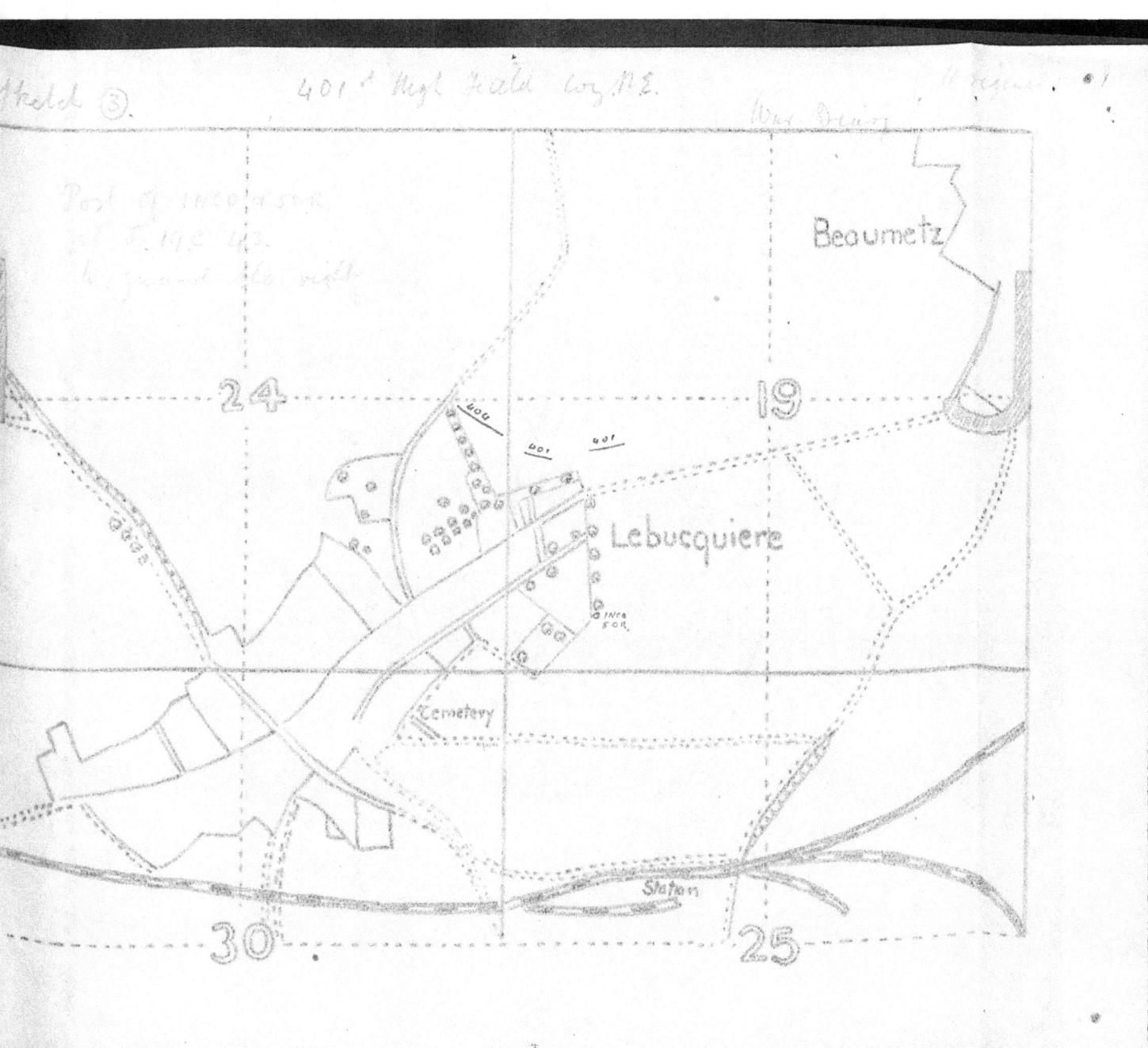

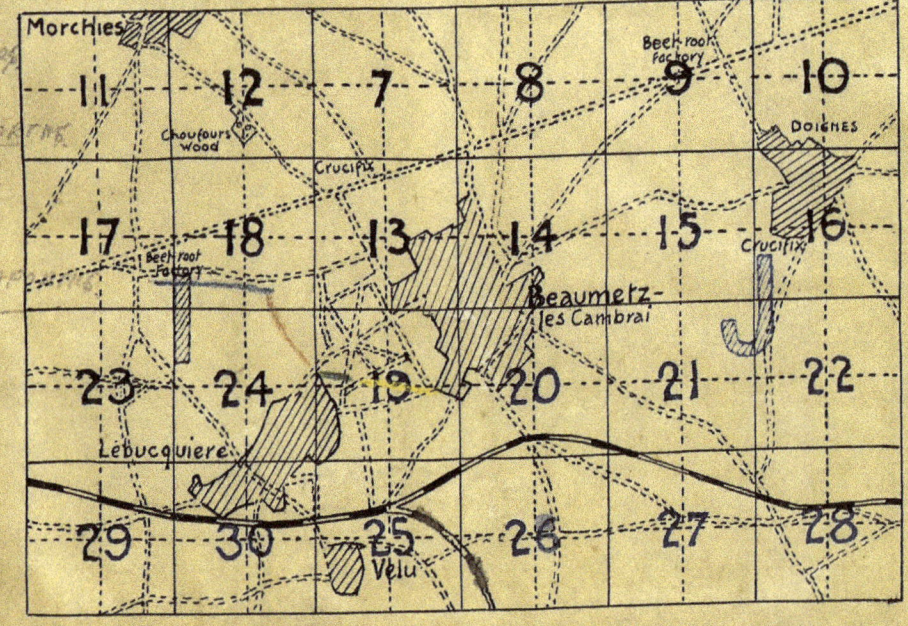

51st Divisional Engineers

WAR DIARY

401st (Highland) FIELD COMPANY R.E.

APRIL 1 9 1 8

SECRET

WAR DIARY

401st (HIGHLAND) Field Coy: RE

April – 1918

W.C. Buckingham
Major RE
1/5/18

Army Form C. 2118.

WAR DIARY
or
INTELLIGENCE SUMMARY. 401st (1/1) Fld. Co. R.E.

(Erase heading not required.)

APRIL 1918.

Instructions regarding War Diaries and Intelligence Summaries are contained in F. S. Regs., Part II. and the Staff Manual respectively. Title pages will be prepared in manuscript.

Place	Date	Hour	Summary of Events and Information	Remarks and references to Appendices
GONNEHEM	1.4.18 – 4.4.18		Am not billets at GONNEHEM. - Employed getting Rolls, kit insp., drill and musketry for Equipment and Stores lost during German offensive. 2nd Lt. D. G. SANDEMAN R.E.(T) joined the Company from R.E.B. Depot for duty. 1.4.18	
	4.4.18		Moved billets to CAMBLAIN CHÂTELAIN (3 miles West of BRUAY) Inspected by Divisional Commander en route.	
AUCHEL	5.4.18		Moved billets to AUCHEL at short notice - Employed Company in drill etc while at AUCHEL and attended LEWIS GUN Instruction from 154th Inf. Bde. Lewis Gun Instr. in LEWIS GUN	
	5.4.18		2nd Lt. D. A. B. ROBERTSON R.E.(T) reported for duty from R.E. Base Depot.	
	7.4.18		2nd Lt. W. GAULD R.E.(T) reported for duty from R.E. Base Depot, 2nd Lt. S. C. MOSS reported 400th (1/1) Fld. Co. R.E.	
CENSE LA VALLÉE	8.4.18		Moved from AUCHEL to CENSE LA VALLÉE	
L'ECLEME	9.4.18		Moved to L'ECLEME - German attack developed on PORTUGUESE front from GIVENCHY Northwards.	
	10.4.18		Defensive system along LA BASSÉE CANAL reconnoitred and reported on. Pontoon bridge consisting of 5 bays - one trestle and stone pontoon piers in canal on LA BASSÉE Canal in front of HINGES by No. 4 & No. 3 Sections (x which No. 3 Section remained at HINGETTE and took own responsibility for demolition of 2 Road bridges on LA BASSÉE Canal at HINGETTE and PONT D'HINGES from 480th (1/1) Fld. Co. R.E.	
	11.4.18		Same Section took over responsibility for demolition of Bridge over Canal at AVELETTE from 552 AT Co. RE. The Company less above section standing by at L'ECLEME	
	12.4.18		Company moved forward to prepare 3 road bridges and one footbridge on LA BASSÉE CANAL between FACAUT WOOD and ROBECQ (marked A B C & D 3 in plan.) for demolition. The Section which had responsibility for demolition of bridges over the Canal in front of HINGES ordered to hand over their responsibility to 529th Fld. Co. RE of 1st the 3rd Div.	

2353 Wt. W2544/1454 700,000 5/15 D. D. & L. A.D.S.S. Forms/C 2118.

Army Form C. 2118.

WAR DIARY or **INTELLIGENCE SUMMARY.**
(*Erase heading not required.*)

Instructions regarding War Diaries and Intelligence Summaries are contained in F. S. Regs., Part II. and the Staff Manual respectively. Title pages will be prepared in manuscript.

401st (W) Field Coy.
APRIL 1918

Place	Date	Hour	Summary of Events and Information	Remarks and references to Appendices
	12.4.18 contd		Instructions were received at the same time as the above, to hold the line of the Canal until the line in addition to arranging out its above work on bridges. On arrival at the Canal it was found that a Field Coy of the 3rd Div had already prepared the footbridges (B on sketch) for demolition and that they were not prepared to hand them over without instructions from their own R.E. The road bridge (C on sketch) west of the Bow bridge was being prepared at the time of our arrival by the 404 (W) Field Coy R.E. However responsibility for the demolition of the bridge was taken over, firing arrangements for this bridge were completed. The bridge on the extreme right of the sector (Canal) taken over was prepared for demolition by the Company and handed over off the bridge (A on sk.) just west of PACAUT WOOD. The preparation for demolition of the Road Bridge on the extreme left of the sector (D on sk.) the ROBECQ – LEQUEME road was taken in hand but was handed over to 400 (W) Field Coy R.E. before it was completed. The Section (No 3) which had worked on the footer bridge and had now handed over responsibility for the demolition of the bridges in front of HINGES was still in Reserve. At about 5 p.m. an order was received to take over responsibility for demolition of the Road Bridge over the Canal South of ROBECQ (D on sketch) and also the bridge ½ mile west of ROBECQ on the ROBECQ–BUSNES road (E on sk.) This was done and the two Sections (1+3) which were no longer required on the duties of 3/CRE were withdrawn to BUSNES. At the time Major W.E. BUCKINGHAM had taken over the duties of 3/CRE and handed over the Command of the Company to Capt W.C. GLEGG R.E. (T). The Germans were holding part of PACAUT WOOD and the VILLAGE of RIEZ-DU-VINAGE at the time and were using M.G. fire and bombs occasionally to the Bridgeheads A + B. The evening was quiet till nightfall. The Coy carried out recces for demolition of bridges in ROBECQ from ...	
	13.4.18		61st Div Engineers were ordered to take over responsibility for the demolition of bridges in ROBECQ from ... The Road bridge over the river (just East of ROBECQ Church) which was already prepared for demolition was taken ...	

Army Form C. 2118.

WAR DIARY
or
INTELLIGENCE SUMMARY.
(Erase heading not required.)

401st Fld Coy RE
APRIL 1918 (3)

Place	Date	Hour	Summary of Events and Information	Remarks and references to Appendices
	13.4.18 contd		At 1 am and then at 4 am the bridges over the Canal South and South East of ROBECQ (C & D on plan) were blown over to the 3rd Div. The Company was now responsible for the demolition of one bridge in ROBECQ (at R on plan), of one bridge 1000' APART 100D (A on plan) and one bridge taking the ROBECQ - BUSNES Road over the Canal (E on plan) — about 5000'. The three intermediate bridges on this canal being under the 3rd Div. Engineers. No 4 Section was ordered back to BUSNES in the evening.	
ROBECQ			At 7 pm on the same day orders were received that the Company was at 5 disposal of FLEMINGS FORCE and to move from BUSNES to just West of ROBECQ (Q on plan) in Section in ROBECQ). The Section in ROBECQ commenced preparing a further bridge and culvert in ROBECQ for demolition. Sites for bridges over the stream West of ROBECQ for (field) communications were reconnoitred (at R' & R" plan).	
ROBECQ	14.4.18		Preparation of above bridges and culvert in ROBECQ for demolition was completed. Two small road bridges and a culvert West of ROBECQ referred to above in the evening were commenced, one of which was completed. In the afternoon the bridge 1000' West of PACAUT WOOD (A on plan) was turned over to a Fld Co R.E. 4th Div (getting others of Sythean Aqueduct at canal near 6th BRASSERIE (N. of ROBECQ) were reconnal. and were considered too much a civilian difficulty — the projecting from each east not be demolished as the Canal bank would have been taken.	
	15.4.18		Major W.E. BUCKINGHAM R.E. resumed command of the Company.	
	16.17.4.18		The wood bridge over the river West of ROBECQ was completed and a further 2 foot bridge in ROBECQ (R' on plan) and 3 South of ROBECQ (N. O. & P. on plan) was completed, that ... the first one while the road was being felled. They were built in pairs of 2 and 3 logs cut approx 2'6" apart and sawn to form a they bridge to make them unconspicuous, and they were not within eye of the enemy. Three bridges were prepared for demolition by the Company. Stones being slung under them in wire netting and a fire of palter burnt placed ready at hand. A further bridge on the Lillers to CARVIN road 1 mile N.E. of ROBECQ was also prepared for demolition he suggested.	

Army Form C. 2118.

WAR DIARY
or
INTELLIGENCE SUMMARY.
(Erase heading not required.)

401ˢᵗ Fld Coy RE
APRIL 1918 (4)

Place	Date	Hour	Summary of Events and Information	Remarks and references to Appendices
	17.4.18 to 24.4.18		[Entry describing important bridges, 2 sappers and an infantry runner posted together with a patrol. Bridges kept covered by but not actually manned, with waterproof sheets...] From 17.4.18 — same as from that date until 24.4.18 when the Company moved out of the line. Company was continuously in section together with French and Belgian troops in front of posn held by 154ᵗʰ Inf. Bde along the CAUDNE – ROBECQ road, about 1000ˣ East of ROBECQ — and along the Rearns Line which runs along the outskirts of ROBECQ. Considerable clearing of the field of fire, draining, and revetting of trenches was carried out. A small amount of new helpers was also carried out. Some heavy revetting work was also carried out in the perimeter of a new permanent RESERVE LINE with trench dug 4½ ft deep & 3' high, and banks 4'6" above ground level, was completed with good overhead protection for parties. The Posts were made to face about 30° of fire step, with an traverses in entries giving shelter to 6" bombardment and 50% of defenders – Posts to hold no less of 1 NCO & 6 or 7. Camouflaged from Enfiladed mixed & Trench Island specially constructed for revetting with materials had to be cut for the revetments from trees to be felled in a farm on the North side of the Canal West of ROBECQ to the South side of the Canal. In this day also the responsibility for the demolition of Railway & Road Bridges over the Canal was taken over from 3 bridges being the posn at D.F.+C on the above set stages had been previously prepared. The total number of bridges for which the Company was responsible for demolition was Rm 8 rly 4 on the Canal S.W. ROBECQ and 1 at CARVIN Road – ruly East of ROBECQ. Whole company was carrying out the above work on the embankment of ROBECQ. "E" Company, whose centres on available parties, was forcibly subject by the bombing of morn standing by ...	

Army Form C. 2118.

WAR DIARY
or
INTELLIGENCE SUMMARY.
(Erase heading not required.)

401st (1/1st FD) Coy RE

APRIL 1918 (5)

Instructions regarding War Diaries and Intelligence Summaries are contained in F.S. Regs., Part II. and the Staff Manual respectively. Title pages will be prepared in manuscript.

Place	Date	Hour	Summary of Events and Information	Remarks and references to Appendices
			whole was carried out between FACAUT WOOD and the ROBECQ – CALONNE Road and in the neighbourhood of RIEZ – DU – VINAGE.	
			On 18-4-18 when the Germans attacked 4 men were wounded by shell fire, 4 other men were wounded later in the day on 18-4-18 and 2 on 20/4/18.	
			While carrying out the above work the Company was attached to 154th Inf Bde. which was holding part of line in 61st Divn area. Tools were therefore left with CRE. 61st Div. in consequence and all the work carried out.	
BOURECQ	24/4/18		The Company moved back to BOURECQ (about 4 to ST HILAIRE Rly) 400 & 1/404 H. FDd Coys. RE moved up (1100 first) to carry on work in the forward area.	
	25/4/18 – 30/4/18		Company employed on Baths, Training, and repair of vehicles. Training included Squad Drill; Saluting; Rifle Exercises; Box Respirator drill, & Range Practices. Football matches against A.S.C. + Divs.	
			Reinforcements recd. during month: 60 O.R. from R.E. Base Depot. Casualties: 13 O.R. wounded. Strength: 7 off. 192 O.R.	

H. G. Buckingham
Major RE
O.C. 401st (1/1st FD) FD C. RE
1/5/18

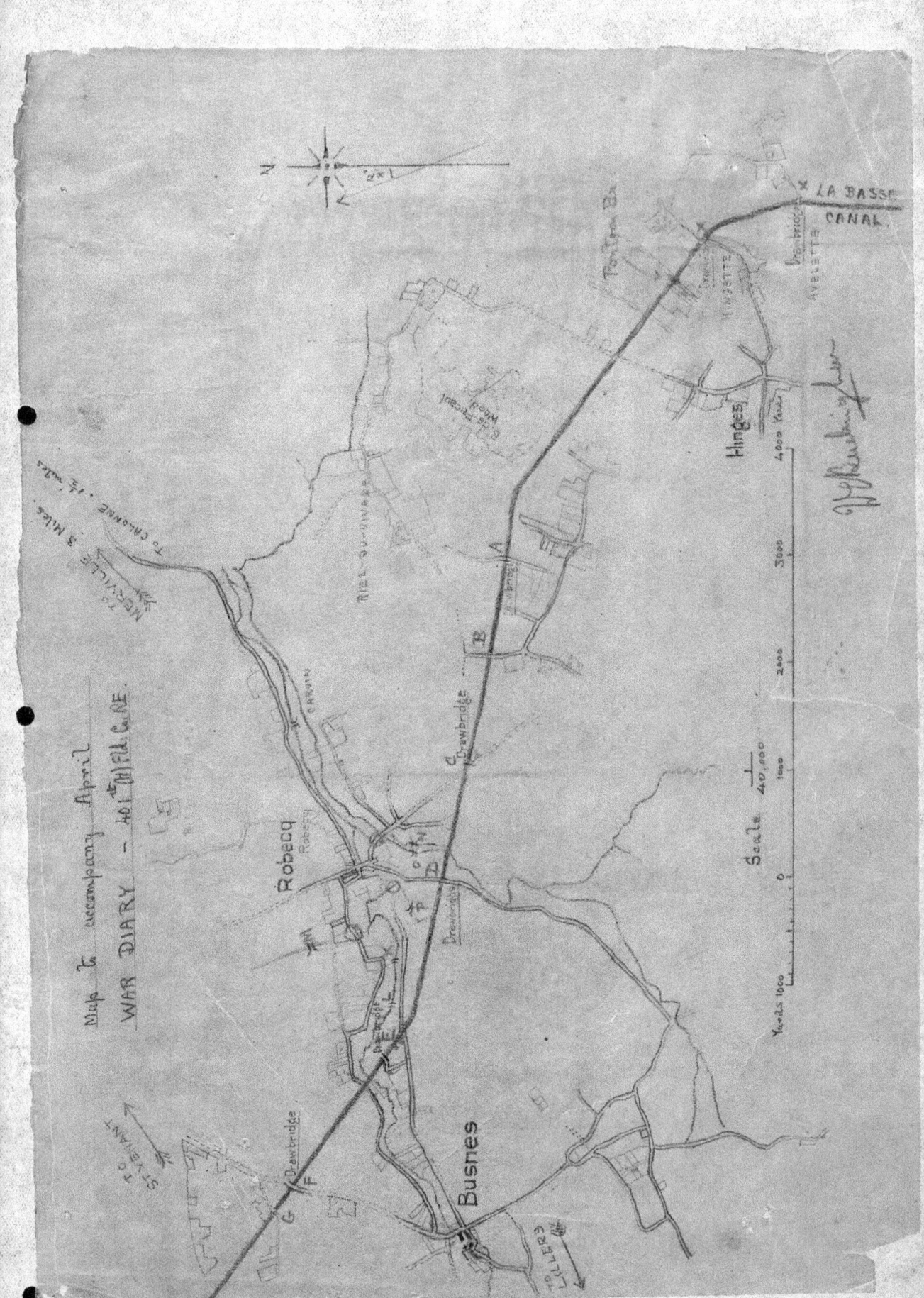

CONFIDENTIAL.

WAR DIARY for MAY, 1918.

of the

401st (HIHGLAND) FIELD COMPANY, R.E.

Army Form C. 2118.

401 st (H) Fd. Co. R.E.

WAR DIARY
or
INTELLIGENCE SUMMARY.

MAY - 1918

(Erase heading not required.)

Instructions regarding War Diaries and Intelligence Summaries are contained in F. S. Regs., Part II. and the Staff Manual respectively. Title pages will be prepared in manuscript.

Place	Date	Hour	Summary of Events and Information	Remarks and references to Appendices
BOURECQ	1/5/18 to 3/5/18		Company reorganising in rest billets. Training and recreation. Repair and painting of Company Transport continued. 2/5/18 Football against A.S.C. 1/5/18 Lecture Party at BALMORAL'S given an entertainment at BOURECQ - also rugby parties carried out in afternoon. 3/5/18 Further training - "Company Shoot" on Range - Major W.E. BUCKINGHAM M.C. On 2/5/18 a Scheme was worked out (and found useful) for meeting the situation in the ROBECQ area in the event of a further German advance.	
MARDEUIL	4/5/18		Company moved at short notice to MARDEUIL. XVIII Corps area (about 4 mls N.W. of ARRAS). Co. moved in bulk, also Coy. for new Div. H.Q. in new area on 5/5/18 (8) Div. Stamp near from the Canadian Div. Allocated huts, area etc. in new area. Headquarters of Coy. Transport moved by road via DIVION. Left at 11.30 P.M. 4/5, arrived MARDEUIL about 8 miles first day, 14th miles 2nd day.	
	5/5/18 to 11/5/13		Company employed in making Nissen Huts about 1/2 mile N of MARDEUIL billets & find billets in hill south, 1st, 2nd, & 3rd buds constructed to new Div. H.A. and later occupied & HQ in MARDEUIL. New Div. H.Q. consists of about 7 billets in hut, tents and various huts for Servants. Company for bearers 60 per day was ordered - also erected for 14 tabernacle NISSEN HUTS was erected, also 7 tabernacles 14 × 12 between . In addition to the above a great hut was built (not built) R. & G.C. - Officers' various shelters and officers' tents (traffic) and oil and artillery. Party of 20 men laying down aerial from station (enemy would interfere & so carrying out connection by day happy assumed. On 11/5/14 2/Lt. ROBERTSON arrived in (preparing from R.E. N.H.) This occupied the week of area to feet wash and disc. Finest in the Div. Bootes at SCRIE - The impact of the parts of was 21/6/24 & all decided on dome office and lengths is the fac months large was sent for from days of Company, dim D13 agents of task out as Exercise units the perm of to field it formed, fill 16 given in prepa for oaking 4 Decker to quit for for reception.	
	11/5/18		Advanced recoverhing parties were out. Lack of 4005 (H) Fd. G. RE. & OTPY. Field Ann Sector such as under Company Cmdr. now.	

Army Form C. 2118.

WAR DIARY
or
INTELLIGENCE SUMMARY.
(Erase heading not required.)

Instructions regarding War Diaries and Intelligence Summaries are contained in F. S. Regs., Part II and the Staff Manual respectively. Title pages will be prepared in manuscript.

Place	Date	Hour	Summary of Events and Information	Remarks and references to Appendices
	11/5/18 and nights		During night of 11th–12th May, 154th Inf. Bde. took over OPPY SECTOR from 153rd Inf. Bde. (approx 2300ˣ front) Two Battns. (N[o]. 1 & 4) moved to advanced billets in BRIERLEY HILL TRENCH between the BROWN and GREEN lines, 2700ˣ behind the front line. That Battns. [in?] over the work of two (M) F. Coys. R.E. in the Sector. Work in hand was (1) Completion of recognition and Great hoarding on AIRPLANE (Gavrelle Trench) in front of POST LINE (2) Repairs & upkeep of communication "HOUSE ALLEY" C.T. (3) Reconstruction and reconnaissance of POST LINE (present line) (4) Construction of dug out in TIRED POST. (5) Two bridges where railway crosses Sunken Road (about 200ˣ behind front line were prepared for demolition, and required R.E. work in sup- and maintenance work + inspection. (6) Maintenance and upkeep of advanced water supply pipe lines west of Railway, referred in depot. Also Sulphur line, machinery.	
ECURIE	12/5/18		The time a day was carried in effort taking our front and rather, improvements, in places and improvements to places and improvements. The Garmont [Garrison?] of Bn. (M) Fed G R.E.	
	13/5/18	10.00ˣ by our 2 Sections in above and for back loading of ammn 4.30 (M) Fed G R.E.		Orders received to arrange that Battn (2 & 3) from ECURIE to relieve Battns 1/4 in POST LINE & 400 on night and two reserve Brigade on receiving orders to advance having 1 O.R. 200 and one officer from battery unit forward to front of the Lie of M.E.F. to arrange 11/7/18 done 13/7/18 signed with 21/5/18.	
	21/5/18		Work in Post Line was handed over in 404th (M) Fed G R.E. – 550ˣ on the were got out on the following nights and truly hammered down. 300ˣ of wire was rescued west of POST LINE 185 Tm to be used to heave and hiding over these days enabled it as were duplicate over POST LINE supply light.	
	20/5/18 23/5/18		Deepening of defensive through an in front all steam calibres of the Bde. half of the Sec. have now all being aligned	

154 Inf Bde. Intelligence OPPY SECTOR. A.D.S.S. Forms/C 2nn.

WAR DIARY
or
INTELLIGENCE SUMMARY.

(Erase heading not required.)

401st (M) Fld. C. R.E.

MAY — 1918 —

Army Form C. 2118.

Instructions regarding War Diaries and Intelligence Summaries are contained in F. S. Regs., Part II. and the Staff Manual respectively. Title pages will be prepared in manuscript.

Place	Date	Hour	Summary of Events and Information	Remarks and references to Appendices
	24/5/18 to 31/5/18		The programme of work settled on by 15th & 19th Divl staffs was put in the hands of the Divde. The whole Scheme of the Ponds & interior of the Front line trench was also carried out. What the trench however was found unsuited by Bdes H.E. Fires still bombarding on 28/5/18. The 4"main giving the water supply was to the system too precarious. Drills, sidings, & new deep wells just behind the Front line were filled up for training purposes.	
			After having over the work in the POST LINE &, most of 404 Fld. C. R.E. on 21/5/18, the Section (H+4) returned to ECURIE for rest.	
			Units in mid Div. were employed as working party for R.A.M.C. off the Subway on the ARRAS–LENS Road behind ECURIE and ROELINCOURT and are also taken in divisions to the Range for the Divl Rifle & Pistol – & LECTURES. Range & Camouflage are carefully made to prevent men being fired at. Men were held in the open. Erection of wirefeller at ECURIE BUTTS was started. Walles reported on 28/5/18 from 1st Army School of Cookery to divide and Instruction in cooking.	
			Casualties during month – 1 O.R. killed (still in) 1 O.R. wounded (still in)	
			No. 4/20/49. C.S.M. HUTTON R reported for duty 15/5/18	
			1 N.C.O. + 10 O.R. on 17/5/18 from R.E. Base Depot. 2 O.R. on 22/5/18	
			Reinforcements {	
			4 O.R. on reinforcement leave to UK Strength – 7 officers 207 O.R.	

W.S. Rushington
Major R.E.
O.C. 401st (M) Fld. C. R.E.

2353 Wt. W2544/1451 500,000 5/15 D. D. & L. A.D.S.S. Forms/C 2118.

Army Form C. 2118.

401st (W) Fld. C. RE

JUNE - 1918

WAR DIARY
INTELLIGENCE SUMMARY
(Erase heading not required.)

Place	Date	Hour	Summary of Events and Information	Remarks and references to Appendices
ECURIE	1/6/18		Rear Headquarters in Nissen Hut Camp at ECURIE. Transport lines in same locality. Work - 2 Sections in Dug Out at Advanced Billets in BRIERLEY HILL TRENCH, working on front line system. 2 Sections in Billets at ECURIE and working in Reserve Brigade Area. Company permanently in LEFT BRIGADE area - OPPY SECTOR - 2 sections forward + 2 sections back as above. Reliefs carried out every 5 days - sections doing 10 days in line and 10 out. At beginning of the month the main work in the forward area, was the excavation of a portion of BOW TRENCH just South of and running parallel with the trench currently back to the point known as the PIMPLE. The portion of ARLEUX ROAD, + also BOW TRENCH at this point. Also stretches of new trenches were completed to Div: section. Further stretches of BOW TRENCH were also completed to the Div: Section where stay back was previously very narrow. About 15 enemy holes were also made in BOW TRENCH and its continuance of Avoy unit in its trench which in the field line, were boarded over 5 or 6 steps down to form dubby holes.	
	4/6/18		On 4/6/18 the 153rd Inf. Bde. relieved 151st Inf. Bde. (sector was then largely concentrated on the integrity out of BOW SUPPORT trench to its correct Divisional Section. In places this trench had been badly knocked about shortly on May 27th when the Germans attacked further South. Posts of the Bow trench were working under supervision of its Company. On the night of 9/10 a gas beam attack was carried out discharged from 2250 cylinders opposite at the points A + B on plan alongside the Railway. Work was favourable about 3 miles per hour. No hostile retaliation in particular.	
	9/6/18			
	1/6/18 -15/6/18		In the back area during the first half of the month one section was employed in pulling down at ECURIE and re-erecting to slightly outside, owing to hostile shelling of ECURIE. The sections erected an ADRIAN hut above ground level on B + T Mt Camp in two rows about 3' apart. Hut type at about 5' above L general section was put up at stage and the cross arrived to belong to. Each section in its turn was employed in part of the time. The work was completed in 13 days at one of its section as an Advanced Dressing Station, between ROCLINCOURT and ECURIE. Subway system up to 1' with 150' of gallery to be an outlook.	
	16/6/18		154th Inf. Bde. relieved 153rd Inf. Bde. in OPPY SECTOR.	
	14/6/18		Ribbons presented by Corps Commander at ECURIE - Sergt TAYLOR - Belgian Croix de Guerre, L/Cpl CRUICKSHANK Mil Medal	

2353 Wt. W2544/1454 700,000 5/15 D. D. & L. A.D.S.S. Forms/C. 2118.

WAR DIARY
or
INTELLIGENCE SUMMARY

Army Form C. 2118.

401st (H.) Fd. Co. R.E.

JUNE — 1918

(Erase heading not required.)

Place	Date	Hour	Summary of Events and Information	Remarks and references to Appendices
H.O.T.B	17/6/18		A New Support Trench to POST TREnCH as shown in Red on plan — (continuous Rel'ne) was started from TIRED ALLEY to AIRPLANE SWITCH and later (anything) was marked out in front for infantry to connect TIRED ALLEY and AIRPLANE SWITCH by. This trench was completed with fire bays and duck boards between TIRED ALLEY and end of month.	
	18/6/18 20/6/18		2nd D. de B. ROBERTSON R.E. was slightly wounded in leg by shell splinter at our M.W.T. & evacuated. Instead of holding line in case of attack to be by defended localities, each locality having sufficient dug outs for the garrison. There were three such localities on the Lft Brigade front along the SUPPORT LINE viz "FACTORY locality"— It is doubtful later. The above three localities on the plan. The point of each locality is about 500" in rotten line. R.I.d. shelter lines in the plan. The point of each locality is about 500" in rotten line. No special trenches are being dug, which would put away their position, in connection with this Company started two dug outs CASTOR DUG OUT (B.16.b.3.4) on 21st inst. and "RUM DUG OUT (B.23.a.1.9) on 24th inst. the embrasures of both of them was practically completed by the end of the month. Three parties were also employed in fire steps in trenches with the above localities. Reconnaissance carried out to determine routes and stabl. of all dug outs in existence.	
	27/6/18		2nd Lt J.R. McEWAN R.E. joined the Company for duty from R.E. Base Dept. During the latter half of the month the Section in our M.W.T. was employed in making dug overs for the Russian Rough Camps. The fire places for the men to take the Baths of the "Cabin" type 7 of these were completed. 154 F. Fd. Co. R.E. 152 F. Fd. Co. R.E. R.R. joined the above under unit returned in connection with the localities stone shelter was employed on.	
	28/6/18		Casualties during month 1 officer + 4 O.R. wounded. Reinforcements received during month 1 officer + 25 O.R. 5 O.R. on leave to U.K. (Seven officers plus 3 months O.R. after (2 mths) Strength of Coy. 7 officers 206 O.R.	

W. G. Buckingham.

O.C. 401st (H.) Fd. Co. R.E.

1/7/18

Divisional Engineers

51st (Highland) Division.

401st FIELD CO., R.E.

JULY, 1918.

WD 42

═ SECRET. ═

WAR DIARY

401ˢᵗ (Highland) Field Coy. R.E.

for JULY 1918

W.G. Buckingham
Major R.E.
O.C. 401 (Hd) Fd C.␣E

Army Form C. 2118.

WAR DIARY
or
INTELLIGENCE SUMMARY.
(Erase heading not required.)

401st (Highland) Fd. C, RE

JULY, 1918

Instructions regarding War Diaries and Intelligence Summaries are contained in F.S. Regs., Part II. and the Staff Manual respectively. Title pages will be prepared in manuscript.

Place	Date	Hour	Summary of Events and Information	Remarks and references to Appendices
ECURIE	1/7/18 to 10/7/18		In billets at ECURIE & working in left Brigade Sector (OPPY SECTOR). Continued and completed excavation of SUPPORT TRENCH to POST TRENCH between TOMMY ALLEY and TIRED ALLEY, as shown on plan last month. Continued construction of Priestleys at rear entrances to Dug-outs in BOW SUPPORT where included in defensive localities. Continued construction of two new dug-outs. Connecting gallery between two entrances of CASTOR DUG-OUT carried 4 feet in each. Connecting gallery between entrances of RUM dug-out in OUSE LOCALITY partly completed. Continued excavation of Bgde H.Q. dug-out and construction of M.G. emplacement at exit from LILY ELSIE. Dug-out in front of Bde. H.Q. completed with two 100 gall. tanks. Men Water Point at FACTORY completed. Patrolling of Water Points and Pipe Lines continued – charges for demolition of Bridge patrolled + tested and maintained. Demolitions. In back area – Further areas were constructed in Battalion camps and R.A.M.C. dug-out was completed. Road Mine at MADAGASCAR CORNER tested and maintained. Camp at ECURIE continued to be shelled with H.V. Gun – one shell burst under ground half under officers' mess without damage. Capt. R.D. NIVEN to hosp. sick. 2/7/18. 2nd Lt McEWAN wounded at duty. 2/7/18.	
	10.7.18		Handed over all work and camp to "A" Coy. 10th Battalion Canadian Engineers.	
	11.7.18		Company moved by light Railway to LA THIEULOYE and (20 miles) and marched on 6 miles to BEUGIN near BRUAY.	
	14.7.18		Started training programme on 12/7/18 & 13/7/18 + resumed morning order for men. Men billeted at OURTON and transport refused.	
	14.7.18 15.7.18		Advanced party proceeded to BRYAS on cycles to entrain for XXII Corps area. 2/Lt PEEBLES admitted to hospital sick. Company marched with transport to BRYAS. Left Camp 2 a.m. Entrained 6.30 a.m.	
	16.7.18		Company detrained at ROMILLY about midday. Company transport was sent on at once to FONTAINE ST DENIS. Horses shall have arrived to take the Company forward from around to Company bivouaced in full put into train for night 16th/17th.	
	17.7.18		Company embarked about midday in 8 buses + went via FERE CHAMPAIGNOISES + VERTUS to South of CHOUILLY (50 miles) arrived there about 6.30 p.m. bivouaced night in wood during heavy thunderstorm and rain. (French Cavalry attached on this day.)	

2353 Wt.W2544/1454 700,000 5/15 D,D.&L. A.D.S.S./Forms/C. 2118.

Army Form C. 2118.

WAR DIARY
or
INTELLIGENCE SUMMARY

401st (Highland) F.M. C. R.E.
JULY - 1918.

(Erase heading not required.)

Place	Date	Hour	Summary of Events and Information	Remarks and references to Appendices
CHOUILLY	19/7/18		Moved to DIZY MAGENTA through behind REIMS Plateau (5 miles behind front line)	
BELLE VUE	20/7/18		153rd & 154th Inf. Bde. attacked on 2½ mile front at 8 am. South of MARFAUX, 9 miles S.W. of REIMS at first the attack was successful but counter attack forced 153rd Inf. Bde. back through the BOIS DE COUTRON which had been captured by them.	
NANTEUIL	21/7/18		Company moved into SARBRUGE WOOD South West of NANTEUIL with transport. Area shelled but little damage done. Casualties in Company 2 O.R. killed and 11 O.R. wounded. Large numbers of small water springs in NANTEUIL and CORMOYEUX, many of small output far from sufficient. Men were moved forward to work with small parties of Infantry operating in BOIS de COUTRON against German M.G. nests clearing 150" × 25" in wood behind Infantry to maintain communication and telephone lines. RE to clean pathways in front of Infantry, covering party of 3rd Royal Scots. Orders received for RE to remain up and assist Infantry in attack following morning. No 3 & 4 Sections finally heavily shelled while waiting.	
	23/7/18		At 6 am. 152nd Inf. Bde. attacked North of the BOIS DE COUTRON on 1400× front, bluejackets ESPILLY and BOIS D'AULNAY - distance about 1000". 154th Inf. Bde. with which Company was working, on their left were to push forward at same time without Barrage.	
	23/7/18		401 Company was employed in 4 parties working in conjunction with 7th A. & S.H. 8th Royal Scots and 4th Gordon Hdrs. Their work was to make narrow pathways leading to the front line, parallel to the infantry advance, as that the infantry could more [?] advance and maintain communication in the woods. The wood to (BOIS & COUTRON) had out many thick & almost impassable. Hostile barrage at zero hour was very heavy also some shell of our own barrage fell short on our own troops. Heavy hostile shelling continued throughout the day. No advance was made in the 154th Inf. Bde. front. 152nd Inf. Bde. took the BOIS D'AULNAY but were held up short of ESPILLY. Casualties in the Company on this day were Lieut Rankin killed II wounded, (5 or) 1 missing believed wounded Company employed four tanks in the wood where required. buried at [?]	

Army Form C. 2118.

WAR DIARY
or
INTELLIGENCE SUMMARY.
(Erase heading not required.)

Instructions regarding War Diaries and Intelligence Summaries are contained in F. S. Regs., Part II. and the Staff Manual respectively. Title pages will be prepared in manuscript.

401st (M) Field C. RE = JULY - 1918 =

Place	Date	Hour	Summary of Events and Information	Remarks and references to Appendices
NANTEUIL	24/7/18 25/7/18		Company employed clearing pathways through wood leading up to Battalion Headquarters also where required along front line part. Notice boards were erected along pathways. A Bridge to take Inf. in single file was also made over small stream.	
	26/7/18		Further clearing and also Prisoner Cage made near NANTEUIL. Capt. R.D NIVEN returned from Hospital & 153rd (S.) Fd. Amb., on R.D. 62nd Div. and French attacked at 6 am.	
	27/7/18		Company were detailed to make tracks in direction of advance along through the BOIS DE COUTRON between the existing roads and through the wood and the track east- total length 1400 ↑. One section started a tr. known as the Second Objective had been taken.	made good progress (No Tks)
			No. 3 Section relieved No. 1 Section. It about 1 pm and completed its task before dark. Task started 400 from road and finished 380" from road through wood. The Germans however had withdrawn before the attack developed and detailed about the BOIS d'ECLISSES.	
			At CHAMBRECY. When following up to see the situation a reconnaissance was made for water and a spring & well found.	
	28/7/18		Company moved to Northern corner of the BOIS de COUTRON, North West of NAPPES and rested in the outskirts and roads until 2nd Lt. SANDEMAN went to Transport lines.	
	29/7/18 30/7/18		Company worked on 4 water points and 1 mile of road between LA NEUVILLE and CHAUMUZY. Reconnaissance made for road to CHAMBRECY.	
	31/7/18		Company moved back from BOIS de COUTRON to woods South of NANTEUIL.	
			C.	
			Casualties for month 4 OR Killed 30 OR wounded 2 OR missing. Reinforcements 11 O.R. from R.E. Base Depot.	

N. G. Buckingham
Major R.E.
O.C. 401st (M) Fd. C. RE

SECRET

WAR DIARY

401st Highland Fld. Co. RE

AUGUST - 1918

Army Form C. 2118.

WAR DIARY
or
INTELLIGENCE SUMMARY.

(Erase heading not required.)

404th (Highland) Fld. Co. R.E.

AUGUST 1918

Instructions regarding War Diaries and Intelligence Summaries are contained in F. S. Regs., Part II. and the Staff Manual respectively. Title pages will be prepared in manuscript.

Place	Date	Hour	Summary of Events and Information	Remarks and references to Appendices
NANTEUIL	1/8/18		Company moved with transport by route march from NANTEUIL to DIRY (15 miles). Weather very hot. 3 men fell out. Company marched with 152nd Inf. Bde. Ambulance gave us FLAVIGNY. On arrival at DIRY, Company bivouacked South West of station.	
	2/8/18		Company arrived in bivouac at DIRY. Two Packs and Truck loads of equipment fitted from 404th (H) Fld. Co. R.E. MOUSSY. Advance party entrained at YPERNAY with 154th Inf. Bde.	
	3/8/18		Company entrained with transport at DIRY station in train with No 2 Coy A.S.C.	
	4/8/18		Company detrained at CALONNE at about 11:45 p.m.	
	5/8/18		Company marched to AUBIGNY during night of 4th/5th distance of about 15 miles.	
AUBIGNY	6/8/18		Company rested and scrubbed equipment & rifle and S.B.R. wet etc	
	7/8/18 – 15/8/18		Company carried out Training Programme	
	8/8/18		2 Lt H.P.J. PEACOCK joined Company from R.E. Base Depot. Training included Recruits Training, Rifle Exercises, Drill, Pontoon Drill, use of Pneumatic Compass and Map-reading. Grenade, Anti-aircraft and Trench Exercises were taken together on Range. Training over a Lewis Gun Frame was also given. Lectures by Coy Officers and N.C.O.s and also carried out a Practice on 30 yd range. In addition to the above trainable reports were carried out to Range particularly the Range South of AUBIGNY known as Tangent and Ribeauville Figure range. This must for 152nd Inf. Bde. It was unfortunate that the supply of reinforcements from the Base did not join the Company until the end of the above short course of training.	
	15/8/18		Orders were received from CRE to send Advanced Party to take over billet of 412th Fld. Co. R.E. at ECURIE and then Advanced Party cuts in the CUTTING at B.27.d.2.6. South East of BAILLEUL and the work they had in hand in the GAVRELLE Sector. Advanced party moved on cycles.	
ECURIE	16/8/18		On 16/8/18 the Company moved in 4 lorries to ECURIE, the Sector moving on to Advanced Billets by Light Railway in the afternoon. The 412th Fld. Co. RE having only been in the Sector a short time, no definite programme of work was taken over. Work however taken in hand was the digging and provision of splinter proof protection of less than 200 yds.	

Army Form C. 2118.

WAR DIARY
or
INTELLIGENCE SUMMARY.
(Erase heading not required.)

401st Highland Fld. Co. R.E.

AUGUST – 1918.

Instructions regarding War Diaries and Intelligence Summaries are contained in F. S. Regs., Part II. and the Staff Manual respectively. Title pages will be prepared in manuscript.

Place	Date	Hour	Summary of Events and Information	Remarks and references to Appendices
ECURIE & BAILLEUL			tanks in the BROWN TRENCH at H.3.B.4.6 and the repair of the 2" wide line leading to it. The deepening and widening of the BROWN TRENCH and RAILWAY COMMUNICATION TRENCH, where required and flaying of trench boards in the trenches was also undertaken at certain points where this had not been completed. The defences of the line by the system of defensive localities which had been started when the 51st (H.) Div. was previously in this sector, but which had not been entirely by other Divisions was again taken in hand. The work involved being the formation of Fire Steps immediately at the entrances of all dug-outs in the formation and the completion of Dug Out accommodation for the garrisons. This work was taken in hand for STERLING POST. Specially carefully sited fire steps to cover as far as possible the trenches leading to the posts were also constructed. While in the sector it was decided that the Garrison of Resistance should fall back from the POST TRENCH to the BROWN TRENCH behind BAILLEUL. This necessitated the completion of the excavation of GULLY ALLEY and the formation of suitable Fire Steps in it. This was completed before moving out of the Sector. The reclamation of some old German Dug Outs in the Sunken Road in B.21.d was also taken in hand. Responsibility for the demolition of bridges at B.27 a.0.3. and B.21.C.9.8 was also taken over also a Road Mine at MADAGASCAR CORNER West of ECURIE and the Pumping Plants between ECURIE and ROELINCOURT. Stones were taken to TOWY DUMP by Light Railway and from this point up to the line by horse transport. On 25/8/18 when the front line was advanced by the Brigade on our right a 154th Bde. Armd. defensive flank, saphers were sent forward to reconnoitre and inspect an objective "Rookery Trench". None were found. On 27/8/18 154th Bde. handed over the Sector to 8th Div. and 4 Sections of the Company were moved to POINT DU JOUR Redoubt to work that evening on Defensive localities in the area recently captured from the Germans. More plans to be still in German hands, namely GREENLAND HILL.	
	27/8/18			

WAR DIARY
or
INTELLIGENCE SUMMARY
(Erase heading not required.)

Army Form C. 2118.

401 st (Highland) Fd. C. R.E.

AUGUST — 1918

Place	Date	Hour	Summary of Events and Information	Remarks and references to Appendices
POINT DU JOUR & SCARPE VALLEY 15 No. 0S.	28/8/18		At COPPER TRENCH, the most Northern of the two localities a considerable amount of work was done improving dug out entrances and machine gun emplacements leading out of dug outs also in digging out and few attempting the trench. On the evening of this day one Section (No.4) was moved up with 2 platoons of the 8th Bn. Scot Fusrs. to Battalion H.Q. East of FAMPOUX to follow up infantry attack on GREENLAND HILL which took place at 6.30 am on 29/8/18.	
	29/8/18		The attack was successful and the final objective on the Eastern slopes of GREENLAND HILL was gained in about 80 mins giving an advance of about 3/4 mile. Extent of attack is shown on dotted green on tracing. The attack was followed by very heavy hostile shelling. In the morning the ground was reconnoitred to see what work was required and an old German trench just behind the crest of the hill was dug out to form the main line of Resistance and fortified work on its forward slope being impossible in day light from the main line of Resistance.	
	30/8/18		The following day 30/8/18 two Sections were moved forward to a dug out near Brown Line of GREENLAND HILL to form defensive locality on forward slope of GREENLAND HILL & East of FAMPOUX to dig out two pillboxes of Resistance. This is shown in Red on tracing. Fwr steps were also made in COPPER TRENCH to form a defensive locality and dug out entrances and machine gun emplacements were repaired.	
	31/8/18		Work on defensive localities was continued. The line WELCOME — WHISPER — WAX — EMB — CURSE SUPPORT — CORK was reconnoitred as a forward line of Resistance. Trenches have good field of fire but in bad repair. WELCOME is out of direct hostile observation. Remainder however is under direct hostile observation.	
			Casualties during month — 1 Officer, 1 O.R. wounded. Reinforcements " " — 1 Officer, 2/Lt. H.P.N. PEACOCK D.C.M. M.M. from R.E. Base Depôt 3/8/18 O.R. 46. O.R. Reinforcements received from Base during month. Leave 1 Officer and 7. O.R. went on leave during the month. — Periods between leave, Officers — 7½ months O.R. — 14 "	

N.E. Buckingham Major.
O.C. 401 (HD) Fd. C. [O5].

2/9/18

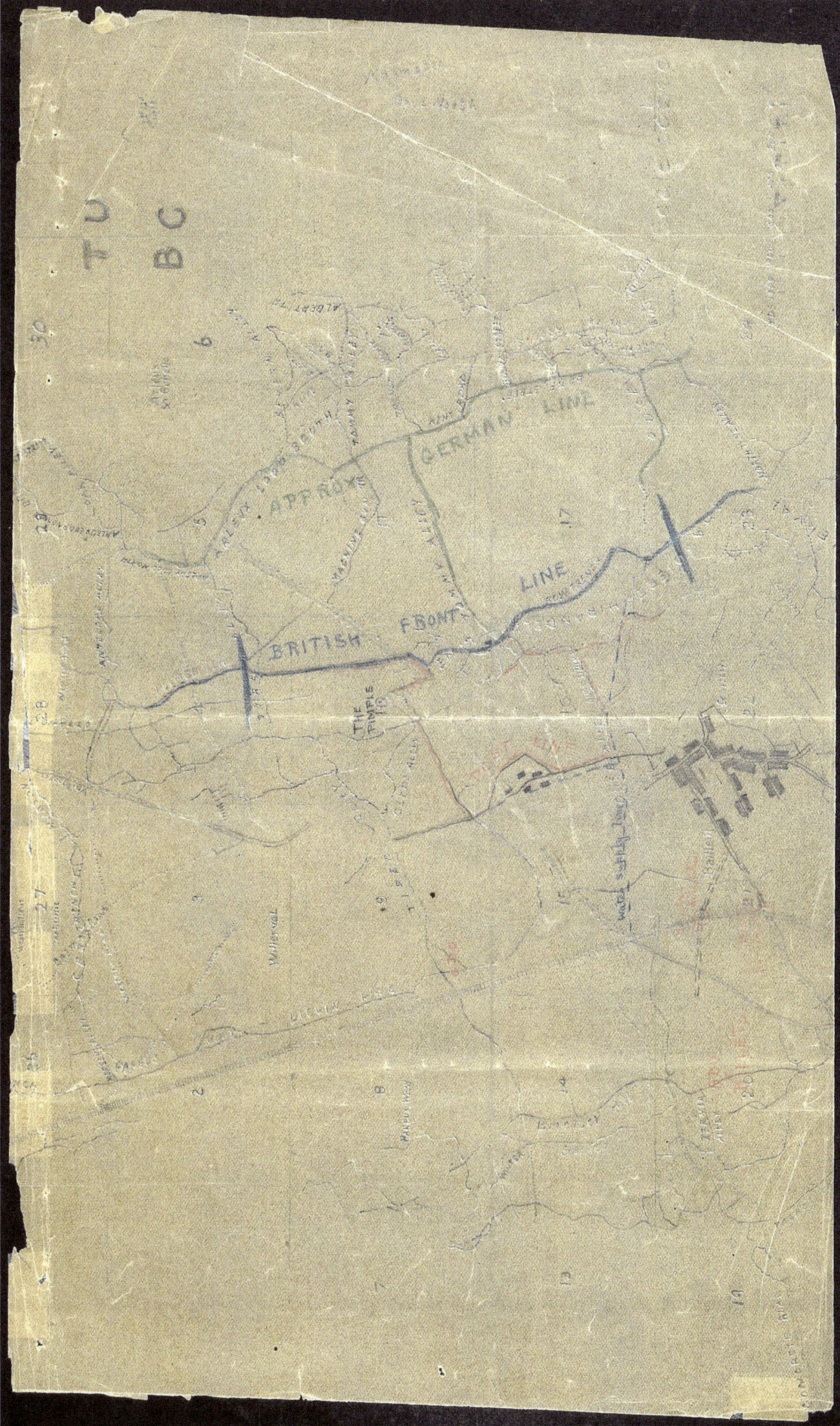

FAMPOUX.

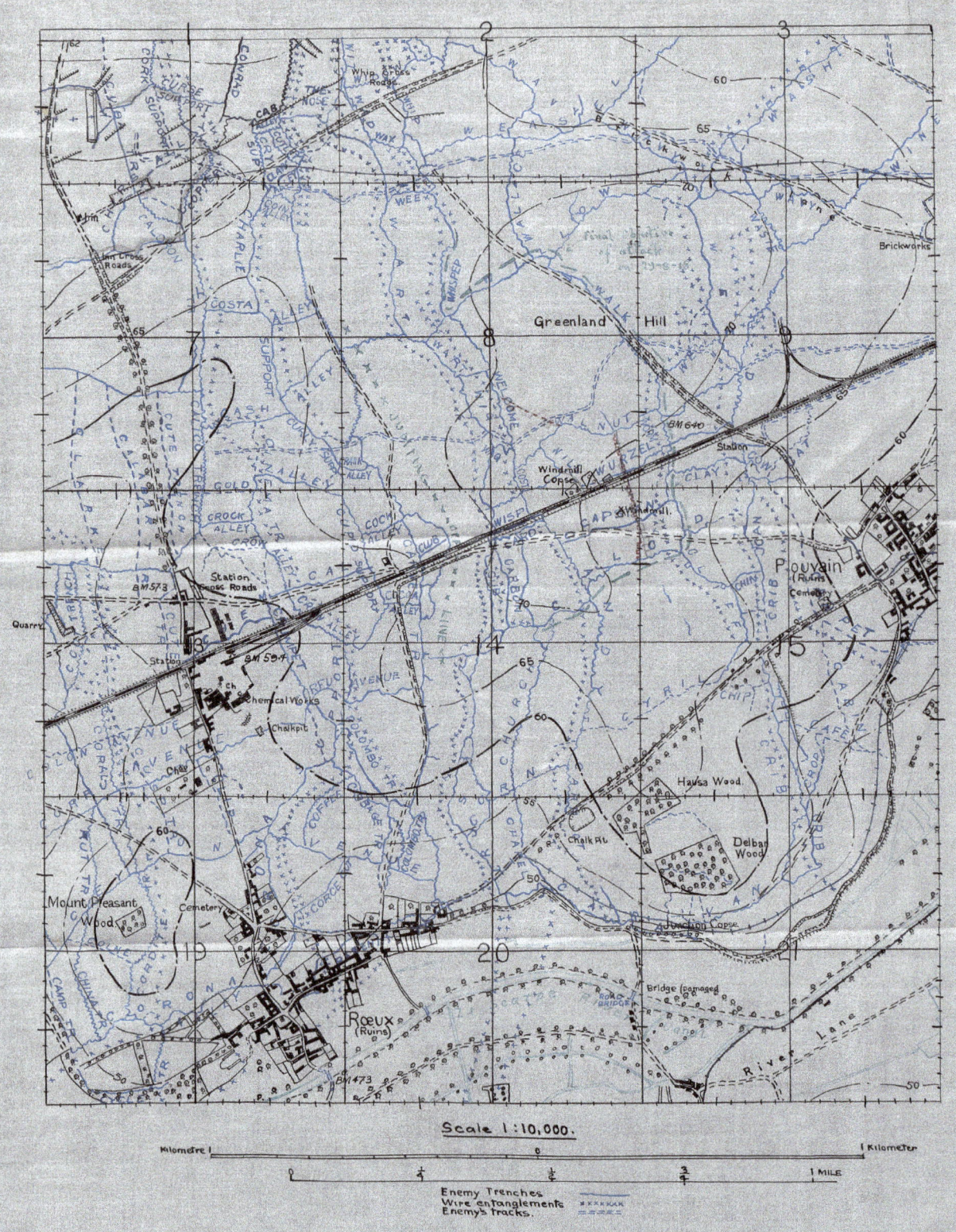

Vol 44

WAR DIARY

OF

401st (HIGHLAND) FIELD COY. R.E.

FOR

SEPTEMBER 1918

VOL. XLV.

WAR DIARY
or
INTELLIGENCE SUMMARY.
(Erase heading not required.)

401st (Highland) Field Co. R.E. Army Form C. 2118.

SEPTEMBER – 1918.

Place	Date	Hour	Summary of Events and Information	Remarks and references to Appendices
ECOIVRE & FAMPOUX area	1/9/18		Transport lines at ECOIVRE. H.Q. & 2 sections at POINT DU JOUR in dug outs and shelters. 2 sections in dug outs about 1 mile East of FAMPOUX.	
			Work – Consolidation of Defensive locality in GREENLAND HILL recently captured and work on communication lines of Resistance along WELCOME – WHISPER – WAX – CAB – CURSE SUPPORT – CORK Hostile artillery active along front and in the 2 sections billets in front of FAMPOUX	
	2/9/18		Work as above. Two hostile artillery activity throughout the day & through night on front line and FAMPOUX area at night. Major W.E. Buckington M.B.E., L'transferred & his Co. Lieut-Maun, Capt. J.G. Christie assumed command to Transport lines ECOIVRE and back – work on [illegible] in defense locality in GREENLAND HILL.	W.B.
	3/9/18		as above. Hostile artillery active on front and in [illegible] area. Major W.E. Buckington proceeded to the line.	W.B.
	4/9/18		Work on defensive locality in front, in [illegible] and in [illegible] line. 2 sections moved back to bivouac one mile [illegible] of FAMPOUX on coming out for a rest. Hostile artillery [illegible] very active at T.1.d. & occasional bursts on [illegible] outposts in line. T.6.c. T.7.a. – T.11.a. 6 other [illegible] injured in afternoon near Comp. T.14.a.4.4. & T.14.c. Hostile artillery active on R. Wing front in the 2 sections billets in front of FAMPOUX. 2/Lt. I. G. Davidson returned from 7 days leave from BOULOGNE	W.B.
	5/9/18		Work of deepening & widening trenches and of putting wire in Defensive locality in GREENLAND HILL continued. The work was much interrupted at night by hostile gas shelling. Deepening and widening trenches of Defensive locality. WAY – WHIP – WHISPER continued. Deep dugout entrances in all tunnels were started with a certain amount of work being carried.	W.B.

WAR DIARY
or
INTELLIGENCE SUMMARY.

Army Form C. 2118.

401st (Highland) Field Coy R.E.

SEPTEMBER – 1918.

Place	Date	Hour	Summary of Events and Information	Remarks and references to Appendices
			Bonnelle deploying enemy at T.1.c.8.6, CORSE SUPPORT, reported on several all improved (spelling of dump & dug outs) Bivouac area for men INN CROSS ROADS, I.7.n.3.3. 2nd Govt in the making at I.7.a.7.9. a children playhad dugout. Commenced ground levelled and track laninged to site.	
6/9/18				
7/9/18			Elwe worked on track - dug out, well and improvised later [illegible] Another site started of dugout at C.L.J. [illegible] on [illegible] R.E. I. & 11g T [illegible] — POINT DU JOUR, on site [illegible] billetin g & stables close to site S.17.a & — TEMP O.C. x.	
8/9/18			[illegible] upon the jobs - work done in GREENLAND HILL dug outs for [illegible] Coys S. O.V. Map hunted for stabling. Red sprinklers seen in trenches near I.7.d.7.9. Stabling will form to be provided.	
10/9/18			[illegible] One [illegible] of [illegible] to hunt at POINT DU JOUR with stabling [illegible]	
12/9/18			Another 0 of [illegible] located to the [illegible] [illegible] [illegible] of [illegible] I.c.6.6. on [illegible] T9 & [illegible] I.c.6.6. on [illegible] T9 & [illegible] R.E. [illegible] located [illegible] ("TELEGRAPH hillerville) [illegible] New battalion from Trenches of Monorail I.5.d.9 & I.11.28. also ross I.7.h.7.9	

Army Form C. 2118.

WAR DIARY
or
INTELLIGENCE SUMMARY.

(Erase heading not required.)

401P/(My Stud)/of Field/76 SEPTEMBER 1913

Place	Date	Hour	Summary of Events and Information	Remarks and references to Appendices
			280th Sy. Formed and made standard angles Plate 1st no 1 gale	
			Company railing target plates. TECNIE and TATEN engineering	
			Stores Map Sh 36 a/db 4 1/10 000 R.E. Map engine materials supplied by	
			Holmes Mac.y of AB-b-28-d 1/2500 R.E. Map engine materials	
			Maintains & AB-b-d 1/5000 as 13th Septr.	
PETIT SERVINS	13/9/18		Company moved to PETIT SERVINS and took over billets	
	14/9/18		Company engaged in refitting and training. Training included infantry drill, musketry and training, transport inspection, service drill, lectures on reports, map reading,	
			permanent compass and demolitions, two parties pushed on for range-experimental trench sheet revetue constructed and tested by infantry, and	
			experimental field gun pit to carry of 6" Howitzer to be constructed at PRESENT CAPELLE	
			and moved to reconnaissance.	
ST. NICHOLAS	23/9/16		Company moved to dugouts near MAISON BLANCHE, near ARRAS-BAILLEUL road.	
ROMAIN VILLE			Company took over from 57th Field Cy. R.E. 49th Division, superintendence for demolition	
near			of bridges over RIVER SCARPE from ATHIES & ST CATHERINE (ARRAS), J. bridges	
			on ARRAS-LENS Railway Ad of senior maintain for ST CATHERINE STA	
			MAISON BLANCHE, fifteen bridges & level crossings in all.	

Army Form C. 2118.

WAR DIARY
or
INTELLIGENCE SUMMARY.
(Erase heading not required.)

Army Form C. 2118.

4012 (Highland) Field Company R.E.

SEPTEMBER 1918.

Instructions regarding War Diaries and Intelligence Summaries are contained in F. S. Regs., Part II. and the Staff Manual respectively. Title pages will be prepared in manuscript.

Place	Date	Hour	Summary of Events and Information	Remarks and references to Appendices
			The demolition charges were gradually cleared by the 179th Tunnelling Coy R.E. under Corps arrangements.	
			L road through PELVES & the RIVER SCARPE, I.20.d.95.to I.27.b.4.3.6. reported to Division Gd. HQrs.	
			Our own Company Transport horses & horses enlisted at SPINDLE FACTORY.	
			ST. NICHOLAS.	
			Third inclinometer fixed & wire cut instd.	
			Company some Field Coy Rly R.E. during the period on cost & water supply of C.R.E.	
26/9/18			H.B. & I section of Company moved to E.d up to in RAILWAY EMBANKMENT at H.13.d.6.6. Where work continued. Proved line near INNs CROSS ROADS, reconnoitred and a drain to complete the restoration (the mine). This work has not commenced.	
27/9/18			2 Section employed in reclamation & improvement of FAMPOUX Rwy & H.18.c, H.18.d, I.19.b & PIEUX. Sandbags and engine head were filled in a sandbag trench around. From 6" to 1 ft. of hard clayed bricks debris & cement from the road and 6 8 Dym. spread & repaired by Rwly Coy at Front	

2353 Wt. W2544/1454 700,000 5/15 D.D. & L. A.D.S.S. Forms/C. 2118.

WAR DIARY
or
INTELLIGENCE SUMMARY.
(Erase heading not required.)

Army Form C. 2118.

401st (Highland) Field Coy by RE
SEPTEMBER 1918

Place	Date	Hour	Summary of Events and Information	Remarks and references to Appendices
	27/9/18		Party of men in charge of an N.C.O. on daily work continued on which task however was interrupted at about 10.30 Sweetwater run the stretcher of 132nd D.I. Brigade prior to entry. Made sketch of PLOEGSTEERT in rather monumental ruined condition. Village has monumental devastation. City halls are ruined. Very sorrowful state of the village. Remains of 2 brass from each crucifix are attached, dispatched to R.E. 3 have lubricated H.B. d B.G. properties Div. H.Q. Being that the party cannot encounter the back temple or even work of H. Parcel, R.E. of manufacture that the armour of responsibility in this country East of GREENLAND HILL the thorns of an enemy interval. Casualties during the event 5 O.R. wounded, 1 O.R. prisoner (Sar Sargent)	
	29/9/18		Reinforcements 20 O.R. received for base depot. 19 O.R. received from base heavy draft. Leave, 1 Officer and 31 O.Rs and one has long draft (Candidates Leave Officer 12 months). O.R. 13½"	

401st
(HIGHLAND)
FIELD COMPANY. R.E.
No.
Date 2/10/18
D.D.S.T. A.D.S.S. Forms/C. 2118.

[signature]
O.C. 401st (Highland) Field Coy R.E.

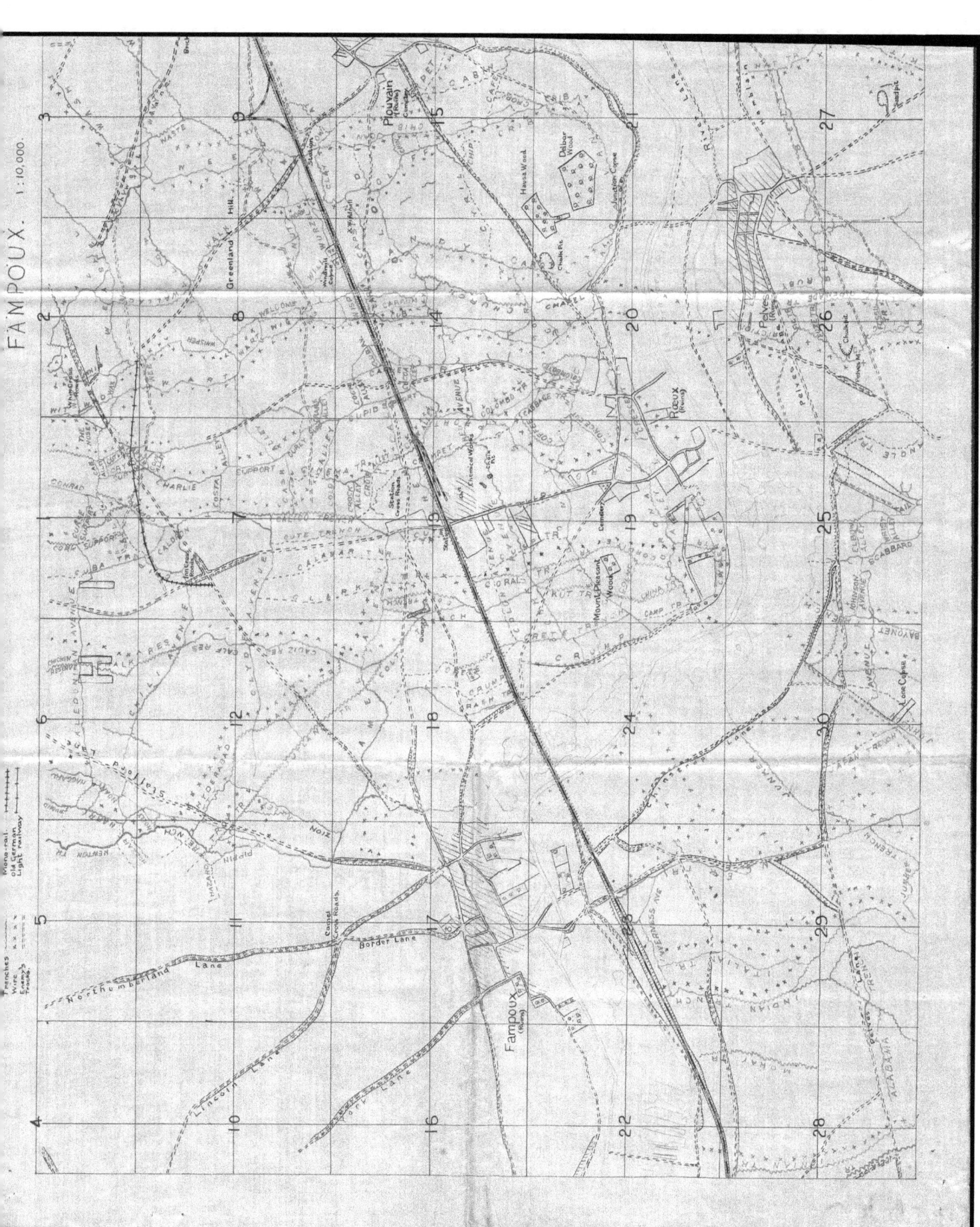

FAMPOUX. 1:10,000.

SECRET

Vol 45

WAR DIARY.

401st (Highland) Field Coy. R.E.

OCTOBER – 1918.

WAR DIARY
or
INTELLIGENCE SUMMARY

Army Form C. 2118.

2016 (Highland) Fld. Cy. / R.E.

OCTOBER 1918

(Erase heading not required.)

Place	Date	Hour	Summary of Events and Information	Remarks and references to Appendices
ST. NICHOLAS	1/10/18		2 Sections of Company employed on repairing FAMPOUX - ROEUX Road, I.15.c., I.16.c. 2 Sections employed on erection of Prism Hut. Hut at RAILWAY EMBANKMENT at I.N. 8156. Future Divisional Head Qrs. Erection of stables for Div. H.Q. at I.N.b. 6 9 6 commenced.	
FAMPOUX			Reconnaissance of roads between FAMPOUX, ROEUX and 12 DUTCHY Roads by 2 officers and details to report to C.R.E.	
			Work on Hut Stables for 2nd Field Cy. R.E. 8.5 Division.	
LE PENDU	2/10/18		Company marched to LE PENDU Camp, North West of MONT ST. ELOI.	
Camp	3/10/18		Company employed on stables and repairs of equipment, fatigues and in-lying and training	
			in junction drill.	
	5/10/18		Major Buckingham returned to Company from A/C.R.E.	
	7/10/18		Company moved to INCHY-EN-ARTOIS by Motor Lorry. Should have moved with 154 Inf. Bde. at 16.30 but insufficient Lorries were provided (about 18 [?] of number asked for). 6 Lorries eventually arrived at 21.30 hrs. — Accommodated in huts & tents. — Arrived 8/10/18 about 04.00 hrs.
	9/10/18		Carried out Company Training. Company Drill etc. at INCHY-EN-ARTOIS	
	10/10/18		Company and Transport moved to 1 mile East of FONTAINE-NOTRE-DAME - by march route via MŒUVRES.	
	11/10/18		Company and Transport moved to point about 3/4 mile N.E. of ESCAUDOEUVRES north of CAMBRAI on night of 11/10/18 154 Inf. Bde. moved into the line taking over from 6th Can. Inf. Bde.	

Army Form C. 2118.

WAR DIARY
or
INTELLIGENCE SUMMARY.

(Erase heading not required.)

401st (Highland) Fld. Co. R.E.

OCTOBER 1918

Place	Date	Hour	Summary of Events and Information	Remarks and references to Appendices
THUN ST MARTIN (HAGENEAU)	11/10/18		On the same evening parties of 1 N.C.O. + 3 sappers were sent to each Battalion & the Brigade to look for booby traps and delay action mines + also to report and take H.Q. for Area when occupation is effected in front Battalions.	
	12/10/18		Company moved to THUN ST MARTIN with half Company harboured 154th Inf. Bde. attached West and East of THUN.	
	13/10/18		Reconnaissance of Roads, Bridges + water supply in IWUY arrival was + 4 Samples of water sent to Field Division. Report of road blown from THUN ST MARTIN to IWUY (East side) taken in hand. Division reported to one point where Germans had blown 5, craters at entrance to IWUY. Large German dump taken at IWUY with large stock of R.S.J. NAILS, STOVES, small amount of timber, no explosives. Sound found, to + connected.	
	14/10/18 to 15/10/18		154th Inf. Bde. attacked at 07.00 hours but failed to capture LIEU ST-AMAND. 154th Inf. Bde. moved back and being being lined in front line by 153 rd Inf. Bde. Contact [illegible] of water supply in IWUY and reconnaissance AVESNES LO - SEC for water and [illegible] samples from 9 wells.	
	16/10/18		Enabled shower baths in THUN-ST-MARTIN for troops. Also made watering But for horses in same village.	
	17/10/18		[illegible] Found a carrot with worms. Report to dentist. Found 1 booby trap in road near IWUY. Only one which has been [illegible] in Coys. area. [illegible] in front of Rl. of Rly. Trk [illegible] tracks, of IWUY + [illegible] 154th Inf. Bde. moved into the W. & S. side of Duisery front 4 officers attached to 154 Inf. Bde. to Coy. for Liaison duty.	
	18/10/18 to 21/10/18		Continued making direction to THUN-ST-MARTIN Road - IWUY Road when enlarged by explosion of [illegible] ammunition dump. Made 10 light but piers from the heavy rail parallel to the forward behind attacking Infantry for stream to cross the River SELLE just north of HASPRES, carrying parts required [illegible] to [illegible]	

2353 Wt.W2544/1454 500,000 5/15 D.D.&L. A.D.S.S.Forms/C.2118.

Army Form C. 2118.

WAR DIARY
or
INTELLIGENCE SUMMARY.

401st (Hull) Fld. C. RE

OCTOBER 1918

(Erase heading not required.)

Instructions regarding War Diaries and Intelligence Summaries are contained in F.S. Regs., Part II. and the Staff Manual respectively. Title pages will be prepared in manuscript.

Place	Date	Hour	Summary of Events and Information	Remarks and references to Appendices
AVESNES LE SEC	20/10/18		On morning of 21/10/18 15th Bn. advanced against only slight opposition to high ground E of River SELLE.	
	21/10/18		Company moved with transport to AVESNES-LE-SEC. Reconnoitred NOYELLES and HEU ST. AMAND for water supply. Reconnoitred site of demolished bridge in NOYELLES.	
			Commenced erection of Trestle bridge over RIVER SELLE at NOYELLES.	
NOYELLES SUR SELLE	24/10/18		Company moved with forward part to NOYELLES. On 23rd light foot bridges were placed across the river to admit.	
	24/10/18		51st (H) Div attacked and advanced to ST. PYTHON & YNIS.	
	25/10/18			
	26/10/18		Bridge at NOYELLES completed. — 3 15' spans + 2 14' spans.	
	28/10/18		Decking 6" Poplars 2½" thick. Bearers 12"× 13", 6"× 5"× 25' R.S.J. Wheel & shore at road ½ — 11½ inches. Road width approx. length up to 1st bridge 7' 1" width. Footway 111' width 48' lightly made up contains. All material taken from former heavy traffic IRON + TILLOY.	
	29/10/18		Orders for Division to be relieved by HP Divn — 15th Bde & 1st details Wer H.Q. Finished new Bridge at NOYELLES and WATER SUPPLY and to H.Q. 458 Fd. & Q. R.E. and dismantled bridges at HEU St AMAND.	
	30/10/18		Remainder of Division moved back to their area. Company quite work of assoon with some details. Free road over Canal & bridge for repair + being	

WAR DIARY
or
INTELLIGENCE SUMMARY

Army Form C. 2118.

401st (M) Fd. Co. R.E.

OCTOBER 1918

Place	Date	Hour	Summary of Events and Information	Remarks and references to Appendices
MOYELLES SUR SELLE			SAPPERS.	
			Worked road, near bridge, after of being Lt. gather to take part in Railway track and repair with silver from J. Erquet.	
			Work and also on large amount of ruts and one foot.	
			Work Regt. demolition charges at Iwuy. Held ready.	
			On 5/10/18, 6/10/18, 7/10/18 about 03.00 hrs on 31/10/18 to hold & 60 men provided to remain proceed to forward area of from 5 & 1D Coys. at a mile to check up the about 350 ft of gun pits and foul in support of 5th Div. advance.	
			Water & steel decking. Bridge over 27 ft. wide by Lake double Railway track with fifteen 2'1" bls. and 18" wide under this side.	
			Entanglement was made to cut — 8'0 × 10' to 12" hedge way through on one side at quality & passable.	
			Practically all the cutting was completed by 09.00 hrs on 1/11/18 when we handed over to 51st Fd. Co. R.E. 56th Div. also 1½ miles of the garden site field. has laid up with 4 5 loose leaves.	
			Strength of Coy. 7 Officers 206 OR	
			Reinforcements during month. 6 OR	
			Casualties during month. 1 OR Died of wounds	
			Leave — Officers on leave to UK during month. Capt W.C. GLEGG (7 nights leave nominal)	
			Lt. D.G. SANDEMAN (7)	
			2/Lt W.F. GOULD. (7)	
			OR generally from 30 to 35 OR being on leave. (13 nights each but travel)	

W. G. Harding
Major RE
O.C. 401 (M) Fd. Co. RE

1/11/18

SECRET 98 46

WAR DIARY.

401st (Highland) Field: Coy. R.E.

NOVEMBER
1918

W.L. Buckingham
Major O.C 401 FW CME
1/12/18.

WAR DIARY
or
INTELLIGENCE SUMMARY.
(Erase heading not required.)

401st (W) Fld. Co. R.E. Army Form C. 2118.

NOVEMBER – 1918.

Place	Date	Hour	Summary of Events and Information	Remarks and references to Appendices
NOYELLES SUR SELLE	1/11/18		Handed over work in forward area – closing demolished Railway bridge near FEMARS – to 572nd Fd. Co. R.E. (56th Divn.)	
PAILLENCOURT	2/11/18		Company moved to PAILLENCOURT. – 6 & 7 mules – with transport.	
			Company employed on Training etc. 1 Section employed repairing billets of 153rd Inf. Bde in HORDAIN and IWUY (Nos. 1 & 3 Sections) put into windows and roof tiles replaced. Year and old barn 1 Section employed 2 day completing bridge over canal Mord at ESCAUDOEUVRES (3/11/18 & 4/11/18) Temporary roof 36'×36' with tarpaulin covering was placed over CINEMA hand at THUN L'EVEQUE and roof was Training in Battle drill (sections) Football Leagues, Reconnaissance, Demolition, it was also any. Squad Drill and Company Drill Football Matches played against 404th Fd. Co. – also v. Black Watch. Educational Training (Staff v. Letters game etc.) Maps, Lewis Bumper & Gun. Practice Telegraphy "Demonstration", "Letter Exchange".	
	13/11/18		Divisional Cross Country Race – 3rd 4th 5th places found by Coy. (Capt Ross & Smith). Our R.E. team was	
	Dec 7/11/18		Maire & Municipal Council of VALENCIENNES should representatives of XXII and Canadian Corps for Liberation of their town. – 3 O.R. from 401st and Fd. C attended ceremony. 401st officer from 404th Fd. Co. R.E. Committee stayed at 08.30 hrs on 11/11/18. Hostilities ceased 11.00 hrs on 11/11/18. Remainder in billets at PAILLENCOURT. Company employed on maintenance of bridges over canal between ESCAUDOEUVRES and ESTRUN	
	14/11/18 to 30/11/18		2 Carrick? amount of work done repairing & cleaning houses, erecting doors and new window sills, fitting & laying floors in width large number of roofs repaired, also some new windows built in.	

WAR DIARY or INTELLIGENCE SUMMARY

Army Form. C. 2118.

401st (Highland) Fld. Co. R.E.

NOVEMBER 1918

Place	Date	Hour	Summary of Events and Information	Remarks and references to Appendices
	27/11/18		Inoculation 2nd Camp made in Quarry & Buildings & begn gun practice carried out. Dancing Platform & Latrines made for Divisional Sports in ground between PAILLENCOURT and TROIS VILLES. Preliminary Events of Divn. Sports seen on 27/11/18. Heats for 5 mile Football & relay race were won. Divisional Sports took place (Championship won by 7th Field Coy).	
	30/11/18		Elsewhere Capt. Muir attended Educational Officers' details of arrangements in schools collected. First Classes given on 21/11/18 after which classes held almost daily in English, German & French.	
			Strength of Coy. 7 Officers 303 O.R.	
			Reinforcements during month 1 Officer (Lieut MORHAM) joined on 3/11/18 to replace 1st Lt Ford (to UK on 7 months leave) 7 O.R.	
			Officers to UK during month II Lt & J.R. McEWAN - (plus 7 weeks) II Lt H.P.J. PEACOCK (" 7 ")	
			Officers on leave to France at one time (Officer 12 months service short leave)	
			O.R. generally 15 to 20 away on leave at one time.	

W.G. Buckingham

1/12/18

SECRET.
WD 47

WAR DIARY.

401st (Highland) Field Coy. R.E.

DECEMBER – 1918.

H E Buckingham
Major 115
401 (H) Fd. C. 115
O.C. 401

WAR DIARY

401st (Highland) Field Coy, RE   Army Form C. 2118.

INTELLIGENCE SUMMARY. DECEMBER 1918

Place	Date	Hour	Summary of Events and Information	Remarks and references to Appendices
PAILLENCOURT	1/12/18 to 31/12/18		Company remained at PAILLENCOURT. Educational Classes held in French, German, Shorthand, Arithmetic, English, Algebra, Geometry and Electricity and Magnetism and Building Construction and Mathematics (Inter-Section and Inter-Company Sport commenced & a number of matches played also Div. Cross Country Run (monthly). R.E. 5th Place. (401 took 2nd, 3rd & 10th place). Repair of Billets in THUN-ST-MARTIN and THUN L'EVEQUE and also in PAILLENCOURT carried out; also maintenance of Bridges over canal from ESTRUN to THUN-L'EVEQUE. Drill and Rifle Exercises and Range Practises preliminary to Instn. No. 402640 L/Cpl. J. STRACHAN 401st (H) Fd C RE T.F. awarded its Meritorious Medal. Strength of Coy. 7 Officers 194 O.R. To O.R. for Demobilisation - 5 O.R. (Coalminers) 1 O.R. (King Service) To O.C. Reinforcements Base for Demobilisation - 1 O.R. Home Officers - Pte H.P.J PEACOCK returned from leave. O.R - generally 26 O.R away on leave at a time. (14 days to 10 NLC since Nov. 1914) Passed in Educational Courses - 2 O.R.	

H.E. Buckingham Major 16
O.C. 401 (H) Fd C. RE
1/1/19

WO 48

WAR DIARY
OF
401st (HIGHLAND) FIELD COMPANY R.E.
FOR
JANUARY 1918

Vol. XXXX 18.

WAR DIARY or INTELLIGENCE SUMMARY

Army Form C. 2118.

401st (M) Fd. Co. R.E.

JANUARY – 1919.

Place	Date	Hour	Summary of Events and Information	Remarks and references to Appendices
PAILLEN-COURT	1/1/19		Holiday. Capt. W. Cavanagh R.E. and 2/Lt. Donaldson R.E. left on leave. HOUDENG-GOEGNIES will to-morrow carry on as billeting area.	
HOUDENG GOEGNIES	2/1/19		Coy. H.qrs. and 2 sections moved by motor lorry to HOUDENG-GOEGNIES. 2 sections arrived & transported at PAILLENCOURT, continued repairing billets and decoration of Hangars etc. for	
	3/1/19		2 sections at HOUDENG-GOEGNIES employed on repairs in billeting latrines, bath room etc. for	
	4/1/19		1st & 2nd Bn/I. Rifle Bde. Arrangements made for technical stores for Frenchmen at LA LOUVIÈRE and for civilian workshops for certain trades.	
	7/1/19		2 sections moved by motor lorry from PAILLENCOURT to HOUDENG-GOEGNIES. Where work continued.	
	8/1/19		Coy. Transport arrived at above area on 8/1/19. Erected in each Coy. latrine, Tables, forms, huts for infantry men were constructed. Education classes & instr. to 1st Educational commenced on 27/1/19 & from 10 am with infantry battalion. Return for discharge re-training reveals at various Dumps.	
	18/1/19		Cancelled chambers for repair of parting of 152 Rl. Bde. at 5 p.m. on 16/1/19 on Coy. employment, recommenced later company work in football netting etc. near intervened. General situation satisfactory.	
	29/1/19		Lieut. Col. Hon. Major M.E. BUCKINGHAM, M.C. R.E. went on leave on 16/1/19 O.R. – 11 Coy. on leave. 2/Lt. BESCHURCH, R.E. joined Coy. for duty on 20/1/19	

WAR DIARY
or
INTELLIGENCE SUMMARY.

(Erase heading not required.)

401²(H) Field Coy RE

JANUARY – 1919

Army Form C. 2118.

Place	Date	Hour	Summary of Events and Information	Remarks and references to Appendices
HOUDENG -GOEGNIES	1/1/19		To U.K. for Demobilisation – 1 Officer, 2/Lt D.G. SANDEMAN, R.E. 41 O.R's	
	31/1/19		Reinforcements received – 6 O.R. Proceeded on Educational course – 2 O.R.	

a/O.C. 401st (Highland) Field Coy, R.E.

Major R.E.

WAR DIARY

OF

401st (HIGHLAND) FIELD COMPANY R.E.

FOR

FEBRUARY 1919

VOL L.

WAR DIARY
or
INTELLIGENCE SUMMARY
(Erase heading not required.)

Army Form C. 2118.

401st (Highland Field) Coy. R.E.

FEBRUARY – 1919

Place	Date	Hour	Summary of Events and Information	Remarks and references to Appendices
HOUDENG-GOEGNIES BELGIUM	1/2/19 to 28/2/19		Company employed on completing and improving Cash: horses, field ovens, latrines etc. in 152nd Inf. Brigade area. One Minerva (Nut) van received for 4th Gordon Hrs. and also a double horse hut was hastily erected for aero battalion. Group Rapid demobilisation of the Brigade and of this division was started and the two huts were dismantled on 20/2/19. Education was continued until the 6/2/19 when demobilisation of company took away the majority of the students, administration. Big hole clay to building construction taken by Lt. Penwick, D.C.M, M.M also closed early in the month. Subsequently our personnel in continuing company efforts on the game reason. Towards the end of the month all other men were employed in clearing up Camp and in moving C.R.E's dump at HOUDENG-GOEGNIES to Corps dump at MONS. Major H.T. Buskinghan M.C was struck off the strength to 2nd on transfer to Scottish Command. Capt. R.O. Brixen was struck off the strength to 2nd on 31/1/19. Leave party extended pending demobilisation 2/Lt. 73. C.S. Church was transferred to 228th (H) Fd. Cy. R.E on 1/2/19. Leave during month – NIL. O.R To U.K. for demobilisation and demobilised in U.K. 75 O.R Reinforcement received. NIL. Proceeded in Zibertini corner – NIL. 7/. K. N. Norham proceeded to U.K. on 15/2/19 on 1st Dispersal Draft, as D.C.O. Number of horses in company strength reduced by 30. " " " mules in company strength reduced by 22.	Nothing

G.B. 401st (Highland) Field Coy. R.E.
Strength [illegible]

Vol 50

WAR DIARY.

401st (HIGHLAND) FIELD COY. R.E.

MARCH - 1919.

VOL. LI.

Army Form C. 2118.

401st (Highland) Field Coy. R.E.

WAR DIARY or INTELLIGENCE SUMMARY.

(Erase heading not required.)

MARCH - 1919

Place	Date	Hour	Summary of Events and Information	Remarks and references to Appendices
HOUDENG GOEGNIES BELGIUM	1/3/19 to 21/3/19		Company employed in clearing up and in moving stores from C.R.E.'s dump, HOUDENG, HOUDENG & MONS. Lt. K.N. MORHAM returned from leave on 14th inst. and took over command of 401st (Highland) Field Coy R.E. on 20th inst. Recommendation in respect of Cancel from HOUDENG to mine SENEFFE, made and submitted to C.R.E. for information of War Office.	
MANAGE.	22/3/19 to 31/3/19		Company moved to MANAGE on 22/3/19, for commence of entrainment of Cache. Billets at time complete and general check of cache equipment made before including to complete establishment. 14 O.R.'s to 64th Field Coy R.E. (Army of Occupation) on 16/3/19. 14 O.R. (Cache B) to U.K. for demobilization on 19/3/19. 3 O.R. on leave during month. Company reduced to Cache A on 19/3/19. All horses sold in districted to remount depot by 25/3/19. Cycles and surplus stores handed over to chance. Lt. K.N. MORHAM and 2nd Lt. T.R. McEWAN transferred to 400th (Highland) Field Coy. R.E. on 26/3/19.	

K. Stewart Clegg Capt.
401st (Highland) Field Coy. R.E.

www.ingramcontent.com/pod-product-compliance
Lightning Source LLC
Chambersburg PA
CBHW081426300426
44108CB00016BA/2309